Cross **Examinations**

Cross **Examinations**

Readings on the Meaning of the Cross Today

MARIT TRELSTAD

Editor

To Tove and Kai

that you may know grace

Library of Congress Cataloging-in-Publication Data
Cross examinations : readings on the meaning of the cross / Marit Trelstad, editor.
   p. cm.
ISBN-13: 978-0-8006-2046-2 (alk. paper)
ISBN-10: 0-8006-2046-1
1. Jesus Christ—Crucifixion. 2. Holy Cross. 3. Crosses. I. Trelstad, Marit, 1967-
BT453.C755 2006
232.96'3—dc22

                         2006011939

Contents

Part I

THE CROSS IN RACIAL AND GENDER OPPRESSION

Part II

THE CROSS: GOD AND THE SUFFERING WORLD

Part III

THE CROSS: IMPERIALISM, VIOLENCE, AND PEACE

Contributors

RITA NAKASHIMA BROCK is an award-winning author and scholar who has worked for over two decades in the field of feminist theology. Among her books are *Journeys by Heart: A Christology of Erotic Power*; *Casting Stones: Prostitution and Liberation in Asia and the United States* (with Susan Brooks Thistlethwaite); and *Proverbs of Ashes: Violence, Redemptive Suffering, and the Search for What Saves Us* (with Rebecca Ann Parker). She has served on the Board of Directors of the American Academy of Religion and was a founding board member of the *Journal of Feminist Studies in Religion*.

ROSEMARY P. CARBINE is Assistant Professor of Theology in the Department of Religious Studies at the College of the Holy Cross, Worcester, Mass., where she specializes in Christian systematic/constructive theology, particularly feminist, womanist, and *mujerista* theological anthropologies. Through fellowship support from the Women's Studies in Religion Program at Harvard University Divinity School, she is currently preparing a manuscript regarding the intersections of gender, theology, and public life, entitled *Ekklesial Work: Toward a Feminist Public Theology*.

DOUGLAS JOHN HALL is Emeritus Professor of Christian Theology, McGill University, Montreal. He is the author of some thirty books, including an award-winning trilogy on *Christian Theology in a North American Context*. His most recent works are *Bound and Free: A Theologian's Journey* and *The Cross in Our Context: Jesus and the Suffering World*.

S. MARK HEIM is Samuel Abbot Professor of Christian Theology at Andover Newton Theological School in Newton Centre, Mass. His books include *Saved from Sacrifice: A Theology of the Cross*; *The Depth of the Riches: A Trinitarian Theology of Religious Ends*; and *Salvations: Truth and Difference in Religion*. He is a member of the Faith and Order Commission of the National Council of Churches and the World Council of Churches and has edited several works in ecumenical theology.

JAY B. MCDANIEL is Professor of Religion and Director of the Steel Center for the Study of Religion and Philosophy at Hendrix College in Conway, Ark. His books include *With Roots and Wings: Christianity in an Age of Ecology and Dialogue*; *Living from the Center: Spirituality in an Age of Consumerism; Gandhi's Hope: Learning from Other Religions as a Path to Peace*; and *A Handbook of Process Theology* (coedited with Donna Bowman). His interests are in interreligious dialogue, religion and ecology, process theology, and the Christian dialogue with Buddhism.

CYNTHIA MOE-LOBEDA is on the faculty of Seattle University's Department of Theology and Religious Studies and graduate School of Theology and Ministry. She lectures and consults nationally and internationally in theology and ethics, focusing on issues of economic justice, ecological ethics, and public church. She is author of *Public Church: For the Life of the World*; *Healing a Broken World: Globalization and God*; and coauthor (with Ched Myers et al.) of *"Say to This Mountain": Mark's Story of Discipleship* and *Saint Francis and the Foolishness of God* (with Marie Dennis et al.).

JÜRGEN MOLTMANN is Professor Emeritus of Systematic Theology at the Evangelisch-theologische Fakultät der Universität Tübingen, Germany. Among his books are *The Theology of Hope*; *The Crucified God*; *The Trinity and the Kingdom*; *The Spirit of Life; Science and Wisdom;* and *The Coming of God: Christian Eschatology,* winner of the 2000 University of Louisville Grawemeyer Award.

SUSAN L. NELSON holds the Director's Bicentennial Chair in Theology and Culture at Pittsburgh Theological Seminary. Her books include *Beyond Servanthood: Christianity and the Liberation of Women; Healing the Broken Heart: Sin, Alienation, and the Gift of Grace*; and *The Other Side of Sin* (coedited with Andrew Sung Park). Her research for this project was funded by the 2003–2004 Lilly Theological Research Grant.

JAMES N. POLING is an ordained minister in the Presbyterian Church (U.S.A.), a pastoral psychotherapist, and Professor of Pastoral Theology, Care, and Counseling at Garrett-Evangelical Theological Seminary, Evanston, Ill. He is the author of many articles and books, including *The Abuse of Power: A Theological Problem*; *Deliver Us from Evil: Resisting Racial and Gender Oppression*; and *Render unto God: Economic Vulnerability, Family Violence, and Pastoral Theology*.

MARY M. SOLBERG is Associate Professor of Religion at Gustavus Adolphus College, St. Peter, Minn. She is the author of *Compelling Knowledge: A Feminist Proposal for an Epistemology of the Cross*, translator of Walter Altmann's *Luther and Liberation: A Latin American Perspective*, and coeditor with Kathleen A. Culhane-Pera et al. of *Healing by Heart: Clinical and Ethical Case Stories of Hmong Families and Western Providers*.

MARY J. STREUFERT is Director for Justice for Women for the Evangelical Lutheran Church in America (ELCA), having previously held a Lilly Fellowship in Humanities and Theology at Valparaiso University. Her essays are found in the journals *Feminist Theology* and *Currents in Theology and Mission*, and her "Re-Conceiving Lutheran Christology" is forthcoming in the Princeton Theological Monograph Series. She earned her Ph.D. in religion at Claremont Graduate University.

DEANNA A. THOMPSON is Associate Professor and Chair of the Religion Department at Hamline University in St. Paul, Minn. She is the author of *Crossing the Divide: Luther, Feminism, and the Cross,* and has recently been teaching and writing about the phenomenon of *The Da Vinci Code.*

MARK LEWIS TAYLOR is Maxwell M. Upson Professor of Theology and Culture at Princeton Theological Seminary. Among his books are *Religion, Politics, and the Christian Right: Post-9/11 Powers and American Empire; The Executed God: The Way of the Cross in Lockdown America*; and *Remembering Esperanza: A Cultural-Political Theology for North American Praxis*. His essays and organizing focus are on U.S. policy in Mesoamerica, U.S. criminal justice, and antiwar peace work.

JOANNE MARIE TERRELL is Associate Professor of Ethics and Theology at Chicago Theological Seminary and an ordained elder in the Michigan Annual Conference of the African Methodist Episcopal Zion Church. She is author of *Power in the Blood? The Cross in African American Experience*. As an African American, Christian, and womanist rooted in the church, her research interests include a focus on Christian origins and their potential for enhancing future developments in black, feminist, and womanist theologies on questions of doctrine.

MARIT A. TRELSTAD is Assistant Professor of Religion at Pacific Lutheran University. Her work has appeared in several volumes of theology, including *Constructing a Feminist Cosmology: Conversations with Nancy Howell,* and in numerous journals, including *Dialog: A Journal of Theology.* In her scholarship concerning the teaching of religion and in the field of theological anthropology, she advocates empowerment, respect, and communal responsibility in multiple avenues of theology: Christology/soteriology, the doctrine of God, anthropology, pedagogical theory, feminist and process theologies, and contemporary applications within such areas as pastoral care and counseling.

ALICIA VARGAS, a native of Cuba, is Assistant Professor of Multicultural and Contextual Studies and Director of Contextual Education at Pacific Lutheran Theological Seminary in Berkeley, having previously taught at St. Olaf and Vassar Colleges. She most recently contributed to *Lutero al Habla*, a new edition of Luther's works in Spanish. The focus of her work is the contextual encounter of Lutheran theology with the Latino community in the U.S.A.

J. DENNY WEAVER is Professor Emeritus of Religion and Harry and Jean Yoder Scholar in Bible and Religion at Bluffton University, Bluffton, Ohio. Among his publications are *Becoming Anabaptist: The Origin and Significance of Sixteenth-Century Anabaptism*; *Teaching Peace: Nonviolence and the Liberal Arts* (edited with Gerald Biesecker-Mast); *The Nonviolent Atonement*; and *Keeping Salvation Ethical: Mennonite and Amish Atonement Theology in the Late Nineteenth Century.* The organizing focus of his research concerns the roles of violence and nonviolence in shaping theology.

DELORES S. WILLIAMS is Paul Tillich Professor of Theology and Culture Emerita at Union Theological Seminary, New York. Her research and teaching have focused on the emergence of womanist theology in addition to theological doctrines and the critique of popular and technological cultures. She is widely influential in the areas of womanist, feminist, and black theology. Her publications include *Sisters in the Wilderness: The Challenge of Womanist God-Talk.*

Preface

THE CENTRAL SYMBOL OF CHRISTIAN EXPERIENCE, the cross of Jesus, today elicits an enormous range of interpretations and emotions. It has itself become something of a religious and theological lightning rod, a vortex in terms of personal lives and within the work of constructive Christian theology. Many positive and negative experiences come to be identified with the symbol of the cross. And, in theology, all categories of thought collide in the cross: Christology, theological anthropology, the doctrine of God and the Trinity, soteriology, sin, atonement, eschatology, and so on. The heat of the burner gets turned up to "high" on all fronts. And, in all instances, interpretations of the cross are intensely connected to the personal, social, and religious contexts of the interpreter.

There is no doubt that the cross has shaped people's lives in positive ways—liberating them in ways they never thought possible and revealing a vision of love and compassion that gives hope in situations of suffering. For other people, the cross may be oppressive in that it can serve to justify patterns of abuse through upholding silent suffering as redemptive or because it has been used as a symbol of racist or nationalist aggression. Indeed, one person may hold conflicting images of the cross that speak to different aspects of one's experience. This volume examines both liberating and oppressive uses of the cross symbol. No book thus far has brought together the major voices contributing to this conversation in one volume so that academic and general audiences can compare the positions and issues raised. This book combines original articles never published with reprinted material from fundamental, defining texts on the subjects of the cross, Christian atonement theory, and Christian understandings of salvation. Each author situates her or his reflections in terms of the issues of gender and racial oppressions, human or environmental experiences of suffering, or issues of imperialism, violence, and peace.

Asian-feminist, womanist, and feminist Christian theologians initiated the current wave of debate over the cross and thus the book begins by engaging that discussion. Their critiques of redemptive suffering and sacrifice added to another line of critique of cross interpretations that had been brewing since early in the twentieth century. In light of World War I and II, many theologians had condemned the use of the cross in war as a military or nationalist symbol and this critique has been revived in recent years. Along this line, Douglas John Hall declares that the cross is a symbol of suffering, humility, and love rather than an image of triumph and thus it provides a much-needed antidote to attempts to use Christianity as an imperialistic tool. Beyond feminist critique or appropriation of the cross, other significant cross examinations have developed and are coordinated in sections two and three of the volume: "The Cross—God and the Suffering World" and "The Cross—Imperialism, Violence and Peace."

This volume emerged from a summer conversation, or should I say friendly debate, with Hall. He insisted, and I agreed, that if Christianity took a theology of the cross seriously, it would provide a needed corrective to current trends that equate Christianity with the United States' obsessions with freedom, power, and even conquest. I insisted, and he agreed, that the image of the cross and theologies of the cross still served to oppress many women by insisting that sexism or abuse was their "cross to bear." Together, we discussed how the cross spoke different messages in different contexts. On an international scale the cross may speak gospel but when transposed into personal lives, it may speak only oppression. We began to speak in terms of macro-contexts and micro-contexts and their influence on cross interpretations and he encouraged me to put this into writing. I realized it would be even better to invite multiple voices to the table to see what arguments and commonalities the conversation would elicit. I am glad they all came and I have learned much in the process.

My thanks and gratitude are extended to multiple people and organizations for their support of this project. The Wabash Center for Teaching and Learning in

Theology and Religion provided a generous fellowship grant that funded months of full-time writing to develop this book. Thanks also to my many colleagues in the Wabash Summer Workshop for Undergraduate Teachers in Religion who pressed us to set goals and paths for achieving them. These conversations were very fortifying. In joining this book's conversation, the contributors have developed excellent pieces and I thank them for their willingness, insight, and openness to editing and suggestions. The interchange and conversation with these authors was my favorite part of the process. I also am thankful for my encouraging, vitalizing religion department at Pacific Lutheran University where we push each other to be good human beings as well as engaged scholar-teachers. My particular thanks go to department members Samuel Torvend and Alicia Batten who read my drafts and provided valuable insight and questions. Almost every page of this volume was combed by my copyeditor and friend Scott Larson whose comments, humor, and corrections were helpful beyond words. My many thanks to Susan Nelson who agreed to be a mentor for me in the editing process. She answered my many questions, responded to drafts, and provided wisdom, encouragement, and expertise. Jack Verheyden and Marjorie Suchocki were willing to once again take up their roles as my teachers and mentors and pushed me to clarify my own thinking, and I am ever thankful for their commitment to my scholarly development. My thanks to Douglas John Hall who told me to write this and to Michael West, senior editor at Fortress Press, who helped shape the volume in significant ways and encouraged me with supportive persistence to keep at it. I am also grateful to all at Fortress who have worked hard to accommodate images, procure copyrights, and keep the volume moving forward to print.

My own writing, theological convictions, and Christian faith find their deepest roots in the love and grace my parents have given me. Thanks is inadequate to express my gratitude for this foundation, for our shared love of theological conversations, for our continuing growth together, and the assurance that questions are the fun stuff of faith. My thanks, also, to my dear friends and family in whose love and presence I am inspired. Thank you to Tove and Kai, who keep me grounded in practical life and insist on playing with worms, dancing, and reading books together endlessly. Above all, I thank Bjorn Larsen, my love, my companion, who is an invigorating, insightful, funny conversation partner and an excellent copyeditor. With two small children in our house and two full-time jobs, he created space and time for me to write and never complained when it took me three hours to write one good paragraph.

Introduction

The Cross in Context

Marit A. Trelstad

At the beginning of Christianity there are two crosses:
One is a real cross, the other a symbol.
Jürgen Moltmann, "The Cross as Military Symbol for Sacrifice"

IN THE PAST THIRTY YEARS, significant theologians and movements within theology have disagreed on the appropriateness of the cross as a symbol of Christian faith. The symbol provokes criticism or support depending on the cultural and personal context of the interpreter. The key critiques that set the stage for the debate over cross interpretations came from feminist and womanist theologians who claimed that the cross reinforces both victim passivity and violent oppression as the locus of the gospel. Many critiques of the cross assert that it supports systems of oppression by demanding self-sacrifice and suffering from the weak while at the same time justifying or, worse, sanctifying oppression and abuse by the powerful. In these ways, they posit that it could be used to support racial and domestic violence or nationalistic, imperialistic uses of the cross.

At the same time, other leading theologians have claimed that a theology of the cross is crucial today for two main reasons. First, it is a symbol that opposes the "prosperity gospel" present in Western cultural and economic philosophies that support individual prosperity despite mass human need. Second, a theology of the cross may encourage Christians to know reality through the eyes of suffering and therefore to address the world's needs compassionately and appropriately. One side of the debate over interpretation of the cross claims that the cross continues long-standing forms of human suffering while the other side claims that the symbol of the cross realistically acknowledges and critiques human-created suffering, thereby offering potential alleviation of suffering. Feminist theologians land on both sides of the debate. Delores Williams's article reprinted in this volume and Jürgen Moltmann's *The Crucified God* (on which he reflects in one essay here) are seminal works that represent these contrasting theological perspectives on the cross. Thus, these writers provide the anchor essays within two sections of the volume.

The volume's three sections address the main categories of cross interpretation that have emerged from gathering these theological voices together: the role of the cross in racial and gender oppression, the cross and the suffering world, and the cross as tool of imperialism, violence, and peace. Some essays work primarily with the symbol of the cross itself and how that symbol functions in society. Others offer analysis of the "work" of Christ's death on the cross to reconcile God and humans and, in doing so, they consider the strengths and weaknesses of traditional atonement theories within the Christian tradition.

All authors in this volume address how the cross and Christian understandings of atonement and soteriology are understood in light of a faithful engagement with contemporary issues. All authors examine the issue of the cross and salvation from within the context of Christianity. Many address the cross's impact on lived Christian faith explicitly. Some authors think the cross or crucifixion is the necessary starting place for Christian understandings of justice, salvation, or God's presence in the suffering world (Moltmann, Hall, Vargas, Moe-Lobeda). Others question the cross as the focal point for Christian understandings of redemption and offer alternative emphases within the Christian tradition (Williams, Trelstad). Approaching the subject of the cross through visual art or Christian liturgical practice provides yet another tool of analysis on the meaning of the cross historically and today (Brock, Nelson, Taylor). Because Martin Luther (1483–1546) specifically wrote about the perspective a "theologian of the cross" brings to both God and the world, his framing of the cross has been significant for multiple contributors (Hall, Solberg, Vargas, Streufert, Thompson, Trelstad, Moe-Lobeda).

This project does not present all contemporary soteriological proposals or theological interpretations of the cross. Instead, it seeks to display soteriologies and interpretations of the cross that explicitly address current social and environmental concerns. Some authors affirm traditional understandings of the atonement, even as they employ contemporary sociological, philosophical, and theological methods. Thus, they provide fresh perspectives on traditional approaches (Heim, Thompson, Solberg, Terrell, Poling). Others expand significantly on traditional approaches, urging new avenues of development in light of today's theological questions and issues (Weaver, Carbine, Streufert, McDaniel). From the conversation between these theological works, it is evident that there are new patterns of cross examination emerging that suggest a distinctive "liberationist" atonement theory, expanding previous categories of atonement theory.

The Importance of Context for Theological Interpretation of the Cross

The meaning of the cross has shifted and changed throughout the two millennia of Christianity. Indeed, it continues to change, depending on the context in which it appears. Burning crosses on the lawns of black North Americans evidences the evil of racism. Crosses on homes, cars, and public properties can simply indicate the religious affiliation or identity of an individual or group. In the front of a church, it signifies belief that centers in the crucified and risen Jesus Christ. In front of the media's cameras, it has become popular simply as a matter of fashion. In crusades, wars, and nationalistic fervor, it has supported a call to unity against an enemy and has often carried an anti-Semitic and anti-Muslim sentiment. In Latin America in the last thirty years, the cross has carried the message that Jesus was on the side of the oppressed in their suffering and struggles against repressive governmental regimes. The contexts that shape one's interpretation of the cross are limitless and each offers a distinctive meaning for theological reflection. One person may hold both positive and negative associations with the symbol, providing conflicting interpretations of the cross as simultaneously both salvific and oppressive.

Even from the beginning there are two crosses—the historical event of Jesus' crucifixion and the theological interpretation of that event. Theological models of atonement and any image of the cross itself automatically reflect interpretations of Jesus' crucifixion and therefore are, fundamentally, religious symbols. In his classic book *Dynamics of Faith* Paul Tillich addresses the nature of symbols in religious life. Tillich claims that religious symbols are "created or at least accepted by the collective unconscious of the group in which they appear."[1] Additionally, they are "[l]ike living beings, they grow and die. They grow when the situation is ripe for them, and they die when the situation changes. . . . They die because they can no longer produce response in the group where they originally found expression."[2] An evolution of meanings surrounding the cross is offered in Rita Nakashima Brock's essay, in which she contrasts the crucifix to previous images of the cross as a baptismal symbol. From another perspective, Delores Williams offers that cross interpretations have always changed in relation to their interpreter's contexts, and thus womanist theologians are likewise invited to interpret the cross in light of their experiences. Tillich's writing on symbols highlights the hermeneutical importance of understanding the context wherein a symbol such as the cross appears.

The scope of one's contextual perspective also shapes one's interpretation of the cross. When one views the imperialistic tendencies of a whole nation or overall environmental abuse of the earth, one may hold the cross to be an antidote to pride. When one views the personal effects of domestic violence and sexual abuse, one may say that the punitive image of the cross furthers the abuse. There is a difference here between *macro-context*, in terms of the nation and planet, or *micro-context* in terms of individual lives. What makes theological sense in one context may be essentially nonsense in another. Likewise, a theological message and symbol that is intended to serve justice and liberation may become oppressive when transplanted into a new context. Moltmann's two chapters offer an example of the cross seen in two lights, bringing two different messages—one oppressive, another liberating and comforting—as he recounts the use of the cross in militarism or the cross image as it conveys the powerful, suffering love of God.

Simply put, the vantage point from which one sees the cross influences one's interpretation significantly. Each author in the volume speaks from a particular context and set of concerns that shape her or his interpretation of the cross. The context, scale, and scope of the issues addressed influence an author's theological interpretation of the cross as well as their affirmation or rejection of traditional understandings of atonement.

TRADITIONAL MODELS OF ATONEMENT

In his 1931 book *Christus Victor*, Swedish theologian Gustav Aulén describes atonement theory in terms of three main categories or types. This categorization has provided the framework on which most subsequent discussions of atonement have been based. Reviewing centuries of theology, Aulén asserts that all atonement theories fall under three main understandings of Jesus' role in reconciling humankind to God: Anselm's satisfaction theory, Abelard's moral example theory, and the *Christus Victor* (Christ the Victor) or "classic" theory, to use Aulén's words. To Aulén's categories, some have added various additional traditions of interpretation, including Athanasius's (c. 297–373) theory of redemption through the incarnation and Origen's (183–253) understanding that Jesus' death was a ransom that God paid to the devil to reclaim humans who were captive due to their sins. Origen's work informs the *Christus Victor* type of atonement theory.

Within the work *Cur Deus Homo* ("Why God Became Human"), St. Anselm of Canterbury (1033–1109) proposed the "satisfaction" atonement theory that Jesus, through the cross, reconciled humanity to God by satisfying God's honor. Being a God of justice, God cannot tolerate sin or injustice that has not been corrected in some way. In other words, human sin, part of our "fallen" character, is irreconcilable with God's righteousness and perfection, God's character, and thus the relationship between God and humans cannot be mended. Anselm posits that God chooses to become human in Jesus, thus merging God and humanity, and therefore provides a bridge whereby humans can be made right with God. As a perfect or righteous human, Jesus' self-sacrifice on the cross is able to compensate God's honor in a way that sinful humans cannot. Reformers in the sixteenth century often adopted Anselm's model in their depiction of "forensic justification," which imagines atonement through legal metaphors: humanity is proclaimed guilty of sinning against God and yet Jesus stands in for the accused, taking the blame as well as God's rejection and punishment for this crime. This kind of logic is found in quite another context within Susan Nelson's chapter, where a Holocaust survivor and artist depicts himself carrying the cross "as an act of expiation.... 'someone has to pay the price.'"[3]

Peter Abelard (1079–1142) rejected Anselm's idea that Jesus' death was necessary for the forgiveness of human sin. God could have reconciled humankind to Godself in another manner and had done so in the past through the forgiveness of sin without any sacrifice. Thus, Jesus is not required to die to satisfy either the devil's dues or God's own honor or system of justice. God instead chooses this particular mode of reconciliation or atonement, Jesus' death, in order to demonstrate the great depth of God's love for humanity. In response to this demonstration of God's love through self-giving, humans would be inspired to greater acts of love and tender charity. Therefore, Jesus' death serves as a moral example or influence that elicits human faith and conversion. Neither Anselm nor Abelard understood Jesus' death on the cross in terms of God's owing the devil a ransom because to do so would have granted the devil too much power in relation to God.

The *Christus Victor* model takes two different forms. The first, as mentioned in reference to Origen, sees God as paying a ransom to the devil for human sin. Another version of this first form depicts God as offering Jesus to the devil as a "payment" for the release of a captive and sinful humanity, but the offer is like a worm being offered on a hook. Only God knows that the bait holds the barb that will undo the devil when it is taken. C. S. Lewis depicts such a model in *The Lion, the Witch, and the Wardrobe* in his famous book series *The Chronicles of Narnia*. The evil forces are undone by "falling for" the bait of innocent blood (see S. Mark Heim's essay in this volume). A second form of the *Christus Victor* model depicts Jesus' death in light of a battleground between cosmic forces of good and evil, where the death of Jesus suggests the conquest of evil but the resurrection affirms the ultimate sovereignty of God.

J. Denny Weaver aptly describes the complications and questions each model presents in his discussion of the questions, "Who or what ultimately needs the death of Jesus?" and "Who ultimately killed him?"[4] Is it the devil, God, or human sinners who need Jesus' death? Does God plan and execute Jesus' death or is it the mob or the devil? For further description of Aulén's models, the reader may look to the essays by Williams and Weaver where the three main types of atonement theory are explained further.

THE CROSS IN RACIAL AND GENDER OPPRESSION

Considering the cross and its meaning for human suffering, the primary critique of past soteriologies and atonement theories has come from feminist and woman-ist writers. These critiques have considered how the image of the cross functions in light of the still-prevalent physical and emotional abuse that many women face. Feminist theology has maintained that human sociological systems are supported and justified through philosophical and theological claims. Indeed, our interactions with one another seem to mimic how we understand God's relation to humanity. The difference is simply that of scale. Thus, the image of the cross and redemptive suffering become controversial because they affect not only our religious convictions but our social relations as well.

If we glorify passive suffering as redemptive through the image of the cross, we may inadvertently justify abuse and convey the impression that it is women's Christian responsibility to bear silently suffering, abuse, or torture. Considering that roughly 30 percent of women can expect to be beaten or abused within their lifetime, this is a substantial concern.[5] "This is my cross to bear" is one of the most common justifications women give as to why they deserve to be beaten or why they cannot leave an abusive situation. Suffering and abuse are understood as necessary, unavoidable, and potentially redemptive based on Jesus' suffering and death.

Feminist critiques of the cross image and atonement theories coordinate in four major issues. First, glorifying the cross potentially treats suffering as though it is God-given and inevitable. This makes the loving character of God in relation to the world dubious and also models God-human relations on a patriarchal model of relationship that idealizes the roles of hero and helpless victim. Second, it valorizes passive suffering as redemptive. Third, the weight of "redemptive" suffering is borne primarily by the oppressed and disadvantaged, and it is promoted and preached most often by those who stand to benefit from the suffering of others. Finally, it may lead to a human neglect of our individual and collective responsibility to end suffering and hold perpetrators of violence accountable.

God's character and love are drawn into question if God is imagined as demanding death or suffering, either as a moral example or as a price to be paid against the power of evil. A relationship that demands the subservient self-destruction of one member is a highly questionable form of love. Additionally, the relation of God to Jesus and, subsequently, God to humans is depicted solely in terms of hero and victim. In a hero-victim relation, even if it claims to offer protection and salvation, there is an inherent disregard of the presumed victim's self-agency. The patriarchal fantasy of the knight in shining armor requires a victim who is passive physically, spiritually, or intellectually. Hero models emphasize the prowess and independence of the hero himself and the indebtedness of the recipient. Thus, Jesus' vicarious suffering becomes critiqued as an appropriate theological or anthropological model since it could disable one's own ability or confidence to stand up to oppression.

An example of these critiques is present in the work of Asian American feminist theologian Rita Nakashima Brock and feminist theologian Rebecca Ann Parker. In *Proverbs of Ashes: Violence, Redemptive Suffering, and the Search for What Saves Us*, they interpret "the crucifixion not as an inevitable outcome of God's will, but as an act of state-sponsored violence. Jesus accepted the cross, . . . not because it was God's will, but because it was the necessary price for speaking truth to a corrupted world."[6] Jesus is the incarnation of God working with the Christian community to empower the struggle against death and oppression. Parker describes her own shift away from believing in a sacrificial atonement model in the following words,

I recognized that Christianity had taught me that sacrifice is the way of life. I forgot the neighbor who raped me, but I could see that when theology presents Jesus' death as God's sacrifice of his beloved child for the sake of the world, it teaches that the highest love is sacrifice. To make sacrifice or to be sacrificed is virtuous and redemptive.

But what if this is not true? What if nothing, or very little, is saved? What if the consequence of sacrifice is simply pain, the diminishment of life, fragmentation of the soul, abasement and shame? What if the severing of life is merely destructive of life and is not the path of love, courage, trust and faith? What if the performance of sacrifice is a ritual in which some human beings bear loss and others are protected from accountability or moral expectations?[7]

Womanist, Asian-feminist, and feminist theologians have all voiced concerns about the cross justifying the suffering of women.

While gender and racial oppressions are connected, some contemporary theologians have specifically focused on the cross in relation to the history of racism in the United States. In Kelly Brown Douglas's book *What's Faith Got to Do With It? Black Bodies/Christian Souls*, she outlines ways in which black Christians have drawn theological connections between lynchings and Jesus' death on the cross.[8] Jesus' passive suffering was used to encourage black Christians to accept slavery as their cross to bear. Douglas's work is discussed in Terrell's chapter within this volume. And yet, even as the image of the cross has represented and reinforced racism against black Christians in the United States, Douglas and others depict how black communities have turned this image around to challenge their oppressors. Black Christians reclaimed the cross as a sign that God was with them in their struggles for liberation by identifying with Jesus who suffered at the hands of the powerful and by highlighting God's clear siding with slaves and the oppressed in the Exodus and other biblical stories. In light of all these perspectives, one needs to examine the liberating or oppressive potential of the cross image.

Joanne Marie Terrell and Delores Williams provide two womanist perspectives within this volume. Terrell's article addresses the cross and sacrifice in light of the lynching of Emmett Till, whose violent death sparked such outrage that it helped galvanize the civil rights movement. Williams's essay critiques traditional atonement theories that interpret Jesus' death as vicarious suffering in light of black women's historical and contemporary experiences of surrogacy and suffering. Rosemary Carbine's essay also addresses womanist perspectives on the cross through an analysis of the work of M. Shawn Copeland. In light of these feminist and womanist critiques, James Newton Poling writes about how Jesus' death on the cross may serve as an exemplar that counters male social pressure to participate in domination and violence. Applied in this way, he proposes that the cross can lead men to resist taking patriarchal, dominating roles in relation to women.

Mary Streufert, Deanna Thompson, Rosemary Carbine, and Marit Trelstad all approach cross interpretation through the lens of feminist theology. Streufert examines atonement theory's traditional claim that Jesus' death brings life and she argues that women's experience of pregnancy and birth may offer an alternative life-for-life model of interpretation. Thompson provides significant conversational bridges between Martin Luther's theology of the cross and feminist theology. While acknowledging the critiques feminism has leveled against the cross image, she affirms the theology of the cross as a positive resource for feminism. Analyzing the writings of Roman Catholic feminist theologians and womanist theologians, Carbine offers an eschatological theology of the cross that places the cross in light of the overall context of Jesus' life ministry and the kingdom of God. Both the incarnation and eschatological hope of Christians provide resources for a feminist theological anthropology and interpretations of the cross. As the last voice in this section, Trelstad offers that the cross is not the locus of God's saving work but rather signifies human rejection of God's covenantal love. Despite this, God extends grace and love to humanity based on God's own commitment to love. Thus, discussion of God's saving work begins in understanding God's nature rather than in atonement theory.

THE CROSS: GOD AND THE SUFFERING WORLD

In the 1960s to early 1970s, several branches of theology simultaneously turned their attention to the role of God in a suffering world. This subject was approached from varied theological perspectives that each addressed specific issues and contexts: European and North American theologians addressing the horrors of World War II, Latin American liberation theologians engaging economic and military oppression, North American black theologians reflecting the ongoing civil rights struggles of the 1950s and 1960s, and emerging feminist theologies exposing the widespread oppression of women. Seminal works in each area were published within five years of each other: Jürgen Moltmann's *The Crucified God* (1974), Gustavo Gutiérrez's *A Theology of Liberation* (1971), James Cone's *Black Theology and Black Power* (1969), and Mary Daly's *Beyond God the Father* (1973). This is tantamount to an evolutionary leap in the field of theology and these lines of conversation have shaped the study of religion ever since. In each of these movements, Christian theologians have struggled to understand the human capacity to participate readily in evil, the experience of massive suffering and oppression and its implications for faith, and God's power and goodness in the face of evil (theodicy).

In *The Crucified God,* Moltmann explicitly addresses the role of the cross in depicting God's presence within the suffering humanity faces. Reflecting on the German concentration camps of World War II, he offers the notion of "theopathy": that God suffers on the cross and subsequently is united with humans in suffering. Here he argues against some Christian doctrines that affirm the impassibility and apathy of God, that God cannot change or suffer the effects of human action. In response, he states that the passion of Christ is central to Christianity and this is, in essence, the image of the suffering God. On the cross, God is revealed within and connected to suffering.

While God feels and suffers the effects of humanity, Moltmann claims that this does not challenge the sovereignty of God. God's suffering is purely voluntary, moved by love. Only by entering evil and weakness can God transform it. In his later writing, *The Trinity and the Kingdom: The Doctrine of God* (1980), he quotes a preacher and writer from World War I, G. A. Studdert Kennedy, who wrote, "It's always the Cross in the end—God, not Almighty, but God the Father, with a Father's sorrow and a Father's weakness, which is the strength of love. God splendid, suffering, crucified—Christ. There's the Dawn."[9] In commenting on Studdert's ministry and theology, Moltmann addresses the political importance of affirming that God suffers alongside humanity. If God is not understood through suffering love, God is too often assumed to be on the side of the powerful, the one who "blesses the violence and weapons" of war.[10] He states, "What was able to stand the test of the battlefields of Flanders and created faith even in the hells there was the discovery of the crucified God."[11] He claims that affirming God's suffering takes the idea of the atonement much further than simply a remission of sins. Atonement instead deals with a primary issue in human existence. The cross is not only punishment for sin but also God's accepting the weight of human suffering voluntarily. While Moltmann's first piece in this volume recaps and updates his work in *The Crucified God,* his second essay addresses the abuse of the cross when it is used to sanction nationalism and militarism.

While theologians such as Gustavo Gutiérrez and Juan Luis Segundo had already developed the foundations for liberation theology, Moltmann's work in *The Crucified God* further underscored a widespread trend in theology to understand Christ's death on the cross in terms of God's participation in the suffering of the world. Theologies emphasizing God's presence in suffering have had a trickle-down effect on an international scale for several decades. Christian anti-apartheid movements in Namibia in the 1980s, for example, were inspired especially by James Cone's work in books such as *God of the Oppressed* (1975).[12]

Here, Moltmann's reflections on *The Crucified God* serve to introduce others who also examine the issue of "The Cross and the Suffering World" today. Moltmann writes, "*The Crucified God* is in essence a book about believing in God after the cross of Christ. What we can say about God 'after Auschwitz' depends on what we can say about God after the crucifixion of Christ, hearing the dying Jesus' cry of abandonment: 'My God, why have you forsaken me?'"[13] He discusses his classic book in the context of his own life and World War II, the assassination of Martin Luther King Jr., and Latin American liberation movements. Building on this theme, Mary Solberg reviews Martin Luther's epistemology of the cross and how it can address today's experiences of anxiety and suffering. Latina theologian Alicia Vargas also uses Luther's theology and understanding of the cross as it provides a sounding board for United States Latina experiences of oppression and struggles for justice. Susan Nelson's essay builds on Vargas's insight of the cross as displaying a deep message of God-with-us. Through the artwork of Marian Kolodziej, who depicts Christ's suffering within the context of the German concentration camps, Nelson argues that visual images of the crucifixion may offer a way for people to experience God's presence and offer paths of healing and reconciliation to move beyond suffering.

The works of Cynthia Moe-Lobeda and Jay McDaniel examine the image of a suffering God and the cross from an ecological perspective. Like others in the volume, Moe-Lobeda finds Luther's theology of the cross to be a useful tool for acknowledging the depth of the environmental crisis as well as providing some paths toward healing. Utilizing a framework of "red" and "green" grace, Jay McDaniel offers that acknowledging suffering—both human and nonhuman—leads to opportunities for creative, positive transformation through shared experiences of suffering and resurrection.

THE CROSS: IMPERIALISM, VIOLENCE, AND PEACE

This section of the volume centers on two main issues: violence and imperialism as they are justified or questioned by Christian understandings of the cross. Considering the role of violence in Christian ideas of atonement, one may ask whether and how death and violence evidenced in the cross are linked to salvation and redemption. If death and suffering were necessary for God's reconciliation with the world, are they still redemptive or saving today? Does Christian theology continue to support the idea that killing and self-sacrifice are the way to reach peace?

On the issue of imperialism, many of the essays affirm an essential shift in Christian interpretation of the cross when Constantine adopted Christianity as the imperial religion. At the Battle at the Milvian Bridge in 312 C.E., Constantine was inspired by a vision that assured that he would conquer in the name of Christ and thus he ordered the Chi-Rho sign for Christianity to be placed on his soldier's shields. This was the first notable event in a subsequently long and dark history in which Christianity became fused with violent imperialistic interests. Even as Constantine's support of Christianity undoubtedly contributed to the success and continuation of this relatively new religion, Christianity's new role in supporting an empire affected its self-understanding ever since.

From this point forward, empires used Christianity across the globe to support military invasions, wars, and conquests of various people who did not adhere to its beliefs. Conquering in the name of the cross, whether in the Crusades or the European colonial invasions beginning in the fifteenth century, Christians created a self-justifying rationale based on connecting the symbol of the cross to conquest, including the unqualified "good" accomplishment of conversion and the often violently procured victory of an empire. Not surprisingly, both religious and military victory resulted in furthering the material wealth of the conquerors. Moltmann and Hall's essays herein directly or indirectly ask that the reader consider this pattern in light of today's global domination by the Christian-identified United States.

The cross has been used for centuries as a rallying point for anti-Semitic movements and whites have used it also to bolster the oppression of black and native peoples in North and South America. At multiple times across the span of its history, Christianity has mounted attacks against Jewish people using the same recycled justifications. One of the most notable of these justifications states that the Jews killed Jesus, which somehow justifies Christian violence against them. This argument is evident in the writings of Reformers and Catholic theologians who supported persecution of the Jews as well as their expulsion from several nations in Europe, in statements supporting the twentieth-century Holocaust, and in current Arian-supremacist literature. Of course, this argument forgets the fact that Jesus himself was Jewish, along with his mother, his disciples, the apostle Paul, and almost all of the early followers of Jesus who became the early church.

Along with anti-Semitism, several of the essays discuss the use of the cross to support racial injustice and violence in the United States. Considering this history of Christians using the cross as a tool of oppression, one may ask whether the symbol ultimately serves to feed such a history or whether the cross and Christian atonement theories provide a counter-message that those employing the cross for ill have ignored.

The first three essays in this section, by S. Mark Heim, J. Denny Weaver, and Rita Nakashima Brock, examine the cross and Christian atonement theory in light of the connections between violence, sacrifice, and redemption. Heim's essay leads the section and provides a foundation for the discussion by utilizing René Girard's theories on the cyclical nature of violence and the role of sacrifice in ameliorating conflicts within a community. In light of Girard's proposals, Heim examines Christian interpretations of the atonement and whether Jesus' death exemplifies the conflict-sacrifice-peace cycle or whether it demands that Christians end the perpetuation of such cycles of violence. Heim's goal is to make sense of the Christian claim that the work of the cross is good and necessary for human redemption even while killing and crucifixions are clearly evil and violent. Weaver's essay provides a broad basis for understanding main issues and questions raised within traditional Christian atonement theories and the ways that Christian theology has been used to perpetuate violence. He claims that the once-and-for-all nature of Jesus' crucifixion supports a contemporary Christian call to peaceful living. Brock's article engages the history of symbolic representations of the cross. While images of the cross were once linked with baptismal imagery, the cross came to depict Jesus' violent death as Christians increasingly sought to justify their own violence as redemptive.

The second set of essays in this section addresses the cross symbol in relation to nationalism, militarism, and imperial conquest. Douglas John Hall employs Luther's theology of the cross to underscore the image of a God who transforms the world through suffering and thereby challenges nationalistic, imperialistic images that depict God solely as almighty and triumphant. Jürgen Moltmann's short essay here reminds the reader of how the cross was used in the context of World War II Germany and elsewhere to support nationalism and war. Finally, Mark Lewis Taylor builds on his work in *The Executed God* as he addresses torture in light of Jesus' crucifixion, Christian eucharistic practice, and political resistance.

NEW DIRECTIONS FOR CROSS EXAMINATION AND ATONEMENT THEORY

> "More than 50 million people were systematically murdered in the past 100 years—the century of mass murder.... In sheer numbers, these and other killings make the 20th century the bloodiest period in human history."[14]

While Aulén's models have dominated theological discussion of atonement for nearly a century, many essays within this book suggest that the context of cross examination has shifted in some significant ways, due in part to our increased global awareness of escalating systemic oppression and violence. Even as we have developed the technology to "achieve" the bloodiest century, we have also been made aware of genocide and oppression across the globe and have considered our involvement in perpetuating some of them. The context of the last century, combined with the influence of liberation theology (see above), has influenced Christian theological interpretation of the cross. While most theologians in this volume may not identify themselves as liberation theologians, several of them assume foundational tenets of liberation theology as normative while overlooking some of the traditional questions posed within atonement theories. Thus, while some scholars have claimed that liberation-based theologies can fit under the *Christus Victor* model, several assumptions and approaches stretch Aulén's category to the point that it is no longer fitting. These changes ultimately merit a new "liberationist" category of atonement theory.

In that liberation-based theologies generally assume that God's suffering through Jesus' death on the cross assures a defeat of evil because of the resurrection, one may find some consonance with the *Christus Victor* model of atonement. But other elements of this atonement theory are lacking and no other category offered by Aulén contains a more fitting model. Was Jesus' death *necessary* as a part of God's plan for salvation or was it the result of state-sponsored violence? The *Christus Victor* model implies that God uses the crucifixion as a method by which to conquer evil. And even though Abelard's model states that Jesus' crucifixion was not *necessary* for atonement, he still affirms that God *chose* Jesus' death on the cross to reveal God's love for humanity. In all of Aulén's categories, God is the one who essentially allows or causes Jesus' death on the cross because it is the mechanism by which God becomes reconciled with the world. Likewise, some liberation theologies may claim that God chooses to enter suffering and thereby can transform and end it.

Several essays in this volume, however, assume that the cross is the result of state-sponsored violence and was not necessarily planned or caused by God for the world's redemption. Most of the essays do not even entertain the question of whether Jesus' death was *necessary* as a part of an overall plan of God to reconcile Godself with the world. This may sound radical, but Christians often have asserted human-caused interpretations of Jesus' death by stating, for example, that it was the fault of the mob or religious authorities who demanded Jesus' death. Often, however, these same Christians contradict themselves by simultaneously believing that the cross was a part of God's plan, thereby essentially God-caused. Even while most essays do not discuss the necessity of the cross, almost all see it as profoundly important for Christian faith. For example, some claim the cross reveals the nature of God and God's presence in suffering.

Other common characteristics found across multiple essays include social interpretations of sin and salvation. Despite a wide variety of interpretations, the cross has always engaged Christian understandings of sin and the "fallen" nature of humanity. There is a definitive theological shift across the essays to understand sin primarily in terms of *systemic evil* (racism, sexism, anti-Semitism, torture, and imperialism) rather than personal, individual sin. Consequently, salvation is also conceived in social categories rather than primarily emphasizing the salvation of individual souls for an afterlife. Within many essays of this volume, salvation is seen in terms of a this-worldly liberation from injustice and oppression. Even as Jesus was resurrected, oppressed people can be assured that repressive economic systems and tyrannical governments do not have the last word. Since liberation from oppression involves the transformation of a social system, salvation is necessarily also social and involves the whole community of faith or an extended network of people and relationships. There is a further call to Christians to participate in the body of Christ, as the church, and live out the vision of the kingdom of God. As stated earlier, each author in this volume examines the cross in light of social contexts or issues and thus these most likely influence his or her interpretation. Nonetheless, redemption, the work of Jesus on the cross, sin, salvation, and God's reconciliation to the world are being conceived in ways that require an additional atonement framework.

A new liberationist atonement category includes theologies that conceive God's reconciliation with the world and Jesus' death on the cross in light of an understanding of sin primarily as systemic evil, and salvation chiefly as liberation from injustice. These lead to the understanding that Jesus' preaching of the kingdom or realm of God and his challenges to the dominating, oppressive empire of his day were significant and were at least partly responsible for his crucifixion. By God's suffering through Jesus on the cross, however, God feels the world's suffering and this is at least one way by which God is reconciled to the world. Jesus' death may or may not be deemed necessary or the only way through which this reconciliation occurs, depending on the author. Theologies holding a liberationist interpretation of Jesus' death span disparate fields within the study of religion and are a growing trend present beyond the scope of this volume of essays. For instance, Stanley Hauerwas displayed elements of such an approach in his 2006 essay "Why Did Jesus Have to Die?" Here he writes, "Jesus was put to death because he embodied a politics that threatened all worldly regimes based on the fear of death."[15]

This challenge to Aulén's models is not new, as many of these same characteristics are found in the work of the Social Gospel movement and of thinkers such as Walter Rauschenbusch. Founding thinkers associated with Aulén's three categories of atonement theory (Anselm, Abelard, Origen, and the Reformers) were simply not operating with an understanding of salvation as primarily social justice. Additionally, Jesus' relationship to the political and religious powers of his day was not so directly influential on atonement theories even if it had significant impact on understandings of grace, as in the Reformation. These themes are not emphasized in the moral example, substitutionary, or *Christus Victor* atonement models, as they have been traditionally understood. To stretch Aulén's models to fit is to distort them to such an extent that they become unrecognizable.

In interpreting the cross through the lens of social injustice, some of these proposals for cross examination also signal a break from popular discussions of the cross today and some traditions of theology that focus predominantly on personal sin and individual actions. Additionally, they provide a countercultural message in an individualistic society that likes to imagine salvation as pertaining to individual souls who are disconnected from the fate of other humans or the rest of creation. While most significant theologians of the Christian tradition have never divorced individual salvation from the overall hope for the realm of God, some thinkers have approached the Christian doctrines of election and atonement through a more individualistic lens. In this volume, the pendulum swings the other direction—by addressing the cross, atonement, and salvation in terms of live, pressing social issues, and thus offering fresh and varied perspectives on the meanings of the cross today.

Part One
The Cross in Racial and Gender Oppression

1

Black Women's Surrogacy Experience and the Christian Notion of Redemption

Delores S. Williams

OFTEN, AFRICAN AMERICAN WOMEN IN church and society have characterized their oppression as unique. Some black female scholars define this uniqueness on the basis of the interfacing of racial, class, and gender oppression in the experience of black women. This interfacing of oppressions is not unique to black women's experience, however. Jewish, Hispanic, Asian, and other women of color in America can also experience that reality. My exploration of black women's sources has revealed a heretofore-undetected structure of domination that has been operative in African American women's lives since slavery. This structure of domination is surrogacy, and it gives black women's oppression its unique character as well as raises challenging questions about the way redemption is imaged in a Christian context.

TWO FACES OF SURROGACY

On the basis of African American women's sources it is possible to identify two kinds of surrogacy that have given rise to the unique character of black women's oppression: *coerced surrogacy* and *voluntary surrogacy*. Coerced surrogacy, belonging to the pre–Civil War period, was a forced condition in which people and systems more powerful than black women and black people forced black women to function in roles that someone else ordinarily would have filled. For example, black female slaves were forced to substitute for the slave owner's wife in nurturing roles involving white children. Black women were forced to take the place of men in work roles that, according to the larger society's understanding of male and female roles, belonged to men. Frederick Law Olmsted, a Northern architect writing in the nineteenth century, said he "stood for a long time watching slave women repair a road on a South Carolina plantation."[1] During the antebellum period this coerced surrogacy was legally supported in the ownership rights by which slave masters controlled their property, for example, black women. Slave women could not exercise the choice of refusing the surrogacy role.

After emancipation the coercion associated with antebellum surrogacy was replaced by social pressures that influenced black women to continue to fill some surrogacy in the postbellum period. The difference was that black women, after emancipation, could exercise the choice of refusing the surrogate role. Because of this element of choice, postbellum surrogacy can be referred to as voluntary surrogacy, even though social pressures influenced the choices black women made as they adjusted to life in a "free" world.

A closer look at these two modes of surrogacy in the two different periods (antebellum and postbellum) provides an in-depth view of the differences between the two modes.

COERCED SURROGACY AND ANTEBELLUM REALITIES

In the period before the Civil War coerced surrogacy roles involving black women were in the areas of nurturance, field labor, and sexuality.

The mammy role was the direct result of the demands slavocracy made upon black women's nurturing capacities. Standing in the place of the slave owner's wife, mammy nurtured the entire white family. A long and respected tradition among many Southern whites, mammy was an empowered (but not autonomous) house slave who was given considerable authority by her owners. According to the existing scattered reports of mammies and how the tradition operated, we know many Southerners thought "Mammy . . . could do anything, and do it better than anyone else. Because of her expertise in all domestic matters, she was the premier house servant and all others were her subordinates."[2] According to historian

Deborah Gray White, Eliza Ripley, a Southern white woman who received nurture from a mammy, remembers her as

> a "supernumerary" who, after the children grew up, "managed the whole big and mixed household." In her [Eliza Ripley's] father's house, everyone was made to understand that "all applications" were to go through Mammy Charlotte. "Nobody thought to go to the judge or his wife for anything..."[3]

The testimony of ex-slaves themselves also attests to the value and power of mammies in the slaveholders' household. Drucilla Martin remembers "that her mother was in full charge of the house and all 'Marse' children."[4] Katherine Eppes of Alabama said that her mother "worked in the Big House, 'aspinnin and 'anussin de white chillun'."[5] Eppes also claimed that the slave owner's wife was so fond of her mother "that when she learned that the overseer had whipped the woman whom everyone called 'Mammy,' she dismissed him and gave him until sundown to remove himself and his family from the plantation."[6]

Mammy was not always so well treated, however. Frederick Douglass tells of his grandmother, who was mammy to a white family. When she became too old and frail to work, "they took her to the woods, built her a little hut with a mud chimney, and left her there to support and care for herself. As Douglass put it, 'they turned her out to die.'"[7] And there is the awful fate of one mammy named Aunt Betty, told by ex-slave Jacob Stroyer: "She had nursed her master through infancy, lived to see him become a drunk, and then became his victim when, during one of his drunken rampages, he took his shotgun and killed her."[8] Nevertheless, the mammy role was probably the most powerful and authoritative one slave women could fill. Though slave women in their coerced roles as mammies were often abused, they were also empowered.[9]

This was not the case for slave women laboring beyond the "big house," that is, the slave owner's dwelling. In the area of field labor, black women were forced into work usually associated with male roles.[10] Feminist scholar bell hooks claims that on large plantations "black women...plowed, planted and harvested crops. On some plantations black women worked longer hours in the fields than black men."[11] What this amounted to, in terms of coerced surrogacy, was black female energy substituting for male energy. This results in what hooks refers to as the masculinization of the black female.[12]

In their autobiographies some ex-slave women describe the masculine work roles black women were forced to fill. Bethany Veney tells of helping her cruel slave owner haul logs, drive out hogs, and set posts into the ground for fences.[13]

Louisa Picquet tells of slave women who drove ox wagons, tended mills, and plowed just like men.[14] Another ex-slave, Mary Prince, tells of a slave woman who drove cattle, tended sheep, and did general farming work in the fields.[15]

Unlike the mammy role of the female house slaves, the masculinized roles of the female field slave did not empower black women in the slave structure to the extent that mammies were empowered. In the fields the greatest amount of power a slave could hold was in the position of slave driver or overseer. Usually, only males could ascend to these roles. Thus, the driver was a male slave. Though a few black males served as overseers, this role was usually filled by white men of lower social class than the slave owner. Females who filled the masculinized roles in the fields were less respected than mammies and drivers. Field women were not often given recognition for their service, seldom realized the endearment of the white folks as did some of the mammies, got worse food and clothing, and often received more brutal punishment. These masculinized female field slaves were thought to be of a lower class than the female house slaves, who usually did "women's work" consisting of cleaning, spinning, cooking, sewing, and tending to the children.

More than in the areas of nurturance and field labor, coerced surrogacy in the area of sexuality was threatening to slave women's self-esteem and sense of self-worth. This is the area in which slave women were forced to stand in the place of white women to provide sexual pleasure for white male slave owners. The Victorian ideal of true womanhood (for Anglo American women) supported a consciousness that, in the area of sexual relations, imagined sex between free white men and their wives to be for the purpose of procreation rather than for pleasure. Many white males turned to slave women for sexual pleasure and forced these women to fulfill needs that, according to racist ideology concerning male-female relations, should have been fulfilled by white women.

In her narrative *Incidents in the Life of a Slave Girl,* Linda Brent presents a vivid description of her slave owner Dr. Flint, who tried to force her into one of these illicit female slave/slave master sexual liaisons. Brent escaped his advances by fleeing from his house and hiding for seven years in a crawl space in the roof of her grandmother's home.[16] The octoroon slave woman Louisa Picquet was not as fortunate as Linda Brent. Louisa was purchased by a Mr. Williams when she was about fourteen years old. He forced her into sexual relations with him. From these relations four children issued.[17] Another slave woman, Cynthia, was purchased by a slave trader who told her she would either accompany him home and become his "housekeeper" or he would sell her as a field worker to one of the worst plantations on the Mississippi River. Cynthia thus became the slave trader's mistress and housekeeper.[18]

There was in the antebellum South a kind of institutionalizing of female slave/slave master sexual liaisons that was maintained through the "fancy trade." This was a special kind of slave trading involving the sale of what were thought to be beautiful black women for the exclusive purpose of becoming mistresses of wealthy slave owners. Though New Orleans seems to have been the center of this trade, it also flourished in Charleston and Columbia, South Carolina; St. Louis, Missouri; and Lexington and Richmond, Virginia.[19] The famous octoroon balls that occurred in New Orleans allowed rich white men to meet and purchase these black women, who became their mistresses and often bore children by these slave owners.

Beyond this special kind of arrangement, slave owners also frequented the slave quarters and established sexual relations with any female slave they chose. The slave woman in either kind of arrangement had no power to refuse this coerced surrogacy in which she stood in the place of the white woman. Sometimes these slave women hoped for (and were promised) their freedom through sexual liaisons with the slave master. But more often than not their expectations were futile, and they were "sold off to plantations where they shared the misery of all slaves."[20]

All three forms of coerced surrogacy illustrate a unique kind of oppression only black women experienced in the slavocracy. Only black women were mammies. Only black women were permanently assigned to field labor. Only black women permanently lost control of their bodies to the lust of white men. During slavery, black women were bound to a system that had respect for neither their bodies, their dignity, their labor, nor their motherhood except as it was put to the service of securing the well-being of ruling-class white families. In the United States fierce and violent struggle had to afflict the entire nation before Southern slave women would experience a measure of relief from coerced surrogacy roles.

Voluntary Surrogacy and Postbellum Realities

When the American Civil War ended and the master-slave relation was officially terminated in the South, black people tried to determine for whom or what black women *would not* stand in place. They were especially anxious to relieve black women from those coerced surrogacy roles related to field work and to black women's sexuality involving black female/white male sexual liaisons. Ex-slave women themselves are reported to have said "they never mean to do any outdoor work, that white men support their wives and the [black women] mean that their husbands shall support them."[21] Black men were just as anxious for black women to quit the fields. According to historians Carter G. Woodson and Lorenzo Greene, "The Negro male when he worked for wages . . . tended to imitate the whites by keeping his wife and daughters at home."[22]

Of even greater concern to black males and females were their efforts to terminate the forced sexual relations between black women and white men that existed during slavery. Inasmuch as marriage between African American women and men became legal after freedom and droves of black women and men came to official locations to be married,[23] sexual liaisons between white men and black women could be curtailed, although white men (without regard for black marriage) still took advantage of some black women. bell hooks points out that after black reconstruction (1867–1877) "black women were often coerced into sexual liaisons with white employers who would threaten to fire them unless they capitulated to sexual demands."[24]

Nevertheless, there was not nearly as much sexual activity between black women and white men after slavery because black women themselves could refuse to substitute for white women in providing sexual pleasure for white males. Nancy White, a contemporary black female domestic worker, testified about refusing this role of playmate to white male employers:

> I've had to ask some [white man employers] to keep their hands off me and I've had to just give up some jobs if they got too hot behind me. . . . I have lost some money that way, but that's all right. When you lose control of your body, you have just about lost all you have in this world.[25]

Nancy White makes it clear that some white female employers approved of black women standing in their places to provide sexual favors for their husbands. White says:

> One day that woman [her white female employer] told me that she wouldn't be mad if I let her husband treat me the same way he treated her. I told her I would be mad . . . if he tried to treat me like I was as married to him as she was.[26]

Nancy White goes on to describe her method of declining this surrogate role her female and male employers wanted to assign her. Says White: "I had to threaten that devil [the white male employer] with a pot of hot grease to get him to keep his hands to himself."[27]

While black women and men did realize a small measure of success in determining the surrogate roles black women would not fill after emancipation, certain social and economic realities limited black women's power to choose full exemption from all surrogacy roles. Poverty and the nature of the work available, especially to Southern black families, demanded black women's participation in some of the most strenuous areas of the workforce. There was also the attempt among newly freed black families to adopt some of the values of the people they took to be "quality white folk" during slavery.[28] This meant that efforts were made to influence black women to choose to continue in two of the surrogate roles they had filled during slavery: substituting female power and energy for male power and energy, and acting in mammy capacities.

After emancipation black women chose to substitute their energy and power for male energy and power in the area of farm labor. Greene and Woodson tell of urban Negro male laborers in 1901 who saved money and invested in farms. "It was not uncommon...to see Negro mechanics owning well-kept farms, which were cared for chiefly by wives and families."[29] The United States Census of 1910 reported that 967,837 black women were farm laborers and 79,309 were farmers.[30] Also, in 1910 Addie W. Hunton reported that

> More than half of the 2,000,000 wage earning women of the [black] race are engaged in agriculture from its roughest and rudest form to its highest and most attractive form....The 15,792,579 acres owned and cultivated by Negroes, which with buildings and equipment and rented farm lands reach a valuation approaching a billion dollars, represent not only the hardihood and perseverance of the Negro man but the power for physical and mental endurance of the woman working by his side. Many of the farms owned by colored men are managed entirely by the women of the family while these men give themselves to other employment.[31]

It was, however, the surrogate role of mammy that some black males and white people consciously tried to perpetuate into the future beyond slavery and reconstruction. In Athens, Georgia, in the early twentieth century, Samuel Harris, the black principal of Athens Colored High School, dreamed up the idea of starting the Black Mammy Memorial Institute in that city. With the help of prominent white citizens this institute was chartered on September 19, 1910, and was authorized to operate for twenty years. According to a brochure published by the Black Mammy Memorial Association, the institute was to be a memorial where men and women learn... how to work and to love their work; where the mantle of the "Old Black Mammy" may fall on those who go forth to serve; where the story of these women will be told to the generations that come and go; where better mothers for homes will be trained; a building from which those who go forth in life may speak louder in their works than their words.... The MONUMENTAL INDUSTRIAL INSTITUTE to the OLD BLACK MAMMY of the South will be devoted to the industrial and moral training of young Negro men and women. The work that is to receive special emphasis is the training of young women in Domestic Art.[32]

Obviously the prominent white citizens wanted to perpetuate the mammy roles so that the comfort of the white family could be assured by a type of black female servant who (after slavery) was properly trained in the skills of nurturing, supporting, and caring about the well-being of white children. Not so obvious, but probable, is the suggestion that to the black man Mr. Harris, black women trained in the mammy skills could learn to organize and manage the black households in the same way that the slave owners' households were organized and managed. This meant that the black family had to become more patriarchal in its structure and values in order to resemble the slave owners' households.

Mammy had a variety of skills that could accommodate this process. She was skillful at exerting authority in the household while being careful not to offend or usurp the power of the patriarchal authority figures: the slave master and his wife. Mammy was skilled in about every form of what was thought of as women's work: sewing, spinning, cooking, cleaning, tending to children, and so on. Hence she could train female children in this work. According to Deborah Gray White, mammy was often the advisor of the slave master in business matters. With regard to the quality of relationships in the master's family, she knew how to be a diplomat and a peacemaker who often healed relations that had gone awry. The mammy skills could promote and support black males as they became the patriarchal heads of the black household after slavery. And the black family could therefore resemble the patriarchal model of family sanctioned in mainline American society.

One could also suggest that the institution of Mothers of the Church, which developed in some black churches after emancipation, has kinship with the mammy tradition. Like the antebellum mammy, a mother of the church exerts considerable authority in the church family. But more often than not she uses her power in such a way that it does not challenge the power and authority of the patriarchal head of the church, usually a male preacher. She is sometimes called upon to be a healer of relationships within the congregation. She is well versed in and knows how to pass along the church's highest values for living the Christian life. Her power and influence often extend beyond the church into her community because she has been empowered by one of the central authority agents of the community (the black church) to provide care and nurture for the children of God.

Black women's history of filling surrogacy roles has fed into negative stereotypes of black women that exist until this day. From the mammy tradition has emerged the image of black women as perpetual mother figures, religious, fat, asexual, loving children better than themselves, self-sacrificing, giving up self-concern for group advancement. The antebellum tradition of masculinizing black women through their work has given rise to the image of black women as unfeminine, physically strong, and having the capacity to bear considerably more pain than white women. These kinds of ideas helped create the notion of black women as superwomen. The sexual liaisons between white men and slave women created the image of the black woman as Jezebel, as one "governed almost entirely by her libido . . . the counterimage of the mid-nineteenth-century ideal of the Victorian lady."[33] Hence the surrogacy roles black women have filled during slavery and beyond are exploitative. They rob African American women of self-consciousness, self-care, and self-esteem, and put them in the service of other people's desires, tasks, and goals. This has serious implications for Christian theologians attempting to use black women's history as a source for constructive theology.

From Black Woman Surrogate to Surrogate Jesus

One of the results of focusing upon African American women's historic experience with surrogacy is that it raises significant questions about the way many Christians, including black women, have been taught to image redemption. More often than not the theology in mainline Christian churches, including black ones, teaches believers that sinful humankind has been redeemed because Jesus died on the cross in the place of humans, thereby taking human sin upon himself. In this sense Jesus represents the ultimate surrogate figure standing in the place of someone else: sinful humankind. Surrogacy, attached to this divine personage, thus takes on an aura of the sacred. It is therefore altogether fitting and proper for black women to ask whether the image of a surrogate God has salvific power for black women, or whether this image of redemption supports and reinforces the exploitation that has accompanied their experience with surrogacy. If black women accept this image of redemption, can they not also passively accept the exploitation surrogacy brings?

I recognize that reflection upon these questions surfaces many complex theological issues; for instance, the part God the Father played in determining the redemptive, surrogate role filled by Jesus the Son. For black women there is also the question of whether Jesus on the cross represents coerced surrogacy (willed by the Father), voluntary surrogacy (chosen by the Son), or both. At any rate, a major theological problem here is the place of the cross in any theology significantly informed by African American women's experience with surrogacy. Even if one buys into German theologian Jürgen Moltmann's notion of the cross as the meeting place of the will of God to give up the Son (coerced surrogacy?) and the will of the Son to give up himself (voluntary surrogacy?) so that "the spirit of abandonment and self-giving love" proceed from the cross "to raise up abandoned men,"[34] African American women are still left with this question: Can there be salvific power in Christian images of oppression (for example, Jesus on the cross) meant to teach something about redemption?

Theologians since the time of Origen have been trying to make the Christian principle of atonement believable by shaping theories about it in the language and thought that people of a particular time understood and in which they were grounded. Thus, most theories of atonement, classical and contemporary, are time-bound (as well as ideologically bound with patriarchy) and do not respond meaningfully to the questions of people living beyond the particular time period. For instance, Origen (183–253 C.E.), capitalizing on people's belief in devils and spirits, provided what Lutheran theologian Alan Richardson speaks of as a ransom theory, claiming that the death of Jesus on the cross was a ransom paid by God to the devil for the sins of humankind.[35] This view of atonement declined when another age dawned. Thus, Anselm emerged in the eleventh century and spoke of atonement using the chivalric language and sociopolitical thought of his time. He shaped a theory describing sin as the human way of dishonoring God. People owed honor to God just as peasants and squires owed honor and loyalty to the feudal overlord. However, men had no power to render satisfaction to God for their massive disloyalty to God through sin. According to the codes of chivalry in Anselm's time, one atoned for a crime either by receiving punishment or by providing satisfaction to the injured person. Since God did not want to punish humans forever (which the sin deserved), and since humans had no means to render satisfaction to God's injured honor, the deity, Godself, made restitution for humanity. God satisfied God's own violated honor by sending the Son to earth in human form ultimately to die on the cross.

There were also the moral theories of atonement associated with Abelard (1079–1142). Since the church in Abelard's time put great stress upon the penitential life of believers, it was reasonable for Abelard to see Calvary as "the school of penitence of the human race, for there men of all ages and races have learned the depth and power of the love of God."[36] These moral theories of atonement, as they are often referred to,[37] emphasized God's love in the work of atonement and claimed that, when humans look upon the death of Jesus, they see the love of God manifested. The cross brings repentance to humankind and shows simultaneously God the Father's love and the suffering human sin inflicted upon that love. The moral theories of atonement taught that the cross was "the most powerful moral influence in history, bringing to men that repentance which renders them able to be forgiven."[38]

As the Renaissance approached and the medieval worldview collapsed, the Anselmian and Abelardian ways of understanding the atonement began to fade. The Renaissance was a time of great interest in the revival of ancient law. So it was reasonable to expect the Reformers to work out their theories of atonement in legal terms grounded in the new political and legal thought of the sixteenth century. Thus, Calvin and others spoke of the justice of God the judge, of the divine law of punishment that could not be ignored, and of the infinite character of human sin that deserved infinite harsh punishment. But, according to the Reformers, God is both just and merciful. Therefore, in infinite mercy God provided a substitute who would bear the punishment for human sin. Jesus Christ came to offer himself as a substitute for humans. He took their punishment upon himself. Thus, the Reformers provided a substitution theory of atonement.

While these theories of atonement—ransom, satisfaction, substitution, and moral—may not be serviceable for providing an acceptable response to African American women's questions about redemption and surrogacy, they do illustrate a serviceable practice for female theologians attempting today to respond to this question. That practice (as shown by the theologians above) was to use the language and sociopolitical thought of the time to render Christian principles understandable. This fits well the task of the black female theologian, which is to use the language and sociopolitical thought of black women's world to show them that their salvation does not depend upon any form of surrogacy made sacred by human understandings of God. This means using the language and thought of liberation to liberate redemption from the cross and to liberate the cross from the "sacred aura" put around it by existing patriarchal responses to the question of what Jesus' death represents. To find resources to accomplish this task, the black female theologian is led to the Scriptures.

The Synoptic Gospels (more than Paul's letters) provide resources for constructing a Christian understanding of redemption that speaks meaningfully to black women, given their historic experience with surrogacy. Jesus' own words in Luke 4 and his ministry of healing the human body, mind, and spirit (described in Matthew, Mark, and Luke) suggest that Jesus did not come to redeem humans by showing them God's love "manifested" in the death of God's innocent child on a cross erected by cruel, imperialistic, patriarchal power. Rather, the spirit of God in Jesus came to show humans *life*—to show redemption through a perfect *ministerial* vision of righting relationships. A female-male inclusive vision, Jesus' ministry of righting relationships involved raising the dead (for example, those appearing to be lost from life), casting out demons (for example, ridding the mind of destructive forces prohibiting the flourishing of positive, peaceful life), and proclaiming the word of life that demanded the transformation of tradition so that life could be lived more abundantly. Jesus was quick to remind his disciples that humans were not made for the Sabbath; rather, the Sabbath was made for humans. God's gift to humans, through Jesus, was to invite them to participate in this ministerial vision ("whosoever will, let them come") of righting relations. The response to this invitation by human principalities and powers was the horrible deed that the cross represents—the evil of humankind trying to kill the ministerial vision of life-in-relation that Jesus brought to humanity. The resurrection does not depend upon the cross for life, for the cross only represents historical evil trying to defeat good. The resurrection of Jesus and the flourishing of God's spirit in the world as the result of resurrection represent the life of the ministerial vision gaining victory over the evil attempt to kill it. Thus, to respond meaningfully to black women's historic experience of surrogacy-oppression, the theologian must show that redemption of humans can have nothing to do with any kind of surrogate role Jesus was reputed to have played in a bloody act that supposedly gained victory over sin and/or evil. Black women are intelligent people living in a technological world where nuclear bombs, defilement of the earth, racism, sexism, and economic injustices attest to the presence and power of evil in the world. Perhaps not many people today can believe that evil and sin were overcome by Jesus' death on the cross; that is, that Jesus took human sin upon himself and therefore saved humankind. Rather, it seems more intelligent to understand that redemption had to do with God, through Jesus, giving humankind new vision to see resources for positive, abundant relational life—a vision humankind did not have before. Hence, the kingdom-of-God theme in the ministerial vision of Jesus does not point to death; that is, it is not something one has to die to get to. Rather, the kingdom of God is a metaphor of hope God gives those attempting to right the relations between self and self, between self and others, between self and God as prescribed in the Sermon on the Mount and the golden rule.

Though space limitations here prohibit more extensive reconstruction of this Christian understanding of redemption (given black women's surrogacy experience), there are a few things that can be said about sin in this kind of reconstruction. The image of Jesus on the cross is the image of human sin in its most desecrated form. This execution destroyed the body, but not before it mocked and defiled Jesus by publicly exposing his nakedness and private parts, by mocking the ministerial vision as they labeled him king of the Jews, by placing a crown of thorns upon his head, thus mocking his dignity and the integrity of his divine mission. The cross thus becomes an image of defilement, a gross manifestation of collective human sin. Jesus, then, does not conquer sin through death on the cross. Rather, Jesus conquers the sin of temptation in the wilderness (Matt. 4:1-11) by resistance—by resisting the temptation to value the material over the spiritual ("One does not live by bread alone," v. 4); by resisting death (not attempting suicide—"if you are the Son of God, throw yourself down," v. 6); by resisting the greedy urge of monopolistic ownership ("the devil . . . showed him all the kingdoms of the world and their splendor; and he said to him, 'All these I will give you, if you will fall down and worship me'," v. 9). Jesus therefore conquered sin in life, not in death. In the wilderness he refused to allow evil forces to defile the balanced relation between the material and the spiritual, between life and death, between power and the exertion of it.

What this allows the black female theologian to show black women is that God did not intend the surrogacy roles they have been forced to perform. God did not intend the defilement of their bodies as white patriarchal power put them in the place of white women to provide sexual pleasure for white men during the slavocracy. This was rape. Rape is defilement, and defilement means wanton desecration. Worse, deeper and more wounding than alienation, defilement is the sin of which today's technological world is most guilty. Nature—the land, the seas, the animals in the sea—are every day defiled by humans. Cultures such as Native American and African have been defiled by the onslaught of Western, patriarchal imperialism. The oceans are defiled by oil spills and human waste, destroying marine life. The rain forest is being defiled. The cross is a reminder

of how humans have tried throughout history to destroy visions of righting relationships that involve transformation of tradition and transformation of social
relations and arrangements sanctioned by the status quo. The resurrection of
Jesus and the kingdom-of-God theme in Jesus' ministerial vision provide black
women with the knowledge that God has, through Jesus, shown humankind how
to live peacefully, productively, and abundantly in relationship. Humankind is
therefore redeemed through Jesus' life and not through Jesus' death. There is
nothing of God in the blood of the cross. God does not intend black women's
surrogacy experience. Neither can Christian faith affirm such an idea. Jesus did
not come to be a surrogate. Jesus came for life, to show humans a perfect vision of
ministerial relation that humans had forgotten long ago. As Christians, however,
black women cannot forget the cross. But neither can they glorify it. To do so is
to make their exploitation sacred. To do so is to glorify sin.

2

Our Mothers' Gardens

Rethinking Sacrifice

JoAnne Marie Terrell

What might have been? He's never far from my mind. I was reading in Scriptures where the Lord Jesus Christ was scarred. His visage, his face was marred beyond that of any other man, and Emmett came to me. I said, "Oh my God, what a comparison." The spirit spoke to me as plainly as I'm talking to you now. And the spirit said, "Emmett was race hatred personified. That is how ugly race hatred is." I said, "Oh." I had to sit down. It struck me really hard. If Jesus Christ died for our sins, Emmett Till bore our prejudices, so . . .

Mamie Mobley, Mother of Emmett Till[1]

Why I'm not good enough? Harpo ast Mr._____
Mr._____ say, Your mammy.
Harpo say, What wrong with my mammy?
Mr._____ say, Somebody kill her . . .
[Harpo]: It not her fault somebody kill her. It not! It not!

Alice Walker, *The Color Purple*[2]

33

Jesus Crucified and Christ Glorified

What might have been? Why I'm not good enough? What wrong with my mammy? The above citations instance the experiences of African American males Emmett Till, a mid-twentieth-century lynching victim and martyr (d. 1955), and Harpo, a fictional character in Alice Walker's controversial novel. Till was a fourteen-year-old boy accused of whistling at a white woman. When his body was discovered, he had been shot and beaten, his neck rigged with a gin-mill fan around it. Harpo's mother, Annie Julia, had been shot and killed, like my own mother, by a jealous lover. Each crime disclosed demonstrates how inextricably linked are the sufferings of African American women and men and their children.

Mobley's question implicates the brutality of white racism in the interdiction of a well-intended life. Drawing the comparison with Christ's suffering, she also implicates (or absolves) God, invoking the hermeneutics of sacrifice. Harpo's questions evoke the legal stipulation that would have effected chattel slavery for life: *partus sequitur ventrem*, that is, "the child follows the condition of the mother." Stigmatized by his mother's fate, he was powerless to overcome his own social alienation and win the approval of his beloved Sofia's father.

Mobley cites the fourth song of Deutero-Isaiah's Suffering Servant songs (Isa. 42:1-2; 49:1-6; 50:4-11; 52:13—53:12). The specific verse Mobley quotes simulates royal imagery by drawing its antitheses: The king is supposed to be good looking; for example, Saul is lifted up because of his singular handsomeness (1 Sam. 9:2); the Servant, on the other hand, has no attractive features. Whereas the king is divinely chosen and anointed, the Servant is "inhumanely disfigured," perhaps with leprosy, a condition that suggested divine disfavor in that context. This antiroyal, righteous sufferer motif runs throughout the passage and, together with the atoning work, death, and resurrection of the Servant, accounts for the Christian appropriation of the Songs to describe Jesus' career and significance. In Jewish interpretive tradition the Servant is usually identified as the Jewish people or a "remnant" thereof; nevertheless, the Songs provided a blueprint for the *imitatio Christi* for the church in persecution and slavery, and they still guide African Americans' apprehension of Christian kerygma and doctrine.

Like the Servant, Jesus, and the Jewish people, African Americans have been devalued, marred, and killed by the violence of oppressors. Given their experiences of massive collective suffering, the notion that divine disfavor is operative contributes to the ambiguity with which persons in both communities understand their relationship to God. Although the love ethic in the Black

Church is predicated on the theme of righteous suffering and is sustained by the compensatory mechanisms of promise, it is unclear if Mobley appeals to it prescriptively and thereby absolves God concerning Emmett's death. Yet it is abundantly clear that she recognizes the destructiveness in the human agency of those responsible. Thus, her comparison of Emmett's suffering with that of Christ's strikes me as having been made not as an inflated or sanctimonious claim but descriptively, in consequence of genuinely living in the theodical question. As one standing within the interpretive tradition of the Black Church, Mobley's willingness to be taught by the Spirit is likely an affirmation of the goodness and sovereignty of God in opposition to white supremacy.

Mobley's image of God, reflected in the face of her mutilated son, as well as Walker's conceptualization of God, recall the dual images of Jesus crucified and Christ glorified and my family's experience of plantation farming. Just as the cross and the cotton-picker's croker sack evoked in me the same reaction of resentment to suffering, when I looked again on the cotton fields of North Carolina, a more attractive picture emerged from a second, skewed image of that crucifixion through circumscription. Like the triumphalist God, plantation labor also fascinated me, for two reasons: (1) because the element of surprise was always great among the mass of folks working together, and (2) because the opportunities to marvel at nature were simply rife. Like the juxtaposed images of Jesus crucified and Christ glorified, like croker sacks/white overseers/aching backs and sun/sky/singing voices/variegated insects/smells of earth, Mobley's and Walker's images of God present me with something fascinating to behold and ponder in the light of my black, womanist, and Christian commitments.

MULTIPLE CROSSES: QUESTIONS WITHIN A CHRISTIAN TRADITION OF SACRIFICE

My rather large family picked cotton and other crops regularly to supplement my stepfather's Air Force income and support ourselves during those early years of his and my mother's volatile relationship. Perhaps among other workers we were a bit elitist, owing to the grandeur we attached to his station. Yet we understood that because we were black and had few other options in the labor force, ours was an imposed lot that neither matched our social and political ambitions nor allowed us to address fully our spiritual and intellectual needs. Economic stress also highlighted my stepfather's inability to fulfill the patriarchal expectations society placed upon him. Thus, race and class oppression, concretized in the experience of plantation labor, reduplicated itself in the often violent interrelations of my family. Once more, I was frightened and repulsed by "the cross"—this time, of plantation labor—because I was sure that this kind of sweat, pain, and toil would be my destiny, portending little agency in a world that held out so many prospects for fun as well as purposeful living. The mean conditions seemed *prescribed* for black people, and I internalized this as an affront to my personal dignity and human potential. Even though I could not name these realities as a child, I understood them. As it was with me then, so it is with me now: the overwhelming sentiment in my heart and mind is that of resentment toward black delimitation and the devastating effects it has had and continues to have on black families' lives.

My resentment has foundations in the African American collective experience of slavery. Beginning in the seventeenth century, European colonists effected the rise of agrarian capitalism on the backs of children, women, and men of African descent through the imposition of chattel slavery and the gradual elimination of indentured servitude. Three, nearly four centuries later, this unpacked, encoded memory of my collective experience, adumbrated in the cotton fields of North Carolina, disclosed bales of resentment in my precocious, even "proto-womanist"[3] soul and stimulated my desire to examine the history and the burden of "the cross" of slavery. I have sought to understand both the black collective experience and my family history as they impinge on my spiritual and intellectual life by linking them to the story of Jesus. Just as the image of a cross recalls for nearly all Christians the physical and psychic injury Jesus sustained for us, the image of a croker sack recalls for me the physical and psychic injury my own and other black families sustained for the benefit of white families and southern agrarian economies, from slavery to the present.

Critical inquiry by some black theologians has broached the theme of unjust suffering and queried the adequacy of Christian theological anthropologies[4] for understanding black peoples' plight. Broadly, they addressed Christian sacrificial tradition with this question: How is the gospel message of the atonement, or reconciliation of sinners with God through Jesus Christ's death on the cross, to be construed by black people, who are similarly persecuted and simultaneously indicted as sinners?[5] Although they did not hold monolithic christological views, black theologians identified their communities' seeming fascination with the cross as *theodicy*,[6] attempts by black Christians to understand the evil they encountered in white power structures and white people, who also claimed to be Christians.

One task of this essay is to survey the works of black theologians and discuss the liberative import they found in the gospel that enabled them to remain both black and Christian.

With feminist theologians, womanist theologians have recently identified the motif of Christ's *surrogacy* (on which hinge traditional theories of the atonement) as problematic in the confession of faith not only because of its utility in sanctioning women's oppression[7] but also because of its similarity to the historical circumscription of black women in surrogate roles in relationship to white men, white women, and their children.[8] Moreover, black women have been historically obliged to be surrogates for black men: in slavery, working in the fields, doing what was considered "man's work"; in the post-slavery labor force, assuming the traditional role of "provider" through whatever employment whites made available. In postmodernity,[9] perhaps singularly owing to the targeting, censuring, and scapegoating of young, black men through the criminal justice system, black women continue in surrogate roles as providers for their families, as "mothers and fathers" for their children. Black women, too, have begun to question Christian sacrificial tradition: Does the image of Jesus as a surrogate figure have salvific power for black women, or does it reinforce the exploitation that accompanies their experiences of surrogacy? Are there ways for black women to be of service in churches and in the communities that are nonproscriptive and nonexploitative? In other words, is the profession of faith in the cross inimical to black women's self-interests? Or, is there power in the blood?

My penchant for theological reflection began at an early age, as I tried to understand the circumscription of black families in the southern work force. My family was embroiled in a complex of issues that often resolved in domestic violence, some of which stemmed from the economic and social stress we were experiencing, some of which stemmed from both my parents' profound self-alienation and social alienation. My mother's story, in particular, is that of a woman who, for the better part of her short life and for all of my life with her, lived in deep grief over personal losses too numerous and painful to recount. Lost in a fog of addiction, after several failed marriages, miscarriages, and broken relationships, she, like Harpo's mother, was shot and killed by her lover. Her murder attests to the insidiousness of sexism within the African American community and to the truth of the radical critique of the hermeneutics of sacrifice put forth in the little ditty that some Black Power advocates sang in opposition to the civil rights movement, which I take liberty to paraphrase here: "Too much love...nothing kills a [woman] like too much love."

Building on Abelard's insight that Christ's example teaches and saves us, I believe that anyone's death has salvific significance if we learn continuously from the life that preceded it. I often resort to my mother's garden—her life story—which for many years I regarded as a tragic tale that had moralistic theological import at best. Whenever I have failed to heed the lessons I have learned, it reflects the fact that I had neglected to tend her garden. Sometimes, I have to admit, I very nearly forget the "rose" that she was—sweet, fragile, beautiful, funny, boisterous, quiet, complicated—much like Margaret Avery in her depiction of Shug Avery in the movie *The Color Purple.* Although her self-alienation was evident long before I was born, in light of her considerable gifts of music, poetry, intellect, and humor, upon my mother's demise I was compelled to ask as a grieving child Mobley's question, "What might have been?" As a consequence of my own alienation, I have been compelled many times to ask Harpo's questions. As a religious person and as a scholar in the tradition of "faith in search of understanding," I search wholeheartedly for answers to them all. The personal crosses I have borne form the basis of my engagement in proto-womanist and womanist reflection on the cross in the African American experience. As a black/woman/person with roots in the poor and working classes, I bring all of my experiences and insights to bear on my womanist theological reflection, in hope of *sacramentally* witnessing to who and what God is in me.

The Social Context of Womanist Christology

African American women share in the historic experience of race and class oppression with black men and other people of color; class oppression with poor white women and men; and gender oppression with all women. With black men they bore the cross of slavery and, in the post-slavery work force, the stigma of the servant class. Many southern African American women (and men) still wear, in their hands, on their backs and knees, the stigmata impressed by the sun, thorns, and other hazards of nature, relics of their not-so-distant sharecropping past.

In postmodernity, with all people of color, black women and men share the cross of systemic racism and the issues endemic to it, especially the thwarting of the embarrassingly simple ideal of social, economic, and political parity with whites—debates over which impugn the humanity of colored peoples the world over, the deprivations of which undermine their prospects for survival, liberation, and creative self-expression. With all women, black women still die daily on the cross of sexism and the issues particular to it, including physical domination, economic injustice, political marginalization, and jeopardized reproductive rights—debates over which impugn the capacity of women to be full moral and social agents, the associated deprivations of which undermine the ability of women to participate fully in the imaging and construction of their own lives.

African Americans have always wrested humanity and agency from their proscribed existence, in conversation with the faith traditions they inherited from both Africa and America. From the days of slavery the very intransigence of their life circumstances helped shape the community's image of the divine as an embattled God and its image of Christ Jesus as a liberator from the seemingly demonic forces arrayed against it. The Bible provided mirrors of their experiences in stories of exile, enslavement, and exodus. In various and sundry ways Jesus was a prime exemplar of how to live in communion with God and neighbor in a context of oppression.

Womanists locate resources for doing theology in the *survival* and *liberation* traditions of the African American religious community. Consistent with the christocentrism of the Black Church, the evangelical thrust of black theology, along with critical insights on racism and classism in nationalist perspectives, the theologians I have focused upon have taken on the challenge of making the good news of and about Jesus relevant to all elements of a community forged in and forging ahead in crisis, bringing their own experiences of sexism to bear as well. Kelly Brown Douglas explores the *roots of the Black Christ* and Christ's significance for African American women. Jacquelyn Grant focuses on *Black Church* traditions that have informed African American women and sustained them in their spiritual, social, and political witness, yet maintains a stringent critique of racism, sexism, and classism in the society, the academy, and the Black Church. While varieties of womanist theology are critical of black theologies of liberation, they do not oppose the project of black liberation; they place a more nuanced emphasis on the goal of *survival* and *quality-of-life* issues for African American people, male and female. Delores S. Williams expresses this view of the womanist enterprise.

Black women have been immersed in totalistic ontological assault in sexism, racism, heterosexism, and classism. Abusive men and control-driven persons raped, battered, and killed them. All these phenomena provided the seedbed of womanist christological reflection, having left black women with little choice but to develop theological perspectives that pertained to their need for *bodily* redemption. The development of this crucial insight on embodied theology would become especially important for black lesbians, who had been stratified out of any consideration as partners in theological and social discourse with heterosexual women and men. Like Mary, a number of black women "kept all these things in [their] heart[s]" (Luke 2:51).

Atonement Theories in Womanist Perspective

Throughout Christian history the idea that Jesus Christ died "for our sake" has been alternately rendered as "on our behalf" or "in our stead" or "in our place," highlighting the surrogacy motif in scriptural and apostolic witness concerning Jesus.[10] Surrogacy has raised concern in feminist and womanist discourse over the nature of the relationship between God and Christ, inciting a controversy that poses several issues of grave concern for traditional theories of the atonement that purport that God *required* Jesus' death. These include the *ransom* and *satisfaction* theories, which synergized in the *substitution* theories of Protestant Reformers.[11] In the early church the prevailing mythos that the world was beset by competing principalities and powers gave rise to the belief that Jesus' death was a "ransom" paid to the devil.

Unfortunately, rather than purport a meaning of Christ's death that empowers Christian adherents to be countercultural, *sacramental* witnesses, the entrenchment of its own power and authority seems to have been the goal of the church since Constantine. In the fifth century Augustine used the weight of imperial authority to crush the Donatists in their opposition to the Catholic Church. In the Middle Ages Anselm consented to the class arrangements of feudalism, using it to model the divine-human relationship. During the Peasant Revolt of 1525 Martin Luther stood against German peasants' demands for equitable economic conditions and political autonomy in favor of "the magisterial sword and secular [Roman] law as the only bar to a relapse in barbarism."[12] In colonial and slaveholding America the church in collusion with the state imposed the hermeneutics of sacrifice because it was effective in inculcating docility among would-be insurrectionists and maintaining civil order. In the early years of the twentieth century President Woodrow Wilson (1913–1921) implemented Jim Crow laws in order to maintain the illusion of white supremacy and separate, unequal institutions, which, of course, included the church. In the era of civil rights and Black Power most white churches roundly ignored the abuses that state authorities heaped upon the black masses. And in postmodernity attitudes laced with sexist and heterosexist innuendo and rhetoric pervade black and white pulpits, negatively affecting the enactment and enforcement of laws protecting women and homosexuals. Thus, the church is historically guilty of inflicting and perpetuating abuse, allying with oppressors and imposing the hermeneutics of sacrifice on subjugated peoples in order to justify the abusive policies of the state and of its own ministerium.

Through the historical unfolding of atonement theories and the hermeneutics of sacrifice the Christian emphasis on Jesus' role as a surrogate/scapegoat has supported "violence, victimization, and undeserved suffering"[13] and lends credence to the charge of "divine child abuse" leveled by Asian American feminist Rita Nakashima Brock.[14] It is notable, though, that the church has developed no single doctrine or teaching on the atonement, only a number of theories that have different weight from communion to communion. Many people in black churches harmonize theories of the atonement, in much the same way that Christian tradition harmonized Synoptic and Fourth Gospel accounts of Jesus' life and ministry. Given that this syncretic model emphasizes Jesus' surrogacy as the means of spiritual liberation, often without a concomitant or necessary stress on political liberation, the doctrine begs for fresh interpretation so that it might have more liberative relevance for black Christians. Womanist theologians have taken up this challenge. In the process of formulating a Christology "from below," they stress the deeds of the historical Jesus and not the idealized Christ, in keeping with the liberative traditions of the religious community.

Kelly Brown Douglas

Kelly Brown Douglas, a systematic theologian and an Episcopalian priest, has explicated the emergence of the "Black Christ" in African American nationalist thought as a precursor to the development of a constructive womanist Christology. The nationalist offering of the Black Christ focused on the recognition or reimaging of God/Jesus as biologically black.[15] According to Douglas, Robert Alexander Young gave one of the earliest arguments for the blackness of God, whom Young believed would send a messiah to redress the wrongs blacks experienced in slavery. This messiah would be "born of a black woman." Douglas states that African Methodist Episcopal Bishop Henry McNeal Turner was among the first to identify the need for blacks to image God in the likeness of themselves, ascribing an ontological significance to the community's reimaging project. Whereas Young and Turner more directly linked the issue of Christ's/God's blackness to opposition to oppression, Marcus Garvey was one of the first to affirm blackness as a biological characteristic of the historical Jesus.

Despite these early attempts to state the significance of God/Christ in relationship to blackness, the Black Christ did not emerge as a formal category for theological reflection in the *liberation* approach until Black Power met with black theology. Contemporizing the relevance of the gospel for the oppressed, black theologians in the late 1960s framed their christological question in this way: Who is Jesus Christ for us today? Although their responses varied, they emphasized Jesus' suffering and stated mission of liberating the oppressed (cf. Luke

4:16–20) as those factors that characterized the essence of his identity, which led many of them to conclude that Christ is black.

Although Douglas locates the earliest warrants for the Black Christ in slave religion, for the slaves the concept had less to do with Jesus' presumed biological race and more to do with those with whom he identified during his lifetime and who they were: the poor and despised. Douglas cites the Lukan Gospel as important evidence of Jesus' liberating ministry. While the other Synoptic Gospels similarly relate Jesus' liberating acts, they are peculiarly in evidence in the Gospel of Luke. The slave community responded affirmatively to these stories and traditions. Moreover, Jesus' own experience of suffering was a reflection of the slaves' suffering, as Douglas attests:

> Essentially, through the cross the slaves' experience and Jesus' experience converged. The suffering of slavery and the suffering of the cross were synonymous. The crucifixion confirmed to slaves that they were one with Jesus, and more importantly, that Jesus was one with them.[16]

As I see it, suffering points up the need for holiness, experienced as wholeness. In this light holiness is agency; it is spiritual power for enduring, resisting, and overcoming the causes of suffering. In the liberationist anthropology of my inheritance and training, the emphasis on human agency is integral to the salvific event expressed in the incarnational thesis *and* the salvation to be derived from following Jesus' example. In their practice of telling and retelling parts of a *whole story* the community affirms the two natures of Christ Jesus, who charges them to be wholly holy and empowers them to fight their oppression. As Jesus was innocent, when the community responds to the call to holiness, highlighting its members' innocence, it exposes the egregious nature of the crimes against them and against God, in Christ, and confirms the ultimacy of their liberatory claims. Thus, in my and Douglas's liberationist perspective, the cross is not taken up apart from what the rest of the story affirms; namely, that Jesus was God *incarnate*, who lived, struggled, and died in suffering solidarity with society's victims.

Jacquelyn Grant

Jacquelyn Grant, a systematic theologian and an ordained elder in the African Methodist Episcopal (AME) Church, builds upon the Johannine christological presupposition that Jesus is God-become-human. As she notes, little distinction is made between Jesus and God in the hymnody, confessional utterances, and theological understandings of the Black Church. The image of Jesus as the divine co-sufferer comports with black Christians' continuous attempts to compare Christ's suffering and death with their own. Like Kelly Brown Douglas, Grant affirms the liberation perspective that Jesus/God is on the side of the oppressed,[17] making a similar claim that the experiences of black women in slavery replicated Jesus' suffering. Thus, Christ's identification with "the least of these" in his own context meant that he identified with those who were "the least of these" in their contexts. Surviving, resisting, and overcoming slavery; living in and finding ways to express themselves artistically despite the strictures of the servant class—black women encountered in the stories about Jesus one who identified with them and empowered them in and through his (1) incarnation and lowly birth, (2) ministry to the poor, sick, and outcast, (3) shameful and wrongful death, and (4) victorious resurrection. In postmodernity, Jesus' whole story remains a message of freedom for black women, inspiring "active hope" in their struggle for liberation from the burdens of the "tri-dimensional phenomenon of race, class, and gender oppression."[18]

Among womanists, Grant consistently lifts up the image of Jesus as the "divine co-sufferer." For Grant, that Jesus Christ was born, lived, struggled, and died among the poor was an affirmation that his ultimate victory is theirs to appropriate. That "Christ came and died, no less for the woman as for the man"[19] was an affirmation of black femininity, indicating that Christ's significance lay not in Jesus' maleness but in his humanity. For Grant, the bold declaration that "Christ is a black woman" carries a step further black theologians' assertion that "Christ is black" by radicalizing black women's conceptual apparatus for imaging God. More important, in helping black women view the divine impetus in/as themselves, her formulation takes seriously the challenge of making the good news of and about Jesus ever more relevant to African American women. Taken together, as black women are unable to do otherwise, these assertions have implications for understanding the atonement as God's option for, and empowerment of, black women. They allow black women to recognize the self-identified Christ in all their particularities. Christ's empowerment of black women lends greater, not less, universal import to the gospel, since they embody all these realities.

Delores S. Williams

A systematic theologian and lay preacher in the Presbyterian Church (U.S.A.), Delores S. Williams matches the theme of black women's surrogacy to traditional views of the atonement, which cite Jesus' death as a vicarious sacrifice for the sake of sinful humankind. As Williams has pointed out, surrogacy is that structure of domination that gives black women's oppression its unique character.[20] Owing to the unique ways black women's bodies have been exploited in and since slavery, naming black women's experience as surrogacy is more apt than any other ascription given by black theologians.

At the controversial 1993 "Re-Imagining Conference" sponsored by the World Council of Churches,[21] Williams appraised the implications of reimaging God/Christ at the "cultural root," a project that the African American community has historically undertaken in order to counter the idolatrous images proffered in racist propaganda (and which were themselves *re*images).[22] Williams herself undertook the effort to unmask the "defects" of the community's various depictions of the reimaged Christ. While the slaves signified a Christ/Jesus who "supported and fitted into a culture of resistance," Christ remained, nonetheless, white, powerful, and male until black theologians reimaged Christ as black. Williams lifted up, out of her own religious experience, *another* reimaged Christ, a "relational" Jesus, who was "shrouded in poverty" and who was "female and male indexed" (as Jesus was regarded as "poor little Mary's son"). Yet Williams questioned the adequacy of even this reimaged form, since it does not attend to the needs of Mary's daughters. Williams posited the need for womanist theologians to reimage Jesus and the significance of the "Christian pageant" continuously through the lenses of their experience, because the "androcentric telling of African American history"[23]—and Jesus' story (!)—obfuscates God's/Jesus' empowerment of women. For example, the confession that the Spirit came through a woman's body means that the "feminine is incorporated in the very being of Jesus." This example of a *re*-reimaged Jesus provides a view of the incarnation that is "serviceable" to women (empowering them to see the divine impetus in/as themselves) and that "energizes" the church, as this signification of the story provides further testimony to the character and creativity of God.

I agree with Williams that Christians need to look more carefully for the life-affirming images in the ministry of Jesus, such as the mustard seed and the fishes and the loaves. At the Re-Imagining Conference, when asked, "What is to be our theory of the atonement?" and, "For what did Jesus come?" Williams demurred, lifting up these images as more faith inducing than that of a suffering God:

> Those are the kinds of images we need for our religion. I don't think we need folks hanging on crosses and blood dripping and weird stuff. I think we really need to see the sustaining, the sustenance images, the faith that we are to have.

The fish and loaves, the candles we are to light, that our light will so shine before people so that we can remember that this message that Jesus brought, I think, is about life, and it's about the only two commandments that Jesus gave; [they were] about love.[24]

SACRAMENTAL SACRIFICE: TRANSFORMING THE LANGUAGE OF SACRIFICE

Although Williams takes issue—as I do—with the notion that God required the death of the Son, Jesus, this understanding of the significance of the atonement belies other testimony in Scripture that God indeed sent Christ, but for more honorable purposes. Scriptural passages (John 3:16–17) confirm what Williams seeks to affirm: "Jesus came for life" and to demonstrate the utter feasibility of life in love and honor. In light of their witness, I agree with her claim that "there is nothing of God in the blood of the cross," if she means by that that there is nothing of God's *sanction* in violence.

The Fourth Gospel consistently sublimates the context of death with the promise of eternal life for believers in Christ Jesus. This spiritualizing tendency of the Fourth Gospel is significant because of its impact on the lives of African American Christians (and all Christians) and because of the images of Jesus that emerge from there and their import for black faith. Certainly, as their confessional utterances confirm, black people know Jesus through the testimony of John: Word, Light, Lamb, Son of God, Door, Good Shepherd, Way (and Way-maker), Friend, Sovereign Lord. The community that attested to these ascriptions about Jesus was a community under siege that, like radical black activists, proffered agape, sacrificial love, to *itself*. "I give you a new commandment, that you love one another. Just as I have loved you, you also should love one another" (John 13:34). Unfortunately, this focus is lost in the harmonizing tendencies of Eurocentric biblical discourse, which in each of its attempts to find the "historical Jesus" has sought to posit monolithic views that have little to do with the liberation of African Americans and even less to do with their experience of Jesus.

Sacrifice understood as the surrender or destruction of something prized or desirable for the sake of something considered as having a higher or more pressing claim is not genuinely that unless it involves one's own agency. The central story's grounding in Hebraic faith and liturgy sheds light on the early church's confession that Jesus' death was *once for all*. Because God desires mercy and not sacrifice, there should never really be any reason for the act of sacrifice. Yahweh's institution of the sacrificial system and Jesus' self-sacrifice are thus construed as the disclosure of God's mercy. Despite the melodramatic quirks in the telling and retelling of this story, Judeo-Christian traditions attempt to signify God's unwillingness to trivialize the blood/life/loss of any creature.

In light of this, the belief that God, in Christ, shed God's own blood elevates the meaning of the *once-for-all* nature of Christ Jesus' death. The divine-human dynamic in the story signifies that there is *something* of God in the blood of the cross, confirming the commonly held belief among African Americans that Jesus is the "divine co-sufferer," as Grant attested. Contrary to the church's historical attempts to impose the hermeneutics of sacrifice on any people whom it or the state would subjugate, this is not sanction for anyone's or any group's victimization. Rather, it highlights the egregious nature of every historical crime against humanity and the Divinity. Thus, the cross is about God's love for humankind in a profound sense.

I believe that Christians need to ponder the implications of Christ's death continuously, because the drama testifies to the exceedingly great lengths to which God goes to advise the extent of human estrangement. It is no slight on the intelligence of black women when they confess this; rather, it reflects on what they say they need and what they say Christ's real presence, mediated through the gospel, provides—redemption and release from the self-alienation and social alienation they experience in their workaday lives. Gospel singer Helen Baylor's *Helen's Testimony* is a stirring account of her deliverance from drug addiction through Christ's agency.[25] She attests that there *is* power in the blood, even in the name of Jesus.

For many Christians, while the image of a crucifix signifies awareness of a God who suffers with us in our experiences of suffering, the image of an empty cross signifies faith in the possibility of our own resurrection. Williams disparages this distinction because "too often, Christians are thereby taught to believe that something good can result from violence."[26] Yet the reality of violence in black women's lives informs their theodical attempts to ascribe meaning to their suffering and to affirm the divine assistance to gain victory over it. For many, the struggle is ongoing. That is not to say that "violence, victimization, and undeserved" suffering are redemptive, but that suffering and merit are unrelated, just as love and merit are, and that we who suffer can be redeemed. This is the singular significance of God's self-disclosure in every aspect of Christ Jesus' walk with us. When black women can see the truth of this revelation, self-love becomes imminently possible. Williams affirms that the cross and crucifixion are "symbols of realism . . . reminders of what can happen to reformers who successfully challenge the status quo . . . [and] of the struggle that lies ahead"[27] for those who are likewise engaged. Perhaps that is redemptive for a survivalist, but for many survivors of violence, the crucifix is a supreme reminder of God's *with-us-ness* (that is, of God's decision to be *at-one* with us; or, better said, of the fact that we are already *at-one*). The empty cross is a symbol of God's continuous empowerment. This is why I believe that the continuous intercession of the spirit of Christ must become integral to womanist reckonings of Christ Jesus' significance. Not the resurrection but Christ's intercession signals the end of the gospel story and the beginning of Christ's significance for us, "on our behalf."

POWER IN THE BLOOD

As I have tried to indicate, I am aware of the problematic nature of the language of sacrifice, the potential and actual abuses thereof; nevertheless, I have cited from my mother's story in order to posit a transformed, *sacramental* notion of sacrifice that has saving significance for the African American community and for black women in particular. Mobley, for example, channeled the pain of her son's death into community service, lecturing for the NAACP (National Association for the Advancement of Colored People), eventually becoming a schoolteacher. When asked, she professed not to harbor bitterness toward Roy Bryant and Big Jim, W. J. Milam (the men who killed Emmett), nor towards whites generally. While [she] did not *profess* love for Milam and Bryant, she *confessed* that her son's death did not nullify the biblical command to love the neighbor and testified that it was God's empowerment that enabled her to keep it. This is what I think it means to witness sacramentally to the character of God: loving one's own, not loving others uncritically, and, most important, not being defined by one's victimization but by one's commitments.[28]

In developing a sacramental understanding of sacrifice as a dimension of holistic spirituality I also take cues from the slave community, which proposed in song, "Lord, I want to be a Christian [love everybody] in my heart." I will to love all of creation, in accordance with the womanist sensibilities Walker describes in her image of God. Although I situate myself within the radical tradition of black theology, my personal praxis is pacifist activist, not merely because I believe it is sound strategy enhancing my prospects for survival, liberation, and creative self-expression, but because I believe that there are some things that are worse than dying—namely, killing—for one's cause. Worse yet is killing without cause, a most horrible transgression of the Oneness in which I delight. Nevertheless, I cannot in good conscience proscribe the liberative options of any people engaged in protracted struggle because I believe in self-defense as a human right that in no way reflects on the capacity to love another.

In my *sacramental* model the aim is to foster human freedom and to garner holistic spirituality from whatever sources are revealed. Thus, I do not seek to enjoin one image of God. Rather, God is, as revealed in Christ, loving and challenging, humane and sovereign, culturally engaged yet countercultural, personal, a healer and a mystic, a co-sufferer and a liberator. This has dramatic implications for women who are embroiled in abusive relationships; who remain in them for economic reasons and/or because their own self-concept is debased by the misogynistic norms of the church and the culture; who are themselves vulnerable to the murderous impulses of patriarchally driven persons; and who may be conflicted about defending themselves physically and/or emotionally.[29] Yet, in the imposition of sacrifice, the first word of Jesus (in the Gospel of Mark), *repent,* is appropriated privatistically, so that the sinfulness of oppressors is never construed as a major issue.[30] I would argue that this is a conveniently missed exegetical consideration, along with Jesus' own profound militancy in his oppressive context.

In the early church's appropriation of the language of sacrifice Jesus' death on the cross was said to have been the pouring out of God's own life, ending sanction for sacred violence, *once for all.* This claim could only be made in the light of the whole story about Jesus, including the incarnation, ministry, suffering and death, resurrection, and continuous intercession of the Holy Spirit. However, the martyrdom ethos in which Christianity was baptized virtually guaranteed that its central image would become the cross. This reality lent ultimacy to their claims concerning sacrifice. In truth, the martyrs evinced a *sacramental witness;* they sought to demonstrate bodily the utter feasibility of life in love and honor, as their association with Jesus had taught them.

Perhaps the cross is central to black Christian identity because black Christians suffer, like Jesus and the martyrs, unjustly. The cross in the African American experience *is* theodicy. Moreover, the death it points to is the way of all flesh. I do not think that the problem is with the imagery per se; the cross, in its original sense, embodied a *scandal,* that something, anything, good could come out of such an event. Seen in this light, Jesus' sacrificial act was not the objective. Rather, it was the tragic, if foreseeable, result of his confrontation with evil. This bespeaks a view of Jesus and the martyrs as empowered, *sacramental,* witnesses, not as victims who passively acquiesced to evil.

As I stated before, anyone's death has saving significance inasmuch as we learn continuously from the life that preceded it. My baptism into the ethos of sacrifice compels me to reflect on it as a vital component of my self-understanding as a religious person and as a person in community. Although I may never be required to give up my life for the sake of my ultimate claims, the peculiar efficacy of my mother's sacrifice as well as the Christian story prevent me from discarding the idea altogether, particularly the notion of sacrifice as the surrender or destruction of something prized or desirable for the sake of something with higher claim, a potentially salvific notion with communal dimensions that got lost in the rhetorical impetus of the language of surrogacy. Yet I believe that in the final hours of her life, I became a higher and more pressing claim to my mother—more important than her addiction, more important than her companion, more important, even, than her life, which he had threatened on more than one occasion. I speculate that this prevented her from challenging my abusive father figure sooner.

I believe that continuous learning will be facilitated for oppressed Christians by always situating the call to sacrifice in historical context; by employing liberative hermeneutics, taking note of dissonances within the text, the experiences of the community, and the community's understandings of God. My mother's ultimate sacrifice and those of countless other black women who suffer abuse and die at the hands of patriarchal, violence-driven persons—whose deaths go unreported and underreported, unprosecuted and underprosecuted—are potentially liberating for women if we learn from their experiences, if we see how they exercised or did not exercise their moral and creative agency. This seems a much more relevant view of the atoning worth of women's blood. Although it is true, as some feminists assert, that women's blood-loss has been devalued in Christian sacrificial tradition, Jesus' own life and *sacramental* example of affirming the intrinsic worth of women enable humankind to see women's blood as sacred.

3

The Cross and Male Violence

James N. Poling

MALE VIOLENCE AGAINST WOMEN IS a global problem. Every year, all around the world, grassroots organizations and women's networks raise awareness and inspire change through imaginative action to overcome different forms of violence against women. Such awareness and action campaigns have brought about the World Council of Churches' "Decade to Overcome Violence (2001–2010)," the worldwide campaign entitled "On the Wings of a Dove," and annual events such as "16 Days of Activism Against Gender Violence" and the United Nations International Day for the Elimination of Violence against Women.[1] Witnesses from every culture and continent are reporting high levels of physical assaults, rapes, and emotional control of women by actions of individual men who are fathers and husbands, as well as other relatives, both male and female, and by official government decrees and actions. War, poverty, and massive migrations make the world and the home even more dangerous places for women and their children because they destroy the order and discipline of local communities. Throughout most of the church's history, however, male violence against women has not been thematized as a theological and ethical problem. I will argue in this essay that understanding and challenging the history of interpretation of the cross is one way to prevent male violence against women, and that this is a particular obligation of the present generation.

The cross of Jesus Christ was a violent event and its interpretation over the centuries has been ambiguous. For men who live in patriarchal societies, the cross gives mixed messages. On the one hand, the cross is a symbol that legitimates male dominance in human community. For many centuries, the cross has been symbolic of the church's authority as a patriarchal institution. Jesus died as a man on the cross and brought salvation for humankind. Therefore, most churches have argued, only men can serve as governors and ritual leaders in the church, modeling a form of governance for all society, including the family. Theologians have taught that male headship over women is established by God the Father and his only Son, Jesus, and any challenge to male dominance is a challenge to God himself. One can see the cross as a symbol of a natural patriarchal order that must be supported by the interactions of men and women.

On the other hand, the cross is a symbol of accountability for men, a sign that God rejects domination and brings judgment on those who engage in violence. In his Pentecost sermon, Peter encouraged his listeners to identify with those who were responsible for the cross: "Jesus of Nazareth ... you crucified and killed by the hands of those outside the law. ... God has made him both Lord and messiah, this Jesus whom you crucified. ... Repent and be baptized every one of you in the name of Jesus Christ so that your sins may be forgiven and you will receive the gift of the Holy Spirit" (Acts 2:23, 36, 38). In the passion narratives, the religious and political authorities are unmasked as villains more concerned about power and control than about justice and love. In the end of the biblical story these villains are discredited by the resurrection and the birth of an evangelistic church that the authorities cannot control. One can interpret the cross as a judgment on all forms of domination and violence that exist in human societies, including male domination and violence against women. "The discipleship of the cross makes a ... difficult demand: the application of nonviolence to every sphere of life."[2]

Observing these two interpretations of the cross, how can we counter the negative effects of male dominance and its effects on the health and salvation for women and men and encourage interpretations of the cross that give priority to safety for women and accountability for men? This is a question for Practical Theology, an academic theological discipline with the task (one among others) of evaluating Christian doctrines and practices in terms of their consequences for individuals and communities of faith in dialogue with other branches of theology concerned with questions of truth.[3] In other words, the ways that Christian doctrines and practices affect the everyday lives of ordinary people need to be considered alongside questions of truth; that is, whether the doctrines and practices conform to the revelation of God in Scripture, history, and rational thought.

Clarice Martin, black womanist New Testament scholar, describes the difference between hermeneutics of truth and hermeneutics of effects:

> "Hermeneutics" is not simply a cognitive process wherein one seeks to determine the "correct meaning" of a passage or text. Neither are questions of penultimate truth and universality solely determinative of meaning. Also of essential importance in the interpretive task are such matters as the nature of the interpreter's goals, the effects of a given interpretation on a community of people who have an interest in the text being interpreted, and questions of cultural value, social relevance, and ethics.[4]

"What is at stake in hermeneutics is not only the 'truth' of one's interpretation, but also the effects interpretation and interpretive strategies have on the ways in which human beings shape their goals and their actions."[5] This form of hermeneutics involves a rhythm or dynamic interplay between biblical texts from the canon and the lived faith and experience of communities of faith. An interpreter cannot understand Jesus by studying the Bible in isolation, but must be immersed in a community of faith that practices the faith today. Without participation in a practicing community faith today, one cannot comprehend the spirit of Jesus in the past or the present. The truth of Jesus in Scripture is revealed in ongoing discipleship in the name of Jesus.

THE CROSS AND VIOLENCE AGAINST WOMEN

The vocation of practical theologians is to understand how the stories, teachings, and practices of our religious institutions affect persons. We need to know how religion functions at the level of conscious and unconscious formation of perceptions and behaviors; that is, how the symbols, ideas, and rituals about God oppress or liberate the human spirit using the criteria of theology itself. If the ideas and practices of religious communities are damaging individual believers and their families according to Christian norms, then we have a responsibility to bring these realities to the attention of religious leaders for reexamination. For example, if certain forms of theology increase the suffering of women and children by refusing to address issues of rape and sexual violence, then we must raise prophetic voices to protest such theologies. If certain ideas and practices liberate persons, leading to healing and transformation and bringing about a more just society for everyone, then we need to bring that feedback to our religious communities. For example, if some survivors of violence against women find Jesus to be a faithful companion in their journey toward healing, we need to understand their piety and bring it to the attention of the church.

Religious rituals and beliefs that shape practices of the church over many years become models that consciously and unconsciously influence our inner reality.[6] Figures in these dramas become internal objects that organize our religious experiences. How does the cross influence the religious imagination of believers? In the story of the cross, there are various figures available for the religious imagination. "In the final scenes of the story we see the defecting disciples, the disillusioned crowd, and the hostile authorities, all juxtaposed to Jesus, who alone goes the way of the cross."[7] Thus, one has many options for reading oneself into the story. One can identify with Jesus, the innocent righteous one who was unjustly killed by his enemies. Many people find Jesus to be a compassionate figure who understands their own suffering and reveals a God who is compassionate with those who suffer. One can identify with the disciples who were frightened for their own lives and betrayed their loyalty to Jesus by denying and hiding from Jesus' enemies. One can identify with the religious and political leaders who persecuted Jesus and were responsible for his death. Or one can identify with the crowd who worshiped him but turned against him in the end.

According to narrative theory, any and all of these religious identifications are possible in the story of the cross.[8] We need to understand how these identifications can lead to ambiguous interpretations of the cross—as a symbol that legitimizes male dominance and violence against women and as a symbol of accountability for men.

One example of the cross as a symbol that legitimates male violence against women is clergy sexual abuse, which has become the focus of so much public attention in the last decade. The most common scenario of clergy sexual abuse is a male clergyman with a female parishioner or with a child.[9] What happens when pastors and counselors sexualize their ministry relationships? A sexual relationship between a male clergyman and a female parishioner replicates the drama between a patriarchal God and an obedient, self-sacrificing Jesus standing in for a sinful humanity. A relationship that was supposedly based on the healing needs of the parishioner becomes reversed so that the parishioner serves the sexual needs of the clergyman. In religious terms, the clergyman has taken the place of God who is all-knowing, all-powerful, and all-loving, and the parishioner has taken the place of Jesus who takes on the sins of humanity, submits her will to God's, and sacrifices her life unto death on the cross for the sake of the relationship.[10]

In family violence, a similar drama is enacted. Given the negative and conflicting images of women in many churches and their responsibility to be obedient to an all-loving Father God and his Son, Jesus, Christian faith means that men are closer to God than women, that the proper relationship of women to men is subservience, and that the traditional values of submission and obedience are the essence of Christian faith. The following are quotes from women who grew up as incest victims in Christian homes and their report of what they learned from the Christian teaching they received:

> You must love your neighbor. Not much attention was paid to standing up for yourself (Ellen). You must always be the first to forgive and you must do so seventy times seventy times (Judith). You must always serve, serve God. Sexuality before and outside of marriage is bad (Margaret). Faith and standing up for yourself are conflicting concepts (Theresa). You must sacrifice your own needs and wants, you mustn't resist, mustn't stand up for yourself, must serve God, mustn't be your own person with your own ego (Amy).[11]

The images of Jesus' obedience to God, his sacrifice of his life for the Father God, and his ongoing service to divine authority are references to the cross. What is troubling about these illustrations is that certain interpretations of the cross clearly create the occasions for sexual and physical abuse of women and children because of their images of the trinitarian God in relationship to human families. Survivors of abuse are saying that an abusive God and abusive clergymen do not contradict the church's theology. The images of abuse are inherent in the symbols themselves. A church that preaches God's love but projects the evil of the world onto women and other marginalized groups is preaching an abusive God.[12]

THE CROSS AND ACCOUNTABILITY FOR MALE VIOLENCE

In contrast to these examples, many contemporary theologians argue that the identification of the poor with the suffering of Jesus on the cross gives the cross power for survival and liberation in situations of oppression. Sharon Thornton's *Broken Yet Beloved: A Pastoral Theology of the Cross* draws on theologians Dorothee Soelle and Douglas John Hall: "The cross stands as a powerful symbol of the suffering of people and of their yearning to know love."[13] She gives many examples of oppressed people, especially women, who feel God's solidarity with their suffering when they meditate on the cross. One example is Mercy Amba Oduyoye from Nigeria: "Women in Africa know that they will need to be ready to risk even death in order to resist death.... 'They face the cross in the hope that the humanity of women will rise from the silence and peace of the graveyard.'"[14] For those who are oppressed, the cross is empowering since it moves the suffering person toward community and empowerment.

> For those who suffer historical injuries...[the cross] reveals the political, ideological, and economic factors that impact people adversely.... Seeing the relationship between one's own suffering and the social conditions that create and perpetuate it can help people find new descriptions and alternative meaning for themselves.[15]

Likewise, Thornton suggests that the cross can be a symbol of liberation for those who are responsible for the suffering of others.

> For those who hold power over others in a particular society, the political cross speaks the word of judgment and demands change, usually in the form of relinquishment of power and control, followed by acts of reparation for past wrongs.... It pronounces judgment in the hope for *metanoia* on the part of the abusers. Judgment speaks the word that only God is God, and no one else is God.[16]

This interpretation is close to my own understanding of the cross and I will explore this possibility through an actual case study. Last spring, one of my students presented a verbatim transcript of a pastoral interview with a nine-year-old boy who was struggling with issues of male violence in his life in relation to the cross. Because the verbatim is lively and vivid, I will present it first and then conclude the essay with commentary on the possible constructive images of the cross herein. My goal is to show how the cross can be a symbol of male accountability in a world overcome by male violence.

A CASE STUDY

The context of this conversation is a middle-class white congregation in the midwestern United States. Jack (fictitious name) lingered after a Bible study and Sharon engaged with him. "On the Sunday following Easter, I taught Jack's class about Peter spreading the news that Jesus was alive. On Easter Sunday, the lesson was the passion story leading up to Easter, which included Peter's denial. After class, Jack approached me and asked if he could ask me some questions he had."[17]

Sharon: Hey, Jack, what's up?

Jack: I wanted to ask you about Sunday school. You said some things that I want to know more about. (*He fidgets somewhat, so I sit down with hopes to make him feel more relaxed. He sits down too.*)

Sharon: Please feel free to ask me whatever is on your mind.

Jack: Thanks. Well . . . you said that Peter was telling people about Jesus coming back to life because not everyone knew. And you also said that those people who followed Jesus were hiding because they didn't want to be arrested.

Sharon: You're right, Jack. You see, they were afraid that if the Romans found out they knew Jesus and followed him, they too would be arrested and maybe put to death.

Jack: And that's why Peter pretended he didn't know Jesus earlier.

Sharon: Yes, Peter denied Jesus because he was afraid he would be punished.

Jack: But now that Jesus is back from the dead, Peter isn't scared anymore and is telling everyone. And . . . that's what I don't get.

Sharon: What don't you get, Jack?

Jack: Well, if Jesus is back to take care of the disciples, why are they still . . . being beaten up? You used a word that I don't remember . . .

Sharon: Persecuted? This means being mistreated by another person or a group of people.

Jack: Yeah, that's it. I mean, Jesus is alive, so that means there's nothing to be afraid of anymore. It means that the Romans were wrong . . .

Jack: (*face scrunches up*) I remember how you said in class that people who believe in Jesus are picked on and beaten up.

Sharon: Yes, that's right. People in Jesus' time and people today are persecuted because of their beliefs.

Jack: I remember how Billy said there are kids at school that make fun of him because he's Christian.

Sharon: And you thought that was wrong.

Jack: Yeah, because being Christian means believing in Jesus. And Jesus was a good person.

Sharon: You thought it was wrong that Billy was made fun of because he believes in Jesus and tries to do the good things Jesus teaches us.

Jack: Yeah, like being nice to others, helping people who are hurt, not saying mean things. All Billy did was not want to tease this girl.

Sharon: When a person teases someone to hurt their feelings, that's wrong. These kids may not understand that they are hurting a person with their teasing.

Jack: I see lots of teasing at school, lots of mean teasing. I think they know that it hurts. (*looking sad*)

Sharon: I think you're right, Jack, I think there are lots of people who know that teasing can hurt, and yet they do it anyway.

Jack: And Billy knew it was wrong, so he didn't want to do it. Because Christians shouldn't do mean things that hurt others; that's what Jesus says in the Bible.

Sharon: And those kids started to be mean to Billy because they thought his behavior was strange; not normal. Now Billy could have pretended, so they wouldn't make fun of him—

Jack: No, because then Billy would have done what Peter did when Jesus was arrested.

Sharon: You're right, Jack. In a way, Billy was like Jesus, standing up to those who wanted to persecute this girl and taking the teasing in her place.

Jack: I know the girl he mentioned. She's Jewish.

Sharon: Do you think that makes it okay for her to be persecuted?

Jack: No, because while I know Jews don't believe in Jesus, Christians are supposed to love all people. And besides, Jesus was Jewish, right?

Sharon: That's right.

Jack: So Christians really shouldn't make fun of Jews because that's like making fun of Jesus.

Sharon: Just like you said, Jack, Christians should love all people, because Jesus taught us to love our neighbors as ourselves. And anyone and everyone is our neighbor.

Jack: (*pausing for a long time*) I was at the playground on that day. I didn't do anything. I think I was like Peter.

Sharon: (*smiling gently*) Sometimes it's hard to stand up for others, especially when we risk being persecuted.

Jack: It's not easy, doing what Billy did. My big brother can't come to take care of me.

Sharon: No, he can't, but your love for your brother can give you strength. And your faith in Jesus can help you when you're struggling with what you should do.

Jack: Jesus takes care of us just like my brother takes care of me.

Sharon: That's right (*smiling*), and standing up with Billy is very powerful. It shows those bullies that more than one person thinks their behavior is wrong.

Jack: Yeah, I see what you mean. (*Jack's mom arrives to pick him up.*) Thanks a lot, I feel better now.

Sharon: I'm glad, Jack, please know you can come to me anytime you have a question, or just want to talk. Good luck at school.

Jack: Thanks.

The central issue for Jack is male violence against Billy and an unnamed girl in the class. Apparently he witnessed a situation where the girl was being teased and bullied by a group of boys. Jack was impressed when Billy stood up to the bullies and supported the girl even though he put himself at risk of being bullied or physically hurt. According to Sharon, "In a way, Billy was like Jesus, standing up to those who wanted to persecute this girl and taking the teasing in her place." Billy put himself at risk in order to support a marginalized person and stand in solidarity with her against abuse. In Jack's and Sharon's religious imagination, Billy was acting like Jesus on the cross, refusing to back down when threatened and standing up for justice. In the process he directed the violence away from the girl and toward himself, thus sacrificing himself for the sake of justice. This could be interpreted as *a sacrificial image of the cross*.[18] It is an example of a boy standing up to other boys who are in the process of learning about male violence against women. The bullies are testing their ideology of male dominance and practicing their skills of power and control. Without someone to confront them with a nonviolent ethical claim, they will learn that violence is effective in getting what they want and acceptable within their peer group as a form of human interaction.[19] With Billy's challenge, there is at least a possibility of ethical debate about what kinds of behaviors are tolerated within the peer group of boys and girls. Billy's action should not be judged by its effectiveness, just as Jesus' crucifixion cannot be judged as an effective short-term political strategy. Rather, it should be evaluated for its integrity and its potential for creating an alternative religious imagination about the value of nonviolence and support for the causes of gender justice.

The critical moment for Jack was disclosed when he said, "I was at the playground on that day. I didn't do anything. I think I was like Peter." In his religious imagination, Jack was like Peter, the disciple who denied Christ in order to protect himself. He was afraid because of the potential violence from which his older brother often protected him. However, his identification with Peter was not a positive image for him because it convicted him of wrong—"It's not easy, doing what Billy did. My big brother can't come to take care of me." His decision to be a passive bystander in the face of male violence was indicted by the cross, a symbol of accountability for those who choose violence and use it to control the lives of others. In the moment that Peter denied that he knew Jesus, he was not acting out of faith, but fear. He did not understand the importance of Jesus' decision to submit to the crucifixion as a revelation of God's commitment to justice and the possibility of human transformation for the future. At that moment, Peter could not see the possibilities for new life because of his fear. Jack identified with this moment in Peter's life when he betrayed his own values and let his fear control his behavior.

I worked in pastoral counseling with child abusers and women batterers for fifteen years and I can testify to the constant presence of fear. Even though I was working with men who had been convicted of crimes of violence and were coerced into psycho-educational programs, they still had the ability to intimidate me with group solidarity in favor of male dominance. As Jack said, "It's not easy, doing what Billy did."[20]

Jack was troubled by the contradiction between fear and faith. On the one hand, he understood that after the resurrection the disciples were not afraid of persecution because they believed Jesus would protect them. On the other hand, he had personally experienced a moment of fear when he was afraid of confronting other boys who were bullying a girl in his class. How could he be confident and unafraid one moment, and then afraid in another moment? Does this mean that his faith in Jesus is not real?

Sharon helped him to tell his story and express his confusion about his own faith and courage. In the process, Jack came to understand Peter as a liberating figure for him. The same Peter who was afraid at the cross and denied his teacher was transformed after the resurrection and was able to act without fear in the face of severe persecution. Even though Jack did not support Billy and help confront the bullies at school, he could be like Peter and learn from the experience. Perhaps the next time he could do better. Sharon also confirmed his ethical analysis that the male violence against the girl at school was wrong and somebody should do something about it. At the end Jack was relieved because he understood himself better as a faithful Christian and felt empowered to act in the future.

THE CROSS: JUSTICE, MYSTERY, AND ETHICAL ACTION

I submit that this story illustrates one possible way that the cross can help hold men accountable for their participation in male violence. It confirms my own Christology, namely, that Jesus died on the cross because of his solidarity with the oppressed people of his time and his courage to confront the forces of domination and violence. He died as a direct result of his commitment to justice and his resistance to evil.[21] Because of his faithfulness to his loving commitment to the people, Jesus revealed the loving justice of God, the creator of the universe. In Christ, we see God as a God of love, power, and justice who never abandons those who suffer because of evil forces. At the same time, Jesus becomes a model for human belief and action. Because Jesus was faithful and showed God's faithfulness, we can have courage in difficult situations to stand up for justice and love. The cross can empower us to engage in ethical actions in solidarity with those who are vulnerable. Thus, the cross discloses the nature of God and empowers those who believe in God.

This example from one pastoral conversation does not resolve the many ambiguities of the cross, nor does it counteract the many ways in which the cross has become a sanction for personal and military violence over the world. But perhaps it gives a way to help us understand why the cross continues to be a redemptive and comforting symbol for some persons who are oppressed and for some persons with power who seek to become nonviolent. We must continue to work to discern the truth and the effects of the cross in the lives of Christian communities and not settle for an interpretation that solves only our personal confusion.

The issue for this essay is whether the cross can function for men as a symbol of liberation from the false consciousness that protects our power and privilege and hides our pain and suffering. Theologian Ellen Wondra suggests that, in disclosing the relationship between God and humanity, Christology functions in two ways: manifestation and proclamation. In *manifestation* Jesus Christ provides a firm foundation for faith and practice. Jesus is "'the decisive re-presentation' of God and of the authentic character of human existence."[22] This is a hermeneutics of confession that trusts personal and corporate experiences with Jesus. In *proclamation* Jesus Christ shatters all theology and religious experience: "Here, the sacred or divine is encountered as a power that shatters, defamiliarizes, or stands over against the human as the radically other which is nonetheless like the self."[23] This is a hermeneutics of suspicion that suspects all authoritative theological interpretations and interpreters, including oneself. In this distinction Wondra helps us understand the cross in faith communities as authentic manifestations and proclamations of the reality of human and divine life.

> Jesus is the Christ because he is the manifestation of the transformation of humanity in the struggle to resist dehumanization, *and* he is the definitive re-presentation of the only God who saves. In the Christ, redemption of all existence is accomplished in principle, but it will be actualized only fully in the future. Thus, the incarnation of God in Jesus the Christ is simultaneously revelation of what has always been the case, vindication of this enduring if concealed and distorted reality, and promise and prophecy of its greater future fulfillment.[24]

Research on this subject brings me to two christological statements. First, the cross is the form of Jesus' resistance to evil as a *manifestation* that human resistance to evil can be trusted because it is the image of God in humans. Faith in Jesus thematizes resistance as a manifestation of "the true relation between the divine and the human (and so the true nature of both divine and human)."[25] Jesus resisted the evil of his day, even to death on a cross, and raises to ontological status human resistance to evil. *Jesus' resistance to evil discloses that resistance to evil is a fundamental attribute of God and humans.* The cross means that we can trust our own resistance to evil as an essential aspect of the image of God in our lives. When Jack felt ashamed of his fear of confronting the bullies and was inspired by Billy's courage to stand up to them, he was responding to some deep truth within his being as God had created him. The story of Jesus' crucifixion on the cross helped him to trust this aspect of his experience and see that another way of behaving was available to him.

Second, the mystery of Jesus' life, death, and resurrection is a *proclamation* that God is a mystery that is beyond all human understanding. *Jesus' relational love and power reveal the mystery of God's Otherness and proclaim that multiplicity and ambiguity are fundamental attributes of divine and human life.*[26] Jesus' death on the cross is a mystery that confronts us with the reality of a God who cannot be understood. Jack could not find the courage to confront the bullies, even when he knew it was the right thing to do. In a sense he was asking Sharon: How do I experience the transformation of Peter who was a fearful coward in one story and a courageous preacher willing to risk his life in another story? How did he change from one kind of person to another? The answer is found in a personal encounter with the living Christ, a transforming moment in which one feels part of the larger relational web, a moment of losing one's self for the greater good, a liminal moment when everything looks different and one embraces a new identity. This second-order change does not come just from one's own sense of goodness and resistance to evil, but from an encounter with a living spirit that gives reason for living and dying.

Jack did not fully understand the way the story lured him into a new future. But we can hope the church will continue to tell the biblical stories in a way that confirms his emerging identity as a disciple of Jesus Christ who has the courage of his convictions to see another way besides patriarchy and male dominance. And I pray that men of all ages and cultures will begin to see other ways of being human and male that can be part of the new community God is bringing into history.

4

Maternal Sacrifice as a Hermeneutics of the Cross

Mary J. Streufert

DURING MY FIRST PREGNANCY, I had the distinct feeling that my body was betraying me. To my acute sorrow, my belly became a purple-and-white-striped watermelon, tightening and ripening in the brilliant summer sunshine. Handel's chorus rang in my head: "By his stripes we are healed," layered over and over in successive parts. That glorious of compositions rang with personal meaning: I wanted to shout, "No! By *my* stripes there is life. By the sacrifice of my body has new life been possible."

Isaiah 53:5 has been used to describe Jesus' salvific suffering and death: "But he was wounded for our transgressions, he was bruised for our iniquities: upon him was the chastisement that made us whole, and with his stripes we are healed" (RSV). As a first-time mother, I could not help but notice that the language used to describe sacrificial death reflects some maternal realities. My personal experiences of physical alteration, psychological and emotional transformation and loss, pain, blood, and the rendering of my flesh brought me face to face with the ideal of sacrifice with which the Christian tradition has predominantly viewed the sacrifice of the cross.

The experiences of carrying, birthing, and mothering two babies have caused me to see things I had not seen previously about how Christians define and interpret Jesus' work of atonement. Physical and existential sacrifice does not always involve physical death. As an alternative view of sacrifice, I am interested in the life-sacrifice of motherhood and how the life-for-a-life model inherent to the mother-child relationship might offer us an alternative model of sacrifice useful for christological interpretation. I propose that a hermeneutic of maternal sacrifice is one way to correct two problems that result from a narrow interpretation of sacrifice in atonement theory: a "sacrifice of glory" and ignorance of a soteriology of restoration.

First, there are concerns over what I have previously named a "sacrifice of glory," in which sacrifice for its own sake is glorified or the endurance of pain or loss is viewed as an end in itself.[1] The violence at the center of traditional categories of atonement is problematic when it is translated into justification and glorification of violence. At root in the broader problem of violence in Western society and Christian practice is an apparent necrophilia that keeps us glued to the worship of death as the water that washes away sin, preventing us from questioning the normativity of sacrificial suffering. This hyper-focus on death results from the heroic paradigm that lies at the heart of appeasement and *Christus Victor* atonement theories.

A sacrifice of glory is further problematic because of the potential misapplication of self-sacrifice. In Western culture in general, a sacrifice of glory is manifest in a variety of ways, including military ideals, but we see a misunderstood paradigm of sacrifice in misogynistic views of female sacrifice. Specifically in Christian belief and praxis, this is especially apparent in relationships of domestic abuse in which women are encouraged to endure suffering because of Jesus' suffering and death and in situations in which sacrifice, of self or others, has been understood as a theological necessity, which in reality benefits those for whom the terms of sacrifice have been construed. Such sacrifice is also particularly apparent in theological justification of slavery and racial servitude.[2]

A hermeneutic of maternal sacrifice likewise reorients Christian theology to a soteriology of restoration[3] that is visible in the Gospels. Love of God, mirrored in the restorative qualities of parenting that seek to bring the child into the folds of interdependent love, respect, and care, restores us, makes us whole. Who a parent is and what she does in her life matters for the life of the child. We might say the same about the person and life of Jesus Christ for us. Indeed, if we understand the person and the work of Jesus' life to be as important as his death, then atonement theory is revealed as more complex.[4]

Who Christians are and how we must act are governed by the concepts of *imago Dei* and *imitatio Christi*. Christians believe we are both made in God's image and called to imitate Christ.[5] If our prime hermeneutic to understand the cross of Christ is through violent atonement, then violence can become our image and what we imitate. Moreover, the preponderance of atonement images in the Christian tradition center on the sacrificial lamb and *Christus Victor*. Although other atonement theories exist in the range of interpretive options, devotional and theological focus continues to be on these images.[6]

In order to situate my argument, I will first point out the cultural ideology of mortal sacrifice in the United States. Next I will discuss the range of atonement theory, commenting on feminist critique of the violence inherent to the predominant theories. Then I will explicate the apparent root of death-for-life sacrifice in the ancient hero motif that travels its way through the New Testament. Having shown that the heroic image carries but one model of sacrifice, I will argue for the hermeneutic of sacrifice inherent in the experience of motherhood. To critical effect, I will explain the positive ways in which another angle on sacrifice at the heart of atonement theory reorients both cultural images of sacrifice and Christian soteriology. Finally, I will turn to recent feminist biblical interpretations of the Gospel of John to edify my proposal scripturally and to open the conversation on the importance of interpreting atonement anew.

CULTURAL NORMS OF SACRIFICE

If mortal sacrifice remains our constant cultural and theological norm, then we fortify violent sacrifice in our society and we lose sight of Jesus' life as a locus of atonement, thus adding divine weight to violent redemption through mortal sacrifice. In other words, the paradigm of *mortal* sacrifice affects how we live, both socially and theologically. It is interesting to note in military ideals a contemporary model of sacrifice.

President George W. Bush clearly assigns sacrifice to those who have either died or been wounded in military service. For example, in a *Meet the Press* broadcast, President Bush argued about the war in Iraq: "Every person that is willing to sacrifice for this country deserves our praise.... [W]e're in a war against these terrorists who will bring great harm to America, and I've asked these young ones to sacrifice for that."[7] To give one's life for the ideals of a government is urged as a worthy, noble sacrifice. We see here that mortal sacrifice is impressed upon us as necessary for good—for "victory."

Lest there be any question that military ideals operate under a paradigm of sacrifice, a highly publicized death in *Time* magazine is a telling example. When football star and U.S. Army Ranger Pat Tillman was killed on the Afghan border in the spring of 2004, he was noted as a hero. His life is said to have defined heroism, and his choice to enlist is described as "that ancient, compelling thing—a sacrifice."[8] That we have glorified the sacrificial death of someone such as Tillman is hardly deniable. The glory of sacrifice runs through these examples of military sacrifice.

THEOLOGICAL NORMS OF SACRIFICE: VARIETIES OF ATONEMENT THEORY

Jesus is likewise the sacrifice for his followers in appeasement or sacrificial models of atonement. Anselm, the most widely quoted champion of satisfaction theory, was trying to understand why the incarnation occurred. His answer comes out of the dichotomy of creational order and disorder caused by human sin. The only way to repair the state of disorder in creation is to make an act of satisfaction, something God does out of divine love rather than punish humanity. God makes the offering to restore order on our behalf, sacrificing God's Son. Although Anselm's theory attests to divine love (because God does not want to punish us), we have theologically taken Anselm's model of restored order and developed it along the lines of penal substitution theory.

Often referred to as the "happy exchange," penal substitution most clearly articulates Jesus' death as a sacrifice for our sin. Through Jesus' death, the sin of humanity is washed away, cleansing us and justifying us before God. By the death of Jesus Christ, we gain Christ's blamelessness and purity; Christ gains our unrighteousness and sinfulness. The majority of Christians "live" the central paradigm of death-for-life each Sunday in liturgy, whether Protestant or Roman Catholic.

What is the source of our focus on sacrificial imagery? The idea of Jesus' death as a sacrifice in the Letter to the Hebrews is developed in subsequent tradition. Augustine, for example, states Christ "was made a sacrifice for sin, offering himself as a whole burnt offering on the cross of his passion."[9] As theologian Alister McGrath notes, the sacrificial nature of Jesus Christ's death became central to Protestant soteriologies.[10] Martin Luther's theology of the cross continues a dependence upon the model of heroic sacrifice. Although from a feminist perspective we can positively observe that Luther's theology of the cross embraces a distinctly empathetic view of God in God's suffering,[11] this understanding of the work of God through Jesus nevertheless depends upon a sacrificial paradigm. Specifically, Jesus must die in order to bring new life. God is only known through the suffering weakness of the cross.[12] According to the Lutheran confessions, by taking our sins upon himself, Jesus Christ is the sacrifice that reconciles us to God.[13] Indeed, according to one interpreter, Jesus on the cross is the fulfillment of the "primitive law of sin and expiation," which God fulfilled.[14] Jesus' heroic sacrifice is the ultimate sacrifice.

Yet another model of atonement theory, *Christus Victor*, relies on sacrifice, but from a victorious angle. From this vantage point, Jesus Christ dies only to be victorious over death and the devil. In other words, by dying and rising Christ is triumphant over the forces that hold us: the certainty of death and the temptation and control of the devil. At heart is the human problem of slavery to sin and death, and by Jesus' death we are freed. Although sacrifice is not as clearly emphasized as in appeasement models, the links to the ancient paradigm of heroic sacrifice are quite readily seen, as will be made apparent below, and the human tendency to emphasize a sacrifice of glory is bolstered by this triumphant theology.

The diversity of atonement theory is clear, and some theologians argue that we need diversity to understand how Jesus Christ atones us with God.[15] Yet I would argue that we are not freed from carefully criticizing the existing theories. One important example is feminist criticism of atonement theories, which has largely concentrated on the problem of violence and death at the center of the atonement. To ignore these important criticisms turns us away from a soteriology of restoration that is found through life-for-life sacrifice.

Feminist Criticism of Atonement Theory

For years feminist theologians have criticized the brutality and violence at the center of atonement theory, arguing against our worship of violence and the practical effects of it in the lives of Christians. On one end of the feminist spectrum, Mary Daly criticizes Christianity as an acute expression of necrophilia, the core of which is misogyny.[16] The Tree of Life, once the symbol of the goddess and her life-giving qualities, was violently appropriated by Christianity's interpretation of Jesus' death on a cross.[17] In essence, she argues, suffering is legitimated through the joy subsequent to the torture of the cross. Although Daly rejects the Christian cross, she raises our attention to the extent to which the cross has been and is used to legitimate suffering. Christians *should* question suffering as an end in itself, and Daly reminds Christians of this in our efforts to seek new ways to understand atonement.

From a reformist perspective, Rosemary Radford Ruether also maintains a critical distance from a violent atonement. Her central focus on redemption as a process of conversion away from systems of oppression to relationships of mutuality implies her criticism of the violence of the atonement. Ruether eschews the idea of redemptive suffering "as some kind of cosmic legal transaction with God to pay for the sins of humanity."[18] What she sees as redemptive in the suffering is not the suffering itself, but the memory of the martyrs to inspire hope and courage to continue to work for justice.[19] She in no way sees Jesus' suffering as a sacrifice for us, existentially or physically. Rather than understanding Jesus' suffering and death as redemptive, Ruether argues that Jesus' death is the result of his commitment to a model of new leadership of service to others.[20] In other words, Jesus' life redeems us, and his suffering is a by-product, not the cause, of redemption. To be reminded that Jesus' life is redemptive is critical in the effort to redirect our focus from a single vision of atonement to a multifaceted view of it.[21]

Recently, Rebecca Ann Parker and Rita Nakashima Brock have criticized atonement sacrifice by laying out the personal costs of living a praxis of self-sacrifice. They argue that violence is theologically sanctioned when we maintain the feudal image of the necessity of violence to repay human disobedience to God.[22] The authors illustrate through stories of abuse, abortion, and racism that this paradigm of salvific violence translates into human lives in devastating ways. For example, Parker tells the story about Lucia, who came to Parker's pastoral office, seeking theological counsel. Lucia's minister at a different congregation had told her that she needed to remain in her abusive relationship with her husband and accept the suffering, just as Jesus had accepted his suffering to save us. This made no sense to Lucia, and neither was it logical to Parker. What was alarming for Parker, however, was that the previous Sunday she had given a sermon emphasizing the necessity of sacrificial love, mirrored in Jesus' sacrificial love. How was Parker to reconcile these—her preaching and her practical advice?

Laying claim to a hermeneutic of maternal sacrifice from a feminist perspective will answer some of the concerns raised by feminist theologians over atonement theory, for it redirects the focus away from death but takes sacrifice seriously. Moreover, it is a potential interpretive stance from which to avoid the practical problems of *imago Dei* and *imitatio Christi* that can lead to harmful application. An important first move, however, is to think about the hermeneutical possibility of maternal sacrifice as a theological norm. Elisabeth Schüssler Fiorenza's feminist hermeneutics point us in the right direction.

Schüssler Fiorenza's work carries two important implications. First, we are confronted with the issue of sacrifice. If Jesus lived the *basileia* of God by festive table and egalitarian healing, as she argues,[23] then Jesus' sacrifice of life has more to do with the kingdom of God and less to do with the redemption of sin. Second, we are confronted with the view of reality in the texts, which she astutely argues is a kyriarchal reality (referring to multiplicative and intertwined privileged male systems of domination).[24] If an analysis of kyriarchal reality in the texts reveals not only how God works in the world through Jesus but also how power is inscribed and reinscribed in the early communities, then the meaning of Jesus' death on the cross has open possibilities. In other words, how we interpret the cross may depend upon cultural paradigms and experience.

What this indicates is that the present range of atonement theory is not comprehensive of all hermeneutical possibilities. Although Gustav Aulén's classic study *Christus Victor*[25] indicates a range in atonement theory, the problem is that the ideal of sacrifice used to understand the cross has been almost exclusively focused on the ancient heroic paradigm, which includes the necessary death of the hero. Studying atonement theory from the perspective of hero worship answers part of the problem identified by feminist criticism and adds to the already existing feminist discourse.

HEROIC SACRIFICE: THE MARKS OF THE ANCIENT HERO AND DEATH-FOR-LIFE

Where does the idea that Jesus must die to save followers originate? We find it rooted in the ancient heroic paradigm. Gregory J. Riley, a scholar of Christian origins, offers an illuminating view on understanding Jesus through the ideals of ancient heroes. Ancient heroes such as Perseus were born of humanity and divinity and held a place in the Great Chain of Being above humans but below gods and goddesses.[26] As a rule, heroes are distinctly characterized by their "example for behavior, . . . courage and distinguished deeds."[27] Specifically, they have remarkable talents, share a destiny interwoven with the fate of others, are often ensnared in a divine drama out of their own control, have divine enemies and human enemies in the form of rulers, and pass through a test of character, eventually dying an early death.[28] Engrained in the consciousness of the ancient world, the hero's life was to be nobly emulated; indeed, living as the hero did prove the quality of one's soul. The story of Jesus, Riley argues, was told from this very paradigm.

The marks of the hero are evident in the Gospels' narrative of Jesus. His remarkable talents are apparent when he performs miracles, heals the broken, feeds the hungry, and commands nature. Jesus' fate, we are to understand from the New Testament, was and is bound with all humanity: if he dies, followers will live. Jesus' divine drama comes to a head when he is put to the test in Gethsemane.[29] Conflict with earthly rulers brings him to an early death, but his death is alleged to have cosmic influence because he battled with the devil and won.

Ancient heroes often rescued a loved one from Hades' House, the underworld of the dead, ruled by Hades, the god of the dead.[30] Layered onto the heroic ideal were Persian Zoroastrian concepts of eschatology, which were pervasive in Galilee.[31] Jesus' eschatological worldview, which divided reality into the present life and eternal life, meant that he perceived his test as the hero to be the sacrifice of his life to make a rescue attempt in Hades' House. What is unique to Jesus is that he descended to Hades' House not to rescue just the select, highly educated few,[32] but the many. In other words, from Riley's perspective, Jesus can be explained as the hero to sacrifice his life in order to bring eternal life to all of his followers.[33]

Positively, Riley's analysis of ancient Near Eastern mythological paradigms sheds light on Christianity's inheritance of necessary religious death. Within this understanding, Jesus must die in order to descend to Hades' House, the very place from which the dead must be rescued. In Christian terms, this mythological portrayal of death came to be described as Jesus' death that conquered death and the devil, flinging the gates of heaven open for "believers," Jesus' followers. What we tend not to see from a Christian position of uniqueness is that this model of heroic death for life is the possible root of Christian atonement theory.

The hero's rescue of a loved one from Hades' House is apparent in both the sacrificial and *Christus Victor* models. In sacrificial terms of atonement, Jesus is both the priest who makes the sacrifice and the sacrifice needed to effect redemption from sin. Similarly, ancient heroes had to give up their lives in order to make the descent to Hades' House on a rescue mission. What differentiates Jesus as priest and Jesus as hero is that in Jewish terms Jesus relieves people from sin; in Greco-Roman terms, Jesus rescues followers from Hades' House into immortality.[34] In the *Christus Victor* model of atonement we readily see the successful hero: death has been overcome for the prize of immortality.

Recognizing that Jesus' story was told in both Jewish and Greco-Roman terms opens up the hermeneutical spectrum. What Jesus did in his life, and what occurred through his death and resurrection, can be interpreted from different understandings of sacrifice. Thus, we see even more clearly the multiplicity of atonement theory, making way for a hermeneutic of maternal sacrifice.

MATERNAL SACRIFICE: THE MARKS OF THE MOTHER AND LIFE-FOR-LIFE

Both the hero and the mother existed before Christian interpretation of the cross, yet the normativity of motherhood is soundly ignored in Protestant theology. Maternal sacrifice, by body and by energy, gives us a view of sacrifice that I think is necessary for a broadened hermeneutic of the cross, which is essential if we are to correct our hyper-focus on redemptive death and if we are to see with new eyes the testimony of a soteriology of restoration in Scripture. Motherhood might serve as a theological hermeneutic because the life of birthing and rearing children lies at the heart of reality for us: without these feats, we would not be. Social critic Kathryn Rabuzzi tellingly states in her book *Motherself: A Mythic Analysis of Motherhood*, "If a society existed in which the way of the mother were the norm, *tales of mothers would predominate the way tales of heroes do in cultures throughout the world.*"[35] Indeed, we're left with the question: Since motherhood *is* the norm, why do we act as if it is not?

Maternal sacrifice might be described in two categories that are not always easily separated: the maternal body and the maternal life—or, "raising children." For one, the courage necessary to endure the physical demands of motherhood is remarkable. For another, the terms of generativity and creativity called to the fore by the demands and joys of raising children, by mothers or fathers, raise questions over the once-for-all terms of sacrifice assigned by predominant interpretation to Jesus' work of salvation.

The physical sacrifice of motherhood is noteworthy. First, consider the possible physical factors of pregnancy: nausea and vomiting, sometimes daily and sometimes disorienting; shortness of breath; stretch marks; hemorrhoids; varicose veins; and high blood pressure, diabetes, and other risk factors that predispose a woman to these chronic conditions once she has contracted them in pregnancy. Pregnancy alone alters a woman's body, which, experienced by women the first time, *is* the beginning of sacrifice for life to come from life.

Childbirth and lactation further alter a woman's body, opening, stretching, and widening her. The prematernal body does not return *in toto*. By woman's stripes is life given. I point out these physical alterations neither in an attempt to receive pity for women who give birth, nor to glorify biological mothers over others. Rather, I am simply pointing out that to live through and accept these physical alterations requires courage—the courage to sacrifice. Women who gestate, birth, and nurse babies are giving life for life. Feminist social critic Naomi Wolf writes:

> Although few women in the West actually die in childbirth today, we deny the many symbolic deaths a contemporary pregnant woman undergoes: from the end of her solitary selfhood, to the loss of her prematernal shape, to the eclipse of her psychologically carefree identity, to the transformation of her marriage, to the decline in her status as a professional or worker.[36]

Although maternal sacrifice does not ordinarily mean mortal sacrifice in industrialized nations, women who choose to be mothers are nevertheless actively sacrificing. As feminist scholar Catharine MacKinnon notes, "To treat motherhood as something that just happens denies a woman's participation in conception, her decision to carry a child to term, her nurturing and sacrifice for nine months, and the labor of birthing."[37] Women are active in this drama, not passive.

In essence, what must be realized, pastoral theologian Bonnie Miller-McLemore points out, is that the creative energy involved in bearing and raising children is a form of generativity, perhaps even the most elemental of all forms of generativity. When the ideal of generativity is weighed in male terms,[38] vocational *productivity* rises like a solo star, leaving "concern for care, procreativity, children, and home as an afterthought."[39] The sacrifice necessary for reproductive and parental generativity leaves little time for vocational "productivity" outside the home.[40] What is put into the life of children oftentimes does not have the dividend of creative energy needed in the short term for one's parallel vocations. Miller-McLemore's point, however, is that we become whole persons by our interdependence, not by our independence. We only truly live the ideal of generativity when we live not as a "separative" self but as an affiliated self.[41] This is indicative of a model of restoration, one in which, I would venture to suggest, people are restored to wholeness in God through each other and to wholeness in each other through God.

SCRIPTURE

The Gospel of John is a ready scriptural partner to the idea that maternal sacrifice as a hermeneutic of the cross keeps a sacrifice of glory in check and is a reminder of a soteriology of restoration. The Gospel of John reflects a notion of salvation free from legalistic sacrifice that feminists might embrace. For example, Parker observes multiple images of moving away from the darkness and cold and into the light and warmth, indicating both transformation and the continuance of life.[42] John 8:12 reads: "Again Jesus spoke to them, saying, 'I am the light of the world. Whoever follows me will never walk in darkness but will have the light of life.'" Indeed, John 17:3 reflects nonviolent atonement: "And this is eternal life, that they may know you, the only true God, and Jesus Christ whom you have sent." Knowing God is in itself redemptive. The remarkable characteristics of salvation in the Gospel of John—continued life, transformation, and nonviolence—ultimately reflect maternal sacrifice.

Such a reading of the text further allows us to see that the Gospel of John is imbued with a soteriological model of restoration. For example, Parker and Brock contend that we need to be saved from the wounds of violence itself, rather than to be saved by violent self-sacrifice from the sin of disobedience to God. Parker in particular relates her experiences of being saved from the devastation of childhood sexual abuse not by further sacrifice or violence, but by restoration. The alternative soteriology they propose is to be saved into the Presence (of God) by the practice of love. Through love the soul is restored.[43] This is a soteriological model of restoration that is not simply material but transcendent.[44] According to Parker, salvation is God-relational: it is a sense of life permeated by the presence of God.[45] Love is what restores our awareness of God's presence.

Parker raises two significant observations from her shared study of John with Brock. First, she points out that the unfolding story of Jesus' death in John is a description of Jesus' antagonists' alienation from God: the hostility toward Jesus grows in the Gospel, and in John 8 Jesus says that people are alienated from the true heritage of God. That is, their alienation from God drives them toward killing Jesus. In a telling summary, Parker relates that in John, Caesar is the god making expiation, sacrificing human life. The Jewish authorities show their allegiance to Rome by giving Jesus up to them (see John 16). Jesus is thus crucified by those who serve Caesar, those who do not serve the God of love.[46] Parker concludes that the theology of expiation is repudiated in John's Gospel.

Second, Parker points out that according to John 17:3, eternal life is to know (to live in intimate relationship with) God. This understanding influences in no small measure the manner in which we understand Jesus as Savior or the role of love in salvation. Parker lifts up three ways in which Jesus is interpreted as Savior of the world in the Gospel of John. First, Jesus is the manifestation of God; in his own body, he is an incarnation of God. The people of John's Gospel had lost the knowledge of the unity of the spirit and the flesh and needed to be born again[47] in order to see the presence of God in all of life. Second, Jesus resists oppressive power; specifically, Jesus resists Caesar and his ways. Third, Jesus gives the life-giving commandment: to love one another as Jesus has loved them. This is the new Torah, the epitome that allows life to be saved. Thus, Parker interprets the path of salvation as the practice of love, which restores us to an awareness of God with us.

A model of soteriological restoration is also apparent in New Testament scholar Sandra M. Schneiders's thesis that the resurrection narrative in the Gospel of John is indicative of transformation and nonviolent atonement. Schneiders's exegesis of the interaction between Jesus and Mary Magdalene shows that Jesus is redirecting Mary's (and others') desire to have Jesus as he was prior to the crucifixion toward "the new locus of his presence in the world, that is, the community of his brothers and sisters, the disciples."[48] No longer should followers look to the physical Jesus, they must rather look to each other—*touch* each other, to find the glorified Jesus Christ.[49] The community is the new place of Jesus' earthly presence. Indeed, "saving revelation," as Schneiders describes it, is what we find in God through Jesus and each other.[50]

What is promised in the Gospel of John, Schneiders argues, is "divine filiation, eternal life in the Spirit springing up from within the believer (4:10-11) and flowing forth for the new life of the world (7:37-39 and 19:34-37)."[51] Just as Parker makes clear, love restores. Yet Schneiders goes on to demonstrate clearly that it is through each other that this occurs, once the glorified presence of Christ is experienced among the brothers and sisters of the community. Indeed, followers are converted toward each other through God. This is transformation.

CONCLUSION: "SO WHAT?"

Allowing for a hermeneutics of maternal sacrifice in atonement theory means three important things. First, Jesus' physical death is no longer seen as an exclusive necessity for new life, given the life-for-life model of the mother-child relationship; we see Jesus' life more clearly as a locus of salvation. What has been criticized as specifically Christian religious necrophilia is turned into *zoophilia*, the love of life. This turns Christians more strongly toward Jesus' life as a potential locus of redemption, for which many feminist and liberation theologians argue. By transferring our soteriological focus from death to life, such as the life given and cared for by the mother, the way to eternal life is no longer exclusively focused upon obedient death but upon God's love as lived through Jesus. Jesus' life, then, is what brings us to knowledge of God, which, according to John 17:3, *is* eternal life.

Second, a new soteriological view afforded by the hermeneutic of maternal sacrifice removes Jesus from a violent center of religion. The result is a different christological paradigm for us to live. The practical effect is enormously significant: we are released from the dangers of a sacrifice of glory, which springs from a misapplication of violent atonement. If Jesus is no longer the sacrifice necessary as a sin offering, then we are released from religious metaphors of violence. Therefore, modes and metaphors of cultural violence, including those of sacrificial abuse and war, are deemed illegitimate. To live *imitatio Christi* is refocused away from a sacrifice of glory to a genuine re-turn to each other, indicative of parental generativity. Jesus' death is no longer exclusively expiation but is also the embodiment of the risk to love. What we do in our re-turn to God (and thus to each other) may result in death, but it will be a death living God's love, just as Jesus' death on the cross can be interpreted. That is, to live out the kingdom of God on earth places one in an ethic of risk that sets one in dire opposition to the kingdom that is antithetical to God.[52]

Last, a practical effect of refocusing sacrificial hermeneutics is that in returning to each other, we embody the life-for-life model of sacrifice inherent to motherhood and are ultimately transformed. As a study of the Gospel of John makes clear, to touch each other in the wake of the resurrection is to find the glorified Jesus Christ. In the same way, a baby must be loved and taken into the human community in order to thrive, to know and to learn the life of interrelationship. What better model of the restorative salvation we find in God through Jesus Christ? The restorative wholeness of relationship, both with God and with neighbor, redeems. Relationship, as the heart of life, indeed, as the heart of the gospel itself, saves.

5

Becoming a Feminist Theologian of the Cross

Deanna A. Thompson

The cross alone is our theology.
Martin Luther

No one was saved by the execution of Jesus.
Rebecca Parker

CONTEMPORARY THEOLOGY PLAYS HOST TO a chorus of voices calling theology to account for its long and thriving history of using the cross of Christ to inflict suffering upon the innocent. Among the alleged perpetrators littering the historical Christian landscape, few loom as large as the Reformers of sixteenth-century Europe, those fathers of Protestantism obsessed with God's wrath toward deservedly damned human beings. Indeed, we need not wade far into the writings of Reformer Martin Luther before becoming submerged in what author Kathleen Norris calls the "scary vocabulary" of Christian speech.[1] Does speaking rightly about God today demand that we abandon the theologizing of bygone thinkers like Martin Luther?

Feminist and other contemporary theologians proclaim that speaking rightly of God requires radical reform of traditional theologies like Luther's. We are often reminded today that all theology is contextual, and many argue that Luther's own contextual preoccupation with wrath, sin, and guilt adds real insult to real injury when spoken to those whose lives bear marks of real crucifixions. Even more pointedly, traditional theories of atonement and theologies of the cross are under attack by feminists and others who work to unmask the damage of these theologies to the wounded, the vulnerable, and the oppressed. Where is the good news preached to the victimized? The responsibility for such oppression and suffering is being laid at the feet of the patriarchal Christian tradition, of which Luther is a card-carrying member. Cries for reform rise up, and they deserve a hearing.

But cries of reform also rose up over five hundred years ago from the mouth and pen of Martin Luther over the oppressive theology and church practices of his own day. Theologians of his day, Luther proclaimed, had bypassed the cross of Christ and were following instead theologies of glory that pursued disingenuous paths to God, paths controlled by religious decrees of the seemingly all-powerful medieval church. Luther glimpsed an alternate reality through the cross of Christ, an alternative vision of what counted as authority, wisdom, and salvation. What Luther accomplished in his Reformation was nothing less than a new way of imaging church, theology, and the Christian's role in society.

The divide between contemporary feminist theologians and Martin Luther is wide. Is it possible to claim both feminism and Luther? Is the divide that separates them crossable? On good days, I believe that both Luther's vision for life with the cross at the center and feminist visions for Christian repentance and healing can be brought together in ways that preserve the integrity of both sides. If Luther's theology of the cross is revisited, feminists will be surprised to meet in Luther an ally for thinking through *how* theologians reimagine and reform dominant, abusive forms of Christianity, and move toward a more faithful, liberating portrait of life lived in response to the gospel message. Those who reside firmly on the side of Luther can learn more from feminists about the nightmarish realities of human suffering and about theology's complicity in the persistence of unnecessary suffering. The divide can be crossed, and this essay is an exercise in crossing and bridge building through examining Luther's theology of reform and how this implies a theological method commensurate with feminism. In addition to this, Luther's theology of the cross offers perspective on feminist interpretations of sin, suffering, and the cross. Finally, claiming the position of a feminist theologian of the cross, I offer four approaches to interpreting the cross today: the cross as critical principle, the cross as mirror, the crucified woman as the location of Christ today, and last, the cross as revealing Jesus who befriends humanity, calling Christians to the vocation of friendship.

LUTHER'S THEOLOGY OF REFORM

My understanding of Luther's theology of the cross is indebted to several formative influences. First, Douglas John Hall's work on an indigenous theology of the cross[2] within North American Christianity first planted the seed for this project. Second, I build upon Walther von Lowenich's argument that Luther's cross-centered approach was integral to his life-long career as a reformer, rather than a passing preoccupation of his monastic days.[3] Third, I am persuaded by Gerhard Forde's recent re-reading of Luther's "Heidelberg Disputation," the foundational text for Luther's theology of the cross, and his claim that, taken in its totality, the treatise tells the cross-to-resurrection story of the sinner brought low, justified, and saved through the cross and resurrection of Christ.[4] With these scholars forming the foundation, I will now present Luther as a contextual theologian of the cross whose life reflects both faithful and not-so-faithful lived applications of this subversive theological approach.

Luther narrates what the cross does to the believer and the enterprise of theology in his 1518 "Heidelberg Disputation." The first part of the story recounts human beings' experience of trying—and failing—to make ourselves righteous before God. This is a failure Luther knew all too well; he wrote often about his experiences of *Anfechtung*, a terrified conscience, due to his inability to fulfill "the law," exemplified for him in the rules and regulations set forth in his monastic order. At this point, Luther argued, the distinction between glory theology and cross theology begins to emerge, for glory theologians put their faith in human ability to move toward God—a fiction, Luther claimed, that ultimately leads to despair (thesis 18). To experience despair over our failure at self-improvement is really, Luther explained, the experience of God's alien or strange work on our prideful selves. The cross of Christ, Luther insisted, judges and condemns all attempts at self-presumption, leaving the Christian humbled and ready to receive the gift of grace.

On one level, Luther's theology of the cross is highly personal and existential. On another level, however, his cross-centered approach narrates a public, corporate story about an alternative to a glory theology that creates a fictitious universe where ecclesial, theological, and monastic institutions come to practice a theology of human power, majesty, and achievement. A critical affirmation of a theologian of the cross, then, is that Jesus Christ's death on the cross tells us that appearances ultimately deceive, that reality is actually hidden *sub contrario*, under its opposite. Precisely where God seems least likely to be—in the shameful event of the cross—there God is, hidden in the suffering. Those theologians of glory who controlled much of the church of Luther's time, however, avoided the cross, wanting instead to "reign with Christ."[5] Thus, for Luther, theologians of glory call good evil and evil good, while a theologian of the cross "calls a thing what it is" (thesis 21), exposing corruption for what it is and demanding reform.

The last part of the story, as Luther tells it in the "Heidelberg Disputation," is that through the cross "the tyrants" (sin, death, and the devil) are conquered, and because of the resurrection, new life in Christ is possible. After the death of the sinner with Christ on the cross, Luther proclaims, the sinner is justified and "raised up" (thesis 24). Now, knowing that salvation comes through what Christ did on the cross, Christians are freed up to "be imitators of God," not as a requirement for righteousness, but as a "stimulant" for loving action in the world (thesis 27). It is precisely this radical notion of Christian freedom that fueled Luther's vision of reformation within medieval Christendom.

Luther's cross-centered vision for theology altered the imagination of late-medieval Christians and provided the foundation for bold and courageous acts of reform. Understood as no longer bound by the regulations of a controlling institution, Luther and his followers championed a theology that freed the Christian for a vocation in the world rather than removed from it. And while we applaud his faithfulness as a theologian of the cross in the ecclesial realm, we also acknowledge his failure to embody that role in other parts of his life, such as during the Peasants' Uprising of 1525 or in giving respect to his Jewish brothers and sisters.[6]

With a thumbnail sketch of Luther's theology of the cross in place, we place Luther in conversation with feminist theologians to see how these distinct per-spectives might be fruitfully combined.

UNLIKELY ALLIES

The cover story of a 2005 issue of the *Christian Century* suggested that a new wave of feminist theologians is emerging who claim the strong and defiant tradition of Luther and other sixteenth-century Reformers when they envision an *ecclesia semper reformanda,* the church as always reforming itself.[7] As more scholars engage in mutually enhancing conversations between Luther and feminist theological visions, *method* becomes an obvious point of connection. It can be argued that Luther shares with feminists a threefold methodological approach: critique, retrieval, and reimagining. I offer here some shared sensibilities that suggest the possibility of a feminist theology of the cross.

To begin, both Luther and feminists utilize what feminists commonly call a "hermeneutics of suspicion," a process of interpretation that recognizes the provisional nature of interpretation and the way in which interpreters presuppose and enforce cultural norms and ideologies. According to feminists, Christian thought and practice overflow with particular theologies of glory—patriarchy, demonarchy,[8] kyriarchy[9]—that employ matrixes of domination in which women live, move, and struggle to be. Feminist theology, in line with Luther's persistence in calling a thing what it is, calls the patriarchal assumptions underlying Christian claims by their real names. Just as Luther's theology of the cross puts everything to the test, including the dominant theological tradition he inherited, so feminists mirror this testing of tradition, scrutinizing its faithfulness to and respect for women.

Second, feminist theologians employ a critique similar to Luther's constant warning of the seductive power of any and all versions of theologies of glory. That which attracts and seduces in a patriarchal milieu is often the same as that which oppresses and suppresses those on the margins. In response, feminist theologians set forth a theological vision from the underside of society, of history, an approach not unlike Luther's destabilizing move to the cross of Christ. Luther returns to Scripture, to Paul's cross-centered vision, retrieving this critical, subversive approach to counter scholasticism's seductively misleading claims. The God Christians come to know through the cross of Christ is the antithesis of the majestic God of the scholastics, who lives and reigns in power and glory. For Luther, God is met in the basest of places, hidden within suffering, pain, and death. In a similar vein, feminist theologians call attention to the forgotten and ignored elements of Christian tradition that highlight the power of women as agents and recipients of God's love. In a tradition guilty of repeatedly denigrating women, feminists uncover and expose God's hidden presence in the most unpredictable of places: in the lives and experiences of women.

Third, Luther and feminist theologians both witness to theology's experiential dimensions. Both understand that theological reflection must be done in constant conversation with the contexts in which they live, responding to the challenges and struggles confronting them. For Luther, theology always stretches beyond mere intellectual exercise to faithful existence under the cross, requiring him to address the unsentimental realities of suffering and death. Similarly, feminists rely

on the contextual category of experience to analyze and assess practical implications of normative claims. Just as Luther determined that attention to the existential dimension of faith was missing from the prevailing theological imagination
of his day, so feminists regard concrete experiences of women as missing from
dominant theological discourse.

Where Luther and feminist theologians stand most closely together is in their
reforming *sensibility* that gets worked out through shared methodological commitments. Both Luther and feminists are allied in their stinging critiques of dominant
traditions. Both are well practiced in leveling a "No!" against the theologies of
glory running rampant in their contexts.

When we allow the conversation between Luther and feminist theologians to
move beyond shared methodological commitments, however, points of difference
quickly emerge. What follows here is an imaginative engagement between Luther
and feminists that should help move us forward toward a feminist theology of
the cross.

DEEPENING THE DISCUSSION: SIN, SUFFERING, AND THE CROSS

Sin and Suffering

Several feminist theologians have argued against Luther's and other traditional
readings of sin, insisting that they represent decidedly masculine patterns of
sinfulness. Stated briefly, if the diagnosis misses the mark for women, feminists
insist, then Luther's call to break the self's curvature in upon itself is not only
off the mark but potentially harmful for women. As one persuaded by Luther's
view of human beings as chronically disposed to sin, I am cautious to embrace
immediately this feminist critique, which often leads, as in the work of Daphne
Hampson, to an exaltation of feminist empowerment. While such empowerment
certainly has its place, feminist ethicist Sallie Purvis casts doubt on such optimistic
feminist soteriologies, stating that in many of our feminist groups "commitments
to cooperate degenerate into attempts to dominate, the common good is lost in
cliques, horizontal violence abounds as the powerless attack one another, and the
most commonly shared experience can be a sense of betrayal."[10] Purvis's point is
by no means antifeminist. In fact, this intrafeminist critique has been deepened by
black feminist bell hooks, who makes visible the way in which privileged white

women fail to attend to the vertical violence that persists among women in their complex identities of race, class, and sexuality. Purvis and hooks lend credence to the cross-centered affirmation that all human beings are ensnared in a complex web of sin and are continuously subjected to the temptation to replicate patterns of domination. Women, like men, experience temptation to sin through the abuse of power, as well as through the trials of broken, wounded relationships. Writer Kathleen Norris suggests we need to communicate these abuses through our language. Norris—in decidedly Lutheran fashion—worries that omitting words like *wretch* from contemporary theological discourse means we encourage neglect of a basic human reality. She asks, "Who never lies awake regretting the selfish, nigh-unforgivable things that he or she has done? . . . It seems to me that if you can't ever admit to being a wretch, you haven't been paying attention."[11] A feminist theologian of the cross must pay attention to women's experiences of personal sin, as well as for collusion with sinful structures external to the self.

But a deeper issue still lurks within this discussion of sin. Many feminist theologians root their understanding of sin not in some generic notion of "woman" but specifically in women whose lives have been shattered by experiences of abuse and oppression. Rebecca Parker, in her book *Proverbs of Ashes,* written with Rita Nakashima Brock, recounts in horrifying detail her preschool experiences of being raped by a neighbor. Just as horrifying is her Christian family's—and her Christian community's—inability to help her deal with this violence committed against her. Parker's indictment against her church and her theology is this: "What my community could not name it could not see. And what the community could not see, I could not integrate. My religious community, most of all, could not see [this violence] because it could not name clearly the violence that happened to Jesus."[12] Parker and others demand that theology respond not just to the "sinner," but to the lived reality of those who are gravely sinned against.

From the vantage point of women like Parker, Serene Jones evaluates Luther's story of justification, noting that the first scene in the drama—and indeed in Luther's theology of the cross—depicts God's wrath fully undoing (crucifying) the subject. This drama begins with a harsh movement against "the pretensions of self-definition and pride," which results in "fragmentation" of the arrogant self. In assessing this drama through a feminist lens, Jones asks, "What happens to the woman who enters this tale having spent her life not in the space of narcissistic self-definition but in the space of fragmentation and dissolution?"[13] She suggests one of two possibilities: in the first scenario, Luther's narrative falls on deaf ears; the story is so foreign that the woman is incapable of seeing herself present in it (that is, unable to identify with its masculine patterns). In the second, more pernicious option, this woman adopts the narrative as her own story, taking upon herself "a script designed for the prideful sinner." She likely will "recapitulate the dynamics of her oppression and self-loss."[14] Again, if she adopts the misdiagnosis of her condition, she will misappropriate the cure.

In response to these problematic and potentially destructive scenarios, it is crucial that a feminist theologian of the cross make distinctions among different kinds of suffering. Luther's concern was primarily with *description* rather than *prescription* of the situation in which humans find themselves. At the heart of Luther's cross-centered vision was the rejection of the way in which "bearing the cross," as prescribed by medieval Christendom, had lost its rootedness in biblical narrative. Suffering under one's own cross should never become a technique or a "work." Christians are not called to sacrifice and suffer in order to be made worthy before God. This is the religious vision Luther experienced and denounced as virtually unbearable; it is precisely the vision he came to reject through his theology of the cross.

The type of suffering of which Luther primarily speaks is the spiritual suffering we experience in light of God's work "against the presumption of our work." We want to heal ourselves, work out our own salvation, and Luther's talk of suffering mirrors quite vividly the psalmist's lament of "bottoming out," of acknowledging our utter dependence upon God. Further, Luther's dialectical approach to human existence and God's alien and proper work allows the possibility to take a deeper accounting of sin as harm done to others. We look to Luther's dialectical approach to Scripture as law and gospel, which he first articulated as letter and spirit. Gerhard Ebeling suggests that Luther realized early on that

> understanding scripture is not something that can be preserved and passed on. As existential life continues, so the understanding of scripture is a continuous task which can never be brought to a conclusion. For there is constant threat that an understanding once achieved will cease to be spirit, and return to being the mere letter, unless it is constantly attained anew and made one's own.[15]

Faced with a woman whose life has been shattered by violence, then, it is conceivable that instead of commending her to be crucified by the law, a theologian of the cross could instead preach a word of comfort regarding God's presence: in Luther's biblical exegesis, for example, he expresses deep concern for the healing of the sinned against. Much in his Genesis lectures affirms that God knows the victims, rages with anger over injustices committed against the innocent, and that God is the One who comforts the wounded, the shattered, as a mother comforts her child.[16]

These aspects of Luther's thought coincide with Jones's vision of retaining Luther's justification drama without having it further damn the crucified woman. Jones suggests that for someone reeling from the effects of sin done against her, she enter the drama in a different scene, namely in the one where she becomes a new creation. Jones argues that "this inversion does not replace or destroy the logic of justification; narrating the story of a sturdy and resilient new creation before turning to the moment of dismantling and forgiveness simply allows the most problematic aspects of justification (its first decentering moment) to be tempered."[17]

This inversion helps preserve what I find at the heart of Luther's theology of the cross: a clarity and conviction that can only be spoken from the resurrection side of the cross. This cross-centered vision for Luther emerges alongside his intensely personal experience of being saved by the Word of God spoken through the cross of Christ. And we cannot forget Luther's dialectical approach to Scripture as law and gospel. In light of this dialectic, I propose that the first word a feminist theology of the cross will speak to the wounded, the vulnerable, the oppressed, is the gospel, the word of hope, without losing sight that each life must also inevitably undergo the undoing by the letter, the law, of any and all attempts at self-sufficiency before God.

The Meaning of the Cross

At the heart of Luther's "experiential *theologia crucis*" is knowing that "we must become Christ to our neighbor, as Christ did for me," and making Christ "personalized and present in our lives."[18] For Luther, a kind of existential unity occurs between Christ and the believer through the experience of faith.

The Cross as Critical Principle. How, then, can a feminist theologian of the cross faithfully communicate the intimate presence of Christ in the lives of Christians—particularly shattered women—today? In order to answer this question, we need to return to the original intent of Luther's theology of the cross. Luther set forth a critical principle into the theological conversation of his time in order to shatter what he saw as the glorious, unfaithful images of God and "man" that were currently proclaimed. Our knowledge of God, Luther insisted, comes only in veiled, hidden, and profoundly unexpected ways through the lens of faith. That God became clothed in human flesh speaks of God's hidden presence in our world.

This vision of God not only upsets human expectations of God, but it also alters the way theology is done. Advocating a theology of the cross as a critical, negative principle to question and chip away at status quo theology and ecclesiology was, Luther believed, the vocation of all those who follow Christ.

Despite the growing popularity and attention given feminist projects, the dominant theological and ecclesial landscape remains in many ways hostile to feminist concerns. Echoing Luther, the critical function of a feminist theology of the cross is to disrupt any and all versions of a theology of glory that suppress and oppress women. Because the gendered identity of Jesus often leads to the theological exaltation of maleness, a feminist theologian of the cross is obliged to call sexism what it is: a distortion of God's hidden presence in human flesh.

The Crucified Woman as the Location of Christ Today. Luther's focus on how a Christian *experiences* Christ's real presence in his or her life led him to critique the effectiveness of scholastic theology when it came to speaking to the mother in the home or man on the street. He was convinced that theology must be done in a language full of dramatic images that speak to everyday persons. He also once implored Christians to "engrave the picture of the cross of Christ on [yourselves]." As contemporary theologians answer the question, "*Where* is Christ today?" I argue that the image of a crucified woman can both judge oppressive theologies of glory and make uncomfortable—while imaginatively suggesting that women as well as men are fully in God's image and capable of bearing the divine.

In the spirit of Luther, I propose that resistance to idolizing Jesus' male identity be presented in the strategic reassertion of the image of the crucified woman as the *location* of Christ today. Because the imaging of Christ has become dangerously synonymous with male identity, the image of the crucified woman has potential to critique the "inherent" link between maleness and divinity. Once it serves that critical, negative function, the crucified woman, in the spirit of a theology of the cross, can then open up, especially for women, new existential pathways and insights into the concrete reality of God becoming enfleshed and embodied in particular human form.[19]

But is the image of a crucified woman necessarily a healing image for women?[20] I contend that the images of crucified women[21] force us to ponder God's hidden presence, God's envelopment of human suffering, in new ways. The crucified woman yells a resounding "No!" in the face of maleness of God, in the face of sexist structures erected in the name of Christ that are too common, too expected. The image of a crucified woman startles us into understanding God's presence hidden *sub contrario*. But the image of the crucified woman stands alongside the full account of the Gospel narrative of Jesus' life, death, and resurrection. The promise that must be pronounced to and with the crucified woman is that the resurrection offers hope to the crucified, that suffering and abuse do not, will not, ultimately have the final word.

The Cross as Mirror. But we still have yet to cross the most difficult divide—the view of atonement. In the face of forceful and varied critiques leveled against traditional atonement theories, contemporary Lutheran theologians attempt to demonstrate that Luther's understanding of atonement differs from traditional satisfaction, *Christus Victor*, or moral influence theories.[22] What is radical about Luther's understanding of the gospel, it is argued, is that Luther reverses the direction of atonement. The message of Christ on the cross is that God comes to us. If a theology of the cross is going to hold to some version of Luther's understanding of the depth of human sinfulness, then humanity must be viewed as incapable of voluntarily moving toward God, unable to overcome its own limitations and secure its own salvation. The message of the cross for Luther is what God does for us.

For Luther, understanding the meaning of the cross is more like looking in a mirror than it is an intellectual assent to this or that theory. Luther claimed that "Christ mirrors our sin, demonstrating what should have happened to us." Because Christ actually became sin for us, Luther asserts, we are freed from having to do the same. In his stressing the uniqueness of Christ's suffering, Luther was delivering the death knell to medieval religious proscriptions that suffering is necessary to become worthy in God's sight. I am drawn here to Luther's invocation of the biblical story of the woman caught in adultery. Luther focused on Jesus' reaction, noting that he did not demand suffering, payment, or sacrifice. Rather, Jesus tells her, "Go and sin no more." Luther then described this pronouncement of Jesus as "laying on her the cross." To live faithfully under the reality of the cross is to live as one who has been justified by God and opened to the brokenness and needs of the world in which one lives.

Feminist theologians are concerned not just with theological language itself, but also with the "effective history" of the images and symbols contained in the discourse. Feminists test Luther not only on his theological claims, but also on how his theology functioned in concrete situations. While Luther's pastoral, devotional orientation succeeded in offering words of comfort to those whose existence was marked by unjust sufferings, we cannot overlook his brutish approaches to the peasants and—later in life—the Jews, often taken in the name of Christ. The feminist theological sensibility of keeping those suffering ones at the forefront of this vision will help mitigate the possibility of following Luther down those destructive paths.

Jesus Befriending Humanity on the Cross. For a feminist theologian of the cross committed to naming the violence specifically toward women that has been justified through appeal to traditional atonement images, a shift in describing the atoning work of Christ becomes necessary. Specifically, I suggest a revisioning of Luther's use of the metaphor of a *frohliche Wechsel,* or "blessed exchange," between the bridegroom and bride to understand atonement. Luther lifts up the image of Christ the bridegroom marrying the "poor wicked harlot," thus taking on all her grievous sins and saving her from rightful damnation. Arguably the power of this biblical image comes from Luther's articulation of the gift character of the husband freely taking on all sins of his wife, thereby endowing her with eternal righteousness. In our contemporary setting, however, much of the power of this metaphor is muted or lost for women and men who cannot move past its sexism.

Rather than a joyous exchange between Christ and the wicked harlot bride, I suggest a metaphor that communicates several key aspects of a feminist theologian of the cross's understanding of atonement. It is the model of friendship—that God's atoning work for us on the cross is done through Jesus' befriending humanity. Drawing on Luther's most beloved Gospel of John, we hear Jesus telling his disciples that "no one has greater love than this, to lay down one's life for one's friends" (15:13). This model is suggested in the spirit of Luther's use of various images—from the devil capturing the bait to the bridegroom taking on the sins of his bride—to convey the meaning of the cross. Luther's theology of the cross was constantly applied and adapted to various occasions, and this occasion for a feminist theology of the cross calls out for another image that communicates the message more effectively to contemporary women and men. In John, the image of friendship is privileged to explain the meaning of Jesus' life and, specifically, his death on the cross. The image of Jesus laying down his life for his friends highlights the gift character that is crucial to Luther's understanding of what God did on the cross. Sallie McFague emphasizes the freely chosen nature of friendship that has not always been a part of the understanding of marriage.[23] Friends freely choose to be in relation to one another. Is that not an appropriate image of Jesus' willingness to give of himself? Jesus was not paying a debt to God. Jesus the Friend acted freely, giving his very life on behalf of his friends. In a related vein, Gerhard Forde argues that the "for us" notion that was so important to Luther

> should be interpreted more on a sense of "on our behalf," "for our own good," or "for our benefit," rather than "instead of us" . . . [which is] oriented solely toward the past. But Jesus' work "for us" in the New Testament is oriented also toward the future. He died not only to repair past damage but to open a new future "for us."[24]

This image of Jesus as intimate friend of his disciples opens up avenues for talking about Jesus' suffering and atonement in ways tightly connected to the biblical story of Jesus' life and actions. The Matthean narrative reports that Jesus' friends included "tax collectors and sinners" (11:19), suggesting that when Jesus lays down his life on behalf of his friends, he bears their sins as well. The image of friendship also points to the role that sin played in placing Jesus on the cross. Jesus' words to Judas in the Garden of Gethsemane are, "Friend, do what you are here to do" (Matt. 26:50). Jesus' friend betrays him with a kiss. Jesus lays down his life for the friends who betray as well as those who remain faithful to him.

The story of Jesus the Friend laying down his life does not provide a guidebook, but it includes some powerful images for how we should live in light of God's work on the cross. "Remaining in the love of Christ" suggests the possibility of a healing vision for those whose present reality is dominated by suffering, negation, and hate, while "loving as Christ has loved us" beckons all Christians to open ourselves up to the devouring needs of others[25] and even to participate in the process of healing. For in the end, Jesus the Friend is not forsaken by God, and therefore we as friends of Jesus witness to the empowering reality of hope given us by the resurrection, a hope beyond all pain and suffering that surrounds us and sometimes swallows us whole.

In the concluding theses of the "Heidelberg Disputation," Luther speaks of how, after dying and being raised with Christ, we are freed to look to Jesus' life as a "stimulant" for loving action in the world. Turning to John's Gospel, where we hear of Jesus' laying down his life for his friends, we see that the narrative lingers with the image of friendship and contains the commands given by Jesus to his friends to "love one another as I have loved you" (15:12). That Jesus gives this command to the gathering of friends suggests that vocational identity is not just personal in character, but corporate as well. Remaining in the love of Christ entails doing so with others. In fact, one can argue that these words become the identifying marks of the Christian community.[26]

THE VOCATION OF FRIENDSHIP AND THE CHURCH AS COMMUNITY OF FRIENDS

Living in the space opened up by justification given through Christ's death and resurrection means living in freedom, called to a vocation of relationship with others in the world. "Faith finds expression in works of freest service, cheerfully and lovingly done...without hope of reward," Luther wrote.[27] Remaining in

Christ's love, Luther believed, meant freedom for the Christian, freedom from bondage to authority as well as freedom to serve all without regard for merit. In assessing Luther's limitations with respect to social reform, critics often point to both his reliance on the language of service as well as his vision of existence as lived out in two kingdoms, where the importance of the temporal realm fades behind the prominence of the realm of God. As a feminist theologian of the cross, I highlight the whole person as wholly present in both realms to avoid slippage into dualisms and I advocate for reform in the language of vocation itself, following the Johannine shift from "servant" to "friend" language. As a feminist theologian of the cross, I appreciate the subversive character of friendship as an operative image for vocation in our contemporary context. This image can express God's hidden presence in a backside manner, through mundane and ordinary relationships. Christians are called to be with others in the body of Christ; more explicitly, Christians are called to be nothing other than the church.

Interestingly, feminist theologians have recently called for the church to understand itself as a community of friends, a vision that builds on the Johannine passages informing a feminist theology of the cross. A feminist cross-centered vision of church builds on Luther's understanding of church as radically other than the hierarchical institution of his day. To call the church a "priesthood of all believers" gives church a communitarian shape.[28] In the Johannine claim that Jesus laid down his life *for his friends,* we are confronted with a view of friendship that challenges conventional understanding.

Within the church community, our vocation is first given to us through baptism. We are baptized into Christ's death, baptized into the story of the cross and resurrection that promises death to the power of sin in our lives. Jesus' friendships often included a shared meal, culminating in the last meal shared with his closest friends. The last supper before his crucifixion, however, is marked not only by friendship but also by betrayal. The Sacrament of Holy Communion recapitulates that meal, including the betrayal and the cross, but, as Rowan Williams asserts, "it does so as the Easter feast."[29] To claim Christ's real presence in the Lord's Supper points to the objective status of Christ's presence as the risen, crucified victim, the one in whom hope is also embodied. The Christ encountered in the meal is the one we encounter as a stranger, as our victim, to whom we confess our sins, admit our brokenness. The hope experienced in the Lord's Supper comes from standing before the risen Christ as a *restored* betrayer, a beloved friend.[30] We are opened to a vocation that calls us into friendship with any and all friends of Christ.

To understand vocation today in terms of friendship, then, takes us into the depths of our world. Living Christian vocation, both individually and corporately, is about bearing our own crosses. This is not an appeal to imitate Christ's suffering or death. Rather, to be the church and to remain in Christ's love for his friends is to be with those who suffer, those who are broken, those who are in pain. At its best, the church is a sanctuary for all such persons. At the same time, Christian vocation calls us into friendships that challenge our identities, both within and outside church walls. Laboring to make ordination more just for our friends who are currently excluded, working for affordable housing with our friends in the community who lack an adequate place to live, lobbying for systemic change in laws for medication distribution for our HIV-positive friends abroad and at home, we are called to embody the friendship of Christ. Living out our vocation of harrowing friendships leads us not only into reigning with Christ but also to conformity to his compassionate, healing humanity as he lived on earth. Bearing the cross of friendship in this world means that suffering comes as an inevitable by-product of justified existence.

This feminist theology of the cross represents one attempt at crossing the divide that exists between reformers in the tradition like Martin Luther and contemporary feminist reformers. Potential exists for new forms of theological, ecclesial, and social reform when contemporary theological thought—particularly in feminist form—rediscovers Luther's turn away from theologies of glory beholden to gods of our own construction toward a theology of the cross and the God hidden in the crucified and risen Christ. This project is just one piece within a much larger conversation between the rich resources of the Christian tradition and the challenging, prophetic forces of feminist theological thought. Let us not pass by this occasion for reform.

6

Contextualizing the Cross
for the Sake of Subjectivity

Rosemary P. Carbine

I've been raising up my hands
Drive another nail in
Just what God needs
One more victim
Why do we crucify ourselves?
Tori Amos, "Crucify"

A MAJOR CLAIM OF CLASSICAL Christology holds that incarnation and redemption are mutually interconnected, or that the person and work of Jesus are
interrelated for the sake of salvation. If Jesus is not fully divine, then he cannot
save. If Jesus is not fully human, then he cannot save human beings, especially if
we take seriously an early Christian principle that "what has not been assumed
has not been healed" (Gregory of Nazianzus). If a fully divine Jesus did not become fully human, then human beings are not truly or totally saved.

Who Jesus is shapes the soteriological significance of what Jesus does; what Jesus does has anthropological significance for the personhood of Jesus and of contemporary Christians. Taking this classical Christo-logic about the mutual interrelationship of the person and work of Jesus as a theological starting point, this essay explores contemporary theologies of the work of Jesus associated with the crucifixion from the perspective of theological anthropology, and attends to underlying understandings of the person of Jesus as well as the human person modeled on the person of Jesus. As we will see, long-standing atonement theologies reflect an essentialist theology of the cross and a static, singular notion of subjectivity based on suffering. By contrast, recent feminist and womanist theologies advance an eschatological theology of the cross, which contextualizes the cross amid many aspects of Jesus' life-ministry for the coming kingdom of God and likewise signifies a multidimensional notion of subjectivity and agency.

ATONEMENT: SUFFERING AND SUBJECTIVITY

Atonement theology is considered a main locus of Christian theological reflection regarding the work of Jesus for restoring right relations between God and humanity. Multivalent atonement theologies emerged in the history of Christian thought (for instance, ransom, recapitulation, battle, satisfaction, substitutionary sacrifice, moral exemplar), but these theologies mainly centered on the soteriological significance of the cross. Yet, traditional atonement theologies hold wide-ranging appeal for contemporary Christians. Mel Gibson's recent film *The Passion of the Christ* focuses on the final hours in Jesus' life and illustrates several atonement theologies. The film features an extended brutal scene of the flogging of Jesus, which recalls satisfaction theologies in which Jesus makes restitution to God in place of humanity by satisfying God's offense at human sin; substitutionary sacrifice theologies that link the severity of Jesus' suffering to God's punishment of sin; and moral exemplar theologies in which Jesus' suffering and death demonstrate God's love and simultaneously provoke repentance and right action.

Also, the cross appeals to many women, especially through female images of a crucified Christ, for instance, the famous sculpture *Christa* by Edwina Sandys. Female images of a suffering Christ hold theological potential; as Lisa Isherwood notes, "Empowering symbols are important to all marginalized groups and there is a certain satisfaction in subverting a symbol that has been part of historic oppression."[1] Gendering the cross exposes the forgotten or silenced suffering of biblical and contemporary women, leading to repentance and solidarity.[2] Crucified Christas resist such suffering, rather than reobjectify it or render it pornographic.

Applying the classical Christo-logic that interconnects the person and work of Jesus, what does religious reflection about the salvific work of Jesus suggest about the subjectivity of Jesus as well as the formation of religious subjectivity through an imitation of Jesus? Atonement theology emphasizes the salvific significance of the suffering and death of Jesus and tends to truncate the reconciling work of Jesus to the cross, thereby sidelining the equally redemptive significance of his life and ministry. In so doing, it addresses the restoration of "vertical" right relations with God, not "horizontal" right relations with humanity.[3] Moreover, separating the death from the entirety of the life-ministry of Jesus can function theologically to glorify and justify suffering,[4] thereby making the suffering of the cross theologically determinative of the person of Jesus. For example, in *The Passion of the Christ*, the life and ministry of Jesus are treated through brief flashbacks that point cinematically to his death, suggesting the misguided theological claim that the incarnation took place for the purpose of the crucifixion, or that Jesus was born to die. Atonement theologies that identify the work of Jesus with the cross are profoundly problematic because they raise troubling questions about the person of Jesus; they suggest a one-dimensional account of the person of Jesus based on suffering that in turn reinforces rather than challenges an imitation of Christ through suffering.

What do women in particular risk in imitating Christ, in patterning their subjectivity on the cross and its long-held theology of redemptive suffering? Interpreting the death of Jesus either to appease God's wrath or to show God's love may theologically sanction violence against women.[5] In addition, substitutionary sacrifice theologies of atonement sacralize rather than stand against women's experiences of social, sexual, and other kinds of surrogacy.[6] Women are put personally as well as theologically at risk when the death of Jesus is disconnected from its historical and theological context. Theologies of retributive and substitutionary suffering ascribe to Jesus a victim identity, which reinscribes rather than resists a victim identity for already oppressed men and women. Identifying with the suffering rather than with the ministry of Jesus may undermine the full subjectivity of women.

In sum, the cross in long-standing atonement theologies describes the person of Jesus and prescribes discipleship. The redemptive work of Jesus, when reduced to the cross, theologically assigns a victim identity to Jesus. Moreover, the cross signifies discipleship in and through suffering itself, rather than through actively struggling *against* suffering *for* full humanity. Can atonement theologies address the work of Jesus Christ without downplaying other significant aspects of his life-ministry? Can atonement theologies avoid essentializing the work of Christ to the cross, and thereby eschew an essentialized subjectivity based on suffering? Does gendering the cross, a symbol of redemptive suffering, redeem women from suffering? How does the cross shape a redemptive subjectivity for women and men that resists rather than reinscribes a singular, static identity based on suffering? Rather than set aside any theological significance of the cross, more contemporary feminist and womanist theologies reinterpret the cross to break theologically troublesome ties between suffering itself and subjectivity. Feminist and womanist theologies articulate an alternative theology of the cross based on eschatology, on the coming reign of God, which, in my view, implies a different anthropology based on dynamically *becoming* rather than statically *being* human.

FEMINIST AND WOMANIST THEOLOGIES OF THE CROSS: BECOMING SUBJECTS OF RESISTANCE

Feminist and womanist theologies take women's daily lived struggles against patriarchal structures and symbols as the starting point of religious reflection. Emphasizing women's experience of struggle safeguards women's subjectivities; it upholds women's right to a theological subjectivity, in which women are not solely objects of suffering but become subjects of resistance. In terms of Christology, feminist and womanist theologies cannot easily appeal to atonement theology because it shapes a suffering subjectivity for Jesus and for women. Atonement theology raises a central theological tension with a widely shared goal across feminist and womanist theologies, that is, to shift women's identities from objects to subjects, from victims to agents, from passive reactors to actively engaged sociopolitical actors.[7]

Advancing the full humanity of women requires a shift from a theological objectification of women to a theological "subjectification" for women. Feminists and womanists support this shift partly through Christology; they reconstruct women's subjectivity by eschewing the ways that the work of Jesus can function theologically to justify suffering as constitutive of Jesus' identity and human identity. On my reading, contemporary Catholic feminist and womanist theologies propose theologies of the cross that unseat essentialist interpretations of suffering through eschatology. In these theologies, the cross is situated within a broader theological and historical context of Jesus' life-ministry for the kingdom of God, which implies a more dynamic, multidimensional portrait of the person and work of Jesus. Rather than an additive approach that lays the life-ministry alongside the death of Jesus, these theologies view the work of Christ through the interpretive lens of the kingdom of God. Eschatology provides a constructive theological perspective from which to gain a better understanding of feminist and womanist reconstructions of the cross and of personhood. From an eschatological perspective, the cross is critically reclaimed as one among multiple aspects of Jesus' life that signify his full humanity as well as his multidimensional struggle for human flourishing. Furthermore, eschatology focuses on resisting and/or risking suffering rather than on suffering itself, and thereby shifts theological anthropology from a static to a dynamic notion of redeemed humanity.

FEMINIST THEOLOGY AND A KENOTIC THEOLOGY OF THE CROSS

Catholic feminist theology engages in a threefold method: to critique patriarchy or "kyriarchy" in religious claims, texts, and symbols;[8] to recover alternate liberating sources in Scripture, tradition, women's experiences, and critical theories; and to reconstruct those claims, texts, and symbols in light of these alternate sources for the well-being of women, men, and the earth.[9] Using this method, feminist theologies of the cross emerge in critical and constructive response to an alleged ontological necessity of the maleness of Jesus in patriarchal Christologies. Elizabeth Johnson illustrates such feminist Christologies.

Christ represents redeemed humanity, but Christology often distorts women's full humanity. As Elizabeth Johnson argues, "the good news of the gospel" has been warped by patriarchal Christology into "bad news" for women.[10] Christology enshrines a static patriarchal norm of redeemed humanity at the expense of women's subjectivity. The maleness of Jesus has generated an "effective history" in Christology that excludes women from identifying with and imaging the divine, from imitating Christ, and from being saved.[11] Patriarchal Christology relegates women to second-class citizens in terms of the image, imitation, and work of Christ. When the maleness of Jesus figures too prominently in theological claims about the salvific work of Christ, women must presume that their redeemed humanity is "covered," "included," or "subsumed" under the male humanity of Jesus.[12]

To counteract patriarchal Christology and construct an emancipatory Christology, Johnson reinterprets Christology through a critical recovery of the Wisdom tradition from a collection of biblical and apocryphal texts. The Wisdom tradition describes a female personification of God, who enjoys divine status; participates in creating, redeeming, and sustaining daily life; and plays the roles of prophetic street preacher and banquet host of justice and peace.[13] Portraying Jesus as Wisdom challenges patriarchal interpretations of the identity, imitation, and soteriological work of Jesus. Feminist biblical scholars and theologians have explored the ways in which early Christian communities utilized the Wisdom tradition to understand the divine identity of Jesus.[14] The female symbol of the divine in Wisdom contests androcentric theological symbols and language for God. And the maleness of Jesus situated within the Wisdom tradition cannot support an ontological connection between a male incarnation of God and an alleged male reality of God. In addition, the male humanity of Jesus, alongside other particular historical features of his person (for example, race, class, culture, religion), are integral to the incarnation but not central to the imitation of Jesus. Focusing on Wisdom's deeds shifts Christology from the person to the ministry of Jesus, which consists of the gospel-based ministry of the historical Jesus as well as contemporary persons that continue that ministry.[15] Therefore, the Wisdom tradition opens up a theological possibility for women to regain their theomorphic ability (to image the divine) and to reclaim their christomorphic ability (to imitate Jesus) beyond the historical limits and patriarchal restrictions of gender.[16]

Furthermore, in regard to soteriology, a critical feminist appropriation of the Wisdom tradition reclaims the redemptive significance of Jesus' prophetic life-ministry for the kingdom of God. Eschatology draws out the salvific meaning of Jesus' preaching and healing practices, table fellowship with oppressed peoples, and inclusive ministry that enabled women to play key roles (as friends, financial backers, advisers, teachers, evangelizers) in bringing about the kingdom of God.[17] Women act as hearers and doers of the eschatological message and ministry of Jesus, by standing in solidarity with him at the cross, signifying "a sacrament of God's own fidelity" to that message and ministry;[18] by witnessing his resurrection; and by being commissioned at Pentecost as "co-workers for the gospel."[19] When the Wisdom tradition shapes soteriology, imitating Jesus goes beyond a static gender identification with a female personification of God, and instead edges toward an active, performative imitation of the ministry of Jesus for the kingdom of God.

On my reading, the ability to imitate Christ and to be saved in Christ is not determined by maleness but by eschatology. Through the Wisdom tradition, the "scandal" of Christology is not the maleness of Jesus but the message and ministry of the reign of God among the least. Gender does not circumscribe the imitation of Christ; rather, the imitation of Christ involves actively participating in his ministry. An *imitatio Christi* is performed, individually and collectively. As Johnson writes, "the beloved community shares in this Christhood...members of the community of disciples are *en Christo*, and their own lives assume a christic pattern."[20] By actively imitating Jesus' life-ministry, any person, community, or movement can be considered another Christ, or a christological sign of the already partly realized but always coming kingdom of God.[21] Mary Catherine Hilkert furthers a performative imitation of Christ in community by claiming that the "scandal" of the gospel is not just the reign of God that Jesus envisioned, preached, and lived, but that "the reign of God is discovered among and entrusted to human persons and communities despite all of our limits." Hilkert develops this eschatological argument: "Because Wisdom has pitched her tent among us and sent her Advocate to seal us in the truth, *we have the power to enflesh the communion that is our final destiny—if only in fragmentary ways.*"[22]

So far, reinterpreting Christology through the Wisdom tradition enables men and women to imitate Jesus/Wisdom by engaging in prophetic action. And conformity to Christ (Gal. 3:26-28; 2 Cor. 3:18) involves active participation in Jesus' ministry, not a static physicalist imitation of his maleness or any other feature of his historical identity. As Johnson writes, "Being christomorphic is not a sex distinctive gift. The image of Christ does not lie in sexual similarity to the human man Jesus but in coherence with the narrative shape of his compassionate liberating life in the world, through the power of the Spirit."[23] Fashioning a redeemed humanity through the imitation of Christ has to do with participating in the work of Christ, in the reign of God.

Emphasizing the eschatological ministry of Jesus sheds new light "onto the whole theological significance of what transpires in the Christ event."[24] An eschatological perspective enables a feminist theology of the cross that takes account of the full spectrum of Jesus' life-ministry for the kingdom of God. In my view, Johnson interprets the cross in an eschatological light to resist any connections between the person and work of Christ that lead to a so-called theological victimology. That is, she avoids interpreting the death (that is, the work) of Jesus as repayment for sin, and avoids figuring the person of Jesus as a passive, scapegoated victim, divinely ordained to die for human sin.[25] Instead, she places a theology of the cross within the broader context of Jesus' life-ministry and utilizes the Wisdom tradition to consider the cross a part of his eschatological message and ministry: "His preaching about the reign of God and his inclusive lifestyle lived and breathed the opposite [of patriarchal dominance], creating a challenge that brought down on his head the wrath of religious and civil authority."[26] From an eschatological perspective, the cross in the context of the life-ministry of Jesus expresses God's ongoing solidarity with suffering while seeking future flourishing.

The salvific significance of the cross itself is not altogether dismissed in this eschatological approach. The cross poses a potent challenge to patriarchal power when reenvisioned through a kenotic Christology, or the divine self-emptying of Jesus (Phil. 2:5-11). A kenotic Christology is a most unlikely source for a feminist theology of the cross and of women's subjectivity; it can block women from developing a sense of self and can equate the imitation of Christ with obedience, suffering, and self-sacrifice, thereby lending theological support to patriarchal constructions of women. In an attempt to offset an uncritical use of kenosis, Sarah Coakley shows that the voluntary self-emptying of Christ carries doctrinal, moral, and political meanings. Building on its political meaning, a feminist kenotic Christology indicates a rejection of worldly power for divine power, or what Coakley calls "power-in-vulnerability."[27] For Coakley, a kenotic imitation of Christ takes place through self-giving or making space for God,[28] and depends on self-surrender or "expansion" into God, rather than on self-abnegation.[29] However, this theology of the cross may not liberate women from patriarchal constructions of women's salvation and subjectivity through submission. It also downplays women's performative roles in promoting the religio-political message and ministry of Jesus. Thus, it may undermine women's ability to lay claim to a more active, dynamic imitation of Christ through undertaking acts of religio-political solidarity.

Also building on its political meaning, Johnson proposes a kenotic Christology in light of Jesus' life-ministry for the reign of God. The cross represents an actual and symbolic challenge to existing religio-political definitions of power as being dominant. In contrast to Coakley, rather than replace being powerful with the refusal of power, Johnson's kenotic Christology shows that power involves the mutual empowerment of God and humanity, engaged in the co-creation of a just society: the cross announces "the kenosis of patriarchy" or "the self-emptying of male dominating power in favor of a new humanity of compassionate service and mutual empowerment."[30] Kenosis as mutual empowerment underscores the real risks of being open to and becoming involved in a prophetic vision and ministry: "The suffering accompanying such a life as Jesus led is neither passive nor useless nor divinely ordained but is linked to the ways of Sophia forging justice and peace in an antagonistic world."[31] A feminist kenotic Christology of the cross bypasses traditional theologies of self-sacrifice that threaten women's subjectivity, while at the same time reappropriates theological claims about sacrifice as a risk of discipleship, of realizing the reign of God.

In sum, feminist theology critically retrieves the cross as a liberative symbol for women's and men's subjectivity when the work of Christ is reconstructed through the Wisdom tradition and its focus on eschatology. The work of Christ expands to include Jesus' whole way of life. The cross is situated in the life-ministry of Jesus for the reign of God, and is treated in the context of political resistance to injustice. The cross is connected to the larger life-work of Jesus, of women, and of communities who resist patriarchal power and who seek to remake the church and world into more kingdom-like places. In terms of theological anthropology, following the way of the cross does not mean passively resigning to suffering and/or internalizing a victim identity; rather, it means becoming human in community, in fleshing out our redeemed humanity in Christ through individual and collective struggles against injustice and for a more liberative church and world. As a political kenotic theology of the cross suggests, becoming fully human in community may come with deep costs; the cross illustrates the costs, not the shape, of discipleship, of redemptive subjectivity. As further explored in womanist theology, suffering constitutes a major part of what it means to be human, but suffering in itself does not exemplify redeemed human nature. Suffering as an outcome of resistance is part of the risk of becoming more fully human in Christ.

WOMANIST THEOLOGY AND AN EPISTEMOLOGY OF THE CROSS

Womanist theology is elaborated in response to the invisibility of African American women in feminist and black theologies. More than a reactionary theology, womanist theology draws on the historical and daily lived experiences of black women, described in Alice Walker's definition of womanism, for theological reflection.[32] Womanist theologians utilize an interdisciplinary method to analyze black women's experiences of God and of resistance to multiple interlocking forms of race, gender, class, and sexual oppression.[33] In womanist Christology, the historical Jesus serves as a theological starting point for christological claims; the gospel-based ministry of Jesus among marginalized peoples takes priority over the "metaphysical make-up" of the person of Jesus. What Jesus does (the work of Jesus) in his life-ministry forms the basis of who Jesus is (the Christ).[34] Like feminists, womanist theologians foreground the ministry rather than the person of Jesus because of the monopoly of maleness and whiteness in long-standing Christologies that reinforce patriarchal, racist, and classist ideologies.

The historical aspects and actions of Jesus are significant to womanist names and images of Jesus as the Christ. Womanist images of Jesus express the prophetic life-ministry of Jesus in solidarity with the oppressed. Portraying Jesus as a black Christ, a black woman, and a black community serves a fourfold function in womanist theology. These images (1) expose hegemonic Christologies that reinforce racist, sexist, and classist ideologies;[35] (2) affirm the subjectivity of black women, men, and communities struggling to reclaim and realize their equal creation in the image of God;[36] (3) constitute a theological site of religious and political accountability;[37] and, (4) highlight solidarity with God in struggles *against* multiple oppressions external and internal to the black community as well as *for* wholeness, personal and communal.[38] In regard to my analysis of Christology and anthropology, multiple womanist personifications of a black Christ help personify African American women and men.

M. Shawn Copeland, in her writings on discipleship, suffering, and freedom, articulates a womanist Christology in which black women image Christ, particularly through the cross. I argue that in her writings the cross functions epistemologically; it deepens a mystical-political consciousness of Christ that leads to praxis of the reign of God.[39] In lifting up black women as an icon of the crucified Christ, Copeland resists the conflation of suffering and subjectivity through eschatology, that is, through connecting the suffering and death of Jesus to his life-ministry for the reign of God. As we will see, reflecting on the sufferings of Jesus and of Christic black women is linked to a knowledge and praxis of resistance and solidarity. As Copeland states, "the power of God in the cross is the power to live and to love—even in the teeth of violence and death."[40]

The cross forms the epistemological basis of Copeland's reflections on disciple-ship. The cross helps retrieve a gospel-based notion of discipleship (for instance, Luke 9:23; 14:27). Discipleship "at the disposal of the cross" involves more than theological knowledge about Jesus; it consists of a mystical-political response to knowing and loving God. It leads to a new "way" of life that is learned by being "exposed, vulnerable, open to the wisdom and power and love of God" and that is lived by "a praxis of solidarity and compassion as well as surrender to the startling embrace of Divine Love."[41]

To understand better this new "way" of life, the cross provides an epistemologi-cal lens through which to contemplate the demands of discipleship. For Copeland, the Gospel of Luke outlines the demands of discipleship in regard to knowledge of God, mystical union with God, and potentially costly praxis. In this Gospel, the inauguration of Jesus' ministry highlights the liberative reality of God; it signals the reign of God for and with the least, including women (Luke 4:18-19; cf. Isa. 61). The Lukan account of Jesus' ministry for the reign of God illustrates key features of discipleship: to be centered in and on a God struggling with the oppressed; to love others concretely, especially (but not exclusively) the oppressed; and to heal broken relations with God and with one another. Combining the mystical and the political, disciples are called to realize actively the reign of God in themselves and in sociopolitical life, as well as to pray for the in-breaking of justice, love, and peace.[42] Besides knowing God and praying for the reign of God, the cross sharpens an understanding of the costs of discipleship. The cross shows God's solidarity with suffering peoples; this solidarity is clarified when the cross is placed in the context of Jesus' life-ministry as well as in its own sociopolitical context. In regard to his life-ministry, the cross continues Jesus' solidarity with the least, which began in his ministry. In regard to the sociopolitical context, Copeland points out that crucifixion played a major role in the Roman military and political theater of violence to deter religio-political insurrection among low-class and subjugated peoples.[43] Contextualizing the cross in terms of Jesus' ministry and its sociopolitical situation reveals the liberative nature of God as well as the risks of discipleship: "The crucified Jesus is the sign of the cost of identification with the poor, outcast, abject, and despised women and men in the struggle for life."[44] Eschatology exacts a cost, because realizing the reign of God takes place in a world opposed to that reign.

Discipleship does not collapse theology and politics. For Copeland, spiritual union with God, described in the writings of Catherine of Siena and in African American spirituals, informs and influences a political praxis of the reign of God. Catherine's description of climbing the stairway of Christ's body shows that meditating on the crucified Jesus is a spiritual pathway to mystical union with God. The African American spiritual "Jacob's Ladder" similarly deals with a spiritual ascent that yields union with God. Spiritual union deepens knowledge of God and demands loving and serving others.[45]

For Copeland, discipleship consists of gospel-based knowledge of God, a spiritual union of love with God, and a praxis of solidarity with the oppressed, all of which is oriented to actualizing an alternate reality, the reign of God. How do black women function as an icon of Christ? In her writings on discipleship, Copeland includes an anecdote about looking at a poor, homeless, and hungry black woman. Similar to the spectacle of crucifixion, Copeland regards the spectacle of this poor black woman an icon of Christ, because she identifies the presence of God among the poor *and* signifies a site of our solidarity with Christ in continuing his ministry. Looking at this black woman entails looking at Christ, looking at our complicity in structural suffering, and looking at a site for struggle against such suffering.[46] On my reading, black women symbolize a rather static icon of Christ that highlights a "performative meaning of discipleship" *for us*, pricking our conscience as privileged peoples and calling us to a critical self-examination of our actions—or lack thereof—in regard to structural suffering.[47] As Copeland writes, "A praxis of compassionate solidarity, of justice-love, and care for the poor and oppressed is a sign that *we* are on the 'way' of Jesus.... These children, women, and men are the only sure sign of his presence among us in *our efforts* to prepare a context for the coming reign of his God."[48] To shift black women *from* objects of praxis for privileged people *to* subjects of their own praxis, we must ask how Copeland retrieves the cross so that black women become a dynamic icon of Christ *for themselves* and engage in a performative discipleship that resists *their own suffering*. Copeland's writings on suffering and freedom reclaim the cross as a theological site of black women's active imitations of Christ.

In her writings on suffering, Copeland examines how black women regained their agency[49] amid the personal and social sufferings of gender, race, class, and sexual oppression during and in the aftermath of U.S. slavery. Slave and ex-slave women's narratives show black women taking an active role in liberating themselves (although they are often recaptured or returned to bondage), in resisting brutal beatings and sexual abuse (although they are often killed), and in seeking freedom by actively collaborating with God (although they doubt God's interest in their lives given their persistent suffering). For Copeland, black women actively resist and manage their suffering, or struggle to make meaning of their lives in response to structural and personal suffering, rather than equate suffering itself with authentic subjectivity or redemption.[50] Just as suffering may despoil or suffuse all of humanity without totally accounting for the meaning of human being, enslaved black women cannot escape the structural evils of slavery, yet their humanity is not totally determined by it; these women are "caught, but not trapped" by suffering.[51] Religion enabled black women to take an agential role in reclaiming their humanity, that is, their self-identity, self-esteem, and bodily integrity. These women "invite God to partner them in the redemption of Black people" and in so doing "freed the cross of Christ... and redeemed it from Christianity's vulgar misuse"[52] to sanction suffering theologically. The cross symbolizes making meaning of life and of humanity through resistance to suffering; it serves as a theological lever to resist and not support suffering.

Resisting suffering restored humanity and freedom to enslaved black women. In her writings on freedom, Copeland argues for a theological anthropology grounded in freedom, defined as the process of crafting a self. Contrary to patriarchal notions of freedom from the body, from others, for self-aggrandizement, and so on, a womanist theology of freedom features freedom of and for bodily integrity; for self-acceptance and self-determination; for self-love in community and solidarity; and for healing.[53] Freedom is construed through an actively embodied subjectivity or "the enfleshing of created spirit through the exercise of freedom in history and society," which upholds the body as a site of "humanity, subjectivity, and agency."[54] Embodied subjectivity contrasts with slavery, which reduced black women's bodies to property; to sites of production, reproduction, and sexual exploitation; and to "parts."[55] The active "enfleshment of freedom" consists of healing fragmentation and seeking wholeness, of freeing mind, body, and spirit in order to redeem and "restore black bodily and psychic integrity."[56]

Becoming "subjects of freedom" is actualized through seeking love and wholeness in oneself and in community, and is mediated theologically through the cross.[57] Copeland conjoins the cross and freedom through the story of Lavinia Bell, who repeatedly attempted to escape slavery but was recaptured, brutally beaten, and even branded. Bell's story and scarred body, especially its "hieroglyphics of the flesh," illuminate the sufferings of slavery *and* the agency of black women in struggling for freedom.[58] The body—of the crucified Christ and the beaten and branded Lavinia Bell—manifests resistance and freedom: "To meditate on Lavinia Bell's broken body is to comprehend the enfleshed meaning of *she who would be free*—free flesh scarred, lacerated, pocked, punctured, riddled with lesions. . . . To place her black broken body beside [Jesus'] crucified body is . . . an expression of the freedom of the human subject."[59] Lavinia Bell serves as a performative icon of Christ. When the crucified Christ is connected to his life-ministry for the reign of God and when the body of Lavinia Bell is linked to her escapes, the suffering occasioned by active struggles for freedom reveals a redeemed humanity. Suffering in the context of resistance and solidarity, and not in itself, embodies redeemed humanity.

In sum, Copeland utilizes several sources—for instance, Scripture, mystical and black church traditions, as well as privilege and abjection—to develop a theology of the cross. Meditating on the crucified body of Jesus or Christic black women deepens knowledge and love of God, which overflows into love of others, a political and risky love expressed in struggles for solidarity and freedom. The cross gives an occasion for an epistemological encounter with God and with others, an encounter that highlights the presence of God and demands a response to that presence by privileged and oppressed peoples. Black women as icons of Christ foster such an epistemological encounter; privileged peoples see a site of solidarity while oppressed peoples occupy a site of struggling for freedom; both solidarity and struggle are ingredient in becoming more fully human. In regard to my argument about Christology and anthropology, putting the cross in the context of Jesus' ministry avoids assigning a victim identity to Jesus and to contemporary persons. And icons of a crucified Christ symbolize a dynamic notion of discipleship and of personhood that resists suffering itself but risks it in the quest for becoming subjects of freedom.

TOWARD AN ESCHATOLOGICAL THEOLOGY OF THE CROSS

This essay has explored the effects of theological discourse about the cross on women's identities. Using the classical Christo-logic that the person and work of Jesus are mutually interrelated, this essay has demonstrated that the work of Jesus, when singly focused on the cross, damages the personhood of Jesus and of women. The theological essentialism of most atonement theologies, which narrows the reconciling work of Christ to the cross, identifies redeemed humanity with suffering. Thus, long-standing atonement theologies settle on the soteriological significance of the cross, to the neglect of the entirety of Jesus' life-ministry and at the expense of a truly redemptive subjectivity for women. Suffering is considered theologically normative for the person of Jesus and for contemporary persons who strive to imitate a Christic model of redeemed humanity. Disconnecting the cross from its theological context of the life-ministry of Jesus and from its sociohistorical context of empire distorts the cross into a theological tool of subjugation rather than redemption.

Traditional theologies of the cross often do not take the larger theological or sociohistorical context of the cross seriously. Contemporary feminist and womanist theologians depart from traditional atonement theologies, but do not altogether dismiss a theology of the cross. Rather, these theologians show that an adequate theology of the cross takes context seriously by turning to the historical Jesus, that is, his life-ministry for the reign of God and the sociopolitical situation of that ministry under Roman rule. My analysis of recent feminist and womanist theologies of the cross reveals a common theological strategy for contextualizing the cross, namely eschatology. The Wisdom tradition for Johnson or certain

Gospel traditions for Copeland function as theological sources to develop what I am calling an eschatological theology of the cross. An eschatological theology of the cross allows feminist and womanist theologians to contextualize the cross in the larger life-ministry of Jesus for the reign of God, and to reclaim the cross as a symbol of the risks involved in bringing about that reign amid oppressive sociopolitical realities. To develop further this new theological intervention initiated by feminist and womanist Christologies, I will briefly sketch out some key features of an eschatological theology of the cross in regard to the work of Christ and theological anthropology.

First, what happens to theologies of the work of Christ when the cross is placed in its theological and sociohistorical context? An eschatological theology of the cross offers a more complete picture of the work of Christ; it avoids a reduction of redemptive work to suffering by identifying the cross as one part of the larger work of Jesus for the kingdom of God. Through the Wisdom tradition and gospel-based prophetic texts, feminist and womanist theologies critically reappropriate the cross by viewing it in light of the life-ministry of Jesus, which goes beyond Jesus and continues in contemporary Christian communities. An eschatological theology of the cross does not empty the cross of all theological meaning, but steers theological interpretations of it toward discipleship. It takes seriously the call to discipleship, to configure actively persons and communities into love and justice that characterize the reign of God. The work of Christ, broadened to incorporate the life-ministry and the death of Jesus as well as the ongoing efforts of Christian communities, supports a performative notion of discipleship, based on struggling against suffering and struggling for the kingdom of God. The cross as one symbol of that work symbolizes prophetic protest against injustice and prophetic praxis for justice, love, and equality in a fraught and frighteningly oppressive world.

An eschatological theology of the cross proclaims that imitating Christ involves struggles for the reign of God, and thereby disrupts the idealization of an *imitatio Christi* through suffering itself. The cross as one symbol of the work of Christ foregrounds a prophetic yet at times personally risky and costly work for this-worldly justice. Eschatology allows an identification with the cross in the context of resistance while avoiding the glorification of suffering itself. Praxis and protest, rather than suffering, allow us to continue the work of Christ and signify the similarity between Jesus and us. With this emphasis on praxis, an eschatological theology of the cross opens up the possibility for figuring the work of Christ with other symbols, drawn from the life-ministry of Christ and from past, ongoing, and future social-justice movements.

Second, what happens to theological anthropology when patterned on an eschatological theology of the cross? As my reflections on discipleship suggest, becoming christomorphic and likewise becoming fully human take place by working for the reign of God. Just as the ministry of Jesus reveals the identity of Jesus as the Christ (that is, what Jesus does discloses who Jesus is), so, too, a performative discipleship discloses the ongoing process of becoming fully human. When the cross is reframed in the context of the life-ministry of Jesus, the reconciling work of Jesus involves an ongoing historical process. A Christology that focuses on the historical Jesus and the larger historical context of his and our saving work[60] suggests that becoming fully human also involves an ongoing historical process in his and our time. As Lisa Isherwood succinctly states, "The suffering Christ is part of the process but by no means the end point of a salvific journey."[61] Thus, the turn to the historical reality of the life-ministry of Jesus warrants a turn to an historicist subjectivity. An historicist subjectivity situates a person in particular sociohistorical contexts; links identity to negotiation among those multiple contexts; and, most importantly, considers identity an ongoing and performed, rather than fixed or static, reality.[62] An eschatological theology of the cross sheds light on a multidimensional, performative understanding of the work of Christ and of personhood.

Eschatology forms the theological basis for a new notion of redeemed humanity. Because redemptive subjectivity is enfleshed and enacted in intrahistorical realities, we always sit on the eschatological threshold of becoming more fully human, catching only fleeting glimpses of it that give us hope in its historical possibilities. Similar to Mary Catherine Hilkert, who claims that realizing our creation in the image of God consists largely of a future reality,[63] becoming christomorphic is largely a future reality, already begun in protest and praxis but not yet fully realized until our lives edge toward resurrection.

Thus, the turn to eschatology offers a more encompassing theology of the work of Christ and an agential, multidimensional notion of personhood, shaped by resistance and also by risks of suffering in seeking to incarnate a more full humanity in the future. To conclude, I highlight the constructive contribution of an eschatological theology of the cross by noting its implications for traditional Catholic theologies of atonement and of subjectivity. An eschatological theology of the cross challenges conventional ways of reading one major document from Vatican II and in so doing discloses an alternate Christology and anthropology.

Among the documents issued at the conclusion of the Second Vatican Council, *Gaudium et Spes* (*GS*)[64] interrelates Christology and anthropology. Jesus represents the model of redeemed humanity (*GS* 10, 22), and the renewal of humanity—

both personally and socially—depends on imitating Christ (*GS* 41). *GS* clings to atonement theologies that stress the salvific significance of the death of Jesus and that closely link full humanity to redemptive suffering: "By suffering for us, he not only gave us an example so that we might follow in his footsteps, but he also opened up a way. If we follow this path, life and death are made holy and acquire a new meaning" (*GS* 22). The cross, or being "configured to the death of Christ" (*GS* 22), represents a primary "way" of following Jesus to achieve full humanity. Major commentaries on *GS* regard paragraph 22 as an interpretive key for the entire document,[65] but in so doing overlook another interpretation of the cross and of humanity.

The emphasis on eschatology in feminist and womanist theologies retrieves a more expansive theology of the work of Christ from *GS* as well as offsets traditional notions of achieving full humanity through redemptive suffering. Rereading *GS* with feminist and womanist eyes, the kingdom of God now figures prominently in its Christology. The life-ministry of Jesus—preaching, healing, and inclusive table fellowship—characterized a vision and practice of the kingdom of God, of actively reconciling God and humanity into a new people (*GS* 32). The constitution identifies the totality of this vision and practice with the "work of Jesus Christ" (*GS* 32).

Moreover, the constitution urges imitations of the work of Christ that actively follow the principles of Christ's life-ministry to bring about the kingdom of God (*GS* 32, 39). Christians are called to "follow the example of Christ who worked as a craftsman" (*GS* 43) in creating and sustaining justice, love, and peace. Imitating a craftsman Christ upholds an agential, dynamic subjectivity in which persons are artisans or "molders of a new humanity" (*GS* 30) in personal and political life (*GS* 55).[66] Becoming human, from this new Christological perspective, is an ongoing historical process; the incarnation spans the entire Christ event and consists of Jesus becoming fully human (without sin) in community from his birth, through his life-ministry, and into his death and resurrection (*GS* 22). Jesus hallowed becoming-human-in-community by actively taking on human life in community as well as by envisioning and seeking to establish a reconciled community of justice, love, and peace (*GS* 32, 38–39). This argues christologically what feminist and womanist theologians suggest anthropologically: personhood is negotiated in community and in relationship to future, more flourishing visions of humanity. But becoming fully human-in-community entails great risk: "Christ's example in dying for us sinners teaches us that we must carry the cross . . . inflict[ed] on the shoulders of any who seek after peace and justice" (*GS* 38). This is one risk worth taking, for our very selves and futures, as well as the future of humanity, are at stake.

Women of the Cross. Anne Ownbey © 1993 Anne Ownbey.

7

Lavish Love

A Covenantal Ontology

Marit A. Trelstad

[Humans], my friends...[are] frail and foolish. We have all of us been told that grace is to be found in the universe. But in our human foolishness and short-sightedness we imagine divine grace to be finite. For this reason we tremble....We tremble before making our choice in life, and after having made it again tremble in fear of having chosen wrong. But the moment comes when our eyes are opened, and we see and realize that grace is infinite. Grace, my friends, demands nothing from us but that we shall await it with confidence and acknowledge it in gratitude. Grace...makes no conditions and singles out none of us in particular; grace takes us all to its bosom and proclaims general amnesty. See! That which we have chosen is given us, and that which we have refused is, also and at the same time, granted us. Ay, that which we have rejected is poured upon us abundantly. For mercy and truth have met together, and righteousness and bliss have kissed one another![1]

Within Isak Dinesen's short story "Babette's Feast," grace is offered in the form of a lavish meal. The mistake of the pietistic, self-denying faithful in the story is that they believe their salvation is based on their submission, humility, and discomfort—but it is not. It is simply given in the form of a feast, of service and love extended, regardless of the recipient's status, need, or asceticism. The message of "Babette's Feast" bears some resemblance to Luther's Reformation insights outlined in his treatise "The Freedom of the Christian." Luther claimed that this treatise contained the "whole of Christian life."[2] Here Luther is clear that the reception of grace does not depend on the status, worth, or choice of the recipient. The lavish love of the giver is all-determinative in terms of the grace and gift offered.

Prior to the meal, the villagers in Dinesen's story fear the meal since it is exotically excessive and unfamiliar. Believing that holiness is related to hard asceticism, they vow that they will neither taste the food nor even acknowledge it. No diners could be more unappreciative of the finest French cuisine. And yet the villagers are transformed by Babette's cooking, and this inside-out transformation leads them to offer forgiveness for past wrongs and to feel as though the heavens are drawing closer to the earth. Likewise, in the first half of Luther's treatise he outlines how grace and salvation have been offered to humankind freely and without limit. The grace is so abundant that he likens the recipient to a lord, a priest, a bride; one shares all that Christ has. Luther's treatise does not depict humankind as demeaned or humbled by God's love but, rather, one is exalted beyond one's natural bearing in life by the gift of relationship that God extends. Grace and salvation, in these examples, are understood to be communicated through the feast Babette offers and the relationship to Christ that Luther describes. Because neither gift is dependent on the nature of the recipients, they also model a theological understanding of salvation through election and covenant extended by God.

In this essay, I offer that God's actions, before and after the crucifixion of Jesus, are the loci of God's saving work. The cross itself does not produce salvation but, rather, God's love as expressed through the promise of biblical covenant is what saves and redeems humankind and creation. Soteriology, the study of how salvation is accomplished, thus begins in God's covenant "election" of humanity and is assured and completed by God's response to the cross. In both the Hebrew Scriptures and the New Testament, God's offer of a covenant relationship leads to a broader vision of salvation that includes restoration, peace, and justice for all creation. This is the kingdom or reign of God of which Jesus preached. In this context, the cross signifies the human rejection of God. Nonetheless, God persists in renewing the covenant, offering an inviolable relationship, and this continues to be extended, even today, despite the crosses and persecutions we inflict on ourselves and others.

All categories in Christian theology collide in the discussion of the cross. The range of possible issues includes one's understanding of sin, salvation, atonement theories, the reason for the incarnation, the meaning of the resurrection, Jesus' own understanding of his impending death as recalled by the Gospel narratives, human and divine responsibility for the death of Jesus, the cross and religious pluralism, and the cross's function in terms of the overall intention of God for creation. Within all these possible avenues, this essay focuses on examining the cross in light of God's covenant with humanity and the corresponding vision of the reign of God, leaving fuller development of connected issues to another time.

I offer here a *covenantal ontology* as the site of "salvation": that human relationship with God is reconciled and restored simply because God chooses to create, love, and redeem creation. Salvation here is primarily understood as the means by which the human-divine relation is reconciled, rather than the means by which human sins are ameliorated. One is assured a relationship with God simply because of who God is and who we are in relation to God. Where theology has often considered the reconciliation of God and humans in terms of soteriology and atonement, I approach the same reunion through the lens of ontology. It is an ontological issue in the sense that who we are, in all avenues of our lives, is created in and by relationships. "Ontology" is evoked here in terms of existentialist and process understandings of being—that one is shaped and created through action and relationship—rather than having an essential, static core that defines one's self. And if God is the fundamental relationship from which we live, move, and have our being, then this covenant shapes our being and existence.

This essay recovers the theological idea of God's election of humankind to be "saved," or reunited with God, prior to any human action. I choose the language of election, rather than that of predestination, in order to emphasize the initial gift of love offered to humanity and the priority of God's action rather than conceiving theology as focused on a final, eternal destination. All human living and ultimate end follow from God's initial acts of grace and love extended. Additionally, election connotes a wider understanding of salvation, situated within social context and communal identity. This is seen in God's biblical election of the Israelites as the chosen people and in Paul's epistles, where he explicates how this election has been extended to the new Christian community.

The writers of the Synoptic Gospels recount that the reign of God, envisioning and enacting the restored covenant between God and God's people, was the focus of Jesus' life and this tenet provides a central focus for Christian theological reflection and faith.[3] An inviolable covenantal relationship of love and acceptance, of God's promising again and again to accompany humankind, is the very meaning of grace. And, in this context, "salvation" means being restored to a right relationship to God, self, and all creation. God's offer of relationship precedes any and all human responses and needs. In light of this, sin is also understood primarily in social terms in the sense that we sin against other people and creation and this affects our relationship to God.

When salvation is understood as based in God's covenant relationship to humanity, three main theological claims emerge. First, salvation comes through

God's offer of a relationship and this action of grace precedes human actions and needs and is not dependent on human character. Second, the human reception of covenant or election involves humanity in an active, responsive relationship both to God and to neighbor rather than necessitating a passive theological anthropology, as some theologies of election have implied. Finally, salvation is primarily social and secondarily individual because the theological idea of election assumes a social context within which a personal relationship to God is possible.[4] The human response to God becomes focused on living into the covenant fully, participating in the vision of the reign of God to which Jesus witnessed.

IN THE CROSS OF CHRIST I WORRY

Both current, popular Christian imagery and many traditional doctrines of atonement locate the site of salvation in Jesus' crucifixion. While this is a meaningful center of faith for many people, it is problematic for both theological and social reasons. In terms of the Christian faith, the *conquering* of death in the resurrection and the reign of God, which Jesus revealed and preached, are ultimately salvific because they restore the covenant and promises of God. Thus, in focusing salvation within the cross event, theology risks losing the larger vision of salvation that involves the renewal of all creation.

From the perspective of feminist theology, the social effect of locating salvation in the cross is also problematic. Some feminist theologies have offered the critique that soteriologies and atonement theories that focus on the cross as the locus of salvation have easily, even if accidentally, supported oppressive theologies. One's theological anthropology becomes skewed toward supporting passivity, humiliation, and suffering as redemptive. This can lead to an odd form of piety that turns too readily from a humbling of oneself to a humiliating and repressing of others, as though salvation or God demands that we come to this relationship "taken down a notch." The emphasis on humility can too easily become a *practice* of humiliation, wherein there is theological justification given for both passive suffering and aggression. While this message has serviced multiple forms of oppression through the millennia, in terms of crusades, slavery, and anti-Semitism, it has also served particularly to perpetuate the oppression of women.[5] Here the cross is seen as problematic because it may inspire human communities to model their own social "solutions" to problems after crucifixions rather than empowering love and relationship.

Because Jesus' crucifixion has often been interpreted as a model of love through passive suffering, theologies of the cross have unintentionally supported abusive models within both human relationships and the God-human relationship. It is not uncommon for victims of domestic violence to remain in abusive situations because they claim that the abuse is "my cross to bear," as though their suffering is necessary for some long-term good. This is backed by the theological understanding that God's method of redemption requires humiliation, beating, sacrifice, and, ultimately, death. From this, one might extrapolate that these elements are redemptive for all time, rather than solely in the cross event. Through this, theology risks depicting God as one who insists on human passivity in the face of denigration and that this humiliation is a necessary condition and result of receiving grace. In this way, the cross is used in ways that destroy the message of grace rather than convey it.

An Abused and Abusive "Theology of the Cross"

One example of a potentially abusive use of a "theology of the cross" is found within Lutheranism, which I claim as my own faith tradition. While Luther created an epistemology of the cross, an increasing number of theologians within the Lutheran tradition have built it into an entire "theology of the cross" over the course of the last century.[6] Luther's epistemology claims that all knowledge of God begins in the cross, with a God who is revealed as humble and suffering rather than by power and glory.[7] By confronting humans with this counterintuitive image of God, the cross humbles humanity by turning our wisdom to folly. His claim here countered, Luther believed, the work of scholastic theologians who affirmed the use of human reason and logic, such as the work of Aristotle, as one tool by which one could attempt knowledge of the divine. Luther himself very rarely uses the actual term "theology of the cross." The few places he writes about a theology of the cross are found mainly in the Heidelberg Disputation and his writings on the Psalms, mostly around the year 1518. Theologian J. E. Vercruysse states that Luther only explicitly uses the terms "theology of the cross" or "theologian of the cross" five times, although his writings on the Psalms and other writings address the importance of the cross for Reformation theology.[8]

There is, however, a crucial difference between an epistemology and a theology of the cross. Luther's epistemology of the cross suggests Jesus' crucifixion as the starting place for understanding God while a theology of the cross suggests that all categories of theology coordinate and originate in the cross event. As a result of this generalizing, comprehensive theologies of the cross risk applying Luther's insistence on the humbling of the human *intellect* to a wholesale application of humility and deprecation regarding *all* human ability.

Potential for damaging theological imagery is compounded when a theology of the cross becomes conflated with Luther's understanding of the function of the law. The meaning of the cross becomes a confused jumble that mixes knowing God through Jesus' suffering on the cross (theology of the cross) with a painful humbling of humans by God. The law is often depicted as humbling and destroying human self-pride because it reveals sinful human nature. Within the Lutheran theological tradition, this process has often been described in violent imagery, claiming that God's law functions to terrify and to strike down, like a hammer that shatters one to the core, leaving humankind desolate and begging for the mercy of God. Once this has been accomplished, grace (gospel) is offered. In his classic text *The Proper Distinction Between Law and Gospel*, nineteenth-century Lutheran theologian C. F. W. Walther discusses this dynamic of law and gospel in preaching. Walther advocates preaching the law in "full sternness"[9] and states that "[i]f you do this, you will be handling a sharp knife that cuts into the life of people. . . . From the effects of your preaching they will go down on their knees at home"[10] and "see how awfully contaminated with sins they were and how sorely they needed the Gospel."[11] Based on Walther, the task of the preacher wielding the law in Lutheran preaching has been summarized: "Drive people to their knees and make them need the gospel."[12]

Whether or not this is the best representation of Luther's own writing on the law and gospel, it presents a problematic image of God's love and grace and the relationship between God and humanity. From a feminist point of view, this cannot help but look like a theology of abuse, based on beating someone up and then offering a bouquet of flowers. The cross, here interpreted in light of the law that condemns, is a tool that humiliates humans. And, if the cross is the work of God and Christ, then it is God who uses this tool against us. While Luther and some theologians may embrace a theology of the cross because it can be *descriptive* and honest in terms of suffering in the world and God's presence therein,[13] the symbol itself is vulnerable to being used *performatively*, enacting the suffering it describes.

In the end, which image of humankind is supported by Christian theologies that claim to depict grace and gospel? That of a free and loved human, empowered to serve, or that of the passive, hammered human stranded at the foot of the cross? Are we offered grace and radically transformed by love or are we destroyed by God's act in the cross?

When God's covenantal love for creation is restored as the locus of salvation, one sees that suffering and humiliation are not linked to salvation but, rather, demonstrate human rejection of God's offer of grace. Thereby, the religious justification for abuse is removed for both victim and perpetrator. One should neither suffer crucifixions passively nor label our own abuse of others as good or redemptive. *God's love, like any good love, does not require humiliation or passivity on the recipient's part.* God seeks a covenantal relationship with humankind that, like the story of the exodus, provides liberation from oppression rather than simply exchanging one relationship of abuse for another. Understanding the cross within its theological and historical setting can provide a broader context for such understanding while, at the same time, addressing feminist concerns over redemptive suffering. Ultimately, the covenantal love of God, revealed in the life of Jesus and in the hope for the reign of God, is the context of the cross and this speaks the gospel of an empowering grace more effectively than the cross alone, especially as it relates to women throughout history.

THE CROSS IN CONTEXT: THE REIGN OF GOD

In our time, several scholars within theology and biblical studies have argued that Jesus' death was the result of Jesus' preaching the kingdom of God in the face of Imperial Rome. New Testament scholars Neil Elliott and Stephen J. Patterson both argue that the cross did not signify an atoning, vicarious blood sacrifice. Early followers of Jesus would have interpreted the cross, and subsequent calls to "take up their own crosses," as a summons to join the vision of the kingdom or reign of God. This would have directly and obviously led disciples to be political dissenters to the Roman Empire. The reign of God was both what Jesus proclaimed and the reason he was publicly executed.

In his essay "The Anti-Imperial Message of the Cross," Elliott argues that Christian theological soteriologies have often misunderstood the meaning of the cross and, as a result, they have misconstrued Paul's writings as well as the crucifixion's theological message. Elliott claims that the cross, for Paul, was first and foremost an instrument of torture reserved for those deemed not worthy of a more "decent" death. Roman citizens were offered other forms of death, such as beheading, whereas crucifixion was reserved for slaves and enemies of the Empire. He argues that Paul's preaching a crucified Christ was a clearly political, anti-imperial message. He writes, "Behind the early theological interpretations of Jesus' crucifixion as a death 'for us,' and behind centuries of piety that have encrusted the crucifixion with often grotesque sentimentality, stands the 'most nonreligious and horrendous feature of the gospel,' the brutal fact of the cross as an instrument of imperial terror."[14]

Because of Paul's Jewish background, he would be keenly aware of the cross as a tool to suppress opposition to the Roman Empire. Reviewing the work of Josephus, Elliott provides multiple examples of the Roman use of crucifixion to squelch Jewish uprising. In 4 B.C.E., for instance, a Roman general simultaneously crucified two thousand Jews suspected of rebellion. Mass crucifixions of Jews continued on through Jesus' time, numbering into the tens of thousands.[15] Thus, Jesus' crucifixion was neither singular nor extraordinary in terms of its historical context.

Elliott argues that Paul's emphasis on disciples sharing the way of the cross makes clear that following Jesus means taking one's place among the slaves, the oppressed, and those challenging the reign of the Roman Empire with the Christian belief in the reign of God. Furthermore, Paul's acquaintance with Jewish apocalyptic hope for the coming kingdom of God would have nuanced the meaning of the cross further. In the cross and especially in the resurrection, Paul sees the beginning of the defeat of rulers and powers of this earth as it ushers in the process in which the reign of God comes to be definitively established. This apocalyptic vision is rooted in the anticipated fulfillment of a long covenant relationship between God and God's people.

The questions at the heart of Paul's theology do not center on how the conscience-stricken individual may be saved, or on how a movement of Gentiles as well as Jews may be legitimized. His questions are the questions of his fellow apocalyptists: How shall God's justice be realized in a world dominated by evil powers? Paul's doctrine of the cross is thus a doctrine of God's justice and God's partiality toward the oppressed. In the crucifixion of the Messiah at the hands of the Roman oppressors, God has recapitulated the history of Israel's exile and brought it to a decisive climax; indeed, in a slave's death on a cross (Phil. 2:8) the enslavement of the whole creation is embodied (Rom. 8:20-22).[16]

If one agrees with Elliott's interpretation of Paul's preaching of the cross, it alters the understanding of the cross's significance since a theological emphasis on the covenant tradition would not necessitate viewing Jesus' death in terms of blood sacrifice. Instead, the cross and God's renewed covenant can be understood as challenging religious and political leaders who claimed religious justification for their own imperial interests.

Patterson, in his article "Consider Yourself Dead: On the Martyrological Understanding of Jesus' Death,"[17] agrees with Elliott that the meaning of the cross in the first century, and for Paul in particular, is linked to defiance of the Roman Empire in light of a new vision of the reign of God. When Paul and the Gospel writers preach the cross, they are encouraging followers to take up the difficult but worthy path of following Jesus, even if it means facing one's death. Patterson argues that within the concept of a noble death, a theme popular in writings before and after the time of Jesus, the martyr is not seen as a passive victim but rather as a defiant, effectual person who is committed to a cause.[18]

Such martyrs, like Jesus and Socrates, were viewed as participating in powerful deaths that had vicarious effects on followers in that they inspired courageous, defiant movements. Thus, Patterson argues that Jesus' death was vicarious, not because it was substitutionary for human sins, but rather because it infected others with zeal for the reign of God. Rather than being a lamb led to the slaughter, Jesus is a political and religious dissident who actively chooses to boldly follow his passionate declaration of the kingdom of God.[19]

Both Patterson and Elliott argue that, in preaching Christ crucified, Paul anticipates the coming reign of God and this inspires new forms of living. Building on this, one can see that the cross acts reflexively, pointing away from death and back toward living. Because of the context of the cross within the hope for God's restored covenant, the focus of attention ricochets back to the faithful, forcing an honest examination of one's beliefs and commitments. Likewise, in following Christ crucified, the way of the cross, Elliot and Patterson claim that would-be disciples were forced to choose actively to risk the costs for embracing Jesus' vision. This is no image of a passive, helpless humanity at the foot of the cross.

RESTORING THE COVENANT: ATONEMENT THEORY AND THE DOCTRINE OF GOD

Traditional atonement theories have most often been based on addressing how God meets the human condition and sin. In Anselm's satisfactory atonement model and Reformation forensic understandings of justification, humans have sinned and need to be both judged and released from condemnation. Jesus takes the punishment that human sinners deserve. Humans have a need that God addresses through the death of Jesus. The atonement models themselves begin with a description of the human condition and, thus, also begin primarily within the category of theological anthropology.

While humans are certainly both fallible and needy, what if we begin our examination of salvation within the doctrine of God rather than anthropology? Stated another way, what if grace is truly understood as dependent on the nature of God rather than the nature of humans? When viewed from this angle, grace and salvation may be seen as based on the nature of God and the nature of God's relationship to humankind, and this offers an alternate, ontological perspective from which salvation is understood.

Abelard's model of atonement could also be understood as beginning primarily within the doctrine of God. As Joanne Terrell writes,

> [In] Abelard's view of the Atonement...he emphasized God's acts of love as the primary and ultimate factors in human redemption....[U]nlike Anselm and Western tradition up to that time, he did not overly stress human sin and unworthiness, and he rejected the necessity of the Atonement to satisfy the demands of justice. In his *moral influence* theory God's own initiative of grace (which he equated with love) prompted God, in Christ, to act on humanity's behalf. God's actions (especially Christ's death on the cross) in turn incite a response of love toward God and neighbor by their salvific potency and example. Abelard believed that God was not constrained to act in this way on human behalf. God was free to effect human redemption in another way, for God had shown the will to remit sin simply through forgiveness.[20]

Abelard claims that God chose to act in grace through the cross to "'arouse us to very great love of God,' teaching humankind by this example that 'true charity should not now shrink from enduring anything for him.'"[21]

In the Hebrew Scriptures, God frees and saves the Israelites because God remembers God's covenant, "I will take you as my people, and I will be your God. You shall know that I am the LORD your God, who has freed you from the burdens of the Egyptians" (Exod. 6:7). This is an ontological statement. God declares a relationship with humanity that shapes their whole reality in terms of both identity and condition. Human salvation and redemption is simply the way things are because of God's choice to love and free humankind. It is not based on any need or quality of our own but rather on God's declaration.

This could be imagined as a parental model of love or grace. Ideally, the parent is faithful and is inspired to love the child based simply on their relationship to one another. "I am your mother; you are my child. That declaration and knowledge is enough to warrant my commitment to your well-being." It has nothing to do with the character or condition of the child or whether the child deserves to be loved and accepted. Of course, not all parental relationships model the choice of limitless love or grace without conditions. Nonetheless, a parent chooses at some point to claim or not claim a child and this commitment to relationship signals a relationship that shapes both parties.[22]

Likewise, God offers and declares love and relationship prior to human response. Essentially, this is the meaning of the theological idea of election. God chooses, declares a relationship with, or "elects" humans prior to their choice. This relationship forms a foundation that profoundly shapes one's being. An ontological change occurs, as it does with any relationship, since we are fundamentally composed of and shaped by our relations.[23] Christian existentialist philosopher Gabriel Marcel affirms that human beings are defined by relationships and claims that fundamental reality is best described as "being-in-society" (as opposed to Jean Paul Sartre's "being-in-itself"). Additionally, he writes that love, grounded in God, is "the essential ontological datum."[24]

THEOLOGIES OF ELECTION

Two Protestant theologians classically famous for a theology of election are Martin Luther and Karl Barth. While Luther did not characterize his own theology using the actual term *election*, theologians within Lutheran heritage have utilized this term to stress that, for Luther, the action of God in grace always precedes any and all human actions. Both Luther and Barth stressed that God declares a relationship with humankind, as witnessed and experienced in the person of Jesus Christ, and this act of grace is wholly determinative in salvation.

Luther's insistence that "works" did not effect or merit salvation led him, theologically, down the path toward affirming that human salvation is accomplished through God's actions alone. Luther's affirmation of the priority of God's action in grace is illustrated in his choice to maintain infant baptism and his strong rejection of "believer's baptism." God's act in grace is performed prior to the infant's ability to comprehend or ask for love and completely independent of human action, worth, or character.

While Luther's theology could be described in terms of God's election, Luther himself did not want to dwell on the idea of predestination. He did not share Calvin's emphasis on the topic of predestination and did not agree with Calvin's "double predestination" (that some are predestined to heaven while others are predestined to hell). Luther asserted that one was to trust God's promise of salvation with confidence and not allow questions of one's own salvation, which may arise in overly thinking about predestination, to direct faith toward doubts that question the promises of God.[25] Indeed, no idea characterizes the whole of Luther's theology or career better than trust and confidence in the grace and promises of God.

Affirming the primacy of God's power and act of free, self-offering love, led Barth, ultimately, to propose a theology supportive of universal election and salvation for all humanity. Barth claims that Jesus' dual nature, containing both God and human, means that he is both the electing God and the one "elected" human. In Jesus' life, death, and resurrection, Jesus transfers this election onto all humans. He writes, "[t]he election of grace in the beginning of all things is God's self-giving in [God's] eternal purpose."[26] Thus, he writes, "There is no condemnation—literally none—for those that are in Christ Jesus."[27] Barth's theology of election, however, is logically able to be extended to all of humanity, not only believers, because he claims Jesus to be the elected human and it is our sharing in the humanity and election of Christ that is salvific. He writes, "Rejection cannot again become the portion or affair of [humans]. . . . For this reason, faith in the divine election as such and *per se* means faith in the non-rejection of [humans], or disbelief in [their] rejection. [Humankind is] not rejected."[28] Thus, his strong emphasis on grace coupled with his understanding of election implies an affirmation of the universal salvation of all humans.[29] Barth was uncomfortable being included among those who affirm *apokatastasis* (restoration or salvation of all humanity and creation in Christ—sometimes called "universal salvation") but, if the love of God is itself *determinative* rather than *determined by* humans, then this is a logical conclusion.

ELECTION AND PASSIVITY: A NECESSARY CONNECTION?

Because the doctrine of election presupposes the primacy of God's actions, regardless of human response or initiative, it has contained the potential of suggesting a "low" or pessimistic approach concerning human ability in general. For Luther, his conviction that humans were passive in relation to God was directly connected to his pessimism regarding human nature. Humans are utterly reliant on God's action due to their thoroughly sinful nature. He makes this point repeatedly in such treatises as "The Bondage of the Will." God is active in relation to humans but never the other way around. Humans are active only "horizontally" in relation to each other. For Barth, the theological motivation for affirming a passive humanity in relation to God's power emerges from his doctrine of God rather than being connected to his theological anthropology; Barth emphasized God's perfect freedom and sovereignty in relation to creation.

If there is a necessary correlation, however, between the doctrine of election and a passive theological anthropology, this depiction of grace would have questionable applicability within feminist theology. It certainly does not depict a relationship of reciprocity that many feminist theologians have advocated in their models of God. Since God-to-human relational models are used to justify human-to-human dynamics, this is especially troublesome. Dorothee Soelle has claimed that the very model of God one uses, if it still assumes a God-human hierarchy in terms of both power and dominance, can perpetuate an active-passive, dominant-submissive model of relationship between men and women as well.[30] A model of a passive humanity in relation to a dominant God additionally runs the risk of asserting that humans should likewise be passive in relation to anyone who asserts a position of God-given authority. Taking these feminist precautions seriously, one must approach the concept of election with care.

Additionally, a strictly active-passive relationship between God and humans poses other issues within the doctrine of God beyond the scope of feminist theology. In his book *The Divine Relativity*, Charles Hartshorne claims that such a strong affirmation of the sovereignty of God may end up depicting God as a tyrant who rules but is completely unresponsive to people.[31] Likewise, theology runs the risk of making multiple practices and ideas of the Christian faith into nonsense since they assume that God is responsive to the world. Hartshorne discusses such practices as prayer, which necessitates a listening, caring, and responsive God.

A completely passive theological anthropology, however, does *not* follow necessarily from an emphasis on the priority of God's acts of love. Here God's love has "priority" in terms of both its sequential priority (God's action in love comes before human response) and its powerful ontological conditioning of human experience. But, overall, salvation through covenant offers an image of an established relation between two or more valued parties, each with something to offer to the relationship. Even if God initiates the relationship, humans are subsequently active, shaping partners in a covenantal love between an "I" and "Thou."[32] Just because one cannot merit or control receiving the love of another does not mean that she or he is rendered entirely passive or faulty in all aspects of the relationship. There is, of course, a type of passive acceptance of another's action and yet it does not demand helplessness as a precondition or continued state. Again, this is much like parental love, determined and offered long before the child is cognizant of or able actively to accept this gift. Passivity only becomes problematic for feminist theology when it is a necessary condition for or result of any relationship. The active love of God is directed to invigorate human action, not suppress it. It fosters and encourages an active-active relationship, even if God's action in love comes prior to human response.

In his book *Process and Reality*, Alfred North Whitehead defines the love of God in terms of God's constant commitment and offering of creative possibility to the world. God's action and love toward creation always precedes humanity's response and it is neither controlling nor dependent on the reception of moral worthiness of people. Correspondingly, there is freedom in each moment for humanity and creation to respond and offer their creativity back to God. The relationship between God and humanity is one of cooperative creativity. God is constantly giving and receiving from the world, regardless of its decisions. God always responds to the world's developing condition with perfect attunement, offering us new possibilities that address and potentially improve our current situation. This, he states, is a different conception of divine love than is offered by much of Western philosophy and theology. Concerning love, Whitehead writes, "It does not emphasize the ruling Caesar, or the ruthless moralist, or the unmoved mover. It dwells upon the tender elements in the world, which slowly and in quietness operate by love....Love neither rules, nor is it unmoved..."[33]

Some images within Luther's "The Freedom of the Christian" also offer an active reciprocity between God and humans that stands in contrast to much of his theology and his cross-related epistemology. The grace of God builds a new intimate relationship with humanity and therefore one is now seen as sharing all the gifts and powers of Christ. Luther writes, "Not only are we the freest of kings, we are also priests forever, which is far more excellent than being kings, for as priests we are worthy to appear before God to pray for others and to teach one another divine things.... Thus Christ has made it possible for us, provided we believe in him, to be not only his brethren, co-heirs, and fellow-kings, but also his fellow-priests."[34] In this treatise, even as Luther maintains his pessimistic view of human nature, one finds a humanity empowered by grace to respond to both God and neighbor rather than being humiliated and passive.

WE'RE IN IT TOGETHER: THE SOCIAL NATURE OF SALVATION

Restoring the context of covenant as the focus of theology affects how one understands salvation and sin as well. In theological discussions of the cross and salvation, there is often a bifurcation of approaches. In North American popular Christianity today, salvation often is depicted in terms of the salvation of individual souls. When this is the understanding of salvation, the cross is likewise viewed through the lens of a personal piety where Jesus' crucifixion is interpreted primarily in terms of its meaning for the individual.

From the standpoint of the Social Gospel movement of the early twentieth century and from liberationist theologies and movements of the last four decades, salvation is seen primarily as a process wherein all creation is renewed and thus these approaches imagine salvation as social and in terms of the reign of God.

Representing this second approach, Walter Rauschenbusch states, "Salvation is the voluntary socializing of the soul"[35] In fact, Rauschenbusch critiques the individual-focused views of salvation as a form of ultimate selfishness, wherein Christians are taught that their own personal salvation is the matter of ultimacy and this self-obsession, he states, illustrates the classic definition of sin rather than salvation.

For the most part, these interpretations of the cross have been proposed as mutually exclusive: salvation is either individual or communal. Nonetheless, a theology of covenant holds together individual and social salvation as two sides of the same coin. Individual salvation is coupled with communal salvation in God's continual choice and election to offer relationship to humans. Following this, communal salvation in the form of justice and love becomes the vocation and ultimate vision for all of society and creation.

Sin, likewise, is understood as social in the sense that our broken relationships on a human-to-human ("horizontal") level affect the human-to-God ("vertical") relationship. Marjorie Suchocki explains this in her book *The Fall to Violence: Original Sin in Relational Theology.* She writes, "Since God must experience the world, violence in creation also entails violence against God."[36] Sin is also social because sin is evident in the world most perniciously in systems of sin such as racism and sexism. As Suchocki elsewhere writes, "Sin as personal indicates a violation of relationships, resulting in a state of alienation from God, nature, one another and self."[37] To the extent that we perpetuate systems of oppression and alienation, we participate in the social nature of sin. How we live and sin against one another breaks the wider covenant relationship with God.

LIVING INTO COVENANT RELATIONSHIP: SALVATION AS CALL TO JUSTICE

> For you are powerful, not that you may make the weak weaker by oppression, but that you may make them powerful by raising them up and defending them. You are wise, not in order to laugh at the foolish and thereby make them more foolish, but that you may undertake to teach them as you yourself would wish to be taught. You are righteous that you may vindicate and pardon the unrighteous, not that you may only condemn, disparage, judge, and punish.[38]

God's covenant itself judges humankind when we witness our actions alongside God's vision for a renewed, restored creation. We are not simply where and who we could be. The vision of the reign of God, of perfect love, relationship, and harmony makes injustice stand out as obvious and unacceptable. Likewise, Elliott and Patterson's proposals regarding the cross state that it functioned to reveal the injustice and sins of the Roman Empire's oppressions while simultaneously witnessing to a new vision of peace and love in relationship to God. Whitehead held a similar notion of judgment between God's vision and our lives. When God feels or receives the actions of the world, God feels these in light of what God envisions as the best possibility that could have been; the felt discrepancy between the two is a form of judgment. Love, fully offered again and again, regardless of our attempts to reject or kill it, carries with it a form of graceful judgment that is stronger, ultimately, than all our acts of retribution or forensic adjudications of right and wrong. As C. S. Lewis points out in his books *Surprised by Joy* and *The Great Divorce*, love and grace can even be painful to accept because of our habituated, self-protective acts of closing ourselves off to lavish love. Likewise, the actions of the pietistic faithful in "Babette's Feast" become clear as people are unable to receive what has been offered all along. Instead, they insist on linking redemption and faith with suffering and personal denial.

Within the framework of the covenant, the cross itself is still profoundly significant even if it is not understood to be the locus of salvation. The cross signifies broken relationships and alienation, God's suffering alongside humanity, the response of the world to the covenant, and what we have left to overcome, along with Christ, to realize the vision of the promised reign of God. Ultimately, the cross acts reflectively, pointing away from itself and insisting that one focus on one's life commitments. Thus, soteriology moves beyond the symbol of the cross to a larger covenantal vision of salvation as a restoration of life and relationship between God and humans. In this covenant model of salvation, God offers a relationship to humanity and the goal of all creation is, subsequently, to live into this covenant fully. Envisioning this goal, early Christians were inspired to acts of defiance against worldly powers that offered privilege through injustice. Likewise, the relationship of grace that God offers humanity today encourages one to counter all systems of sin, such as sexism, and it does not support systems of patriarchal power and abuse of women by encouraging passivity in the face of oppression.

Thus, it is not the cross that saves; it is God's *response* to the cross that saves. God's response is a restoration of life and relationship and this is the meaning of grace. God's action is met by our commitment to save bodies and restore a vision for a renewed creation. Humanity is active in relationship to God and, likewise, to other people as we are invited to live into a covenant relationship with God, surround the crosses of the world, and insist they stop.[39]

Part Two
The Cross: God and the Suffering World

8

The Crucified God

Yesterday and Today: 1972–2002

Jürgen Moltmann
Translated by Margaret Kohl

THE CRUCIFIED GOD, FIRST PUBLISHED in Germany in 1972, "is undoubtedly one of the theological classics of the second half of the twentieth century," wrote Richard Bauckham in his preface to the 2001 SCM Classics edition. "What marks it as a classic is that, when one rereads it several decades later, themes, which were innovative in its time, seem now rather familiar...but also that it still shocks and surprises, enlightens and provokes, with its dialectical sharpness of expression....It is a passionate book, written 'so to speak with my lifeblood,' as Moltmann said of it much later."[1]

I am not sure whether Richard Bauckham is right, but I am certain this book was part of my personal "wrestling with God," my suffering under the dark side of God, the hidden face of God, the *hester panim,* as the Jews say, the godforsakenness of the victims and the godlessness of the guilty in the human history of violence and suffering.

In July 1943 at the age of seventeen, I lay watching bombs rain down all around me in my hometown of Hamburg. Forty thousand people, including women and children, were killed as a result of that bombing or burned in the firestorm that followed. Miraculously I survived. To this day I do not know why I am not dead like my comrades. My question in that inferno was not, "Why is God letting this happen?" but rather, "Where is God?" Is God far away from us, absent, in his heaven? Or is God among us, suffering with us? Does God share in our suffering?

Two questions occur to me at this point. One is the theoretical question about accusing God in the face of the pain of the victims—this is the so-called theodicy question. The other is the existential question about community with God in suffering. The first question presupposes an apathetic, untouchable God in heaven, while the second question is searching for a compassionate God, "the fellow-sufferer who understands us," as Alfred North Whitehead said.

Yes, I remember the catastrophe of my people, the inexorable crime against the Jewish people that has the name of shame, "Auschwitz." I shall never forget the pictures of the dead in the concentration camp of Bergen-Belsen shown to us POWs in England in October 1945. It was so unbelievable, but it was true; the crimes were committed in the name of my people. I shall never forget walking through the remnants and ruins of the death camp of Maidanek, near Lublin, in November 1961. I would have rather sunk to the ground than gone on, and there, all of a sudden, I became certain that these murdered people would live. The horrors over the crimes of the Holocaust had weighed on me and many other people of my generation in Germany ever since the end of the war. Much time passed before we could emerge from the silence that stops the mouths of people over whom the clouds of the victims hang heavy. Did God let this happen? Where is God? Is God far away from the victims of violence, or is God on their side, crying and suffering with them? My book *The Crucified God* was said to be a Christian theology "after Auschwitz." This is true. It was for me an attempt to speak to God, to trust in God and speak about God in the shadows of Auschwitz and in view of the victims of my people. The God-question has been identical with the cry of the victims for justice and the hunger of the perpetrators for a way back from the path of death.

The Crucified God is in essence a book about believing in God after the cross of Christ. What we can say about God "after Auschwitz" depends on what we can say about God after the crucifixion of Christ, hearing the dying Jesus' cry of abandonment: "My God, why have you forsaken me?" The whole book can be understood as a theological interpretation of these words from the Gospels of Mark and Matthew.

I remember April 6, 1968. I was participating in an international "Theology of Hope" conference at Duke University when Harvey Cox stormed into the hall and cried, "Martin Luther King has been shot!" The conference ended immediately and the participants returned home because many cities in America were burning that night. I left a few days later for Tübingen, and I promised my American friends that whenever I returned to their country, I would not speak about the theology of hope anymore but of the cross: "In a civilization that glorifies success and happiness and is blind for the suffering of others, people's eyes may be opened to the truth, if they remember that at the centre of the Christian Faith stands the assailed, tormented Christ, dying in forsakenness. The recollection that God raised the Crucified one and made him the 'Hope of the world' must lead churches to break their alliances with the violent and enter into solidarity with the humiliated."[2] I wrote this in 1970, two years before *The Crucified God.*

And where are we today? Before September 11, 2001, America was successfully globalizing American power and culture with a kind of universal optimism in the new world order, or *novus ordo seclorum,* as it is written on every dollar bill. After the terrorist attacks on the World Trade Center and the Pentagon, a new "age of anxiety" seems to have come over us. In order not to sink into an abyss of despair, we should discover anew the face of the Crucified One in the faces of the victims of violence, the "crucified people," as Jon Sobrino would say. What is the crucial theological question? Should we ask, "Why did God let this massacre happen?" Would this not say that our God is the God of the terrorists, and that they were unconsciously God's obedient servants? Or should we ask, "Where was God in these attacks?" and find God as the suffering God among the victims? Is God not weeping and crying over the death of his beloved children? Jesus wept over the destruction of Jerusalem (Luke 19:41), and so tears rolled down the face of God at Ground Zero as surely as they did over Jerusalem, and we are called to participate in these sufferings of God with all our compassion.

This was and is the decisive question of *The Crucified God.* Is God the transcendent and untouched stage manager of the theater of this violent world, or is God in Christ the central engaged figure of the world tragedy?

In the next section, I will explain the basic themes of *The Crucified God.* Then I will summarize the criticism of Karl Rahner, Johann Baptist Metz, Hans Küng, Dorothee Soelle, and feminist theology. To conclude, I will look into the future of the risen Christ and the coming joy of God.

BASIC THEMES OF *THE CRUCIFIED GOD*

Is God Passible or Impassible?

Is God capable of suffering? If we follow the fashion of Greek philosophy and ask what attributes are "appropriate" to God (Greek: *theoprepes*), differentiation, diversity, movement, and suffering all have to be excluded from the divine nature. The divine nature is incapable of suffering; otherwise it would not be divine. The absolute subject of modern metaphysics is also incapable of suffering; otherwise it would not be absolute. Impassible, immovable, uncompounded, and self-sufficing, the Deity stands over against a moved, divided, suffering, and never self-sufficient world. The divine substance is the founder and sustainer of this world of transitory phenomena. It abides eternally, and so it cannot be subjected to this world's destiny. This is called the metaphysical apathy axiom. We find it in Aristotle's *Metaphysics,* book 12.

If we turn instead to the theological proclamation of the Christian tradition, we find at its center the passion of Christ. The gospel tells us about the suffering of Christ for the redemption of the world; the Eucharist communicates the self-giving of Christ in the form of bread and wine. When Christ's passion is made present to us in Word and Sacrament, faith is awakened in us—the Christian faith in God, not just a certain monotheistic belief. We believe in God for Christ's sake because God himself is involved in Christ's passion story. But in what way? If the Deity cannot suffer, how can we see Christ's passion as the revelation of God? Does God let Christ suffer for/with us, or does God himself suffer for/with us in Christ?

The ability to identify God with the suffering Christ dwindles in proportion to the importance given to the apathy axiom in the doctrine of God. If God is incapable of suffering, then Christ's passion can be viewed only as a human tragedy and there is no redeeming power in his passion. If we want to say both, we end up formulating paradoxes, as did Bertrand Brasnett in his book *The Suffering of the Impassible God.*[3] I think it would be more consistent if we simply stop making the metaphysical axiom of God's apathy our starting point in theology and start from the biblical axiom of God's passion instead, so as to understand Christ's suffering as the *passion of the passionate God.* The word *passion* has the double meaning of suffering and overwhelming feeling and ardor, and the God of Israel is a God full of passion for the life of his people and for justice on his earth.

Why did patristic theology hold fast to the apathy axiom (with the exception of Origen), although Christian devotion adored at the same time the crucified Christ as God? We can see two reasons:

1. God's essential impassibility distinguishes the Deity from human beings, who are subject to suffering, transience, and death.

2. Salvation is the deification of human beings by giving them a share in eternal life. If we become immortal, we shall also become impassible: Apathy is divine nature and the fulfillment of human salvation in eternal life.

Logically these arguments fall short because they take only into account a single alternative: either essential incapacity of suffering or fateful subjection to suffering. But there is a third form of suffering, *active suffering,* which involves the willingness to open oneself to be touched, moved, affected by others—and that means the suffering of *passionate love.* If God were in every respect incapable of suffering, God would also be incapable of love. If God is love, however, God opens Godself for the suffering that love for others brings. God does not suffer, as we do, out of deficiency of being, but God does suffer from love for creation, which is the overflowing superabundance of God's divine being. In this sense, God can suffer, will suffer, and is suffering in the world.

For Whom Did Christ Die?

The traditional answer to this question is that Christ died for sinners. In *The Crucified God* I expanded the question of salvation from the traditional concern with sin to encompass also the contemporary concern with innocent and meaningless suffering. Those with whom Christ is identified in his abandonment and death are the godless on the one hand, and the godforsaken on the other, or, more concretely, the evildoers and their victims. Traditional doctrines of justification are sin oriented; modern liberation theology is victim oriented. Both sides belong together in a world of sin and suffering, violence and victims.

Why did God take the suffering of Christ onto Godself? The first answer is: To be present and beside us in our suffering and abandonment. This leads to a *solidarity Christology:* Christ our divine Brother "emptied himself, taking the form of a slave...humbled himself and became obedient to the point of death—even death on a cross" (Phil. 2:7-8). If God takes this road with Christ and God is where Christ is, then Christ brings God's fellowship to people, who are as humiliated and emptied of their identity as Christ was. Christ's cross stands between the countless crosses that line the paths of the powerful and violent, from Spartacus to the concentration camps and the "disappeared" in Latin American dictatorships. His cross stands between our crosses as a sign that God participates in our sufferings. This was the comforting insight of Dietrich Bonhoeffer in the Gestapo cell: "Only the suffering God can help," as we find in his *Letters and Papers from Prison.* This was the conversion experience of Archbishop Oscar Arnulfo Romero in San Salvador, as described by Jon Sobrino: "In the crucified people of history the crucified God became present to him. In the eyes of the poor and oppressed of his people he saw the disfigured face of God."[4] Christ took upon himself humiliation and passion so that he could become the brother of the humiliated and forsaken and bring them God's embracing presence.

> *And when the human hearts are breaking*
> *Under sorrow's iron rod,*
> *Then there is the selfsame aching*
> *Deep within the heart of God.*[5]

The second answer leads to *reconciliation Christology*. From very early on, Christians saw Christ's passion as the vicarious divine suffering for the reconciliation of sinners. Following the model of the Suffering Servant in Isaiah 53, they saw Christ as the divine Son who reconciles sinners with God through his vicarious suffering. Is this necessary? How does it work? Without forgiveness of sin, the guilty cannot live, for they have lost all their self-identity and consequently also their self-respect. But there is no forgiveness without atonement. Yet atonement is not possible for human beings because the wrong that has been done cannot be made undone or made good by any human act. Only God can reconcile guilty people with their past. How? The Suffering Servant of Isaiah takes away the sins of the people by "carrying the people's sin." By carrying and bearing human sin, God transforms their aggressions into his suffering.

Christ is the brother of the victims and the redeemer of the guilty. He "carries," on the one hand, "the sufferings of the world" and, on the other hand, "the sins of the world."

Both sides of Christ belong together for the redemption of the world, but they are not equal. Victims have a long memory, for the traces of suffering are deeply etched into their souls and often into their bodies too. People who have committed the injury always have short memories. They do not know what they have done because they do not want to know. They are dependent on the memory of the victims if they want to see who they are and be reconciled. They must learn to see themselves with the eyes of their victims.

When I wrote *The Crucified God,* I turned the traditional question upside down. The question traditionally asked is the soteriological question: What does the cross of Christ mean for our redemption? My question was the theological one: What does the cross of Christ mean for God himself? I came face to face with the pain of God the Father of Christ, who suffered with him. If Christ dies with the cry of being forsaken by God, then in God the Father there must be a correspondingly profound experience of his forsakenness by his beloved Son. In 2002 Peter Dudeney from Boston wrote to me: "I remember while reading *The Crucified God* being struck by the realization that Jesus experienced ultimate abandonment and the Father ultimate bereavement and that no one, in whatever extremity, will ever, can ever, be beyond the fellowship of God and the power of the Spirit."

The suffering of the Father is different from the suffering of the Son. The Son experienced dying in forsakenness, while the Father experienced the death of the Son. We can illustrate this with our own experiences. At my end I shall experience dying, but not my own death, while in those I love, I experience death when they die because I have to survive their death. The death of Christ reaches deep into the nature of God and, above all other meanings, is an event that takes place in the innermost nature of God, the Trinity: Do we see at Golgotha a fatherless Son and a sonless Father? "One of the Trinity suffered," said the early church theologian Cyril, and this so-called "theopaschitic principle" is now accepted. I would like to add that where one suffers, the others suffer, too. Christ's death on the cross is an intratrinitarian event before it assumes significance for the redemption of the world. There is a famous medieval image of the Trinity, the so-called mercy seat or chair of grace, sometimes called even "the pain of God." With an expression of intensive pain God the Father carries in his hands the crossbeam of the cross on which the dead Son hangs, while the Spirit in the form of a dove descends from the face of the Father to the face of the Son. This is an image of the Trinity with the cross at the center. What we are shown is the breathtaking scene of Holy Saturday, after the death of the Son on Good Friday and before his raising from the dead on Easter Sunday. There is a mystical moment of silence between cross and resurrection.

It follows from this that a true theology of the cross (Luther) must be a trinitarian theology (beyond Luther). The Trinity is the theological background for what really took place on Golgotha between Christ and the God whom he called in Gethsemane "Abba, my dear father." On the other hand, the crucified Christ is the revelation of the trinitarian mystery of God. Only when we plumb the depths of this pain of God can we grasp the immeasurable Easter jubilation of the joy of God and of the whole creation.

CONSENT

The Crucified God became controversial in the best sense of the word. It stimulated people to think about suffering and the crucified Christ for themselves. I received strong support from Anglican theologians such as Kenneth Woolcombe and Richard Bauckham, from liberation theologians such as Jon Sobrino and

Leonardo Boff, from the Korean Minjung theologian Ahn Byun-Mu, and, to my surprise, also from the Orthodox Romanian theologian Dumitru Staniloae, who found the pain of God included in the concept of the merciful God. Many authors followed me with titles such as *The God of Weakness* (John Timmer), *The Suffering God* (Charles Ohlrich), *The Passion of God* (W. McWilliams), *God and Human Suffering* (Douglas John Hall), *The Disabled God* (Nancy Eiesland), *La Croix de Dieu* (Jean-Louis Souletie), to mention only a few. Numerous dissertations were written on the topic. But what impressed me most were the many personal letters from people in prisons, hospitals, and basic communities in slums, people who have to live in the "shadows of the cross," or in the "dark night of the soul," or among the crucified people of this world. People are still coming to me after thirty years, speaking about the personal consolation they found in this book. When they cried out to God, they found the suffering God at their side.

In 1990, I received a letter from Robert McAfee Brown. He told me a moving story from San Salvador. On November 16, 1989, six well-known Jesuits, together with their housekeeper and her daughter, were brutally murdered in the university there by a group of soldiers. The rector of the university, Father Ignacio Ellacuria, was one of them. Jon Sobrino escaped the massacre only because he happened not to be in the country at the time. The letter continues: "When the killers were dragging some of the bodies back into the building, as they took the body of Ramon Moreno into Jon's room, they hit a bookcase and knocked a book on the floor, which became drenched with the martyr's blood. In the morning when they picked up the book, they found that it was *The Crucified God.*" Two years later I made a pilgrimage to the graves of the martyrs and found my book, *Il Dio Crucificado,* there under glass, as a sign and symbol of what really happened in this place. It gave me a great deal to think about.

CRITIQUE

God Cannot Suffer!

In his last interview, Karl Rahner answered the question of whether or not God suffers rather roughly:

> I would say that there is a modern tendency to develop a theology of the death of God that, in the last analysis, seems to me to be Gnostic. One can find this in Hans Urs von Balthasar and in Adrienne von Speyr; it also appears in an independent form in Moltmann. To put it crudely: It does not help me to escape

from my mess and mix-up and despair [German: *mein Dreck und Schlamassel und meiner Verzweiflung*] if God is in the same predicament [German: *Wenn es Gott genau so dreckig geht*]. It is for me a part of my consolation, to realize that God, when and insofar as he entered into this history as his own, did it in a different way than I did. From the beginning I am cemented into this horribleness [German: *Gräßlichkeit*], while God is in a true and authentic and consoling sense the God who cannot suffer, "Deus impassibilis, and immutable God, Deus immutabilis." In Moltmann and others I sense a theology of absolute paradox of Patripassianism, and to this I would say: What use would that be to me as consolation in the true sense of the word?[6]

I found these statements of Karl Rahner only after his death. So I answered in a kind of posthumous letter. Here are a few excerpts:

I am disturbed by your objection that God "in a consoling sense is the God who cannot suffer." I find no connection between consolation and apathy.... Of course God entered into our history of suffering in a different way; he was not subjected to it against his will. That God does not suffer as finite creatures do does not mean that he is incapable of suffering in any way. God is capable of suffering because he is capable of love. His very being is mercy.... I cannot imagine an impassible God as a God who consoles in a personal sense. He seems to me to be as cold and hard and unfeeling as cement.... What disturbed and shocked me, though, was what you said about yourself: "From the beginning I am cemented into its horribleness." That sounds bitter, cut off, isolated and incapable of movement ... like a life which is unloved and incapable of love. And: With what right do we human beings say that God is "incapable"? Do we not "cement" God in with the negations of this negative theology? If that is the case, then a personal experience of being locked in and a divine image of a *Deus impassibilis* go closely together. How can a God who is locked into his immobility and impassibility become a comfort for the person whose situation also seems to be like that? In that case God would indeed be in the same predicament, and neither God nor human beings could find comfort in eternity.[7]

Johann Baptist Metz followed the argument of his master, Karl Rahner, and added that God must not suffer because the theodicy question—If there is a God, why is there evil and suffering?—must be kept open. At the end we shall accuse God and ask, Why has there been so much evil and suffering in the world? And then God must answer us. A God who has been present in our suffering and who took up his cross for us could not be accused. Metz cannot find the christological answer to his open theodicy question. There is a christological deficit in his fundamental theology.

It is similar with Hans Küng. God is for him—as for Ignatius—*Deus simper major*, the always greater God. In the face of innocent suffering there remains only a "theology of silence." When Aaron's sons were killed by God's fire, the biblical statement is short: "And Aaron kept silent." Küng wants to find the consent of Jews and Muslims. His doctrine of God is therefore without Christ. He is looking for a common belief in the God of Jews, Christians, and Muslims, for a monotheistic world movement. This, however, must not deny that Christians believe in God for Christ's sake.

Did God Kill His Own Son?

The most severe attack on my theology of the cross came unexpectedly from Dorothee Soelle, at that time more a liberal theologian than a feminist, in her book *Suffering*.[8] In my interpretation of the godforsakenness of Christ on the cross she saw signs of a "theological sadism." For me, Christ's godforsakenness was the most profound expression of his solidarity with forsaken men and women. Dorothee, however, read the Passion story morally and rose up in arms against such a "sadistic God" who abandons and sacrifices his "own son." She even compared this God with Heinrich Himmler. This viewpoint was so alien to me that I had not even considered it. But ever since then, the legend has gone around that, in Moltmann's view, "God killed his own son" on Golgotha.

Feminist theologians in Germany and the United States willingly picked up this moral criticism of the theology of the cross as specific "feminist critique" without realizing that this is old Enlightenment criticism against atonement theology, the sacrifice in Roman Catholic mass, and sacrificial morality. More recently this criticism has appeared in the reproach of victimization in patriarchal religions and has been justified by the defamation of the Christian theology of the cross. The "sadistic God" is now turned into a heavenly practitioner of child-abuse (as Moloch of the Phoenicians), on the pattern of the atrocious fathers who abuse their own daughters. I am absolutely against the victimization of sons and daughters, because I myself hardly survived being "sacrificed" for my "holy fatherland" in World War II. As a matter of fact, the Christian theology of the cross of Christ ended sacrificial religions "once for all," just as the Mount Moriah story of Isaac's nonsacrifice stopped child sacrifices as religious requirement (compare again Moloch, the child-eater, or Kali, the boy-eating goddess of Calcutta). Dorothee Soelle (before her death in 2003) and some German feminist theologians have turned more and more to the recognition of the presence of the suffering God in the pains and sorrows of suffering people.

THE CRUCIFIED GOD TOMORROW

I started my theological writing in 1965 with *The Theology of Hope*. This was an interpretation of the resurrected Christ and Easter. The second book was *The Crucified God*, and this was an interpretation of Golgotha and Good Friday. At this point, I decided to balance the two books with a study of the Holy Spirit and an interpretation of Pentecost, so *The Church in the Power of the Spirit* followed in 1975. After establishing this foundation for my theology, I was ready for more systematic books. I wrote my systematic contributions to theology from 1980 to 1999. The secret goal that I was searching for all the time was a theological reflection of the Easter joy and a theological anticipation of the eternal glory in the new creation of all things. The depth of the cross and the height of the resurrection of Christ are not in balance. "How much more...," the apostle Paul always said (Greek: *pollo malon*). "Christ Jesus, who died, yes, who was raised..." (Rom. 8:34); "but where sin increased, grace abounded all the more" (Rom. 5:20). There is a surplus value of the victory over the defeat, of the resurrection over the crucifixion, of grace over sin and joy over pain. Good Friday is at the center of this world, but Easter morning is the sunrise of the coming of God and the morning of the new life and is the beginning of the future of this world. I love the Orthodox Easter liturgy, with the hymn:

> *Now all is filled with light,*
> *heaven and earth and the realm of the dead.*
> *The whole creation rejoices in Christ's resurrection,*
> *which is the true foundation. . . .*
> *Let us embrace one another.*

> *Let us speak to those who hate us:*
> *For the resurrection's sake we will forgive one*
> *Another everything. And so let us cry:*
> *Christ is risen from the dead.*

I finally found this theology of joy and jubilation in my 1995 book on eschatology, *The Coming of God: Christian Eschatology,* in which I do not deal with "the end of the world" and those who may be "left behind," but with the coming of God. I say in the last sentences: "The feast of eternal joy is prepared by the fulness of God and the rejoicing of all created being.... The laughter of the universe is God's delight. It is the universal Easter laughter" in heaven and on earth.[9] This is the promise and the future of the crucified God.

9

All That Matters

What an Epistemology of the Cross Is Good For

Mary M. Solberg

MARTIN LUTHER WAS NOT INTERESTED in salvation. As a working Christian, he had better things to do; as a faithful theologian, he had more important things to write, preach, and teach about. Inheritors of Luther's theological legacy ought to care a good deal more about how we live than about whether we are saved. As justified sinners, how we live should be all that matters to us.

STEPPING OUT ON LUTHER

Luther's *theologia crucis*, or theology of the cross, is not—nor did he ever intend it to be—either a doctrine or a theory of atonement. It is not an article of faith, for Christians in general or even for Christians who name themselves for Dr. Luther (to his profound chagrin, it is said). It does not explain how God redeems human beings—which remained for Luther, as for any self-respecting Christian theologian, a mystery. Nor is it a matter of either faith or salvation.

While Luther said that "the cross alone is our theology" (*crux sola est nostra theologia*),[1] he never wrote much about what he meant by "theology of the cross."[2]

I find it very difficult to characterize Luther's theology of the cross using conventional theological terms. I suppose the term *method* might be least *un*satisfactory. But even that term is too weighty, too substantial, to signal the role *theologia crucis* played in Luther's theological thinking—and in his life. A little later in this essay I will explain how I think it *functions*.

In the best-known expression of his theology of the cross, at the Heidelberg Disputation in 1518, he refers to a "theologian [rather than a theology] of the cross."[3] In a real sense, this is quite in keeping with the central place lived experience has in all of Luther's theology. It also suggests his disdain for theology as speculation and for the pretense that anyone could do theology at a distance from everyday life, which is always lived *coram mundo* (before, or in the presence of, the world) and *coram Deo* (in the presence of God). From my point of view, finally, it undergirds the contention that living, not salvation, is what both theologians and theology ought to be concerned about.

Luther's life story generates this theology, and this particular theology animates that life story. Truth be told, there is nothing generic about anyone's theology. To say that this theology of the cross emerges from Luther's life story in no way keeps it from resonating deeply with someone else's life story, too. I hope that my twenty-first-century attempt to characterize Luther's theology of the cross might allow it to resonate, or resonate more clearly, with the lives of more contemporary Christian believers, theologians among them.

It seems to me that, for Luther, it is almost as if a theologian of the cross is someone who has been struck, as if by lightning, by what God reveals on the cross: namely, God's own self. Sent reeling, the theologian intuits or glimpses, rather than apprehends, that his or her expectations and categories—even the words to articulate who this is on the bloody cross, what is going on here, or anything else one could call reliable human knowledge—have been upended, reversed, short-circuited. There is no human capacity to comprehend the depth, mystery, even scandal, of what is transpiring on the cross. A theologian of the cross, cut loose from all human moorings, cries out—and God, through the gift of faith, grasps the outstretched arms of the despairing human creature. I do not believe that this experience happens only once in a lifetime, Luther's or anyone else's. I believe it happens repeatedly, disconcertingly, and as a gift.

What else could enable a theologian of the cross to "call . . . the thing what it actually is"?[4] Certainly no experience or learning that humankind could dream up. The difficulty of explaining what Luther's theology of the cross actually refers to itself points up the sharp limits of the analogical approach; God's things, even as humans experience and describe them, are not like humans' things. At the same time, human language is all humans have to point to these things. Even if we were constrained only in this way—and not also by our compulsion to run our own lives and save our own skins—we would likely and quickly reify this confounding of our expectations of who and what God is and how God ought to work.

In Luther's theology of the cross, there is nothing to systematize, legalize, or even grasp hold of. In a real sense, there is no content. If there is a way to reflect about it in twenty-first-century, postmodern terms—a way that might help us think more seriously about how we are to live—it may be to consider the *theologia crucis* as, instead, an *epistemologia crucis*, that is, as an epistemology of the cross.

THEOLOGIANS' TASK: FAITHFULLY SEEKING UNDERSTANDING IN ORDER TO LIVE FAITHFULLY

The Christian story begins deep in the history and sacred texts of the Jews. At its heart is the promise of God, the creator, redeemer, and sustainer of Israel, of the body of Christ, of the whole cosmos. That promise is that we are being and will be drawn into the life of God. That all we need to live is being and will be provided by the loving-kindness of God. That whatever happens, we belong to God.[5] That God has and is the last word, just as God had and was the first. That God is faithful, and while all else may change, God's faithfulness will not change.

According to the peculiarly Christian story, which began to be told in the first century C.E., all these promises were enacted in Jesus of Nazareth, a first-century Palestinian Jew. People who heard, saw, and touched or were touched by Jesus— and later, those who heard, saw, and touched or were touched by them—told the story of their encounter with him. Faith told them this One—crucified, dead, and raised by the power of God—was the transparency, the icon, the incarnate child, of God Almighty.

That the promises of God were fulfilled in Jesus in no way meant or means that God's promise is now a precious but closed book. That promise continues to be fulfilled everywhere through the work of the same holy-ing Spirit that brooded over the deep at the beginning of everything. It is the Spirit that makes it possible for Jesus to be a part of people's everyday lives in as many ways as there are variations of the human experience.[6] The followers of Jesus speak and the listeners hear, each in their own language. Interpreting the sacraments, Luther observed that we need something to cling to, and God provided what we needed: God became one of us.

The task of theology, defined so succinctly by Anselm as "faith seeking under-standing," is, in the seeking and through the understanding, to equip us and direct us toward our project as humans, which is to live abundantly, loving God and caring for our neighbor as for ourselves. For Christians, preaching the gospel and sharing the sacraments renew our consciousness of God's creative, redeem-ing, sustaining work: the fulfillment of the promise God incarnated in Jesus of Nazareth and enacts in the everyday lives of everyone who follows in his footsteps. If salvation is different or separate from what animates this kind of living, it is not good news.

Is God's work of equipping confined to the means of grace Christians claim? Is the story of God's mercy and justice, of God's faithfulness and loving-kindness, expressed only in the Christian faith tradition—or accomplished only by Christians who confess the Lordship of Jesus Christ? I do not know with certainty the answer to that question. But I doubt it. Whatever the answer, Christian disciples of Jesus could benefit from seeing more clearly the difference between living *in order to be saved*, whatever salvation turns out to be, and living *as if we are*.

THE CROSSWALK AT RUSH HOUR

For human beings, living is, among other things, a journey into accountability. The journey entails a gradual recognition of the interdependence within which each living thing lives with all others. For creatures that are not human, this interdependence seems to be a given, while humans, who are no less firmly knit into the web of life, seem to have to learn about it. Some people even seem to think they have a choice about all of this.

Despite our knowing this story in the marrow of our bones and in the elec-trochemical synapses of our brains, most of us ignore and sometimes even deny it. We speak approvingly of "self-made men," "patient autonomy," and "original scholarship," for example, and act as if such things actually exist. We say we believe that anyone who works hard can succeed and that those who do succeed evidently worked hard (the corollary: those who did not succeed evidently did not work hard enough). We tell each other how much we value the "right" of every patient to make his or her own health-care decisions. We forget, or never learned, that in health or in sickness, no one is really autonomous, least of all the patient who seeks what only others can provide.

The truth is, we cannot and do not do *anything* in this world by ourselves.

To the given of interdependence we add a peculiarly human dimension: mutual moral accountability. Here, too, however, we seem ambivalent. We imagine our court system, for example, as dispensing society's justice. When arraigned, though, we routinely utter "not guilty" and do our best to ensure we are not held accountable, or held at all. A host of television "lawyer shows" teach us, if lived experience does not, that the most successful attorneys are those who can get their clients off, irrespective of guilt or innocence. Few public officials, when their wrongdoing is exposed, take responsibility or ask forgiveness.

These settings and practices remind us how closely our lives are woven together—not as a matter of choice but as a matter of fact, as constitutive of who we are as consciousness is. Remembering that these things are so ought first of all to produce a singular sort of relief, the kind one feels when a missing child is found. But beyond relief, it also ought to awaken us to the fragility and sensitivity of these relationships, as well as their surprising resiliency. The one thing we cannot afford to be in the dark about, though, is that they make us who and what we are.

A THEOLOGIAN ON THE SCENE

Luther understood theology to be relational at its heart. It had to do not with human speculation about God but rather with human being in relation with God.[7] The *relationship* between God and humankind was the only framework of meaning for contemplating ultimate human destiny, as well as for living daily life in all its mundane details. To try to come to terms with who we are, and who we are in relation to others, outside this framework, will fail miserably in thought, word, and deed. The evidence is all around us.

When Luther observed that humans insist on relying on their own power, he was neither condemning nor prescribing a remedy for human nature. Rather, he was *describing* the human situation: humans' denial of their relatedness—most fundamentally, their dependence on God, and then, their interdependence within the whole created world.

By the standards of his own time or ours, Martin Luther was an activist. His capacity and (apparently) his appetite for work were prodigious. He published volumes of biblical commentaries, lectures, and sermons. He also published tracts and treatises on education (public support for education of boys and girls), economics (charging interest), government (how princes should govern), welfare (how communities should provide for the poor), and a host of other subjects and personages. Luther said something—often eloquently, often with great vulgarity—about practically every controversy, inside or outside the church. Many of them he started himself.

What made it possible for Luther to take such risks, to live so close to the edge, to thunder with apparent fearlessness against or in favor of causes, institutions, and individuals? Martin Luther was not interested in salvation, but rather in living. Commenting on the Reformer's theological and existential project, Gerhard Ebeling writes that, for Luther,

> [t]o know God means to know what God can and does do, not his power and his potentialities, but his power as it is *actually at work in everything that exists* [emphasis added]....But if man has to know...what he is capable of with regard to his salvation, then he evidently knows neither what he is capable of, nor what God is, until he knows for certain that he can *do nothing* towards his salvation [emphasis in the original]. And that very inability permits him to be certain of salvation, which is based upon the act of God alone.[8]

The knowing referred to here is rooted in and sustained by faith, which "is not only the negation of human possibility, but its realization as well."[9] Faith is as far from blindness as sight can be.

ABOUT KNOWING WHAT THERE IS TO KNOW

If Luther had lived five hundred years later, he might have proposed an epistemology, rather than a theology, of the cross. What happens at the foot of the cross entails a radical reevaluation, and a demotion, of human knowing. Here, human notions of "righteousness," or "wisdom," or "justice"—and what others do we have than human ones?—break down. *This* cannot be an expression of God's righteousness, this pathetic human being caught up in the terror and injustice of a real crucifixion. As this good man suffers physical agony and heartbreaking aloneness, *who* would have the unmitigated gall to claim that God is present there? Who can explain this execution scene, who can "know" what this means, what this *is*? Knowing breaks down.

Over the centuries, "the cross" has become an abstraction for Christians, a theological placeholder. Once it was a brutal historical event: the Roman Empire's execution of a first-century Palestinian Jew named Jesus. His tortured death was as real for him and those who loved him as were tens of thousands of other crucifixions that occurred during the centuries before and after his. While crucifixion as an instrument of state terror belongs to the distant past, there are good reasons to use the expression to describe the suffering of millions of marginalized men, women, and children all over the world today.[10] Justice and mercy are as alien to their sudden or gradual deaths—and of as little concern to the powers that be—as they were to countless executions, including that of Jesus of Nazareth, at Roman hands long ago.

Insofar as the spectacle of "the cross" describes what is real in human experience, Luther's figure of speech (*theologia crucis*) suggests an existential disposition— what I am tempted to call a "frame of heart," rather than of mind—that begins by relinquishing (because it must) the illusion of self-made-ness, of certainty and control. It "breaks" with dominant human norms and criteria for knowing.[11]

Knowing, an elusive notion, surely refers to much more than salting away information for possible future reference and use.[12] From lived experience we come to *know* much that matters more and stays with us longer than data. People *know* each other. Children *know* their parents' love—or its absence. Mothers *know* the sound of distress in their children's voices. Good cooks *know* what to add to draw out the special flavor of a dish. All human beings practice and rely on these kinds of knowing as well as others.

Advances in scientific and technical knowing have been accompanied by technological developments that facilitate the accumulation and dissemination of more information than anyone could possibly put to use. Despite these advances, however, the most fundamental, most necessary human activities must be learned anew—taught, nurtured, cultivated anew—by each successive generation, each person. Who has not had to learn how to love, or even to live with, another person? What parent has not had to learn, step by step, how to raise a child? Who knows ahead of time how to "make" peace—with another person, tribe, or nation?

Knowing, and the frameworks we construct to describe how and what we come to know, what knowing is for, who can know, how to distinguish between truthful and deceitful knowing, are part of our daily living. There is much more reciprocity and overlap in the practices of knowing and the practices of everyday living than we are usually aware. Such awareness would be burdensome. At the same time, we do well when we recognize the impossibility of clean and clear distinctions between the living out of what we know and the knowing out of which we live.

Coming to know, and attempting to describe what one knows, entails (and may be enabled by) an implicit conviction that somehow "it all" fits together, makes sense, and that we can *know* at least some of it reliably. Humans share this conviction, something like a common "faith."[13] Our complaints that this or that phenomenon "doesn't make sense" express our underlying conviction that, on the whole, things *do* make sense. People with serious mental illnesses suffer from them as intensely as they do at least in part because of their utter inability to grasp the sense things make; in turn, those who try to treat or alleviate these illnesses are often frustrated by their perplexing senselessness.

BUILDING AN EPISTEMOLOGY OF THE CROSS: WHERE TO BEGIN?

Epistemologies constructed chiefly out of a deep suspicion of power understood as domination, thoroughgoing skepticism about value-free, "objective" knowing, and a passion for moral accountability win few prizes in established academic circles, including those of science, philosophy, and theology. They are novelty items, interesting to talk about from time to time, but probably ill-suited for the serious, if sometimes distasteful, business of learning about the world or running it.

The chief architects of such epistemologies have been feminist philosophers, among them Lorraine Code, Donna Haraway, Sandra Harding, and Elizabeth Kamarck Minnich.[14] They are outraged by the injustice of the centuries-old (and ongoing) exclusion of women from the community of recognized knowers, and by the grave consequences the whole human family suffers because of this injustice. These feminist thinkers ask us seriously to reassess both the scientific and the ethical adequacy of our knowing. Unlike much traditional epistemology, theirs does not question the possibility of knowing, but rather the terms of the enterprise itself. Their self-consciously lived experience of relative or relatively complete marginalization as women equips them to take a critical stance vis-à-vis knowledge-projects-as-usual. In addition, they have made constructive proposals that suggest where and how to look for both better and more just ways of knowing.

Some years ago it occurred to me that there might be affinities between these secular feminist philosophical proposals, on the one hand, and insights and implications drawn from Luther's theology of the cross, on the other. As I set them next to one another, it seemed clear that they had much to say to one another. Their conversation is galvanized by a common concern for the well-being of "the neighbor": our shared environment, a world that cries out for care, justice, and hope.[15]

Luther's theology of the cross, I have argued, functions first of all as a sharp critique of the official theology of his day. He sets it over against a "theology of glory" that he claims characterizes the thinking and praxis of those who represent the church. But his critique is deeper and broader than that. It lays bare and names the pretentious human self-centeredness that corresponds to idolatry and ignorance of God.

In my judgment, we do not give Luther sufficient credit for the uncanny truthfulness of his insight and his remarkable courage in drawing this contrast between "cross" and "glory" as he stood face-to-face with the most powerful political and economic institution of his day. What the Roman church was doing was the sixteenth-century ecclesiastical, political, and theological version of what humans always do, Luther argued: they "believe and act as if they have the power to invent, name, describe, control, and dispense God.... [And t]he god humans invent can be found wherever (human) glory, majesty, and power are most evident, whether in an institution or an individual heart."[16]

While many of us in the twenty-first century have changed the vocabulary or dispensed with God-talk altogether, we are no less adept at mistaking ourselves and our claims for whatever seems to us to be ultimately valuable. We build nation-states and corporations, political movements and armies, in our own image and our own interest; the power and glory that then accrue, we understand as legitimate, and legitimating our God-like projects. Glory-projects have not and cannot have anything truly to do with the suffering, humiliation, and profound vulnerability that characterize life for most of the world's people. Nor do we want them to, despite a vague, chronic sense of guilt about that.

More surprising than the critical function of the theology of the cross, perhaps, is what it *announces*: that "God has become incarnate in the human Jesus, whose life—given the brokenness of reality—led to the cross."[17] Christians' claim that God becomes human, enters human history, in the form of a mere (!) human, anchors all other Christian claims. If there *is* anything to that claim, as Elizabeth A. Johnson puts it, "then it is very important to see what kind of human being God became. If Jesus is God with us, then his story is an answer to the question, 'Who is God?'... We need to put *that* story into dialogue with our own lives today."[18] People who take *that* story and those of countless other human beings seriously have much to come to know and much to risk in the process.

There *is* something quite radical about the notion that God reveals Godself in a real person about whose life, ministry, and death no claims to glory and power are made, and about the notion that God's human incarnation would endure a ghastly execution without a raised fist or a word of hate. No wonder Luther recalled Paul's words in 1 Corinthians, "God chose what is foolish in the world to shame the wise; God chose what is weak in the world to shame the strong; God chose what is low and despised in the world, things that are not, to reduce to nothing things that are" (1:27–28).

Recall that Luther's *locus classicus* for theology is the relationship between humankind and God, with relations among human beings understood as part and parcel of that locus. Luther's understanding of the faithful truth of Paul's words lines up directly with his understanding of theology's task and limits. Theology is not about *God*; it is about how it is with *us*—in the presence of God-in-relation-to-us in the person of Jesus Christ. This is not out-of-this-world theology; this is theology for real life as we live it, in the first, sixteenth, and twenty-first centuries. I wonder: Will we who are privileged ever catch the sense of the African American spiritual, "Nobody knows the trouble I've seen…Nobody knows but Jesus"? I fear we have become addicted to a theology of glory and the epistemology that accompanies it.

One additional observation about how Luther's theology of the cross functions: it helps equip us to risk living as if God really *has* revealed Godself on the cross. Luther contends that one becomes a theologian not by speculating but by living and dying. His own life story shows what he cannot explain:

> the profound correlation between the One who, in suffering, revealed to humans God's nature and intention for them, on the one hand, and those ones who, in their suffering, were enabled to know that nature and intention for them, on the other. This was for Luther true knowledge of God.[19]

For Luther, daily living—a constant dying and rising with Christ—is the medium and testing ground for this true knowledge of God.

CROSS-REFERENCED KNOWING: ITS ELEMENTS

My own "feminist proposal for an *epistemology* of the cross" continues to evolve. Its key elements may be summarized as follows:

• It *engages critically* knowledge claims made by those in positions of *power*. It suspects, with good reason, that the powerful often claim what serves to maintain the status quo, and deny, ignore, or hide much that is of great value. An epistemology of the cross identifies itself as an *epistemological alternative* to claims made or maintained out of power.

• It takes as its point of departure *lived experience*. This entails regard for the *embodied* character of experience; recognition of its *"given-ness"*; acknowledgment that experience is always *interpreted*; valuation of the *particularity* of lived experience; and finally, confidence that "to know truly on the basis of lived experience is to know *from the margins*: of life, of sanity, of dignity, of power."[20]

• It shares with feminist epistemologies great *skepticism about "objectivity"* as it is usually understood; at the same time, it has a distinctive, *partisan starting point*, namely, on the side of the poor, the forgotten-about, the nonperson. From this perspective it glimpses a truthfulness that is both painful and life-giving. Here, an epistemology of the cross "shares with feminist epistemologies the conviction that, to the degree that relatively undistorted and ethical defensible knowing matters, the place of the least favored—at the foot of the cross, in all its contemporary forms—is a better place to start than any place of domination could be."[21]

• *Accountability* is intrinsic to this framework. An epistemology may encourage or hide certain ways of knowing. Engaging critically with power-epistemologies that may hide injustice, this approach *requires awareness* of these realities. It also asks *accountability of itself*; no knower, no knowing, is innocent, unimplicated, in our shared reality. To see this is to accept accountability for who we are and what we know. It generates, finally, a *transformative accountability*, enabling and encouraging change toward justice.

A CASE STUDY: SEPTEMBER 11, 2001

What an epistemology of the cross *is* becomes much clearer as one imagines how it might work in a real-life context. Consider how the elements just described might have disposed you and me as "knowers" in interpreting the events of September 11, 2001.

Nearly 3,000 people died that day. Many were neither Americans nor citizens of this country. In countries around the world, families and friends cried out in grief when they heard—hours, days, or weeks after the planes struck—that their loved ones had perished. Governments sent official condolences. More moving, ordinary people covered fences and sidewalks in front of American embassies all over the planet with signs of shared grief. Not since the death of John F. Kennedy had there been such a global expression of sympathy for the people of the United States. We who watched and wept in shock and grief were—for a moment—one global human family, transfixed, horrified, astonished at our utter vulnerability.

Thinking through these events in light of a cross-referenced framework, imagine the questions to which we might have given voice: Why did we think we were invulnerable? Did these deaths really mean anything? (There were heroes; but so few of those who died, died for any good reason.) Did we have nothing to learn? What might we have learned if we had asked more searching questions, listened to those on the short end of the stick rather than to the powerful? And yes, the $64,000 question: Where was God?

Numerous national cable TV channels covered the story from every conceivable angle, around the clock, for weeks on end. Remarkably, no one in front of a camera or a broadcast mike asked us to think together—soberly, critically, tenderly, honestly—about any of these questions.

A Cross-Referencing Epistemology in Three Parts

An epistemology is an attempt—and only that—to attend to and reflect on a curious sort of activity: knowing. Knowing can be distinguished—barely—but not separated from what we are doing all the time, whatever we are doing. It rarely happens in a sequential, linear, or structured way; it is often circular, cyclical, repetitive, cumulative, selective, and is always partial, particular, situated, reciprocal. Descriptions of it do not capture it; they follow their subject rather lamely, reflecting only a fraction of its restlessness and its energy.

A cross-referencing epistemology—what I have called an epistemology of the cross—describes a three-part movement: coming to know what is the case; acknowledging one's implication in what is the case; and recognizing oneself compelled to act. Each one of these three parts or (to use a musical term) phrases flows from and leads into the others. None "happens" without the others, nor the others without the one. Their relationships are dialectical, mutually shaping, affecting, and generating one another. We will return to this point after elaborating what seems to be happening in each movement.

Part 1

The first part—*disillusionment*—refers to a "coming to know" what is really going on, how things really are, what is really the case. It may be a gradual awakening, a dawning awareness, a coming to terms, a raising of consciousness. Or it may be a rude awakening, as if one is shaken out of a deep sleep, or has had a pail of cold water thrown in one's face. One finds oneself saying, "I had no idea..." and feeling a curious mixture of chagrin, guilt, relief, and disorientation.

Such moments often occur unexpectedly: an experience of traumatic violence; a longtime job lost (along with pension and insurance) in corporate downsizing; a fervent prayer for a loved one's healing not answered; an encounter with people whose suffering neither heart nor mind can make sense of. Never-questioned beliefs tested and found wanting. Unexamined assumptions shredded. Illusions unmasked.

We resist disillusionment, especially when its occurrence reveals what we do not want to see or know: others' suffering, or our own. Our vulnerability to others' unpredictable selfishness or violence exercised against those we love, including ourselves. The limits of our freedom, our control, even our dreams. And the pain and suffering of others who turn out to be fellow human beings after all. Who would choose to be disillusioned, knowing what is in store? Whatever brings about disillusionment must be very powerful and—usually—unanticipated, or we would protect ourselves against it.

Cross-oriented knowing considers such disillusionment a gift. With eyes of faith, we see it that way, too, and thank God. The cross, after all, is the *last* place human beings like us would expect to see God, and yet—if Luther is right—that is precisely where God reveals Godself to eyes of faith.

Part 2

The second part of the movement is *epistemological conversion*, or recognizing one's implication in what is the case. How would it be possible for us *not* to be implicated in a reality as interconnected and interdependent as, in our best and brightest moments, we know it to be? All of us, each of us, "has something to do with" what is going on. Not one of us is *dis*connected from any of it; none of us escapes or can be cut off from our common reality.

Perhaps this is just stating the obvious. So often, though, the obvious is what we forget to attend to, or make a point of ignoring. As long as we remain reasonably comfortable, is it not unduly burdensome to consider ourselves implicated...in *everything* that happens? It seems to me there are a couple of ways to make sense of this. The first way is plainly, even scientifically, a matter of fact. Any one individual's implication may be minimal, he or she may have an almost indecipherable effect on everyone else's reality, but the world *is* in fact a bit different than it would be without that person's physical and social presence in it.

The second way of making sense of it, while no less matter-of-fact, requires a shift in consciousness and in conscience: a shift from seeing that everyone occupies some space somewhere, to recognizing that I am accountable for *where I am*, for the space I occupy. Those on the margins, those in crisis, those who suffer—drug addicts, homeless men, battered women, children with AIDS—"merely by being there, . . . call into question those who approach, challenging their 'being human'; and this radical questioning of what it means to be a human being serves as the historical mediation of our questioning of what 'being God' means."[22] Are these people really human, we ask ourselves? Are they really like us? Are we really members of the same—human—family? Struggling with such a question, if we are willing to take the risk, begins to work an "epistemological conversion" in us, begins to show us that we are implicated, that we *do* "have to do with" how things are in this world.

This step or part of the three-part movement seems more formidable because "conversion" means change—usually significant or even radical change—and because we often associate being "implicated" with the language of crime and punishment. There are no doubt many things we have done indirectly or not prevented from being done, whose consequences we would rather not take any credit for. On a very local level, these may include personal betrayals within intimate relationships; on a global scale, they may involve policies or interventions through which "we" (as in, the United States) have bent other peoples to "our" will, to their humiliation and suffering. To be honest and accountable about these things takes a good deal of courage and just plain grit.

Recognizing the mysterious but fully incarnate way in which God willingly implicated Godself in the life of the world, with consequences as unjust as (Christians believe) they are salvific, an epistemology of the cross inspires, perhaps even enables, us to be converted to the world we live in and to the neighbor who lives there with us.[23]

Part 3

The third part of the movement, *responsive accountability*, or knowing oneself compelled to act, issues from the experiences of disillusionment and epistemological conversion, but it also generates them. The more one pays attention, sees what is the case—in Luther's wonderful phrase, "calls the thing what it actually is"[24]—the more one is drawn into what is going on; the more one is drawn in, the more one feels, and then *knows*, oneself involved; the more one knows oneself accountable, the more one feels compelled to act *with* and *on behalf of* the neighbor(s) with whom one now stands. One could imagine starting out at any one of the three phases, or phrases, and becoming more conscious of the movement of the whole, and how each distinguishable but inseparable step affects the others.

It is easier to think of this third phrase as the one that involves action, *doing* something to respond to the suffering or exclusion of one's neighbors. The more I have thought about this, however, the more difficult it has become to draw even a distinguishing, let alone a dividing, line between "knowing" and "doing," or "knowing" and "living." This is not simply an intellectual or semantic difficulty; as soon as one accepts that there is a wide and rich variety of senses and ways of knowing (recall the earlier discussion of this), one discovers that, for all practical purposes, living and knowing are wedded. At the very least, appreciation of their synergy should require us to clarify more rigorously than we otherwise might what we are talking about when we measure, define, study, or evaluate "knowledge" or "knowers."

Responsive accountability entails solidarity with those who have been excluded, treated as if they are worth less than those who make and enforce the membership standards. Doing what is right should be governed by this criterion, rather than by following the rules. Insofar as living takes this direction, one must prepare to live with change, ambiguity, uncertainty—and in anticipation of transformation. Here again, Christians' formative story explodes off the page: the heart of Jesus' ministry, what he says and what he does, is the "reign of God," which is "very near." Was he able to enact the reign of God because he could imagine it, really see it, in his heart and mind? Preparing to do what disciples do—walk in the footsteps of the one they follow—means preparing for a cross-shaped life in a cross-shaped reality.

How to live with what we know? Freely.

A Christian's job is not to work for salvation, nor is it to save others—unless from injustice, suffering, loneliness, and hunger. It is to live fully, "a perfectly free lord of all, subject to none [and]...a perfectly dutiful servant of all, subject to all."[25] To the extent that an epistemology of the cross assists us in seeing what this might mean, it does its job too.

10

Reading Ourselves into the Cross Story

Luther and United States Latinos

Alicia Vargas

THE GOSPEL IS CENTRAL IN Luther's theology and in the theology and
spirituality of Latinos in the United States. This essay attempts to develop an
articulation of the centrality of the gospel and the cross from Luther's perspective
and a Latino/Hispanic point of view and experience. In doing so I will proceed
from Luther's definition of the gospel as the story, in both content and form, of
the cross and resurrection of Jesus Christ to the experience and appropriation of
that gospel story in the very life stories of United States Latinos. Latinos' way
of reading the gospel and Luther's gospel hermeneutical style find each other in
the confluence of the diverse narratives of marginalization and oppression of the
Latinos in the United States and in the appropriation of the gospel narrative of
Jesus Christ's death and resurrection in that context.[1]

NARRATIVE THEOLOGY: THE GOSPEL STORY AS
EXPERIENCED ENCOUNTER

The gospel is indeed the central item for Luther in the life of the church and
in the life of faith for both the community and the individual. He indicates
this in the early Reformation document, the Ninety-five Theses: the battle over
indulgences will be a battle for the restoration of "the gospel, which is the very
greatest thing" (thesis 55). Luther declares that "the true treasure of the church

is the most holy gospel of the glory and grace of God"[2] (thesis 62) rather than the indulgences that sought to draw upon the treasury of Christ's merits. Luther would never change his conviction of the gospel's centrality, and unpacking its meaning would be his lifework.

That unpacking begins, for Luther, with semantic reflection: "For 'gospel' [*Euangelium*] is a Greek word and means in Greek a good message, good tidings, good news, a good report, which one sings and tells with gladness."[3] This quote contains two distinct points, both of which will be pivotal to this essay: the content of the gospel, that of which it consists, is good news; an immediate corollary of this is that this good news is something spoken of, that is, passed on from hearer to hearer.

Essential to the content of the gospel is, for Luther, the form in which the good news is packaged and comes to the recipient. Indeed, for Luther form and content are inextricably interrelated; in the space of just two pages of text, he reiterates this crucial point four times: "Gospel is and should be nothing else than a discourse or story about Christ"; "Thus the gospel is and should be nothing else than a chronicle, a story, a narrative about Christ, telling who he is, what he did, said, and suffered"; "For at its briefest, the gospel is a discourse about Christ, that he is the Son of God and became [human] for us, that he died and was raised, that he has been established as a Lord over all things"; "The gospel is a story about Christ, God's and David's Son, who died and was raised and is established as Lord. This is the gospel in a nutshell."[4] So, for Luther, the gospel is the good news of Jesus Christ that is given to the recipient in story or narrative form and is passed on from hearer to hearer.

In between receiving and sharing, the gospel story is to be appropriated by the hearer: "Therefore you should grasp Christ, his words, works, and sufferings, in a twofold manner. First as an example that is presented to you, which you should follow and imitate.... The chief article and foundation of the gospel is that before you take Christ as an example, you accept and recognize him as a gift, as a present that God has given you and that is your own."[5] Appropriation, for Luther, is a two-way event between the Christ-narrative and the hearer/reader:

> When you open the book containing the gospels and read or hear how Christ comes here or there, or someone is brought to him, you should therein perceive the sermon or the gospel through which he is coming to you, or you are being brought to him. For the preaching of the gospel is nothing else than Christ coming to us, or we being brought to him.[6]

Luther is here anticipating what philosopher Paul Ricoeur calls a "narrative theology." Central to Ricoeur's concept of narrative theology is how a narrative has meaning:

> ...the *"meaning" of a narrative*... is not confined to the so-called inside of the text. It occurs at the intersection between the world of the text and the world of the readers. It is mainly in the *reception* of the text by an audience that the capacity of the plot to transfigure experience is actualized.

> By the world of the text I mean the world displayed by the text in front of itself, so to speak, as the horizon of possible experience in which the work displaces its readers. By the world of the reader I mean the actual world with which real action is disclosed in the midst of "a web of relationships."[7]

For Luther as for Ricoeur, appropriation of the Christ-narrative—Christ coming to us, and ourselves being brought to Christ—is meaningless if it is not really engaged. Authentic reading or hearing of the gospel is not a dispassionate, intellectualized "story-telling"; it is an engagement of the story of the good news of Christ's life, death, and resurrection in one's own life as really lived and experienced. Ricoeur is again helpful:

> The moment of understanding responds dialectically to being in a situation, as the projection of our "ownmost" possibilities in those situations where we find ourselves. I want to take this idea of "the projection of our ownmost possibilities" from ... [Martin Heidegger's] analysis and apply it to the theory of the text. In effect, what is to be interpreted in a text is a proposed world, a world that I might inhabit and wherein I might project my ownmost possibilities. This is what I call the world of the text....[8]

If this sounds like difficult and challenging work, this act of truly appropriating a text by genuinely coming to it and entering it with one's "ownmost" self and true being, that's because it is. Luther says as much when he talks about faith in the Christ of the gospel story in the opening paragraph of his treatise on Christian freedom:

> Many people have considered Christian faith an easy thing....They do this because they have not experienced it and have never tasted the great strength there is in faith. It is impossible to write well about it or to understand what

has been written about it unless one has at one time or another experienced the courage which faith gives a man [or woman] when trials oppress him [or her].[9]

For both Luther and Ricoeur, the act of understanding is realized only within the bounds of actual lived experience. For Ricoeur, the hearer/reader enters the text-world, taking personal possibilities for new life into that world, from which transfigured experience may arise. For Luther, the divine world, so to speak, as embodied in the gospel story of the life, suffering, death, and resurrection of Christ comes to the hearer/reader and is interfaced with, or incorporated into, his/her life through faith. That interface is realized within the hearer/reader's life as actually lived, experienced; and, in order for new life to come forth from the encounter, Christ's gifts must be experienced and tasted, actually and truly lived and put to use.

Experience for Ricoeur has a narrative quality;[10] so does the very being of the reader/hearer:

> To make a narrative of one's own life is, in a certain way, to posit a beginning, or several beginnings, a middle, with its highs and lows, and also an ending: one has completed a course of study, a project, a book. There is a kind of apprenticeship of beginning and ending and of beginning and continuing whose model is essentially narrative. But unlike a closed narrative, life is open at both ends—whether we think of the obscurity of our birth, which sends us back to the jungle of our ancestors, or that something that is not an ending but an interruption, our death, which is a kind of violence. This open-endedness places us in a situation where we can bring ourselves together narratively only by superimposing in some way a configuration with a beginning, a middle, and an ending. But at the same time, we are always in the process of revising the text, the narrative of our lives. In this sense, we may construct several narratives about ourselves, told from several points of view.[11]

In a strong sense, who we are, individually or collectively as a people, are the stories or narratives that we write and tell about ourselves. Those narratives contain shifts, changes, variations, and revisions throughout the duration and flow of our lives, and no one of them is given pride of place as the definitive story that serves to authenticate, correct, or rule out any other of those stories.

Remarkably, something parallel holds, according to Luther, of the Gospels, and, in fact, explains why we have one gospel in many Gospels. He writes: "Such a story [the gospel] can be told in various ways; one spins it out, and the other is brief"; the gospel story is "a subject which one describes briefly, another more fully, one this way, another that way."[12] The need to bring one's own life-narrative to the gospel-narrative of Jesus Christ in order truly and fully to appropriate it is well illustrated by the highly specific and strongly contextualized nature of Luther's own writing. His biblical and ecclesiological writings are full of discussions that interface the struggles of Luther's own life and ministry in his historical time and place. One can hardly read a page of his biblical and ecclesiological works without coming into serious contact with Catholics/Papists, Turks, Jews, Fanatics, and others, and the items of controversy over which Luther took issue with his opponents. Discussing the Eucharist in an anti-Catholic vein, Luther the radical comes out. When responding to the overly radical proposals of others, however, Luther's more Catholic side comes to the fore. Luther would advocate for the poor and those in need in his communities but he wanted nothing to do with radical, revolutionary justice of Thomas Müntzer and his ilk who claimed to represent the peasants. We can, *á la* Ricoeur, picture the different courses each of these sides of Luther's life ran as partial narratives of his life and ministry, or as narratives of his life told from different contextualized perspectives. Luther always brought these narratives of his life to his ministry as teacher, preacher, reformer, or writer, and his life and ministry always mutually informed one another.

THE CROSS AS OUR STORY

Lutheran theologian Gerhard Forde speaks, in terms very amenable to Ricoeur's thinking, of a merging of stories in Luther's thoughts on narrative appropriation. Speaking of what he calls the "cross story," Forde writes: "Luther . . . projects for us an inescapable awareness of being drawn into the event. . . . Thus the cross story becomes our story. It presses itself upon us so that it becomes inescapable. . . . The cross thereby becomes the key to the biblical story and opens up new possibilities for appropriating—or better, being appropriated by— the entire story."[13] Forde says that the cross story is the key to the gospel story. Forde notes: "The word 'cross' . . . is, of course, shorthand for *the entire narrative of the crucified and risen Jesus.*"[14] A quick comparison of this remark with the above-quoted texts from Luther on the content of the gospel reveals the close identification between the two stories; they are so close in nature to one another that "gospel" and "cross" can almost serve as alternate names for one and the same story. Timothy Lull comes close to voicing this identification when he writes of "Luther's passion for a grace-centered theology of the cross, and his confidence that this gospel is the deep message of Scripture when it is rightly interpreted."[15]

The gospel and cross stories are not simply identical to each other, but that is not far from the case; for Luther, the chief expression of the gospel story is the theology of the cross. Or, to appropriate a term from Forde, the gospel for Luther is "cruciform."[16] This is confirmed by another glance at the earlier-quoted Luther texts on the nature of the gospel: indispensable to them are the key references to the suffering, death, and resurrection of Christ, the cross-events in Jesus' life. The gospel is the center of Luther's theological thought on the life of faith, and the center of the gospel is the theology of the cross.

Luther's gospel hermeneutical dynamics parallel the Latino theological perspective on the gospel and its centrality. For Luther the gospel is the story of Jesus' life in a "cruciform" form, and it is appropriated in the narratives of our lives through faith. Latinos who are theologically related to Luther appropriate the gospel story of the cross in the narratives of our lives as community and as individuals in a context of diversity and marginalization in the United States.

Many have been the attempts at the very definition of United States Latinos. José David Rodriguez reviews some of these definitions by Latino theologians and concludes that "in describing the collective identity of Hispanics in North American society two distinctive elements stand out: on the one hand, the rich racial, ethnic, and cultural background of our origins and evolution; on the other, our continuous subjection to subordination and marginality."[17] These two elements define indeed our story and stories in the United States. And it is also our diversity and our marginalization that are the central and operative points of contact of our stories and the story of the gospel.

We, Latinos/Hispanics in the United States, are diverse in our skin colors, ages, political ideologies, economic classes, and religious pieties. We are so diverse we can't even agree on what we should call ourselves: "Hispanics"? "Latinos"? We all come together as brothers and sisters as we read and rewrite the cruciform story, however. It is paradoxically our diversity that actually activates our self-defining narrative and our mutual recognition of each other no matter where our "jungle of ancestors" is from, and no matter if we are first, second, or third generation, or if we have lived here since before the United States even became the United States. If we are recent immigrants or natural-born citizens, or if we are of Mexican, Puerto Rican, Cuban, or Central American descent, or if we are black, white, or Indian, or if we belong economically to the middle class or not, we all come together as Latinos in our marginalization and oppression. Our plurality generates our common identity because from any social or cultural location that we find ourselves, we see commonality within the experience of blatant rejection at its worst and institutional paternalism at its best. A university or seminary professor

who feels powerless to change a curriculum that perpetuates the marginalization
of her/his people; a factory worker who is prohibited from speaking Spanish on
the floor; a bus boy who is not paid overtime; or a Latino inmate in a correctional
institution who is overrepresented by his ethnic brothers and sisters—all share in
the experience of injustice and social isolation. In the United States, the professor,
the factory worker, the bus boy, and the inmate find a sameness in their differences,
find a unity in their diversity—unity and sameness that is most probably not a
given in their own countries of origin.[18]

Latinos share a "minority culture" within another culture that is dominant in
all the public aspects of our lives. As a community that has to try continuously
to assert its presence and voice, we come together in our faith in the Christ who
was also silenced and killed on a cross. We find our power to continue in the
struggle for self-affirmation in the country where we live within the resurrection
reality that abolished the attempt to exterminate God's hope on the cross. From
the histories of any of the countries where our families or we have come from, we
bring with us a long story of oppression. In most cases, the consequences of the
relentless oppression brought us here or made us a minority in our own native
land now called "United States." Across our diversity, we have brought from
everywhere our stories that were mingled with the blood of Jesus Christ.

In our present and our past we have experienced as a people and as a community
the difficult faith that Luther talks about: the faith that is experienced only in the
midst of oppression and trials, the faith that brings courage in the midst of that
suffering. We Latinos/Hispanics are precisely our stories of that marginalization
and the courage that we experience through faith in the gospel story of the life,
death, and resurrection of Jesus Christ. Our stories find their parallel in the story
of the gospel; our life of marginalization and death by oppression, and our courage
to hope and to continue struggling for our place and liberation in this society—all
of this appropriates the story of Jesus' own life, death, and resurrection. We bring
the "ownmost" of our narratives into the hearing and telling of the narrative of
Jesus' life. We are brought to Christ and Christ is brought to us[19] in our experience
of the gospel.

JESUS PRESENT IN *LA LUCHA* [THE STRUGGLE]

Ada María Isasi-Díaz proposes a *mujerista* theology, according to which Latina
spirituality is a lifelong project of *sobrevivencia* (survival) of the dignity and self-
affirmation of Latina women living in what for them is more often than not

the oppressive socioeconomic context of the United States.[20] In the very helpful ethnographic interviews that Isasi-Díaz conducts to document her study of Latinas' spirituality and liberating praxis, she quotes a Mexican American woman called Lupe who experiences Jesus' presence with her precisely in times of rejection and oppression. Lupe says: "[Jesus] is with me—we are getting *cachetadas* [slaps in the face] together and *aplastones* [crushings] together."[21] And Inez, a Puerto Rican woman living in the south Bronx, also quoted by Isasi-Díaz, is even more explicit in expressing the appropriation of the "cruciform" gospel story in her own life story. Inez says:

> Look, I see Jesus as a perfect example of *lucha* [struggle], as a perfect example who broke with all the institutions and with everything that people followed. I see him as a person who, in difficult moments, I can sit down, read about, reflect on, and it gives me *ánimo* [encouragement] to continue. He suffered; he is a person I admire and contemplate. . . . Every person has leaders, and I think that he is the principal leader for me because of the life he led, because of how daring he is many times. And sometimes when I am in difficult circumstances, I say, "In similar situations, how would Jesus have acted?" And I use him as an example.[22]

Luther said that the gospel story had two dimensions: as example and as gift. Inez is a perfect example herself of a Latina woman who takes Jesus as her *example* in the midst of her oppression and appropriates the *gift* of the power and courage of the narrative of his life into her own. The world of the text is approached by her and "understood" in her own "hearer/reader" world. The *ánimo* that she experiences is derived from the intersection of the two worlds, the two stories, her own and Jesus'.

Inez's spirituality echoes Luther's expression of the centrality of the gospel story and the theology of the cross within it. Inez's theology is not that of glory; the personal power that she gets to continue in *la lucha* [the struggle] is from the cross. The theology of the cross is also very palpable in what Lupe had said earlier. The *cachetadas* [slaps in the face] that she shares with Jesus, because he experienced what she experiences, is what defines her faith narrative, the intersection of her life and that of Jesus. In a theology of glory, we would sing the praises of our own works, but within the theology of the cross, United States Latinas find empowerment and liberation in Christ's suffering on the cross. Thus, the contextualized narratives of suffering of Lupe and Inez can be transformed into narratives of divine presence and inspired struggle for liberation empowered by the gospel story of the cross followed narratively by the resurrection.

Like Inez and Lupe, Latinos who experience the story of oppression and mar-ginalization are predisposed to the appropriation of the gospel story Luther-style. "Reading the Bible in Spanish," as Latino theologian Justo González proposes,[23] comes very near to Luther's contextualized reading and appropriation of the cross-story of the gospel. Luther, of course, did not read the Bible in Spanish or from the exact same perspective of today's Latinos in the United States, but he read it (even translating it first) in German with all of the connotations of the Germany of his time. He indeed read it from the varied contexts of time and place and political and ecclesiological circumstances where he found himself in Germany in the sixteenth century.

And lest we think that Luther was always in the opposite contextual perspective from where the struggling Latinos are now, let us recall other moments than his anti-peasant and anti-Semitic ones. In 1540 Luther recommended in a document entitled "That Clergy Should Preach against Usury" (or profiteering from high-interest money lending) that "we shall scold and condemn usury from the pulpit,"[24] that a minister should not "administer the sacrament to [a usurer] or grant [him/her] absolution as long as he [she] does not repent,"[25] and that the minister should "let the usurer lie as a pagan in death, and do not bury him [her] among other Christians."[26] This is because, according to Luther, the unrepentant usurer "serves mammon, he [she] is unbelieving and he [she] cannot have or receive the forgiveness of sins nor the grace of Christ nor the communion of the saints."[27] These harsh prescriptions may not make Luther a liberation theologian, but they certainly reaffirm his view that the appropriation of the gospel is to happen in one's life. A usurer that would have wanted to be buried in the church might have thought that he/she knew the gospel narrative, but Luther says unequivocally that he/she had not appropriated it in his/her life. And with usurers, or their updated versions of exploiters today, Luther said that one "can never be sufficiently harsh, for they have given themselves over to mammon and the devil. They let us cry out and not once enquire about it."[28]

On the right or the wrong side of the issues, Luther always has a radical stance informed by his own contextualized appropriation of the gospel story. A proclamation of the gospel story akin to Luther's contextualized style will encourage such engagement of the gospel text with the world of the hearer. The proclamation of the gospel to United States Latinos, according to Luther's emphasis on the centrality of the cross-story, will serve as a subversive encouragement that would empower us to keep struggling against subordination and keep reasserting our dignity as a people blessed by Jesus' liberating blood from the cross. The telling of the gospel story of the life, death, and resurrection of Jesus Christ in this way will empower Latinos to continue in the task of appropriation of that story into our stories. Many more deaths and resurrections will occur while the task of appropriation continues, but, no doubt, the Latinos are up to *la lucha*, the struggle. We've been there. We have died on the cross with Christ again and again and we have found there the hope in the resurrections that are the gifts from his cross. In that hope our stories will continue.

Figure 1. *Taking Down from the Stake*, Marian Kolodziej, 1993.

11

Imagining the Cross

Through the Eyes of Marian Kolodziej

Susan L. Nelson

IN JANUARY 2004 MY MOTHER died. Sometime during the year of intense anxiety that preceded her death, I began slowly to carry my tension in my neck and jaw. Six months after her passing, my jaw had settled into what I feared was a permanent clench. I could only barely open my mouth before intense pain halted me. I ate by carefully wedging food between my teeth—relying on my tongue to mash the food before I swallowed. Realizing that one thing could eventually lead to another, I decided to seek help. Fearing a visit to a specialist might result in surgery, and advised that my problem was most probably muscular, I sought the aid of someone who might address the problem of my jaw by attention to the complex web of muscles, bones, and nerves that constitute my entire body.

So it was that one rainy afternoon I found myself lying on my back on a physical therapy stretcher as a cranial-sacral therapist began her intriguing work. You are a religious person, she said (having read on my chart that I teach at a theological seminary). Perhaps while I do this, you can pray to be open to God's spirit working through me.

So she began. Only slightly manipulating my body, she asked me a few questions: Had I received a blow to my jaw? Had there been major trauma in my life? Had my mother experienced some sort of trauma as she carried me in her womb?

I talked and she listened—yes, when I was so very little my mother had been struck with polio and carted off to the hospital in a hearse (the only vehicle available in the midst of the polio epidemic). To my very young self, that had felt like a death. When my mother returned from the hospital, I am told that I bit her toes as her legs lay lifeless on the couch. The therapist, touching a place on my skull, said she could feel something deep within me. You are a person of faith, perhaps you can imagine the cross and picture laying your anger at the feet of Jesus and letting it go.

As a feminist theologian, I have for years carried on a critique of the cross as a model of self-sacrifice and self-denial.[1] I was afraid that her suggestion to lay my anger at the cross smacked too much of an unhealthy self-denial. Still, I was interested in giving the healing process a chance. So I imagined being at the foot of the cross and laying my anger down before Jesus. Suddenly I could hear/remember the words of Jesus spoken from the cross: Forgive them for they know not what they do. Surely, I thought, I can forgive my mother for her vulnerability to disease—it wasn't her fault that she had abandoned me for those many months in the hospital. And as Jesus' words became my own, I could feel a lessening of tension in my side.

On a succeeding afternoon, I felt compelled to tell the therapist, however, that while I thought it was helpful to forgive my mother (even God) for what had happened, my anger was very complex, particularly since expressing anger at my mother had never been an easy thing to do. Rather than thrust my anger at her, I had repressed it (she was already hurt enough) or turned it inward. Sometimes, I admitted, I even had dreams of wanting to push her over a cliff. Perhaps, I suggested, it might be helpful for me to think about expressing my anger toward Jesus (rather than my mother)—even punching him out.

Now these words made me cringe—the thought of pummeling the already bleeding body of the crucified Jesus sounded awful. But then my imagination took another turn, for I remembered that Jesus the crucified didn't stay dead! In some "trickster" fashion—Jesus was Lord of the Dance: "I am the life that'll never, never die."[2] And I realized that my anger would not kill Jesus (as I feared it might do to my mother). I could imagine him laughing at me for thinking that it could.

Now, while my particular flights of religious imagination might seem rather strange, in fact flights of religious imagination are very common in the Christian tradition.[3] The stations of the cross daily offer many Christians an opportunity to imagine themselves before Christ as he suffers on the way to the cross, thereby evoking compassion, contrition, empathy.[4] Hymns like "In the Garden" teach the believer to imagine that Jesus walks and talks with them. Visual images of Jesus throughout the ages have placed him in new places (Jesus among the burghers of Berlin, or a manger placed in a lovely Italian hillside, for example.). And teenagers (and adults as well) often seek to imagine what Jesus would do in situations like their own. While some might claim that the Jesus dressed in human imagination is not the real Jesus (Albert Schweitzer, after all, proclaimed that everyone's Jesus ended up looking like themselves[5]), others have understood that these visual images are ways of inviting viewers to believe/imagine that Christ is for and with them. Such acts can even evoke experiences of healing and reconciliation.

But what interests me about my experience is not only that the imagination can create such images and that the process could be healing, but that there were multiple understandings that the cross evoked. On these occasions I had seen Jesus both as one through whom I could forgive and also as one who could take my anger and not be cowed by it. But on another occasion in my life, when I was in the midst of great emotional pain, I wandered into a church just so I could see a crucifix—an image of Jesus suffering—and know that I was not alone in my suffering. Moreover, imaginings of the cross can take surprising directions. A student, resolved to finally end a battering relationship, has a vision of Christ on the cross looking down at her with severity saying, "I suffered, why shouldn't you?" Unsettled by the image, she meditated for a while until she told the man on the cross that he wasn't really Christ at all.

The cross, it would seem, is a multivalent symbol[6] with multiple meanings available for the religious imagination. This reality needs to factor into our discussion of the viability of the cross (and I would include with the cross images of the entire Passion narrative) as an image to speak redemptively to all people. It would seem that understandings of the cross vary (why else would we have multiple theories of the atonement?), that context matters, and that a people or an individual can imaginatively use the cross in contradictory but satisfying/helpful ways. (Thus suggesting that it is not the cross—a simple fact of history—but certain ways of construing the cross that are at issue as we consider whether or not the cross can work redemptively in all situations.)

The theme of this paper, then, is that the cross can serve multiple interpretive purposes, that context matters in interpreting its meaning and function, and that we thus cannot speak universally about the appropriation of the cross as a symbol in the lives of all people. I will also show that the cross can function redemptively to express an outrage or grief that might not otherwise have a language or a sympathetic hearing.

To make my point, I will focus on the visual testimony of one man—Marian Kolodziej—a Polish, Catholic survivor of Auschwitz. His work both places the cross in the context of trauma (a situation similar to that from which many critiques of the cross have been written)[7] and reveals how the symbol can function in multiple ways.

A Case Study: The Cross at Auschwitz[8]

When Marian Kolodziej was only seventeen years old, his native Poland was invaded by the forces of Nazi Germany. Patriotically attempting to cross the border to join the Polish forces in exile, Kolodziej was captured, imprisoned, and soon thereafter sent aboard the first transport to KZ Auschwitz. There he was subjected to all of the terrors of life and death that Auschwitz has come to mean to the post–World War II imagination: starvation, torture, hard labor, exposure to extreme weather conditions, brutality, death. After relating a time when, forced to collect dead bodies and carry them to the crematorium in a cart, he was irritated when some of the bodies would move because it made his job harder, he said, "Auschwitz turned people inhuman."

Mr. Kolodziej survived Auschwitz and became a set designer for the Polish stage. While images of the horror he had endured emerged often in his work, he never dealt directly with his memories of Auschwitz during his professional career. Then in 1992, after he had suffered a stroke, all the images stored inside began to pour out of him. Taping a pencil to his hand and lying on his belly, he began to draw. His agony became a line drawn with increasing intensity into images of masses of suffering people (Fig. 2).[9] As Mr. Kolodziej drew, he slowly regained his strength and began to fashion his remembrances into an exhibit he entitled "Plates of Memory."[10] The exhibit was then installed into a facsimile of Auschwitz Mr. Kolodziej had himself designed. There is much that can be said

Figure 2. *The Dance of Death*, Marian Kolodziej, 1993.

about the character of Mr. Kolodziej's work,[11] but for the purposes of this essay, I will focus on his multiple uses of images of the passion and the cross to remember and witness to his experience of Auschwitz.[12]

There is a strong tradition in Poland—drawing both from its Roman Catholicism and its patriotic lore—that suffering is redemptive.[13] During the period of martial rule that followed the shipyard strikes in Gdansk, Father Jerzy Popieluszko (a priest at the heart of the Solidarity movement) spoke the following words at a mass for the nation.

> Because of the death and resurrection of Christ, the symbol of shame and humiliation became a symbol of courage, of persistence, of assistance, and of fraternity. In the sign of the cross we seize today upon the fact that there is a great deal of beauty and courage in man. It is by means of the cross that we advance toward the resurrection. There is no other way. And this is why the cross of our fatherland, our personal crosses, those of our families, must lead to victory, to resurrection, if we join them to Christ who has overcome the cross.[14]

Father Popieluszko recognized the shame of those who are rendered powerless by torture, suffering, unjust and systemic systems of oppression. Identifying their suffering with that of Christ, he resolves the shame: your powerlessness is like that of the Christ. And, just as Christ's cross was followed by the resurrection so that evil and death did not have the last word, so by linking the suffering (the crosses) of the people to that of Christ, Father Popieluszko makes their suffering redemptive—it is an investment in victory.

In this theological move, the cross and passion of the Christ are linked eternally in the logic of God to the victory of the resurrection.[15] The part represents the whole, and one viewing either the cross or another's suffering interpreted through the lens of the cross understands the link. Suffering is not meaningless; chaos is not at the heart of things (an understandable fear in the face of radical suffering). It is a moment in God's work of redemption.

Given this cultural context, we must wonder as we consider the multiple uses of cross and passion in Mr. Kolodziej's work whether the cross and passion as he has appropriated them are intended to represent the whole; whether he intends it as a language of resurrection or transcendence; or whether the cross, standing in the stark context of Auschwitz, loses its shimmer of transcendence; whether the image intended to mirror the cry, "My God, My God, Why have you forsaken me?" suggests a flicker of hope (despite its context or even, perhaps, despite the artist's intention).[16]

There are at least three contextual layers to Mr. Kolodziej's work: the raw experience of the camps; the fifty years between his Auschwitz experiences and his stroke, when we can guess from descriptions of concentration-camp sickness that memories, images, and dreams continued to plague him; and the ten-year span of time in which these drawings emerged. We may question whether Mr. Kolodziej used images of the cross and passion to interpret Auschwitz as he experienced it. Some religious imagery may have been useful to him in his suffering. For the purpose of this essay, I will not try to parse which images belong to which level but will focus on the images as they appear in the exhibition. I will, however, note some sequence in the production of certain images for the exhibition.

Christ Crucified

One enters Mr. Kolodziej's exhibit through a dark corridor paneled in rough, dusty planks. On the left, one is greeted by Kolodziej's rendition of Grunewald's crucifixion scene from the Isenheim Altarpiece (Fig. 3).[17] Grunewald's crucified Christ is remembered for the human agony of the Christ, as well as for the starkness of the dead body. As Jane Dillenberger says, this Jesus has died.[18] So, too, in Kolodziej's picture, the Christ hangs dead on the cross, signaling to the viewer that this exhibit is about death. The starkness of the message is enhanced as the artist embeds the crucifixion scene in a sea of suffering persons. (Their nakedness, rather than the traditional striped garments, emphasizing their vulnerability; their skull-like quality suggesting Golgotha.) A broken clock taken from a crematorium clues the viewer that time as we know it was suspended in Auschwitz—the sun is

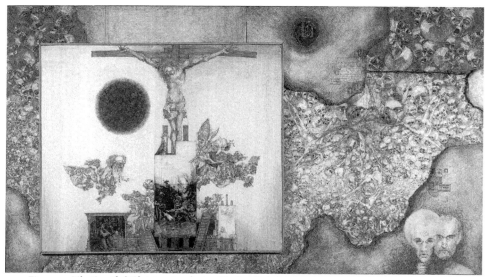

Figure 3. *The Crucified Christ at Auschwitz*, Marian Kolodziej, 1993.

darkened (as the sun often was by the smoke of the crematoria), perhaps a simile to the darkness that is traditionally attested to the time of Jesus' death.

The Isenheim crucifixion is part of an altarpiece—it is only a piece of a larger story it intends to tell—a story that includes annunciation and resurrection (as well as the temptation of St. Anthony). And death in Isenheim is not the last word. As Andree Hayum has shown, medicinal plants are depicted in the topography of the paintings, suggesting to the viewer the promise of healing.[19] If the residents of the hospital at Colmar where this altarpiece was installed saw Jesus suffering their same affliction (the crucified Jesus bears the symptoms of the same St. Anthony's fire from which the patients suffered), then they might also expect that they, too, would share in his resurrection. But Kolodziej's crucifixion stands alone—there is only death.

Surrounding Jesus in Grunewald's work are John and Mary and the Magdalen— all expressing the depth of human anguish. For Kolodziej this empathic anguish is missing save for the disembodied, pleading hands at the foot of the cross—all that remains of the Magdalen. The anguish Kolodziej draws is on the faces of those who suffered and died as Jesus did. One could argue that Kolodziej's use of the cross in this image, in identifying Christ with those who suffered, speaks not only to death, but also to the unjust nature of the death of those at Auschwitz.[20] Like Jesus, they were despised and rejected—with no form nor comeliness that we should desire them.[21] While at Isenheim the images of John the Baptist and the Lamb of God perforated with the cross and bleeding into a chalice point to the theological significance of Jesus' death, Kolodziej's picture holds no such promise of meaning. It is about death so massive that it belies any theological justification.[22]

Christ in Distress

There is an image of Christ found in the artwork of northern Europe that is particularly well-known in Poland. It is called Christ in Distress (Fig. 4).[23]

Figure 4. *Christ in Distress,* Marian Kolodziej, 1993.

Believed to have evolved from the tradition of the passion plays (where the beaten and exhausted Christ is seated while the cross is being made ready for his final torture), it shows Christ in a dejected posture—elbow on knee, arm holding up a heavy head, eyes sad and without focus. This is Christ where all vestiges of power and hope have been drained out of him.

Like most prisoners in Auschwitz, Marian Kolodziej endured brutal beatings and torture that pushed him to despair. (He told me that, in a sense, Christ had it easy: he had gotten to die.) The standing cell in the basement of Block 11 evoked fear in anyone assigned to it. Narrow (it was used to contain four prisoners with no moving room), windowless, it was entered by a hole in the base of one of the walls. Prisoners were forced to remain in this place for hours at a time—sometimes driven into it by snarling dogs. At other times, prisoners were taken to the attic of Block 11 where their hands were tied behind them and then fastened to a hook over their heads, leaving them to hang in a posture designed to wrench their shoulders from their sockets. Or they could be given tedious and seemingly endless tasks (untying knotted ropes in this image) with extreme pressure to complete them. In this place, Mr. Kolodziej imagines himself in the likeness of the Christ—overwhelmed, powerless, a crown of barbed wire on his head: a dumbstruck Christ.

Drawing on the Polish tradition that the Christ in distress represents the whole (including the resurrection), one might expect that Kolodziej's use of the Christ's posture of distress is meant to signal to his viewers that same link to the resurrection that the Christ in distress signals to those who walk the stations of the cross: that the suffering, while undeserved and thus shameful, is not shame at all, but the glory of victory. But there is something about the extent of the destruction, death, and cruelty of Auschwitz that severs the thread of connection. This exhibition, Kolodziej warns, is not about martyrdom. Just as the crucified Christ in our first image lacks the accoutrements of redemption, so the Christ in distress does not harbor hope (despair is, after all, the absence of hope). If there is hope in the viewing, it lies in the hearts of the viewers who, moved by the extremity of the suffering, resolve "never again."

But there is doubleness in this image. Could it also be that in imagining himself as the Christ—putting his face on the Christ—he suggests that his suffering is not uniquely alone? That the visual language giving it expression suggests something of solidarity?

Hanging Christ

Remembering his own experience of torture, Holocaust survivor Jean Amery wrote:

Whoever has succumbed to torture can no longer feel at home in the world. The shame of destruction cannot be erased. Trust in the world, which already collapsed in part at the first blow, but in the end, under torture, fully, will not be regained. That one's fellow man [his torturers] was experienced as the antiman remains in the tortured person as an accumulated horror. It blocks the view into a world in which the principle of hope rules.[24]

In *The Hanging Christ* (Fig. 1), Kolodziej returns again to his experience of torture, this time expressed in the posture of crucifixion. Actually, this image is not a crucifixion; it is a hanging, yet it is arranged in such a way as to suggest crucifixion. Turning the image clockwise ninety degrees, the viewer recognizes the cruciform shape of the artist's body: arms outstretched, head hanging, legs curled to the side.

Using the image of the crucifixion to express the reality of trauma is not an uncommon occurrence. William H. Johnson portrays a victim of lynching in the posture of Grunewald's crucifixion;[25] Marc Chagall portrays Christ as a crucified Jew in the midst of pogrom and the threat of Holocaust.[26] Both artists use the image of crucifixion to evoke recognition in their viewer: these victims are also innocent; their suffering mirrors that of the cross; it should not be. In Chaim Potok's novel *My Name Is Asher Lev*, the artist (a Jew) offends his community because he finds in the cross the best symbol to express the anguish he seeks to convey:

> For all the pain you suffered, my mama. For all the torment of your past and
> future years, my mama. For all the anguish this picture of pain will cause you.
> For the unspeakable mystery that brings good fathers and sons into the world
> and lets a mother watch them tear at each other's throats. For the Master of the
> Universe, whose suffering world I do not comprehend. For dreams of horror,
> for nights of waiting, for memories of death, for the love I have for you, for
> all the things I remember, and for all the things I should remember but have
> forgotten, for all these I created this painting—an observant Jew working on
> a crucifixion because there was no aesthetic mold in his own religious tradition
> into which he could pour a painting of ultimate anguish and torment.[27]

Kolodziej's image evokes a similar recognition. And yet this image is different. The suffering victim is not the Christ, but rather is accompanied by the Christ. Where in the hanging torture, two hands are tied together, fastened to a hook from which the prisoner hangs, in this picture the two hands (both stretched in an agony reminiscent of Grunewald's Christ) belong one to the victim (Kolodziej) and the other to the Christ who, wearing a crown of barbed wire, appears perhaps to murmur (or at least breathe) into Kolodziej's ear. Kolodziej's arm, suspended downward, echoes the posture of Christ in many renditions of the deposition—the arm of the dead Christ dangling like deadweight as he is carefully taken down from the cross. But in this picture, Christ is not dead and the arm of Christ does not dangle; it appears, rather, to hold Kolodziej—lifting him a bit in his pain.[28] It is tempting to place Jean Amery's description of the survivor of torture who, as the pain begins to subside, experiences a moment of ephemeral peace, alongside Kolodziej's image and wonder if there might be a correlation between Amery's experience of surviving torture and Kolodziej's image of the victim being supported, perhaps even comforted, by the Christ.[29] The Christ alive in Kolodziej's imagination is not arrayed in glory—but seems, in fact, to suffer with the crucified. What do we make of a Christ who continues to suffer?

Alan E. Lewis, in *Between Cross and Resurrection: A Theology of Holy Saturday,* offers another interpretive lens through which to view Kolodziej's cross at Auschwitz. Noting "the church's inclination to look for ways of blunting the cruciform sharpness of Christ's earthly destiny...," he argues for remembering the tradition of Holy Saturday—that time between the cross and the empty tomb, when Christ "descended into hell," where "he sank into an unimaginable abyss of evil and horror, to a point of measureless distance and unendurable separation from the love of God."[30] Auschwitz as hell! As human beings continue to create and experience hell on earth, might not the crucified Christ be right there?

Pieta

Marian Kolodziej entered Auschwitz with no training in a trade that might have made him eligible for work assignments that prisoners considered less odious. He was whipped, tortured, and consigned at one time to the cell of death (waiting execution for drawing plans of Auschwitz to be secreted away for the invading allied forces). He endured roll calls, never knowing when the bell was rung whether or not it meant selection for death. He watched as others were brutalized and murdered.

Kolodziej's images of this time seem to have been steeped in decades of nightmares. Bodies are twisted together in agony—the images often pouring off the drawn page, lice become monsters, Kapos take on mammoth proportions, prisoners open their mouths in a thunderous silent scream. These are the images that predominate in Kolodziej's exhibit.

At one point in his imprisonment, Mr. Kolodziej was assigned to the hospital detail where his job was to pull dead bodies off their bunks, spit on their chests, and toss them onto a pile destined for the crematorium. The whole process was dehumanizing for him, not only because of the overwhelming presence of death, but also because he had been raised to show respect for the dead. Then, he says, he came upon the body of his best childhood friend. Refusing to spit on his friend and throw his body on a heap, the young Kolodziej picked the body up, cradled it in his arms, and carried it to the crematorium himself. On the way he was stopped at a barbed wire fence by the sign "Halt, *Verboten.*" He ignored the command. In that moment, he says, he was free.

In his image entitled *Pieta* (Fig. 5), Kolodziej renders his memory of that moment—doing so with the trappings of Christ's passion. In the background, the teeming bodies of victims are shadowed to reflect the image of the cross. One body dangles, arms outstretched like a crucifixion; other bodies resemble the deposition; below the barbed wire the images call forth entombment; and then there are flames and smoke—the fire of the crematorium arranged to suggest the descent to hell.

Figure 5. *Pieta*, Marian Kolodziej, 1993.

At eye level as the picture is exhibited, one stares into the face of Kolodziej (his number 432, like the mark of the beast, inscribed on his forehead) holding the stiff, lifeless body of his friend. The cradling of the body in his arms resembles traditional images of the Pieta. Mary, the grieving mother, conveys to the viewer her grief—modeling for the viewer a response to Christ's death. Other artists have transposed the image of the Pieta to their own contexts to express outrage at tragic death (see, for instance, Japanese artist Taeko Tomiyama's *Pieta of Kwangju*, a memorial to the massacre).[31] But in Kolodziej's rendition, Mary/Kolodziej neither wails nor cries. His eyes, touched with the grief of the moment, show focus and resolve (unlike the usual way the eyes of the sufferers are cast down, shaded in death). "I didn't let this end the way it was supposed to end (and neither should you)."

The visual language of cross, deposition, entombment, Pieta are placed against a background of death. But the image has great light. Resurrection (does not the "language" suggest that is next?) is definitely too transcendent a term to use for this image that captures his moment of defiance, but it seems to me he is conveying here how, in an act of dignity both for his friend and himself, he was able to find or revive his soul.

Neither *The Hanging Christ* nor the *Pieta* were part of Kolodziej's exhibit as it was first shown. Looking at the catalogue from that first exhibition, the stark horror of death is what grips the viewer. These two images seem to be later—they appear in the exhibit after it had moved to its permanent location at the Maximilian Kolbe retreat center. Perhaps the addition of these images from the passion reflects the context in which the exhibit now resides and the community of likely viewers—using intentional Christian images to speak to a largely Christian audience. Perhaps. But these images also suggest a layer of compassion, resistance, freedom that for a moment seem to transcend the context. It is tempting to wonder: Might they not reflect Kolodziej's process of healing as he gives expression to images that have stewed inside of him for so long?

Bearing the Cross

In *The Broken Connection: On Death and the Continuity of Life*, Robert Jay Lifton examines the psychology of a survivor of trauma—"one who has come into contact with death in some bodily or psychic fashion and has remained alive."[32] Among the five themes that characterize the psychology of survivors of trauma, Lifton notes death imprint and death guilt (the other three are psychic numbing, conflicts around nurturing and contagion, and struggles with meaning or formulation).

The death imprint he describes as the "radical intrusion of an image-feeling of threat or end to life. . . . Of great importance is the degree of unacceptability of death contained in the image—of prematurity, grotesqueness, and absurdity."[33] Guilt imprint he describes as "the limited capacity to respond to the threat and self-blame for that inadequate response."[34]

> The soldier whose buddy is next to him, for instance, experiences an image that contains feeling not only of horror and pity but an immediate plan for action—for helping his comrade, keeping him alive, relieving his pain, perhaps getting back at the enemy—or at least a psychic equivalent of any of those forms of action. But under the circumstances —*and all the more so in a massive immersion in death (as in Hiroshima and the Nazi death camps)—both physical and psychic action are virtually eliminated* [italics mine]. One can neither physically help victims nor resist victimizers; one cannot even psychically afford experiencing equivalent feelings of compassion or rage.[35]

Figure 6. *Bearing the Cross*, Marian Kolodziej, 1993.

A survivor, then, Lifton notes, "feels responsible for what one has not done, for what one has not felt, and above all for the gap between that physical and psychic inactivation and what one felt called upon (by the beginning image formation) to do and feel."[36] The survivor's fundamental question, "Why did I survive while s/he didn't?" is an image-centered question: "Why did I survive while letting him, her, or them die?" It is a simple step—because the survivor was not able to imagine a reaction to the trauma s/he has witnessed, to the conclusion that "I killed him" or that "If I died instead, he, she, or they would have lived."[37]

Marian Kolodziej's witness to Auschwitz carries all the signs of his having survived a traumatic experience. There is a grotesque quality to his work.[38] The dejection of Kolodziej's body as he presents himself once again in Auschwitz suggests grief. His image *Bearing the Cross* (Fig. 6) captures many of the themes common to survivors of atrocity. He is plagued by demons (one of which seems to be swallowing the artist), haunted by faces of the dead. In the upper left corner, he implores the heavens for help while monsters surround him and no help arrives, thus conveying his inability to do anything. The vileness of Auschwitz has become a part of all. All of this he bears as a cross formed out of the fence posts of Auschwitz. He struggles uphill, toward Golgotha, but the end is not in sight.

His use of the cross in this image suggests his guilt; immediately over the head of the young Kolodziej is another image of himself taking a bite of an apple, conveying the sense of "the" fall, or his own fall into sin. His cross becomes an attempt to frame his suffering—the weight he carries—as an act of expiation. He said to me in one interview, "Someone has to pay the price." But whereas in Poland, as we've seen, the cross stands for resurrection—redemptive suffering— one feels in this place, instead, a heavy sense of guilt, perhaps self-blame, and responsibility. Unlike the hanging Christ, in this picture there is no one to help him carry the cross.

As a feminist thinker, I argue with this use of the cross. The guilt the artist expresses seems to me more the "false" guilt that plagues a survivor—heaping impossible expectations upon himself. There seems no relief for him in this landscape of Golgotha. But the cross seems to me to express a twofold truth: first, that the artist continues to struggle with his memories and his impotence in the face of trauma; and second, that his exhibition probably reflects both his impotence at the time and his agency in trying to alert the world as to what evil human beings can do to one another. Thus, as Robert Kraft suggests, while traumatic memories may reside permanently in the victims, the victims can use those memories as a witness to call the world to remember and through this action can experience some hope.[39] While the image may not be redemptive for me, it may reflect a redeeming process for him.

CONCLUSION

Noting the effect of trauma such as Auschwitz on its occupants, psychologist Ronnie Janoff-Bulman argues that trauma threatens the world as it is known. Human beings are psychologically unprepared for trauma, she says. "Our fundamental assumptions about the world and ourselves—assumptions embracing benevolence, meaning, and self-worth—generally afford us a sense of relative invulnerability."[40] But trauma ruptures our assumptive world. It "entails a confrontation with mortality, real or symbolic, and with our own fragility. Survivors recognize their earlier assumptions for what they were—grand illusions—and experience the pain and disillusionment that accompany their collapse."[41] However, Janoff-Bulman says, survivors can also heal. To do so they must find a way to interpret their traumatic experiences—a way to "reconstruct new, viable assumptive worlds that are psychologically comforting yet can account for their traumatic losses."[42]

In *Holocaust Testimonies: The Ruins of Memory,* Lawrence L. Langer explores the difficulty survivors have in finding a language to describe their experience of trauma. Deep memory (the memory of the actual event), he says, belies expression. Quoting Charlotte Delbo:

> I have the feeling that the 'self' who was in the camp isn't me, isn't the person who is here, opposite you. No, it's too unbelievable. And everything that happened to this other 'self,' the one from Auschwitz, doesn't touch me now, *me*, doesn't concern me, so distinct are deep memory and common memory.[43]

Deep memory, Langer says, "tries to recall the Auschwitz self as it was then" but does not have the right language; common memory offers a language that functions to "restore the self to its normal pre- and post-camp routines," but is also problematic for it "offers detached portraits, from the vantage point of today, of what it must have been like."[44] Deep memory thus depends on common memory to speak, but also suspects it is "knowing what common memory cannot know but tries nonetheless to express."[45] In his exhibition "Plates of Memory," Marian Kolodziej uses images from the common memory of the church—the passion and the cross—to express for himself and to his viewers the trauma that he experienced at Auschwitz.[46] The cross provides a wealth of meanings—perhaps a new, viable, assumptive worldview—with which to express his deep memory: the starkness of death, the suffering of those who lived through it, a sense of abandonment and despair, an experience of comfort/solidarity, a moment of resistance where he managed to hold on to his soul (resurrection), the constant struggle to bear his memories and pain so that they may be redemptive. The cross—itself a traumatic experience—serves then as a language for him as he seeks to integrate his experience of trauma. If the cross suggests various meanings, then perhaps that is an appropriate way to integrate the disintegrating experience of trauma—the world just doesn't fit together as neatly ever again.

If Langer is correct that common and deep memories stand in tension, deep memory serving to distrust what common memory would speak for it, then we might assume that just such a tension lies in the appropriation of the cross. Yet whereas the tradition has seen the cross as a symbol of hope—tied eternally to the resurrection and the promise of eternal life,[47] Kolodziej's use of the cross to express his experiences of Auschwitz brings us back to the trauma of the cross and to the deep memory that is the primary experience of the church.[48]

12

A Theology of the Cross for the "Uncreators"

Cynthia Moe-Lobeda

THERE IS GOOD REASON TO distrust many theologies of the cross. I do. To other theologies of the cross I owe my hope and therefore, perhaps, my life. The question is, "Which cross and whose cross?" A duo hermeneutic is the obligation of Christian faith: a hermeneutic of trust and of suspicion working together. Led by our forebearers and by Jesus himself, we are a critical tradition, testing our claims and convictions for the extent to which they either pass on the splendid Mystery of God's unbounded and undefeatable love for this good creation and presence with and within it, or betray that good news.[1] So it is with theologies of the cross.

Whose cross and which cross? False crosses have been with us since at least the year 313 when Christianity became the religion of the "known world's" reigning imperial power. The cross of Constantine, for seventeen hundred years justifying war in the name of God, was not and is not the cross of the God revealed in Jesus of Nazareth. The cross of the "white Christ," known most horrifically in the American slaveholders' religion, betrayed and betrays the cross of Jesus Christ.[2] That cross is present today in well-intentioned pictures of the Northern European Jesus, subtly linking whiteness with goodness and saving power. The cross of "bear your suffering meekly," "like a lamb," where it drives abused women and others back into the hands of their abusers is not the cross of Jesus. Nor is the cross of Christian religious supremacy, raised in towns and cities where the faith of Jews,

Muslims, or people of other religious traditions is denigrated. Another cross so focuses attention on Christ crucified that it obscures Jesus of Nazareth, the very point at which "the way" of living to which God calls us becomes most visible and intimately known. To subsume Jesus in the cross seduces us into ignoring the One who teaches us how to live.

The medieval turn to a cross that retains Jesus nailed to it, forever dead or dying, bears other dangers; the risen Christ, alive and breathing in and through creation is lost. The Incarnate One revealed today in a grain of wheat, in the touch of wind or sun on bare skin, and in human goodness, this Christ with us and within us may be pushed under where the cross holds Christ dead and captive on it.[3] False too is the cross that holds the second person of the Trinity so central that, in christocentric fervor, we forget that Jesus called us to worship not him, but the God whom he loved. As Joseph Sittler insisted, "There is no sense in being more Christocentric than Jesus was. And Jesus was not Christocentric at all."[4]

Indeed, false crosses abound, in history and currently. At worst, they have justified domination, exploitation, and dehumanization. The responsibility of "faithful disbelief" includes recognizing and exposing these falsehoods. Yet, that part of the life-giving story without which it would be neither the story nor ultimately and eternally life-giving remains central: the cross and resurrection.

We live in a world of beauty beyond comprehension, a glorious bit of earth and water resplendent with sight, sound, smell, and touch . . . a shimmering sphere created and destined to provide abundant life for all. I love to sleep outside so that when my eyes open, I see emerald and sapphire, or almost magical hues of grey, and my skin feels the breath of moving air. Often, I pretend that I am seeing for the first time the glittering of leaves in the light. It is marvelous and awesome, this fecund and fragile planet. The beauty within ordinary people—in their compassion, tenderness, courage, tenacity, and resilience—is another face of creation's splendor. When my perception is not clouded, I marvel at the depth of simple human goodness.

And this world is tormented. Our world—God's world—is tormented by suffering in multiple forms. This essay is concerned with human-caused suffering, more specifically suffering caused by social structures that bring power or wealth to some of Earth's people at the expense of others and of the Earth itself. Some theological trajectories, among them Catholic social teaching and some liberation theologies, refer to this dynamic as "structural sin." From a moral perspective, suffering caused by structural sin has two forms: that in which "we" are implicated—albeit unknowingly and unintentionally—and that in which "we" are not. This essay pertains singularly to the former.

Today, humanity faces a twofold moral crisis never before known: We are, in the words of John Cobb and Herman Daly, living toward "a *dead* end," destroying Earth's life systems, and building a soul-shattering gap between the rich and the impoverished. "The fact that many people of good will do not see this dead end is undeniably true...."[5] Hear it slowly: The human species, living in the manner in which you and I live, is a threat to life on Earth. Our numbers and our excessive consumption threaten Earth's capacity to regenerate life. God created a planet that spawns and supports life with a complexity and generosity beyond human ken. Never before has a species endangered that generative capacity. *We have become the "uncreators."*

Here I have not space to argue that claim. Others in multiple fields of human inquiry (the life sciences and earth sciences, ecological science, economics, Christian ethics, moral philosophy, and business, to name just a few) have done so convincingly. Here I simply illustrate the twofold crisis with the following voices, revealing first the ecological dimension and moving to the related challenge of economic equity:

The World Meteorological Organization and the United Nations Environmental Programme warn that humanity is conducting an unintended, uncontrolled, globally pervasive experiment whose ultimate consequences could be second only to a global nuclear war. The Earth's atmosphere is being changed at an unprecedented rate by pollutants resulting from human activities, inefficient and wasteful fossil fuel use, and the effects of rapid population growth in many regions. These changes represent a major threat to international security and are already having harmful consequences over many parts of the globe.[6]

The Intergovernmental Panel on Climate Change predicts that the world's oceans could rise by about 95 centimeters by the year 2100.... [I]t is an alarming prospect for many low-lying regions of the planet, in both large and small states.... [S]ea-level rise by even 1 meter will lead to astronomical human and material costs. For example, it could affect over 70 million people in coastal China, and displace up to 10 per cent of the population of Egypt and 60 per cent of the population of Bangladesh.... Sea levels rise due to the thermal expansion of the oceans and the melting of polar ice, as just one consequence of the ecological degradation that leads to global warming.... the primary cause of this is the overwhelming dependence of the world economy on fossil fuels.[7]

Consider also these statistics: "A child born in a wealthy country is likely to consume, waste, and pollute more in his lifetime than 50 children born in developing nations. Our energy-burning lifestyles are pushing our planet to the point of no return."[8] "Every time someone in the West turns on a kettle, he or she is helping to flood Bangladesh."[9]

The environmental crisis is linked to a global economic equity crisis. The United Nations Human Development Programme reports that "The world's richest 225 people have a combined wealth...equal to the annual income of the poorest 47 percent of the world's people."[10] For many, asserts Jesuit priest Jon Sobrino, "poverty means death."[11] Addressing this crisis, Methodist Bishop Bernardino Mandlate of Mozambique, when asked to speak at a United Nations meeting concerning the causes of poverty in Africa, identified as a primary cause the external debt—that is, the millions of dollars in capital and interest transferred yearly from the world's poorest nations to foreign banks and international finance institutions controlled largely by the world's leading industrialized nations. This debt, he declared, is "covered with the blood of African children. African children die so that North American children may overeat."[12] The money spent in debt servicing is then not available for health care, education, or food and water security. Bishop Mandlate's words ring a note of horror in the heart for those of us whose economies benefit from the capital and interest paid by the world's poorest nations.

The reality is gut wrenching for people of relative economic privilege who live in the global North, including me and, I suspect, most of my readers. Our lives are wound up in and benefit materially from social structures and norms that breed deadly economic violence for many whom we fail to see. And everyday life, in the ravenously consumptive and petroleum-dependent mode that we consider normal, threatens the web of life called forth by the One whom we know as Creator of all.

WHAT IS THE CROSS OF JESUS CHRIST FOR A PEOPLE WHO HAVE BECOME THE "UNCREATORS"?

I will argue that, amidst widespread and vast suffering in which we are implicated, and given the threat that our way of living poses to life on Earth, the cross is central if Christians of relative economic privilege in the United States are to *confess* faith in the God whom Jesus revealed and trusted. Luther illumines the implications of "confessing faith"—"If I profess with the loudest voice and clearest exposition every portion of the truth of God *except precisely that little point which the world and the devil are at that moment attacking*, I am not confessing Christ, however boldly I may be professing Christ"[13] (italics mine). Discerning what this means in our particular moment is the work of all who would confess faith in Christ.

Clearly the implications are infinite. It seems that "the devil and the world are attacking" numerous points of "God's truth" at this moment in the brief history of our species' presence on this many-splendored planet. This essay concerns two of those points in relationship to one another. They are the truth-claims that, first, God loves her whole creation, not only the one species blessed with consciousness capable of reflection on itself, meaning, history, and potentiality; and, second, human beings, created in the image of God, are created for and called into intimate lovership with this God. We are to receive God's love and then to bear it into the world. God's love, breathed into us by the Holy Spirit, is creating, healing, liberating, and sustaining the world. Said differently, we are called to participate in what God is doing on Earth, and are empowered for that work by God's Spirit.

These two claims, held together, are "under attack" by the way in which we live. Our life-ways are a menace to Earth's life-support systems (air, water, soil), and are generating a massive and growing gap between those who have too much and those who have too little. For many, poverty is deadly. To live in life-destroying or life-degrading ways, where resistance and alternatives to those ways are possible, is to attack the truths of God's life-giving, life-saving, and life-sustaining love for this world and of our call to love as God loves.

To confess the faith *at this historical moment* is—drawing upon Luther's formulation—to profess or defend these two truth-claims. We cannot defend them in words, if the overwhelming weight of our actions betray those words. To defend these two truth-claims means engaging the pan-human and interfaith "great work" of our day: forging ways of living—at the household, institutional, and societal levels—that Earth can sustain and that build economically just interhuman relations.[14] I will argue that, for Christians, so doing, as an act of faith, is made possible by the cross of Christ. Thus, confessing the faith today is made possible by the cross.

THE QUESTION AND THE PRELIMINARY QUESTION

One question looms: *How* might the cross and our understanding of it do what I have asserted: enable people of faith to work toward ecologically sustainable and socially just ways of life? How might the cross of Jesus Christ contribute to this all-encompassing transformation of society—this re-formation of economic policies and practices, political structures, modes of transportation and recreation, architecture, business, and more?

A response requires a preliminary question: What currently *undermines* our capacity to work toward ecologically sustainable and socially equitable ways of life? What disables our moral-spiritual capacity to live as if indeed, as we claim, God loves this good Earth and its living beings with a love that seeks well-being for all, and we are called to embody that love? In short, what undergirds our astounding moral inertia in the face of Earth's distress and the anguishing poverty of multitudes?

This set of questions—my "preliminary question"—is one of the most important facing humankind at this pivotal point in human history. The question defies simple resolution. Accurate responses will be, of course, highly contextual and perspectival. The context out of which and to which this essay speaks is that of United States Christians who are "relatively secure economically."[15]

That stage set, this essay proceeds in two parts. First I respond to my "preliminary question" by probing four key factors undergirding moral inertia. Subsequently, I argue that a theology of the cross could counter those four factors, thus enabling our capacity to live toward more sustainable and just life-ways. In other words, by indicating how the cross might counter the dynamics that truncate our moral-spiritual power for just and sustainable living, I am suggesting how the cross might, in fact, enable that power.

Four Factors

Multiple factors contribute to moral inertia in the face of economically and ecologically exploitative lives. In previous work, I have investigated two.[16] Others certainly include the power of sin in human life and the practical constraints of time in our time-starved lifestyles. Here I suggest four additional dynamics.

Avoidance and Denial of Our Participation in Structural Sin

Some of us are not engaged because we fail to recognize the role that we play in ongoing sins committed against the Earth and against many people whose lands, resources, and labor are enabling our lifestyles of outrageous consumption levels. We do not see because seeing would be too terrible. It would be too painful to acknowledge the truth, to recognize our implication in profound and widespread suffering and in that which threatens the life of the world today. Over 500,000 children under the age of five died in Iraq between 1991 and 1998 from disease connected to the United States' bombing (devastating water and electrical systems and contaminating the land) and U.S.-invoked sanctions prohibiting medicines from entering Iraq.[17] How could we live with realities like this, if we truly took them in? How could we face the piercing, life-shattering anguish endured by the parents of those children? While human life depends upon the health of Earth's life-support systems (air, soil, water, biosphere), "every natural system on the planet is disintegrating,"[18] due in significant part to massive consumption of petroleum products in the last fifty years. We citizens of the United States, with our blind and insatiable addiction to oil, spew forth over one hundred times the deadly greenhouse gases per capita as do our counterparts in some lands. How will we face our children when they realize what we have done? How can we think the unthinkable, acknowledge the utterly unacceptable?

We, not by intent or will, but by virtue of the social structures that shape our lives, are complicit in both ecocide and economic brutality. It has been said that "to be human is to suffer knowing that we create suffering." "We are haunted," David Tracy declared, by that suffering.[19] Knowing *that* we cause suffering is not new. Knowing that we cause this magnitude of suffering is unprecedented. We have no concrete guidance for living with this knowledge. Human beings are to learn "how to live" from those who go before us. Yet no ancestors have prepared us for this position, for this knowledge of ourselves as the "uncreators."

From knowledge of this kind we flee. *Not seeing*—moral blindness—is far more bearable. Blindness failing, numbness sets in. Where numbness thaws, despair makes sense. We retreat into denial and defensiveness, privatized morality, or overwhelmed exhaustion. Holy outrage and lament are dead before born, and we hide from accountability for systemic sin under the comforting cloak of virtue in private life.

Grave moral danger accompanies avoidance and denial. Crucial moral weight lies in what we see and refuse to see. When good and compassionate people do not see the consequences of life-ways we uncritically accept as normal, natural, inevitable, or divinely ordained, we simply carry on with them.

Denial of Who We Are as Bearers of God's Love

Others, who, in contrast, do dare to face their participation in structural sin, may retreat from public morality for an opposite reason, a denial of *who we are* because of God's saving acts and of *why we are created:* we are friends of God, beckoned and empowered by God to receive her love, and then to live that justice-making, mysterious, and marvelous love into the world. Life is breathed into us for a purpose. We are given a lifework: to receive God's love; to love God with heart, mind, soul, and strength; and to love neighbor as self. We are here to let God work through us, in us, and among us to bring healing from all forms of sin that would thwart God's gift of abundant life for all. This is our vocation as Christ's body on earth today. If the first factor is a failure to see the consequences of social structural sin in our lives, this second is a failure to see the depth and extent of the freedom for which God has set us free from sin to serve the God of life.

A Sense of Powerlessness

For many people, moral inertia in the face of the Earth crisis and the inequity crisis stems from a sense of powerlessness. On some level, perhaps unconscious, many of us perceive that something is terribly wrong; life should not grant unbounded consumption to some while others starve. Yet the systemic forces undergirding that situation and the Earth's degradation seem too powerful for human agency to impact. The sense that "I cannot make a difference" easily overwhelms, and with good reason. It seems impossible or at least difficult to trust that God indeed is luring all of creation toward the reign of God, and that no form of sin ultimately can triumph.

An Anthropocentric Lens

Finally, I suspect that the anthropocentric lens through which we tend to view God's indwelling presence may inhibit the moral power inherent in it. Until recent ecofeminist theologies, feminist theologies of mutual relations, and ecological theologies, Western Protestant theology and ethics have not taken seriously the ancient Christian claim that God dwells within, not only human creatures, but "all things." Failing to consider the presence and power of God abiding in "other-than-human" parts of creation, we fail to consider how that God-presence might nurture human capacity to serve God's work on Earth. Furthermore, anthropocentric assumptions preclude questioning the implications that ecological destruction might have for a faith tradition that locates Christ on the underside of power and in places of destruction and pain. Cruciform Earth does not appear where the abode of the immanent Christ is imagined as singularly human.

To confess Christ is to profess "that little point [of the truth of God] that the world and the devil are at that moment attacking." Today, those include the truths that this Earth is infinitely beloved by God, and that we are called to embody God's justice-making love in all that we do. In our context, defending those truths entails seeking sustainable Earth-human relationships and economic practices and policies that lessen the gap between poor and nonpoor. Having asked what disables our moral-spiritual capacity to do so, we noted four of many contributing dynamics. I am convinced that the cross of Christ and a practiced theology of the cross may counter these four debilitating dynamics, thus profoundly *enabling* moral-spiritual power to strive for justice-making, Earth-honoring ways of being human.

THE CROSS

What has the cross to do with healing these forms of moral inertia? How might the cross counter these disabling dynamics? That is, how might the cross enable God's people to: (1) recognize the extent of our implication in ecological and economic injustice; (2) claim our identity as participants in God's life-giving and life-saving work on Earth; (3) embody a sense of hope and power for that work; and (4) receive the moral power, motivation, and wisdom that may flow from the presence of God inhabiting "even the tiniest leaf"?[20]

For insight, we turn initially to the lived theology of the cross emerging in the last two works of Dietrich Bonhoeffer,[21] and then, briefly, to the long under-considered theology of Christ immanent in all things, as it converges with a theology of the cross. A significant assumption about theological method surfaces in Bonhoeffer's *Ethics* and *Letters and Papers from Prison*.[22] Reflecting Luther, Bonhoeffer demands and demonstrates that theology develops out of the struggle to live the gospel where it is betrayed in each particular time and place. Bonhoeffer was convinced that moral power dies when good people fail to recognize evil in the guise of good. He warns that the moral sensibility of good people easily is warped by their failure to recognize social evil "disguised as light, charity, historical necessity, or social justice."[23] Referring to "fools" who have become passive and complicit in the face of structural evil, he writes: "The fool will be capable of any evil and at the same time incapable of seeing that it is evil. Here lies the danger...."[24] Theology, then, must address the very points at which evil parading as good is attacking the life of the world, disclose evil for what it is, and counter it with prayer and righteous action. So doing, he understands, may be at risk of life, but is in fact life giving. Bonhoeffer's theological method, in this sense, enjoins us to glimpse the meaning of the cross, seek and see where the good news of God's unquenchable and incarnate love for the world is betrayed, and there act in accord with that love.

In *Ethics,* Bonhoeffer struggles to formulate four alternative ethical frameworks. All are theologically grounded and elaborate the following three theological claims inherent in the theology of the cross found in the later Bonhoeffer and in Luther.

These three—held together with a fourth—reveal a theology of the cross capable of countering the morally enervating dynamics identified above.

The Cross Reveals Who We Are: Selves "Curved in on Self"

First, people of relative privilege tend to arrange life around lines that hide from us the cruel impact of structural sin and our implication in it. Our media, zoning policies, investment procedures, commercial activities, vacation and recreation patterns, transportation routines, and other life habits shelter us from those realities. Theologian Simeon Ilesanmi describes the blind ignorance that accompanies economic inequity today: "Those at the bottom are very bad off in both absolute and relative terms.... The conduct of those at the top produces the poverty of those at the bottom." And the former can "avoid contact" with the latter, and thus avoid consciousness of their poverty.[25] I do not *see* the children of Mozambique, for example, who do not eat because their nation's resources go to finance the international debt, a debt structure that brings wealth from the most impoverished nations to the wealthier.

Bonhoeffer's theology of the cross—mirroring Luther's—counsels that the work and ways of God are revealed most fully in Jesus Christ. Moreover, in some way beyond full human comprehension, this One—while known profoundly in life's beauty and joy—is known most deeply in places of brokenness and suffering. Thus, we will know God and glimpse what God is doing most fully, to the extent that we recognize God in the goodness and splendor of earthly life, *and* allow ourselves to be present in profound solidarity where people and creation suffer most.[26] Where systemic injustice breeds suffering, solidarity means seeing that injustice and, in Bonhoeffer's terms, "putting a spoke in the wheel"[27] to stop it.

To be deeply present "with and for" beings (human and other) and places who suffer the ravages of systemic exploitation, and to seek its undoing, is to begin to see the world in reverse, upside down. It is to begin to see that ways of life previously assumed to be good may not be. Daring to follow the gaze reveals ourselves as a people so "curved in on self"[28] that we accept the reality of poverty and ecological degradation without effectively asking, "What are the political and economic structures that make this possible? How are our lives wound up in them and how can we resist?" If being present "with and for" is integral to a lived theology of the cross, then the cross opens eyes to who we are as participants in systemic sin. By enabling that vision, the cross frees up moral power.

Were a theology of the cross to end here, it would not be the cross of Jesus Christ. To behold in the cross the depth of humankind's corruption, and not our salvation, would defy the gospel. It is a realization too condemning to bear unless at the same time we see that precisely there, in the furthest reaches of brokenness, in bondage to evil, the saving Christ is present, is healing, is liberating. The only force that truly can heal creation is drawn instinctively there, and in that place draws forth healing power that we did not know we had. This truth enables seeing the structural brutality of which we are a part without being destroyed by that knowledge. Canadian theologian Douglas John Hall says it well: The central message of the cross "is not to reveal that our condition is one of darkness and death; it is to reveal to us the One who meets us in our darkness and death. It is a theology of the cross not because it wants to put forth this ghastly spectacle as a final statement about life in this world but because it insists that God . . . meets, loves, and redeems us precisely where we are: in the valley of the shadow of death."[29]

This claim is stranger than it seems. God's presence in the depths of our brokenness means that God with grace is present even where "I" am perpetrator of tremendous violence against others. God is present even if I continue with that violence, and even if I have no awareness of God's presence, and have no faith that God is present. A central message of what became known as Luther's theology of the cross and continued in Bonhoeffer's is that where God seems *absent,* there God is. God is hidden in God's apparent absence. The saving power of God is hidden in the form of its opposite (*sub contrario suo abscondita sunt*). "*Nothing* can separate us from the love of God in Jesus Christ" (Rom. 8:39). The power of this claim is immeasurable for those who have glimpsed even momentarily the horror of being an extravagantly wealthy Christian in a world filled with hungry people whose hunger is connected to one's wealth. This saving claim makes possible seeing that reality, rather than pretending that the economic systems that create our wealth are beneficial to all. When reality seems "distorted and sinful, and seemingly Godforsaken . . . a theologian of the cross is not afraid to recognize reality for what it is."[30] In Luther's words, "A theologian of glory calls evil good and good evil. A theologian of the cross calls the thing what it actually is."[31]

The Cross Reveals Who We Are: Bearers of Indomitable Love

This second claim also concerns moral anthropology, yet makes quite the opposite point. While the first revealed our identity as participants in structural sin, this claim reveals us as a dwelling place of the God revealed in Jesus Christ and therefore as *subjects* of Christic love.

A widely accepted theological stream holds that baptized followers of Jesus Christ live in a paradoxical moral reality, corresponding to the "already and not yet" reign of God on Earth. This has been expressed diversely throughout Christian history. In sweepingly general terms: we are alienated from God and as a consequence of this alienation, we will, as individuals and as humankind, betray (to some extent) the ways and will of God; we will participate in sin, live as "selves curved in on self." Simultaneously, we are saved by the work of God in Christ and Spirit. Salvation frees us for loving God, self, others, and this good Earth as "God so loved the world" (John 3:16).

I look for the moral agency implications of this paradoxical moral anthropology as it relates to the cross. While we are implicated in cruel forms of oppression, we also *are body of Christ on Earth.* The living Christ and the Spirit of God abide within and among the people of God. Bonhoeffer, informed by his biblical scholarship and his context, is adamant that the love of Christ—revealed most fully in the cross—has chosen to "abide in" the church (although not only the church). For him, as for Luther, the finite bears the infinite (*finitum capax infiniti*). The "finite" is all of creation. Yet, in a particular way, "the finite" is the church.[32]

In Bonhoeffer's terms, Christ's dwelling in the church "conforms" it to "the form of Jesus Christ," God's overflowing love incarnate as a believing community acting responsibly in the world on behalf of abundant life for all and against what thwarts it.[33] That action requires recognizing social evil, naming it, and "putting a spoke in the wheel" of earthly powers that demand disobedience to God. The power to work on behalf of others and resist social structural evil, even when so doing is terribly costly, is the actual love of God as Christ taking form in the community of faith.[34] Christians as objects of Christ's love become subjects of that love. Faith is both "faith in Christ" and "faith of Christ."[35] This is not, for Bonhoeffer, a matter of effort to "become like Jesus." Rather, it is a matter of the Spirit working to unite human beings (as individuals and as humanity) with God in Christ.[36] That God, who abides in the church, is a God utterly active in history in every dimension of life. And, *as revealed in the cross and resurrection*, it is a God whose life-serving love is indomitable, even when it appears to be defeated.

It is an ancient faith claim—that God's love in Christ is "flowing and pouring into all things" and there offers creating, saving, and sustaining power for the healing of a broken world.[37] Incarnate mystery lives in and among us as justice-making, self-honoring neighbor-love. The church today is called to rekindle that ancient faith claim, to breathe and live in the promise that indeed this God is incarnate in us—mud creatures of the earth,[38] gathered to praise God and "participate in God's mission"[39]—and, in us, is hungering and hastening toward the restoration of this precious and brutalized world. This vision breathes power to open our hearts and minds to the "data of despair"—including our implication in ecological and economic violence—and not drown in it, but rather enter into it on behalf of life abundant for all. In the face of hopelessness or despair, herein lies hope and power for living as body of Christ.

The Cross Ends in Resurrection Hope

The cross speaks hope in the face of despair. For many people, as noted above, moral inertia in the face of ecological and economic violence is born not of failure to see it, but of hopelessness; the forces of wrong seem too powerful for human beings to have an impact on them. Resistance and work toward alternatives appear futile. Despair is sown by a deep sense that things will continue as they are in this world.

The cross and resurrection promise otherwise. The power of God liberating all of creation from the bonds of oppression, destruction, and death is "stronger" than all forces that would undermine God's promise that all shall have life and have it abundantly. We have heard the end of the story, and it is resurrection. Soul-searing, life-shattering destruction and death is not the last word, in this moment or forever. In some way that we do not grasp, the last word is life raised up out of brutal death. In the midst of suffering and death—be it individual, social, or ecological—the promise given to the Earth community is that life in God will reign. So speaks the resurrection.

This message of hope also bears danger. It may lead people to abdicate responsibility for public morality, leaving it in "God's hands." Bonhoeffer's startling dialectic between ultimate trust in God and unwavering critique of liberal Christianity's *deus ex machina* demands otherwise.[40] His ethic of responsible action to disclose and confront evil is grounded in absolute dependence on God and trust in God. "I believe that God can and will bring good out of evil," he writes, "even out of the greatest evil. For that purpose [God] needs [people]. . . . I believe that God will give us all the strength we need to help us to resist in all time of distress."[41] Yet, Bonhoeffer denounces religion's pervasive proclivity for reducing God to "a machine for fixing life's problems" and for leaving action to the agency of God alone. He insists that God's power on behalf of the world is not that of a fix-it machine, but rather is located in God's embodied presence in and with responsible actions by human beings on behalf of life.

Christ Present in "All Things"

Multiple streams of Christian tradition, from its earliest centuries, affirm the *mysterium tremendum* that God dwells within not only human beings, but all creatures and elements. Hear that incarnational claim in a voice not widely recognized for it, Martin Luther: "The power of God . . . must be essentially present in all places even in the tiniest leaf."[42] God is "present in every single creature in its innermost and outermost being...."[43] God "is in and through all creatures, in all their parts and places, so that the world is full of God and He fills all...."[44] "Everything is full of Christ through and through...."[45] "All creatures are...permeable and present to [Christ]."[46] "Christ...fills all things....Christ is around us and in us in all places....[H]e is present in all creatures, and I might find him in stone, in fire, in water...."[47]

If indeed Christ fills Earth's creatures and elements, then the Earth now being "crucified" by human ignorance, greed, and arrogance is, in some sense, also the body of Christ. In every age followers of Jesus the Christ are charged with asking Bonhoeffer's question, "Who is Christ for us today?" Where is the cross today? Where are we lured into denying Christ crucified today? If Earth, as habitation of God, as body of Christ, is cruciform, and if believers took seriously this christological claim, might we be motivated to treat this Earth differently?

Furthermore, God as boundless, justice-seeking love, living and loving not only in human beings, but also in the rest of creation, implies that *other-than-human creatures and elements embody divine agency toward creation's flourishing.* Earth embodies God, that is, not only as creative and revelatory presence, but also as teaching, saving, sustaining, empowering presence—as agency to serve the widespread good. How might moral agency—power to resist social and ecological destruction and to move toward just, sustainable life-ways—be fed and watered in human beings by this God-presence and God-power coursing through "all created things"?[48]

These two notions—of Christ crucified in a crucified Earth, and of God's saving power and presence indwelling the created world—indeed may render moral motivation and moral agency for the long and uncharted journey toward a world in which humankind is not toxic to our planetary home and in which none amass wealth at the cost of others' impoverishment. Pursuing these theological possibilities at the intersection of cross and indwelling Presence may be key to a theology of the cross capable of enabling moral agency in the face of ecological and economic violence today.

In Sum

"If I profess with the loudest voice and clearest exposition every portion of the truth of God except precisely that little point which the world and the devil are at that moment attacking, I am not confessing Christ, however boldly I may be professing Christ."[49] Today, ways of life that we assume to be "good" are destroying Earth's capacity to sustain life as we know it and are generating a massive gap between those who have too much and those who have too little for life or for life with dignity. Two long-standing Christian claims—that God loves creation actively, and that God's people are called and empowered by the Spirit to receive that divine love and bear it into the world—when held together, are "attacked" by those purportedly "good" ways of life.

In this context, and in line with Luther's words, confessing the faith means witnessing to the truth of those claims. We do so by living *as if* they are indeed true. That is, we witness through conversion or re-formation toward ways of being human that nurture rather than threaten Earth's health, and that restructure political-economic systems that buy wealth for some at the expense of life for others. Douglas John Hall's interpretation of "confessing the faith" rings true: In today's context, North American Christians of economic privilege "confess the faith" when, by contemplating life as we know it in light of the faith tradition, "we are thrust into an active engagement with that which threatens the life of our world."[50]

This confession of faith and this ongoing conversion may be enabled by a lived theology of the cross. This essay queried: "How might the cross enable eco-reformation toward life-ways that nurture Earth's health and that build economically just relations with neighbors far and near?" In response, we first noted four key factors that may dissuade us from that lifework, four dynamics that breed moral inertia: (1) the tendency not to recognize our own participation in social structural sin; (2) the tendency not to recognize who we are called and empowered to be as participants with God in God's work on Earth; (3) a sense of powerlessness in the face of systemic forces that seem beyond the ability of human agency to impact; and (4) an anthropocentric understanding of God's indwelling presence. Finally, we called upon a Lutheran theology of the cross to overturn those barriers, turning for guidance to Dietrich Bonhoeffer and to the ancient Christian understanding that God abides within God's creation. The latter opens doors to sources of moral motivation and agency obscured by more anthropocentric notions of God's indwelling presence. Bonhoeffer's lived theology of the cross and resurrection reveals who we are as both perpetrators of systemic sin and bearers of God's liberating and healing love. And it offers assurance that—by the grace of God—our being the latter ultimately will triumph over the former.

13

The Passion of Christ
Grace Both Red and Green

Jay B. McDaniel

Consider the lilies of the field, how they grow; they neither toil nor spin; yet
I tell you, even Solomon in his glory was not clothed like one of these.
Luke 12:27

CHRISTIANS OFTEN SPEAK OF GOD'S grace. For some of us grace is primarily
a doctrine or object of belief. We assent to the idea that we are saved by grace,
even as grace has no correspondence in our emotional lives. But for most of us
this is not enough. We want to feel grace and to live from its healing powers. We
want to drink from the cup of salvation.

My aim in this essay is to present two kinds of saving grace that we can feel
in daily life: red grace and green grace.[1] Red refers to the wine of communion
and to the blood of Jesus on the cross, but I do not mean to limit experiences of
red grace to sacramental contexts or to Christian experience. It is not necessary to
believe in Jesus or even in God in order to experience red grace. Nor is it necessary
to be preoccupied with blood, whether life giving or tragically shed. When the

Buddha invited people to take heed of their own suffering, he was inviting them to enter the world of red grace, even as he did not speak of God or Jesus. Red grace is available to everybody. It is the healing that occurs when we become aware of unwanted suffering in others and ourselves; when we assume responsibility for whatever harm we have done to ourselves and others, some of which originates in unhealthy attachments to finite things as if they were infinite; and when we allow our own sins and sufferings to be transformed into creativity and love. From a Christian perspective, this transformation occurs through the healing power of God's indwelling Spirit, thus named or not.

Green grace is also from the Spirit. Green refers to the lilies of the field, to which Jesus referred when he enjoined his disciples to live simply and gratefully; and more generally to the beauty of the earth and its many living beings, all of whom God declared very good on the sixth day of creation (Luke 12:27; Gen. 1:31). Green grace occurs when we enjoy rich bonds with people, plants and animals, and the earth. In moments when we taste green grace, we experience the Spirit, not as a reality within us or beyond us, but rather between us. It is holy communion itself.

These two forms of grace elicit different but complementary ways of seeing the world. Red grace points to a tragic side of life that all humans must face at one time or another, apart from which there can be no wholeness. And green grace points to the sheer goodness of life, despite the tragedy. While red grace is usually serious and earnest, green grace can have a light and even frivolous side. While red grace deals in ethical categories, green grace is responsive to beauty. Both forms of grace are necessary. Red grace without green grace is morbid, lapsing into a rigid control of others in the name of being holy and pure; and green grace without red grace is naïve, easily lapsing into a self-absorbed narcissism. At its best Christianity is a religion of grace both red and green.

But here there is a problem. Many Christians emphasize the cross so fervently that they—we—subordinate green to red. We forget the animals and plants, the music and friendships, the laughter and frivolity—as if Christianity is *only* about sin and salvation from its consequences. The result is an unhealthy way of living in the world that is harmful to others, neglectful of the earth, forgetful of beauty, and incapable of laughter. My aim is to offer some ways of thinking about the cross that might help people appreciate its wisdom in light of grace both red and green.

I offer my conclusions at the outset. The first is that red grace, when it takes the form of sensitivity to the sufferings of others, is a form of green grace. This means that green grace need not be happy in order to be fulfilling. There is a harmony in shared suffering that is beautiful but painful. This beauty is part of green grace: the sharing of pain so that it does not have to be born alone.

The second conclusion is that red grace prepares the way for the enjoyment of the happier sides of green grace. This is especially obvious when red grace involves forgiving others and accepting their forgiveness. When we have been at odds with others and then become reconciled, we experience a joy that we would not have known otherwise. In Christian language, we have experienced our crosses in isolation, but we have enjoyed resurrection together. And new life, in community with others, is a process of growth and change, never the same at any two instants. Resurrection is a verb, not a noun.

Green grace, then, is not simply the grace of an originally good creation. It is available in the present moment as an existential springtime, a new life that follows a letting go. Usually this new life is forged with help from others: friends and family, dogs and cats, air and water, music and colors. We are trapped in forms of denial or confusion, and our friends listen to us and hear us into speech; our dogs need feeding and our cats pounce on us, reminding us that we are not the center of the universe. We might thank God for these blessings, but we should also thank our friends and dogs and cats. Resurrection, or new life, is not a gift from God alone. It is gift from others. We help resurrect each other.

This emphasis on process reflects two influences that shape this essay: the Christian dialogue with Buddhism, in which I have been a longtime participant, and Christian process theology, of which I have been a longtime advocate. Buddhists help Christians see clearly that human life unfolds moment by moment and that every moment is connected to every other moment in a vast web of creative inter-being. And process theology helps Christians see how each moment is also a place where we can meet God.[2]

BEING SAVED

I have said that we are saved by grace both red and green. This mention of salvation leads us to the question, "Are you saved?" Often, the question is a challenge rather than an invitation, and it puts us on the defensive. It begs the question of what salvation means in the first place.

Salvation need not mean life after death. Instead, it can be experiential wholeness—a harmony and intensity—that can be known in this life and that can be deepened after death. A concern with life beyond the grave is quite legitimate.

Many people die without having tasted a wholeness for which their hearts yearn. Other animals do, too. When the rabbit is chased and then eaten by the fox, the rabbit is terrified and does not want to die.

Nevertheless, the problem for the rabbit and for human beings is not exactly death. Each moment is a living and a dying, and we are never exactly who we were yesterday. The problem is incompleteness. Each living being contains an eros (desire or drive) to survive with satisfaction—to live and to live well—that is frustrated when death comes too early. This indwelling eros is part of God within us, and the desire for salvation is an expression of this eros. The frustration of this desire is what makes the painful and untimely deaths of children so painful to us, even as we recognize that the deaths of older people can be quite good. Accordingly, we understandably hope that the journey of life continues until satisfaction is known, at least for those who die untimely and tragic deaths. Thus, the hope for life after death is not necessarily rooted in a fear of death. It is rooted in a love of life.

If the hope is justified, we can only speculate as to how and why this might occur. Buddhists propose that the stream of experiencing is not precisely identical with the brain and that even as the brain dies the stream can continue in other planes of existence. If they are right, then life after death is a natural rather than a supernatural reality. It is simply the way things work, and as Christians we can rightly hope and trust that God will be at work in the continuing journey, until wholeness is fully known.

But we will not even recognize this wholeness if we do not taste it in this life, and it is the more this-worldly wholeness on which I focus in this essay. This salvation can be defined negatively and positively. Negatively it consists of freedom from what Buddhists call *dukkha*, which is another name for suffering in its many expressions: jealousy, envy, confusion, fear, self-hatred, depression, and guilt. Positively, salvation consists of what the Quakers call "living from the center" in the daily life, in a spirit of wisdom and compassion and in community with others.[3]

Understood in this way, salvation does not occur all at once or once and for all. Instead, it occurs by degrees. But one thing is clear: we cannot be saved alone. Part of being saved lies in awakening to our connections with others, cognizant that we are gathered together in a network of inter-being. If someone asks, "Are you saved?" we should not say "Yes" or "No." We should say, "Sometimes, but you better ask my neighbors, too. If they are still suffering, I'm not saved either. We are in it together."

These neighbors include the animals and plants, the forests and the rivers. There can be no salvation that is not ecological salvation. The whole creation, so often groaning in travail, seeks freedom from *dukkha* (Rom. 8:18-22). This is one reason why Christians can and should be environmentalists. They want to relieve the natural world of unnecessary suffering to which it is subjected through human abuse. Their activism is rooted in red grace. But ultimately this motivation is insufficient. Activism must also be rooted in joy: in a sense of the sheer beauty of a world worth preserving, not only for human use but for its own sake and for the sake of divine delight.

GOD WITH US IN OUR WALKING

In process theology God is within the universe as a reality who can be experienced through feelings as well as ideas, but God is also more than the universe as a transcendent reality whose wisdom and love are not reducible to human wisdom and love. Put simply: God transcends the universe and is immanent within the universe. Conversely, the universe transcends God and is immanent within God. In other words, the universe is more than God and not reducible to God, which means that it has integrity of its own. And yet the many inhabitants—the hills and rivers, trees and stars, people and animals—are inside God as part of the divine life. God is not One-over-many but, rather, One-embracing-many. Red grace and green grace are ways that we experience this embrace. They are what animate the life of discipleship, the life of walking with God.

The word *walking* is a helpful way of understanding the Christian life. After all, Christianity is not exactly a path on which we travel, but rather a way of walking that can accommodate many paths. As we walk in this way, we may have friends who are also seeking to walk in love and who will help us along the way. They include other people and other creatures. They are church for us. We may also have rituals, our spiritual disciplines, such as taking communion and singing hymns and praying before meals. But even in the worst of times, even when the human hands fall away and the spiritual disciplines cease to have meaning, we are not completely alone. God walks with us. One way that God is with us is by calling us in certain directions, relative to the circumstances of our lives. Here God is the indwelling and perpetually adaptive Spirit whose presence we feel through possibilities that change from moment to moment, but that are always in our best interests. Every moment has its calling. But always we are called to love our neighbors and ourselves. The heart of Christian living lies in trusting in this Spirit.

The very fact that we are called means that we are free. In a given moment we can choose this direction or that direction, and no one—not even God—can know exactly what step we will take until we take it. Scientists tell us that we live in a creative universe filled with quantum indeterminacies, which means that if the universe returned to its initial conditions and expanded anew, it might evolve in very different ways. Buddhism and process theology remind us that each moment of our lives is a quantum indeterminacy of sorts—a new beginning—that is inevitably shaped by the past but not entirely determined by the past. The script of our lives cannot be written in advance: not by our genes, not by our environment, not by our past decisions, and not even by God. The good news is not that God knows the future in advance. It is that, whatever steps we take, God will be with us in the walking.

This presence of God pertains not only to the present moment but also to the next moment. As the psalmist puts it, God is steadfast in God's love. This means that even when we fall down, even when we fail to respond to the call of the moment, God does not give up on us. Rather, God adjusts to the new situation and calls us anew, in light of what has happened. This is why we are free to acknowledge that we have fallen down in the first place. We can be honest about our fallen situation, because we know that we are not doomed. The love of God is not all-controlling; rather, it is all-faithful. No matter how we fall or why we fall, God will be present to help us get up again. Moreover, God is walking with all other creatures, too, whether they walk or crawl or creep or fly. Not a sparrow falls that God is not moved.

The defining characteristic of Christianity, then, is not that it has a monopoly on God's love or an exclusive path to salvation, but rather that it takes Jesus as its key to walking in love. This Christ-centered way of walking—the life of discipleship—does not lie in repeating the beliefs or imitating every action of Jesus. Rather, it lies in being open to God in our way and our time as Jesus was in his way and his time, thus extending his healing ministry.

JESUS ON THE CROSS: A WINDOW TO ALL SUFFERING

Jesus' own footsteps took him to a cross. After he died many Christians came to believe that God knew about this cross all along, long before the world was created, and that it was part of a timeless plan. They said—and still say—that God created the world knowing that humans would sin and that these sins would need to be redeemed by a crucifixion. Without this death, they say, human beings could not stand in God's presence at the end of time. In order to stand in God's presence we must be washed in the blood.   .

But this depicts God on the analogy of a political dictator who is too pure to be in the presence of unwashed people. God instead embraces the unwashed from the outset, and we can point to Jesus for support. He took a very strong liking to dirty people, helping people of his time break free from a purity code that separates clean from unclean. He was interested in downward mobility, in identification with the least of these, and displayed a divine reality with similar interests. He hoped others might identify with them, too. Why, then, did he walk toward the cross?

It seems plausible that the idea of dying on a cross emerged for Jesus as it became apparent to him that many around him were not going to hear his call to love. In voluntarily accepting his death, his aim was not to appease God, as if God was unable or unwilling to forgive unless a death occurred. Rather, Jesus' aim was to reveal a deeper dimension of what it means to walk with God. It is to walk in love and to refuse to avenge violence by violence.

If there is wisdom in this alternative way of thinking about the cross, it is important to remember Jesus was not the only person nailed to a cross. Others, too, were crucified by Roman authorities, including two people beside him. Moreover, as painful as it must be to die in this way, crucifixion is not necessarily the most painful form of dying. It took Jesus several hours to die; it has taken tortured prisoners in jails days and months to die, often in excruciating pain both mental and physical. Christians do these others a disservice by saying that no one has suffered as Jesus suffered. Jesus' suffering is best understood, not as the most extreme suffering that anyone has ever undergone, but as a *window to all suffering that anyone has to undergo*. It is like the first noble truth of Buddhism. In order to grow in the spiritual life, we must first look at suffering itself, because this is the root of the problem.

THE CROSS, SUFFERING, AND SYMPATHETIC ACTION

The cross can be approached in various ways, some empowering and some disempowering, and thus the cross holds ambiguous meaning for many Christians today. For a woman who has been living under the rule of an abusive spouse, the cross can be dangerous if interpreted as a call to share in Jesus' suffering. And yet there are certainly times in our lives when we rightly and willingly undergo suffering and endure difficult situations, when in principle we could take an ostensibly easier road. Consider what happens when our loved ones are suffering from debilitating and terminal diseases and they cannot be "fixed" or "cured." The best we can do is to share in their suffering and be with them in a comforting way. Rather than leaving the cross behind, we carry one with them in order to lighten their load. When it comes to the cross and its relevance to human life, *everything* depends on context. Thus, the question emerges: Can *carrying the cross of Jesus* be understood in more active terms, such that, in some circumstances, we carry the cross by learning to love ourselves and to say no to others, including those who harm us?

Perhaps Jesus provides an example. He had to love himself enough to want to be God's messenger, despite more immediate inclinations to the contrary. He had to say no to those who encouraged him to avoid the cross and also no to those feelings inside himself that said the same. If he truly didn't care about himself or his vocation in life, he could have fled to the desert for the rest of his days. Jesus may have felt called to sacrifice his physical well-being for the sake of a larger vocation. But if the deeper call of God—for Jesus and for others—is a call to love, perhaps one can be called to love in different ways: love displayed in self-sacrifice and love displayed in a call to love oneself.

In the twentieth century many theologians have said that Christian love is primarily or exclusively agape. They have defined agape in many ways: as "acting for the sake of the beloved" and as "doing good" and as "self-giving" and as "selfless altruism." And they have distinguished agape from erotic and friendship love by saying that the latter involve personal fulfillment and a sense that the other has value worth appreciating. Agape has been said to have been "above all this," precisely because it lacks any sense of self-satisfaction and appreciation of the value of the beloved.[4]

In more recent times, though, Protestants and Catholics are criticizing this preoccupation with agape. They have criticized the idea that Christian love is exclusively self-sacrificial and neglectful of the value of the other; and they have affirmed that friendship and erotic affection are indeed part of healthy Christian love. In *Love: Human and Divine*, for example, the Catholic writer Edward Vacek argues that God loves the world through friendship and erotic affection as well as through agape, and that Christians themselves are called to embrace all three types.[5]

An evangelical process theologian, Thomas Oord, adds to the spirit of Vacek's approach in a way helpful to our concerns. Oord bypasses sharp distinctions between self-sacrificial love and self-fulfilling love, between other-regarding love and self-satisfying love, and offers an operational definition of love that can be helpful to Christians seeking to understand the kind of love that sympathy for the cross might elicit. To love, he says, "is to act intentionally, in sympathetic response to others, including God, to promote overall well-being."[6] Of course, at face value this definition does not say very much about self-love. But Oord quickly adds that the *others* whom we can love include ourselves. When we appreciate our own achievements in the past, for example, acknowledging some good we have accomplished, we are appreciating who we have been. And when we act for the sake of our own well-being in the future, we are respecting who we can be. Not only others, but we ourselves, are worthy of our love. Intentional action that promotes overall well-being involves caring enough about who I can be in the future to move beyond who I have been in the past. In the case of an abused woman, heavenly love has not initiated the abuse and it cannot prevent it. But it can help her step out of it.

DEATH AND RESURRECTION

For many people, this stepping out of suffering involves coming to grips with it first. It involves a taste of red grace. But this taste has three portions. Red grace occurs (1) when we are mindfully present to the suffering that lies within us and in others; (2) when we acknowledge the ways in which, in some circumstances, we are responsible for some of this suffering that we experience in ourselves and others; and (3) when we allow both of these realities—the suffering and the sin—to help us grow in our capacities for wise and compassionate living, as precipitated by a "letting go" of attachment to finite things as if they were infinite.

The first face—*a mindful presence to suffering*—is important because sometimes we hide from the suffering of others and also from our own, in which case no growth is possible. This hiding can take the form of emotional anesthesia, in which case we actively block out suffering; or it can take the form of debilitating numbness, in which case we hurt so deeply that we cannot feel the pain anymore. Either way it is important, when the time is right, to look at the pain from which we hide. Red grace is the freedom to look at suffering.

The second face—*acknowledging our complicity in suffering*—is important because sometimes, even when we are aware of suffering, we pretend that all of it—whether undergone by ourselves or by others—is the result of others' doing. If we are victimizers, we hide from the fact that we are harming others. We pretend that we are not hurting anyone. On the other hand, if we are victims, we may hide from the fact that, even as others may harm us, we have freedom in how we respond to what they do, either inwardly or outwardly, apart from which we harm ourselves. And if we are ordinary people, we hide from the fact that most of us are hybrids: both victimizers and victims. Red grace is the freedom to accept responsibility for whatever suffering we cause to others and to ourselves.

The third face—*allowing suffering and sin to be transformed into creativity and love*—is important because, in point of fact, we cannot transform suffering and sin all by ourselves. The transformation process occurs only when we let go of the illusion that we are masters of our destiny and thus open ourselves to a healing Spirit at work in the world, within us yet beyond us, whose very nature is to bring new life into the world, moment by moment. In Christianity, of course, this healing Spirit is named God and our openness to it is called faith. Many Protestant Christians emphasize that, in the last analysis, we are saved by grace through faith rather than good works. Here faith need not mean intellectual assent to verbal propositions but rather trust in something more—a pervasive yet nonmanipulative Spirit—that is healing and whole making. Even people who do not believe in God can trust in this Spirit. Red grace is trust in the Spirit.

This trust involves and requires a letting go: that is, a relinquishment of attachment to finite things as if they were infinite. Most of these finite things are inside us. They include legitimate psychological needs that have become central organizing principles of our lives and thus compulsions. Examples include a need to be needed, to receive approval from others, to be perceived as unique and special, to be in control, to be perfectly responsible, to avoid suffering at all costs, to avoid conflict, or to engage in conflict. When we live from a deeper center—when we live from the Spirit—these psychological needs have their rightful place in our lives, each appropriate in different circumstances. But when we allow them to control us, we must let go of them, and the letting go is painful. As Jesus lay dying on the cross, he had to let go of his own need to be in control of his destiny. It was not easy for him and he felt forsaken, even by God. In the case of the woman being abused by her husband, she must let go of her need to be needed by her husband and of her fear of what will happen if she leaves him. At the heart of red grace, though, is the trust that, if we let go, new life will arise in our hearts. Letting go is openness to resurrection, to green grace.

Green grace, then, is the resurrected life itself. We recall Jesus' admonition to consider the lilies of the field but also the quip of Emily Dickinson, who once said that considering the lilies is the only commandment she ever consistently obeyed. To obey this commandment is to seek and enjoy rich bonds with the rest of creation, including animals, plants, other people, and ourselves. Here the word *rich* is a synonym for harmony and intensity.

Harmony consists of rapport or communion with others, including oneself. Especially in relation to people and other living beings, this harmony necessarily includes a respect for differences. Even as we might feel at one with other people, for example, we must also feel *at two* with them so that they can be themselves. This is why *rapport* is a better word than *oneness* to name the harmonious side of richness. Moreover, harmony can include disharmony. Just as in music there needs to be dissonance in order for there to be consonance, so in harmonious relations with others there needs to be tension in order for there to be rapport. Not only sympathy, but also humor, is an important part of harmony.

Intensity has two aspects: receptive and active. Receptively, intensity lies in feeling with others in intense ways, such that they inwardly affect us in ways that enliven our own lives. Certainly this can include sharing in the sufferings of others, in which case the intensity is both painful and satisfying. Nevertheless, sharing in the experiences of others in intense ways is by no means reducible to suffering. We can also share in the happiness of others, and sometimes, for those of us who are burdened by envy, this can be much more difficult. It is no accident, then, that some Buddhists say that sympathetic joy is the most difficult form of love. In any case, for most of us the most intimate expressions of green grace will lie in healthy relations with people: with friends and family, for example. But in our time there is a profound need to remember our bonds with the more-than-human world. Red grace can only take us so far in this remembrance. It helps us understand that we are connected with all creatures of the flesh who suffer and that we share a common plight. Green grace, however, helps us revel in beauty. The enjoyment of green grace includes a sense of sacred awe in the presence of the heavens; a sense of kinship with other living beings; a sense of belonging to a particular portion of land; a healthy relation to our own body; the enjoyment of companionship with other animals. If the calling of our time is to help build communities that are socially just, ecologically sustainable, and spiritually satisfying for all, then the all must include the other living beings. We find our home in this more inclusive consciousness by opening ourselves to green grace. The world cannot be saved by moral earnestness alone. It must also be saved by delight in beauty.

The hope for Christians, then, is that we can live balanced lives in openness to grace both red and green. If we know red grace without green grace, we become preoccupied with sin and suffering at the expense of recognizing the more delightful sides of life. We can share in the sufferings of others but we cannot dance barefoot in the moonlight. If we know green grace without red grace, we neglect the suffering that comes from sharing in the suffering of others and we ignore our own complicity in some of that suffering. We can dance in the moonlight but we cannot take responsibility for our actions. A walk with God includes both kinds of grace, both of which are ways of sharing in the passion of Jesus. We share in his passion on the cross, to be sure, and know the wisdom of red grace. But we experience green grace when we share in his passion for beloved community. The passion of Jesus is more than what happened on the cross. It is also what happened when he turned water into wine at weddings and considered the lilies of the field. The calling of the Christian, saved by these two forms of grace, is to live and die daily with Christ, not only by sharing in suffering, but by enjoying the taste of new wine.

Part Three

The Cross: Imperialism, Violence, and Peace

14

Saved by What Shouldn't Happen

The Anti-Sacrificial Meaning of the Cross

S. Mark Heim

THE ATONEMENT HAS TWO FACES.[1] Numberless people attribute saving transformations in their lives to a belief that Christ died for them, and profess the work of the cross to be the heart and soul of historical Christian faith. Uncounted others see a long list of good reasons to be uncomfortable with the doctrine of substitutionary atonement and to suspect there is something terribly amiss at the very heart of atonement theology generally. Some people belong to both groups at once. This tension, the insistence that atonement must be either the best or the worst feature of Christian faith, or some curious combination of both, is itself a reality in need of explanation.

ADDING UP THE PROBLEMS

The objections to atonement theology are closely woven into troublesome questions about Christianity as a whole. The objections themselves are marked by a curious double-sidedness. Let us consider a few of them. First, few can be unaware that the cross has been the cornerstone of Christian anti-Semitism. The libel that charges Jews with the collective responsibility for Jesus' death draws its virulent strength from the companion assumption that this death was uniquely horrible and uniquely important. Behind this historical evil lie several odd tensions. One is that Christians insist Jesus' death is caused by (and is God's response to) universal human sin, while the "deicide" (killing God) charge turns on the contradictory claim that the Jews alone are implicated in his killing. Another tension is that while Christian anti-Semitism is at times seen as illustrative of a general human propensity to demonize others, it is at the same time often viewed as an unparalleled and distinctive evil, rooted not in generic human failings but in sources peculiar to Christian faith itself.

Second, the language of sacrifice strikes many as empty because it is unintelligible, or offensive because it is morally primitive. The first time I visited the Kali temple in Calcutta, I literally stepped in pools of blood from a sacrificed goat. I was shocked, but I saw the irony in that shock. I had attended Christian worship services all my life that talked and sang regularly about blood. I had never walked away with any on my shoes before. In actual belief, most people are no more likely to regard Christ as a sin-offering who removes our guilt than they are to consider sacrificing oxen on an altar in the neighborhood playground as a way to keep their children safe. Christians frequently conjure up an idea of sacrifice that we can half-believe long enough to attribute meaning to Christ's death. Once it has served that transitory purpose, we drop it as swiftly as possible, since we have no wider use for the category and don't know how to make sense of it. The tension is that Christians seem compelled to understand Jesus' death in terms drawn from the ubiquitous human practice of sacrifice, but at the same time are compelled to recoil from explaining its power simply as an example of the same mechanism found in that practice. This ambivalence goes to the root of the sources themselves. The New Testament insists on setting the cross in a sacrificial frame while it insists no less on removing it from that frame with contentions that it marks the end of sacrifice, the final sacrifice.

Third, an awareness of world religions and mythology has put Jesus' death in an unavoidably comparative context. The Gospels attribute decisive significance to the cross. Yet, since the rise of modern anthropology we know that tales of dying and rising gods are commonplace. Christians are charged with the nearsightedness that comes from standing too close to just one cross in a forest of others. We are told that these dying and rising gods express symbolic truths about the cycles of nature, the quest for psychic wholeness, the healing of inner wounds. And we are often also told that non-Christian myths convey these truths much more elegantly and nonviolently, neither marred by the crude literalism and moralism of the Christian passion stories nor vexed by fixation on an actual historical event. In sum, the Christian story of the cross is exactly like all the others and perversely, uniquely worse than all of them.

Fourth, we readily suspect that emphasis on the cross fosters toxic psychological and social effects. In exalting Christ's death, do we not glorify innocent suffering and encourage people to accept it passively "in imitation of Christ"? If the cross is God's recipe for salvation, do we paint God as a violent and merciless despot? Does the church's theology, which has the divine Father punish his innocent child to redeem the world, look uncomfortably like a charter for child abuse? Is the invitation to identify with Christ's death and suffering a kind of therapeutic malpractice, fostering morbid fantasies? Perhaps the cross should carry a label: "This religious image may be harmful to your health." The tension here is not simply the obvious fact that the cross carried at the head of crusades and pogroms has also hung as the inspiration in hospitals and leprosy clinics and marched in movements for justice, an occasion for acts of love and compassion. Almost identical doctrines have figured in both cases. The tension rests in the further fact that for an image that should be hated by the weak and embraced by the strong, the cross has a perverse tendency to reverse this expectation in actual practice. It is often grasped with passion in barrios and in storefront churches, and just as often distanced coolly in the sanctuaries of the powerful. The supposedly victimizing image seems to tap a perennial recognition and respect among victims. It is far from obvious that the fact that God suffered as a persecuted one represents an endorsement of such suffering instead of an identification with their cause, a reproach to persecutors.

The Gospels themselves seem to echo all this contradiction and ambivalence with an overarching paradox of their own. Someone who wanders into a pew for the duration of Lent may rightly be perplexed by the New Testament's divided outlook on a simple matter: Is the cross a good thing or not? Jesus sets his face faithfully to go to Jerusalem. Jesus teaches his disciples, to their horror or disbelief, that it is a divinely appointed burden that he must be handed up to die. Despite his own reluctance, he goes to his execution out of obedience to God—"not my will but yours be done" (Luke 22:42)—and does not lift a finger to oppose it. He is supposed to die. Yet the Gospels are equally emphatic that Jesus is innocent, that his arrest and killing are unjust, that those who dispatch him are quite indifferent to truth and treat Jesus as a pawn in larger political or social conflicts, that it is shameful for his friends to betray and abandon him. It is wrong for him to die. Jesus sums it up when he says, "For the Son of Man goes as it is written of him, but woe to that one by whom the Son of Man is betrayed! It would have been better for that one not to have been born" (Mark 14:21).

In short, Jesus' death saves the world and it ought not to happen. This is God's plan and an evil act. Which is it? Are Pilate and Judas criminals or saints? It is not only the stranger in the pew who may wonder whether the Bible has its story straight. A reader not bothered by this is not paying attention. Until we have addressed this problem, nothing is going to make sense. Everything worth learning has its tricky passages, like math problems where there's that one point where it's so easy to take the wrong turn. The difference between being right and being wrong is so small, that one last multiplication step and remembering whether it should come out *negative* one billion or *positive* one billion (and that's a difference of *two* billion!). The Gospels have such a passage in the Passion narratives. We must hold on to the problems and add up all the oddities or it won't come out right. This paradox, however, is not an incoherent loose end but the heart of the story itself.

INVISIBLE VICTIMS

Let's think about our problem the other way around for a moment. What would Christianity need to be like to avoid all the criticisms that are made about the shocking execution that is at the center of faith? What if, in place of the Passion narratives of the Gospels, Christians had instead the following text:

> Christ—the living wisdom of God—came down to earth. He visited a great city in the form of a stranger, a swarthy carpenter with a withered leg, in order to call back those who had fallen into ignorance. He taught many things to those who had the inner ears to hear. But those who saw only his outward form did not understand the grace he brought.
>
> He performed many miracles, and the people worshiped him for this reason and made him their king. But still their ignorance was not dispelled, and each house in the city was set against another, and great fires burned there day and night. So Christ prepared his final miracle. One day he called to him Mary, his mother and his dearest disciple. He went into the Temple and ate the bread in the Holy of Holies, that no person is to touch. They lay together there near the altar throughout the night. While they lay there the earth shook, and many in the city were stricken with a deadly disease and the people were afraid. He sent Mary away, telling her that she must return without fail at the first hour and that whatever she found at that time must be cast outside the gates.
>
> In the morning, when the people came to the Temple, seeking to know what evil had been done to bring these troubles upon them, they found nothing but the smallest mustard seed lying near the altar. He had taken the form of a mustard seed, carrying the entirety of divinity within him. All the people

were greatly distressed at this. Priests and soldiers, foreigners and natives, members of every tribe, all were seized with awe, in a kind of trance. Heeding Mary, with one spirit they rushed together to form a procession and carried the seed to a stony hill where they threw it in a great hole that opened there. And each person, without exception, threw in stones to cover it.

Miraculously, the seed immediately grew up into a great tree, and Christ himself was in the fruit of that tree, and everyone who ate of this fruit discovered God within themselves and the joy of eternal life. The people returned to the city rejoicing, and health and peace ruled in those walls.

This is a rich symbolic story, full of allegorical possibilities. There is no offensive violence, no punishment or glorified suffering. Instead of a cross of blood, there is a tree of life. How different things might have been if Christians had made such a parable of spiritual self-discovery their text. We would not be embarrassed by charges of victimization in our Scriptures. We would have the added bonus that the spiritual value of this story is unhindered by concerns with historical reality. That value is no less if we regard the story as entirely imaginary instead of something that actually happened.

Suppose we added just one additional clarification, namely, that this text in fact refers to the events of Jesus' execution, to what actually took place as it is described in the Gospels. In that case, the text is a lie about a lynching. If we were then happy to substitute this text for the Gospels, knowing that Jesus' death is perhaps the one thing about which we are historically most certain, it would say something interesting about us—that we like to avert our eyes from the real victims.

The substitute Gospel we have just considered is not merely a thought experiment. René Girard has attracted a great deal of attention by arguing that to avert one's eyes from the sight of our real victims is a characteristic human act.[2] He contends that in light of this central aspect of human life we can understand the saving character of the cross. The meaning of Jesus' death can be understood only in light of the prototypical "good bad thing" in human culture: scapegoating sacrifice. Girard maintains that central human myths are in fact transcriptions of a consistent kind of violence that he calls the "founding murder." Such murder literally stands at the beginning and in the middle of human society. It makes human community possible.

Girard's account, in brief, is this: social life, particularly in its infancy, is fatally subject to plagues of rivalry and vengeance. Escalating cycles of retaliation are the original social disease. Without finding a way to treat this violence, human society can hardly get started. The ability to break this vicious cycle appears as a kind of miracle. At some point, when feuding threatens to dissolve a community, spontaneous and irrational mob violence erupts against some distinctive person or minority in the group. They are accused of the worst crimes the group can imagine, crimes that by their very enormity might have caused the terrible plight the community now experiences. They are lynched.

The sad good thing that happens as a result of this bad thing is that the scapegoating actually works. In the wake of the murder, communities find that this sudden war of all against one has delivered them from the war of each against all. The sacrifice of one or a few in the role of scapegoat discharges the pending acts of retribution. It "clears the air." This benefit seems a startling, even magical result from a simple execution. The sudden peace confirms the desperate charges that the victim had been behind the crisis to begin with. If the scapegoat's death is the solution, the scapegoat must have been the cause. The death has such reconciling effect that it seems the victim must possess supernatural power. So the victim becomes a god, memorialized in myth.

Rituals of sacrifice originated in this way, says Girard. They were tools to fend off social crisis. And in varied forms they are with us still. The prescription is that divisions in the community must be reduced to but one division, the division of all against one common victim or one minority group. Prime candidates are the marginal and the weak, or those isolated by their very prominence. The key feature is that they are or can be cut off from any support from others. Typically, they will be charged with violating the community's most sacred taboos, crimes so extreme that they could have brought calamity on the whole and so distasteful that no one will side with them. The process does not just accept innocent victims, it prefers them—"outsiders" who are not closely linked to established groups in the society. This, in a nutshell, is Girard's account of the origin of religion. It is identical with the beginning of culture itself, for without some such mechanism to head off tit-for-tat violence, human society could not get off the ground. The violent sacred is our founding "good bad thing," reconciliation in the blood of the innocent.

No one thought out this process, and its effectiveness depends on a certain blindness to its workings. Myth reflects the scapegoat event but does not describe it. Myth is the product of a collective killing that all the actors found completely justified, entirely necessary, and powerfully beneficent. It is the memory of a clean conscience that never registered the presence of a victim at all. The unbroken continuity of consciousness between producers and consumers of the myth from generation to generation ensures the invisibility of the victim as a victim.

So our text about the seed and the flowering tree is an example of what Jesus' death would look like if it were a true myth in Girard's sense. If we suspect there is an execution behind this story, we can see many telltale signs: typical marks of the victim (he has a physical deformity, he is a foreigner), indications of social conflict (fire sweeping the city), traces of the accusations (incest, profaning holy things), the unanimity of the mob violence (stoning and burying the "seed"), and the positive benefits of the death. We can easily see how a ritual would evolve from this story, perhaps the annual offering of a sacrificial victim at the foot of the sacred tree. Above all, of course, what is "mythical" is that the killing has disappeared completely, and no issues of persecution, guilt, or violence are present in the text at all.

Scapegoating is one of the deepest structures of human sin, built into our religion and our politics. It is demonic because it is endlessly flexible in its choice of victims and because it can truly deliver the good that it advertises. Satan can cast out Satan, and is the more powerful for it. Its hold is strongest where it is most invisible. Victims are called criminals, gods, or both. So long as we are in the grip of sin, we do not see our victims as scapegoats. Texts that hide scapegoating foster it. Texts that show it for what it is undermine it.

SAVING FROM SACRIFICE

Jesus' willingness to face death, specifically death on a cross, suddenly looks anything but arbitrary and much more like the "wisdom of God" that the New Testament so surprisingly discovers in the crucifixion. God is willing to die for us, to bear our sin in this particular way, because we desperately need deliverance from the sin of scapegoating. God breaks the grip of scapegoating by stepping into the place of a victim, and by being a victim who cannot be hidden or mythologized. God acts not to affirm the suffering of the innocent victim as the price of peace, but to reverse it.

Note that in the Gospels it is Jesus' accusers who affirm the reconciling value of his death. "You do not understand that it is better for you to have one man die for the people than to have the whole nation destroyed," says Caiaphas, the high priest (John 11:50). In other words, it is expedient that one man should die for the sake of the people. And Luke 23:12 contains this curious note after Pilate and Herod had shuttled Jesus between them: "That same day Herod and Pilate became friends with each other; before this they had been enemies." Jesus' persecutors intended his death to bring peace. It offers a way to avoid an outbreak of violence between Romans and Israelites, between Jews and other Jews. Jesus' death is intended to be sacrificial business as usual. But God means it to be the opposite.

There is a key scene in Mel Gibson's movie *The Passion of the Christ* that represents a dramatic missed opportunity to convey this truth.[3] The moment comes when Jesus is brought back before Pilate and the crowd, after having been whipped and brutalized. The plot moves back and forth a bit, with Barabbas being released and Pilate temporizing. But the situation becomes increasingly volatile. Suddenly, pushing and shoving breaks out in the front ranks, between the Roman soldiers and members of the crowd. That's it. Things snap. Crucify him, Pilate says.

Satan is a visible figure in Gibson's film. Given that choice, this is the one moment Satan certainly should have appeared (but doesn't)... moving in the crowd and saying, "We've got to get rid of Jesus or he's going to bring the Romans down on us." And moving among the Roman soldiers and rulers, saying, "We've got to get rid of Jesus or there will be rebellion and blood on the streets." And nudging up to Peter and John and Mary, saying, "Don't say anything—do you want to get killed like that too?"

The Romans are at odds with the Judean Jews. Jewish factions are at odds with each other. The Romans are afraid of rebellion. The religious leaders are afraid of repression. They all want and expect Jesus' death to have a reconciling effect on this situation. That seems to be precisely what Caiaphas and Pilate have in mind. It makes enemies like Pilate and Herod friends before it even happens. There's nothing like a little redemptive violence to bring us all together.

So is this the way God works? Is this God's plan, to become a human being and die, so that God won't have to kill us instead? Is it God's prescription to have Jesus suffer for sins he did not commit so God can forgive the sins we do commit? That is to compute the oddity of God becoming our victim the wrong way. Blood is not acceptable to God as a means of uniting human community or reconciling with God. Christ sheds his own blood to *end* that way of trying to mend our divisions. Jesus' death isn't necessary because God has to have innocent blood to solve the guilt equation. Redemptive violence is our equation. God is not just feeding a bigger and better victim into this machinery to get a bigger payoff, as the theory of substitutionary atonement might seem to suggest. Jesus' open proclamation of forgiveness (without sacrifice) *before* his death and the fact of his resurrection after it are the ways that God reveals and rejects what Girard terms the "victimage mechanism."[4] Jesus didn't volunteer to get into God's justice machine. God volunteered to get into ours. God used our own sin to save us.

C. S. Lewis, who knew the mythical heritage of the world better than most, saw this aspect of the crucifixion clearly. In his Christian allegory *The Chronicles of Narnia*, the lion Aslan, the Christ figure, allows himself to be killed so that the evil powers will release those they hold hostage.[5] The idea of this exchange the canvas of the liberation of people and their bodies from oppression, provides a very different kind of spirituality of remembrance, one that is earthy, political, social, and alive with meaning for any system that brutalizes and tyrannizes.

Body of Christ as Eucharistic Action: "Acting Up!"

So, third, the Eucharist is a social space of performance. It is a life-context in which the body of Christ "acts up," we might say. This acting up is a corollary of being a community that is marked by a sociality of deliverance. Acting toward liberation is the mark of the body of Christ as the church, as a social presence in history. The bread is broken, the cup lifted, words are spoken. In *Remembering Esperanza*, which sought to think through the Eucharist in relation to the problems of world hunger, the denial/lack of food and drink to so many, I suggested that even the words of institution might be seen as "performative utterances," borrowing a term from philosopher J. L. Austin. The words of institution are not intoned solely as a remembering back, but as that kind of re-membering that is heavily laden with expectation, expectation of deliverance of a groaning people (of hungry people, today), expectation that hearers will perform a distribution of elements not only among themselves but also as food and drink to those in need. Building on this, the eucharistic practice of the body of Christ can be seen as the collective performative force of Christians, moving and on the move, to provide succor and strength to those under repression who are cut off from the social flourishing of soul and body that mark life in the Spirit.

If state torture is an attack on the body that destroys collective life—especially destroying democratic society and virtues, atomizing society, breaking individuals off from one another so that they are subordinate to the state—then torture, from the vantage point of the body of Christ, is seen as the very antithesis of eucharistic practice. It must be affirmed, though, that Christians celebrating the Eucharist in a time of American torture cannot help but be on the move in resistance to it, given what life in the body of Christ is to be.

Again, in his excellent book *Torture and the Eucharist*, Cavanaugh makes the powerful and direct links between the Eucharist and a people suffering torture. His main scene of study is Chile, under the regime of Augusto Pinochet, and the way the church constituted itself during those years of torture and repression. The Eucharist offers, he says, a "counter-politics" that took the form of pursuing three practices in Chile: (1) an announced "excommunication" of Christians who torture or condone torture; (2) an organization of a complex support structure for torture victims, their families, and all poor residents whose activism made them in Luke's account, when the centurion confesses at the moment of Jesus' death, "Certainly this man was innocent" (Luke 23:47). Girard recounts the shock of recognition he experienced in coming to the New Testament after studying violence and the sacred in anthropology and the history of religion. He found in the Gospels all the elements he had come to expect in myths: the crowd coalescing against an individual, the charges of the greatest crimes and impurities. But he was startled to recognize that the reality of what was happening was explicit, not hidden. Here is the same mythic story, but this time told from the point of view of the victim, who is clearly accused unjustly and murdered wrongly. In the Gospels, the scapegoating process is stripped of its sacred mystery, and the collective persecution and abandonment are painfully illustrated so that no one, including the disciples, can honestly say afterward that they resisted the sacrificial tide. The Passion narratives follow the script of sacrifice as diagnosis, not as prescription.

The resurrection makes Jesus' death a failed sacrifice, but of a new kind. When mythical sacrifice succeeds, peace descends, true memory is erased, and the way is smoothed for the next scapegoat. If it fails (because the community is not unanimous or the victim is not sufficiently demonized), it becomes just another killing, stoking the proliferation of violence, and the search intensifies for more and better victims. But in the case of Jesus' death, something else happens. People do not unanimously close ranks over Jesus' grave (as Jesus' executioners hoped), nor is there a spree of violent revenge on behalf of the crucified leader. Instead, an odd new counter-community arises, dedicated both to the innocent victim whom God has vindicated by resurrection and to a new life through him that requires no further such sacrifice. As Girard sees it, this is the good news, the inexplicable revelation, that is found in the Bible.

The revelatory quality of the New Testament on this point is thoroughly continuous with Hebrew Scripture, in which an awareness and rejection of the sacrificial mechanism is already set forth. The averted sacrifice of Isaac; the prophets' condemnation of scapegoating the widow, the weak, or the foreigner; the story of Job; the Psalms' obsession with the innocent victim of collective violence; the Passion narratives' transparent account of Jesus' death; the confessions of a new community that grew up in solidarity around the risen crucified victim—all of these follow a constant thread. They reveal the "victimage" mechanisms at the joint root of religion and society and they reject those mechanisms. Jesus is the victim who will not stay sacrificed, whose memory is not erased, and who forces us to confront the reality of scapegoating.

This is why the case of anti-Semitism is the infallible test for a healthy Christian theory of atonement. One of the crucial things that makes the church a new community is its solidarity, not against some sacrificial victim, but in identification with the crucified one. Christians are as susceptible as others to scapegoating, and have often turned their tradition to sacrificial ends. Our guilt in this regard is underlined by the fact that the gospel prompted Christians who would resist its revelation to create a new version of the old sin. Because the dynamic of Jesus' passion has made it much more difficult to ignore scapegoats or to mystify them in myths, Christians who would be persecutors have put them in plain sight. Jews were scapegoated with the claim that they were the ones who had scapegoated Jesus.

The new sin, for which Christians can claim "credit," was to victimize people by accusing them of being victimizers and thus to make the revelation directed against sacrifice a new rationale for sacrifice. To use the gospel in a mythological way, Christians have to distort the very truth it has given them. The moment we point a finger at some "they" as Jesus' killers, we have enacted the sin that the very particularity of the cross meant to overcome. Christians bear a special culpability for this prompt perversion, with less right to claim that we knew not what we did. Christian history is a struggle between a redemptive resistence to sacrifice and a remythologizing of the gospel. Both focus on the cross, yet the second takes the pattern of scapegoating highlighted there not as the diagnosis of an evil to be overcome but as a prescription for persecution.

WOUNDED FOR US

We noted the tension seeded through the Passion story: Jesus' death saves the world and it ought not to have happened. The tension is there not because the Gospel writers can't get their story straight but because this tension is the heart of the story itself. The cross must be known to be sacrifice, so that we know sacrifice as what is to be overcome. We can see how this paradox illuminates the objections to atonement theology with which we began. We can understand, for instance, why critiques of Christian anti-Semitism may rightly see it both as an exemplification of a universal human tendency and as something distinctively new and specially culpable. Similarly, in terms of the mythological context we can grasp how necessary it is that Jesus' death should closely fit the pattern of the scapegoat's story (it *is* just like other myths) if the story is to be told from the victim's point of view and reversed by God's vindication of that victim (and so become radically different from the others: a "bad" myth). We can note that critics reject atonement theology on the one hand because they say it rests on notions of sacrifice that are nothing but superstition, delusions that make no sense to modern people. It is rejected on the other hand because its sacrificial terms trade in the raw dynamics of violence, vengeance, retribution, and substitution—dynamics so powerful and so real in human life that the great crime of the cross is its threat to inflame them. These are but the two sides of the gospel paradox reflected back against it, for in the Passion the ostensible justification for sacrifice (the sin of the victim and the divine condemnation of the victim) is dispelled as illusion and superstition at the same time that the real violence carried out in service of that illusion is unveiled and opposed. And we can further understand how such dramatically contrasting appropriations of the cross have arisen in history or psychology, since within the Passion narratives themselves the diagnosis of the problem and the divine reversal of it lie but a hair's breadth apart. It is easy to mistake one for the other.

The biblical language of sacrifice and blood (with all its dangers) tells the truth. To want to purge these elements from the story reflects a naïve confidence that we are in greater danger of being corrupted by the bloody language than we are of falling prey to the sin it describes. The good/bad tension is there in the texts because of their frank description of the sacrificial, scapegoating violence that has existed from the foundation of the world. That unifying persecution may in fact at times contain the spread of even more extensive violence. But its victims ought not to be sacrificed. So at the first level, this tension stems from an honest description of our human condition, the way that religion and violence intertwine in our social history.

Becoming subject to this sin, God takes this tension to a second, different level. The peace that depends on sacrifice (the "reconciliation" Herod and Pilate aim for in Christ's death) now also registers as something that ought not to happen. The good part of the "old good bad thing," sacrifice now is seen as part of what is bad in the crucifixion. What is needed is a completely new basis for peace. It is hardly accidental that "peace" is often the first word of the risen Christ in his appearances. It is an apt greeting. If a sacrificial victim were to return with power to those who had persecuted or abandoned him, peace is the opposite of what they would expect. And it is a new kind of peace, peace not based on more victims, peace not "as the world gives," that is now offered.[8] So in the gospel a new kind of tension is stressed, in which it is the entire complex of sacrificial violence—both the "good" peace it brings and the bad violence it uses—that becomes the bad thing. It is God's willingness to suffer the worst this process has to offer to deliver us from it, to deliver us to a new path of peace, that is the good thing.

Christ is wounded for our transgressions. We can hardly deny that Jesus bears our sin of scapegoating, precisely because of its collective and ubiquitous character. Christ died for us. He did so first in the mythic, sacrificial sense that all scapegoated victims do. That we know this is already a sign that he died for us in a second sense—to save us from that very sin. Jesus died in our place, because it is literally true that any one of us, in the right circumstances, can be the scapegoat. As the Letter to the Hebrews says, Christ is a sacrifice to end sacrifice, and he has died once for all. Christ's purpose was not "to offer himself again and again, as the high priest enters the Holy Place year after year with blood that is not his own; for then he would have had to suffer again and again since the foundation of the world. But as it is, he has appeared once for all at the end of the age to remove sin by the sacrifice of himself" (Heb. 9:25-26).

Is Christ's death unique? It is not, since it is crucial to the saving "work" of the cross to recognize that Jesus' death is precisely the same as that of so many other victims. And yet by virtue of this identification it is unique because it is the one of all these deaths that have been happening from the foundation of the world that irreversibly shows us the sin in which we are everywhere enmeshed and in which God has acted on the side of the victims.

It is true that there is a transaction of sorts at the cross. God agrees to be handed over to our sacrificial process, to bear our original sin, and to carry the burden that no human alone can bear. Any human being can be plausibly scapegoated (we are all sinners) and no human can prevail when the collective community turns against her. Nor is it sufficient for Jesus simply to instruct us about our situation, for we are all too fully enclosed in the scapegoating process to be able to break the spell. It is an extraordinary step even to arrive at the awareness of our own susceptibility expressed by the disciples at the Last Supper, when they piteously ask Jesus, "Surely not I, Lord?" (Matt. 26:22).

Only one whose innocence truly can be vindicated and whose power could have offered escape can, by suffering this sacrifice, reverse it. The work of the cross is the work of a transcendent God breaking into a cycle we could not change alone. If we limit Jesus' work to that of a human exemplar, the crucifixion becomes more of a prescription for suffering than if we grasp it as the work of the Incarnate One, done once for all. It is a saving act of God, a victory over the powers of this world, a defeat of death.

Early Christian writers spoke of the crucifixion as basically a trick on Satan. The powers have been tricked. By drawing Christ into the usual sacrificial machinery, the powers have been revealed and broken, because all the traditional means of justifying and erasing the sacrificial violence won't stick this time, and their hold will increasingly be broken.

Is there any point in Jesus dying this particular, specific kind of death? Yes, because his death exemplifies a specific kind of sin we all need saving from, and lays the basis to overcome it. We humans took a terrible thing—scapegoating violence against the innocent or against those who *are* guilty of something but not the demonic effects we claim—and made it a good thing. It brings us together, stops escalating violence, unites us against a common enemy. We overcome our conflicts and make peace by finding a common enemy, by hating together.

God was willing to be a victim of that bad thing we had made apparently good, in order to reveal its horror and stop it. And in so doing God made that occasion of scapegoating sacrifice (what those who killed Jesus were doing) an occasion of overcoming scapegoating violence (what God was doing). It is the same event, but what is happening in that event for the people who kill or accept the killing is not what's happening in that event for Jesus and God. God used our sin to save us from that sin. God did this so that victims of such acts would never be invisible—they look too much like Jesus. God did this so that we would turn to finding some new basis for peace, such as that around the communion table.

This is the razor's edge of interpretation of the atonement, where a small step can lead us far for good or ill. This is why we have what sounds like the same language overlaid on this same event twice, to different effects. Christians say Christ's death is a sacrifice...but to end sacrifice. They say, "blood shed for us," but blood shed once for all. They say, "We are reconciled in his blood," but they mean we have been freed to live without the kind of reconciliation that requires blood, the kind Caiaphas and Pilate and Herod had in mind.

When Christians gather at Holy Communion we see this clearly in the unequivocal reminder of Christ's bloody death. When we hear, "Do this in remembrance of me," we should hear the implied contrast that comes with emphasis on *"this."* Unlike the mythic victims who became sacred models for future sacrifices, Christ is not to be remembered with more scapegoating. *This* is a humble meal and prayer, not a new cross. Christ has offered his very real body and blood so that, at the Last Supper, he can set a new pattern and say of bread, "this is my body," and of wine, "this is my blood." These will serve in the place of sacred violence.

Following that example, Christians believe this meal of the new community is able to accomplish all the peace that sacrificial violence could, and more. In it, we recall a real sacrifice and celebrate a substitutionary atonement. Here on this table, bread and wine are to be continually substituted for victims—substituted for any, and all, of us.

15

Violence in Christian Theology

J. Denny Weaver

IS CHRISTIANITY CHARACTERIZED BY THE medieval crusades, warrior popes, the multiple blessings of wars by Christians over the centuries, wars religious and otherwise fought in the name of the Christian God, support for capital punishment, justifications of slavery, worldwide colonialism in the name of spreading Christianity, corporal punishment under the guise of "spare the rod and spoil the child," the systemic violence of women subjected to men, and more?[1] Or does it reflect its eponymous founder, who is worshiped as "Wonderful Counselor, Mighty God, Everlasting Father, Prince of Peace" (Isa. 9:6); whose Sermon on the Mount taught nonviolence and love of enemies; who faced his accusers nonviolently and then died a nonviolent death; whose teaching of nonviolence inspired the first centuries of pacifist Christian history, was subsequently preserved in the justifiable-war doctrine that declares all war as sin even when declaring it occasionally a necessary evil, and also was preserved in the prohibition of fighting by monastics and clergy as well as in a persistent tradition of Christian pacifism?

The fact that one could plausibly answer both of the previous questions in the affirmative points to the frequent disjuncture between Christian theology and ethics. Christian theology talks about Jesus, but Christian ethics takes its cues from elsewhere, so that Jesus is again and again proclaimed "not relevant" for social ethics.[2] To illustrate how accepting the relevance of Jesus' nonviolence makes an impact on the study of Christian theology, this essay outlines the way that a presumed standard Christian theology has accommodated violence, focusing especially on the central Christian doctrine of atonement, and concludes by sketching a specifically nonviolent understanding of atonement.

I use broad definitions of the terms *violence* and *nonviolence*.[3] *Violence* means harm or damage, which obviously includes the direct violence of killing—in war, capital punishment, and murder—but also covers such systemic violence as poverty, racism, and sexism. *Nonviolence* is identified with a spectrum of attitudes and actions, from the classic Mennonite idea of passive nonresistance to the active nonviolence and nonviolent resistance pioneered by such leaders as Mahatma Gandhi and Martin Luther King Jr., which would include various kinds of social action, confrontations, and posing of alternatives that do not cause bodily harm or injury. That such commitments to nonviolence have generally become separated from theological abstractions can be seen from an examination of one particular sphere of Christian doctrine, the atonement.

STANDARD ATONEMENT MOTIFS

The standard account of the history of doctrine lists three families of atonement images. *Christus Victor*, the predominant image of the early church, existed in two forms, each of which involved the three elements of God, the devil or Satan, and sinful humankind. In the *ransom* version of *Christus Victor*, the devil held the souls of humankind captive. In a seemingly contractual agreement, God handed Jesus over to Satan as a ransom payment to secure the release of captive souls. The devil killed Jesus, in an apparent victory for the forces of evil. In raising Jesus from the dead, God triumphed over the devil, and the souls of humanity were freed from his clutches. This victory through resurrection provides the name *Christus Victor* (or Christ the Victor).

A second version of *Christus Victor* pictured the conflict between Satan and God as a *cosmic battle*. In this struggle, God's Son was killed, but the resurrection then constituted the victory of God over the forces of evil and definitively identified God as the ruler of the universe.

Satisfaction atonement has been the predominant atonement image for much of the past millennium. It suffices for present purposes to sketch two versions of satisfaction atonement. One reflects the view of Anselm of Canterbury, whose *Cur Deus Homo?* (1098) constitutes the first full articulation of *satisfaction* atonement.

TWO MORE QUESTIONS

The description of the history of atonement thus far has followed the standard account. Two additional questions bring to the fore the intrinsically violent elements of these atonement images.

First, a nuance appears when we shift from asking about the object of the death of Jesus to inquire, Who or what needs the death of Jesus? For the ransom theory, one might say that the devil clearly needs the death—it fulfills God's part of the bargain when the devil releases the souls of humankind. For the cosmic battle image, the question makes little sense. For the satisfaction theories, it is God's honor or God's law that needs the death. Without it, the debt to God's honor remains unpaid or unsatisfied, or the penalty required by God's law remains unmet. Finally, for the moral theory, one might say that "we"—sinners—need the death since that is what enables us to perceive the Father's love.

A second question shifts the nuance again and produces an ultimately shocking answer. The question is, Who arranges for or is responsible for the death of Jesus? Or, put most crassly, Who ultimately killed Jesus?

With the two forms of *Christus Victor*, it is obvious that the devil killed Jesus. But God the Father certainly appears to be something less than the source of all love and grace—handing the Son over for Satan to kill as a ransom payment to purchase freedom for God's other children. One can easily sense Anselm's distaste for this motif.

But the situation is not ameliorated when one poses the question for satisfaction and moral theories. Satisfaction atonement pictures a debt owed to God's honor. God's honor not only needs the death, but God also arranges for Jesus to die to pay the debt to God's honor. The image implies that God has Jesus killed in order to pay the debt to God's honor. Here is where we very pointedly see the result of Anselm's deletion of the devil from the three-cornered relationship involving the devil, sinners, and God. With Satan deleted, remaining in the equation are God and the sinners who have offended God. But these sinful human beings cannot save themselves by repaying God themselves. It is thus merely an extension of Anselm's own logic that leads to the conclusion that God is the only one left to orchestrate the death of Jesus in order to pay the debt owed to God's honor. In penal substitution, God's law receives the necessary death that it demands for justice. But again, since sinners cannot pay their own debt, God is the one who arranges to provide Jesus' death as the means to satisfy God's law.

One might ask, Weren't the devil or the mob or the Romans responsible for killing Jesus? But answering yes to that question within the framework of satisfaction atonement points to a strange juxtaposition and non sequitur. Jesus, who is innocent and who does the will of God, becomes sin, subject to punishment. And the evil powers who oppose the reign of God by killing Jesus—whether the devil, the mob, or the Romans—are the ones who are actually doing the will of God by killing Jesus to provide the payment that God's honor or God's law demands. The strange implication is that both Jesus and those who kill Jesus would be carrying out the will of God. In fact, asserting that both claims are true is nonsense. Attempting to avoid the implications of such mutually contradictory claims by cloaking them in a category such as mystery, or by claiming that the acts of God are too big for our categories to contain, renders meaningless any attempt to use theology to express Christian faith.

The moral theory fares no better. Remember that while Abelard rejected the idea that Jesus' death was a payment directed toward God's honor, Abelard agreed with Anselm in removing the devil from the equation. The result is an atonement motif in which the Father has one of his children—the Son—killed in order to show love to the rest of the Father's children, namely, to us sinners.

These observations about the implied role for God the Father in satisfaction and moral atonement motifs help explain why a number of feminist and womanist writers have claimed that atonement theology presents an image of divine child abuse.[5] While none of the classic motifs escapes, the sharpest feminist and womanist critique falls on satisfaction atonement.

I cannot fault this feminist and womanist critique. The two questions (Who needs the death of Jesus? Who authors or arranges the death of Jesus?) reveal problematic dimensions of traditional atonement theology. The problems are particularly acute for satisfaction and moral theories, which have occupied most atonement discussions until quite recently. And these observations are not merely the result of feminist or pacifist radicalism. Most fundamentally, the observations about the role of God in satisfaction and moral atonement motifs simply draw out the implications of Anselm's own move to delete the devil from the atonement equation.

The conclusion from our first round of observations about classic atonement doctrine is that they portray an image of God as either divine avenger or punisher and/or as a child abuser, one who arranges the death of one child for the benefit of the others. Does it then surprise us that Christians envisioning a God who orchestrates violence as part of a divine plan might justify violence, under a variety of divinely anchored claims and images?

Retribution in Atonement

Another set of observations reveals additional violent elements of satisfaction atonement. The several versions all function with the assumption that doing justice or righting wrongs depends on retribution. Sin creates imbalance. Satisfaction atonement assumes that the imbalance is righted or balanced by the punishment of death.

One contemporary version and one historic version of this assumption make clear its presence in satisfaction atonement. The criminal justice system of the United States operates on the principle of retribution. Small crimes require small penalties, while a big crime requires a big penalty. The biggest punishment, namely death, is reserved for the most heinous crimes. The assumption that doing justice is equated with punishment appears in the public disapproval when what is perceived as a big misdeed receives only a "wrist tap" as punishment. With an apparent imbalance between deed and punishment, it seems that justice was not done. The assumption of retributive justice—that doing justice means meting out punishment—is virtually universal among North Americans and throughout much of the world.[6] The assumption that doing justice means to punish underlies satisfaction atonement, in particular the image of penal substitutionary atonement, with an innocent Jesus bearing the punishment we deserve.

The contemporary assumption of retributive justice has a medieval counterpart in the feudal system. I follow R. W. Southern's description of the feudal system and how Anselm's image reflects his feudal worldview.[7] The feudal world was hierarchical with a lord at the top who held the hierarchy together. The stability of the system depended on maintaining the honor of the lord at the top of the hierarchy. An offense against the lord's honor incurred a debt that threatened his authority and thus the stability of the system. In order to restore honor and stability, the debt had to be repaid. Inability to collect the debt challenged the honor and authority of the lord.

It is not difficult to see that Anselm's image of the atoning death of Jesus reflects the feudal worldview. Human sin has brought imbalance and disharmony into the universe. The restoration of harmony, order, and balance requires a payment to satisfy the offended honor of God. Anselm understood Jesus' death as the debt payment that satisfied the honor of God and thus restored balance and order in the universe.

Although Anselm's understanding of satisfaction atonement differs significantly from penal substitutionary atonement, each assumes some form of the idea of retribution. Whereas penal substitution pictures retribution in terms of punishment exacted by divine law, for Anselm it was the offended honor of God that required retribution in the form of the payment of death. The conclusion is inescapable that *any and all versions of satisfaction atonement, regardless of their packaging, assume the violence of retribution or justice based on punishment and depend on God-induced and God-directed violence.*

AHISTORICAL ATONEMENT

Satisfaction atonement accommodates violence in a third way. It structures the relationship between humankind and God in terms of an ahistorical, abstract legal formula. Thus, it concerns a relationship that is outside of human history. Further, when visualizing the birth, life and teaching, death, and resurrection of Jesus, quite obviously satisfaction atonement actually needs or uses only the death of Jesus. These elements—positing a transaction outside of history and involving only the death of Jesus—make satisfaction atonement an image that (with one exception treated below) implies little or nothing about ethics and contains nothing that would challenge injustice in the social order. It is an a-ethical atonement image, with an understanding of salvation that is separated from ethics. In John Howard Yoder's language, it is theology that is "not relevant" for social ethics, or a theology quite compatible with exercise of the sword, or a theology that accommodates slavery and racism.

The particular significance of these observations about the ahistorical and a-ethical dimensions of satisfaction atonement appears when they are considered against the backdrop of the changes in the church that are symbolized by Emperor Constantine. These changes began already in the second century and extended through several centuries in evolutionary fashion. The end result of this evolution was that the church ceased being perceived as a dissident minority group and came to identify with the social order and thus to make use of and express itself through the institutions of the social order. Among other things, the exercise of the sword shows the change in the church's status from a contrast with, to an accommodation of, the social order. Whereas before Christians by and large did not wield the sword and pagans did, now Christians wielded the sword in the name of Christ. Rather than defining what Christians did on the basis of what Jesus said or did, the operative norm of behavior for Christians became what was good or necessary to preserve "Christian society." And in determining what was good for society, the emperor rather than Jesus became the instance of identification.[8]

I suggest that satisfaction atonement reflects the church after Constantine that had accommodated the sword rather than the early church, which was primarily a pacifist church. The satisfaction motif's abstract, ahistorical, a-ethical formula permits one to claim Jesus' saving work while wielding the sword that Jesus had forbidden. James Cone, founder of the black theology movement, notes how such abstract formulas allowed slave owners to preach a salvation to slaves that preserved intact the master-slave relationship.[9] In other words, stated generally, satisfaction atonement separates salvation from ethics. In contrast, the atonement motif presented in what follows both reflects the nonviolence of Jesus and understands ethics as an integral dimension of salvation.

To this point, we have observed three levels of exhibiting or accommodating violence in satisfaction atonement. First, removing the devil from the atonement equation, as did Anselm and Abelard, leaves an image of God who saves by violence and of an innocent Son who passively submits to that violence. That is, its image assumes God-orchestrated and God-directed violence. Second, satisfaction atonement assumes the violence of retribution. Finally, satisfaction atonement's abstract, ahistorical character does not challenge and in fact accommodates violence and violent practices in the social order.

MORE VIOLENCE OF ATONEMENT

To this point, the argument has focused on the intrinsically violent elements of classic atonement formulas themselves. We now turn to observe additional problematic implications of the classic formulas and their application in the modern world.

Focusing on the violence of retribution that is intrinsic to satisfaction atonement brings to the fore the issue of the *image or role of God*. The logic of satisfaction atonement makes God the chief avenger or the chief punisher. In its worst case, as previously noted, it makes God a child abuser. This vengeful image of God led Abelard to reject the idea that Jesus' death was a payment to God's honor. However, the moral influence theory still leaves God the Father offering the Son's death to sinners as the example of Fatherly love. And classic *Christus Victor* has the Father hand over the Son as a ransom payment.

A further component of the violence in classic atonement images is the model of Jesus it presents. In satisfaction atonement, Jesus is a model of voluntary submission to innocent suffering. If the Father needs the death of Jesus to satisfy divine honor, Jesus as innocent victim voluntarily agrees to submit to that violence needed by the honor of God. Or as innocent victim Jesus voluntarily agrees to undergo the punishment deserved by sinful humankind in order that the demand of divine justice be met. Because Jesus' death is needed, Jesus models being a voluntary, passive, and innocent victim who suffers for the good of another.

It is important to underscore for whom these images of God as abusive Father and Jesus as an innocent and passive victim may pose a particular concern. It is an unhealthy model for a woman abused by her husband or a child violated by her father and constitutes double jeopardy when attached to hierarchical theology that asserts male headship.[10] A model of passive, innocent suffering poses an obstacle for people who encounter conditions of systemic injustice or an unjust status quo produced by the power structure. Examples might be the legally segregated South prior to the civil rights movement or *de facto* housing segregation that still exists in many places, or military-backed occupation under which land is confiscated and indigenous residents crowded into enclosed territories (called "reservations" in North America, "bantustans" in South Africa, and "autonomous areas" in Palestine). For people in such situations of an unjust status quo, the idea of "being like Jesus" as modeled by satisfaction atonement means to submit passively and to accept without protest that systemic injustice. James Cone links substitutionary atonement specifically to defenses of slavery and colonial oppression.[11] As seen in chapter 1 of this volume, Delores Williams calls the Jesus of substitutionary atonement the "ultimate surrogate figure." After depicting numerous ways in which black women were forced into a variety of surrogacy roles for white men and women and black men, Williams says that to accept satisfaction or substitutionary atonement and the image of Jesus that it supplies is to validate all the unjust surrogacy to which black women have been and still are submitted.[12] Such examples show that atonement theology, which models innocent, passive suffering, supports rather than challenges violence in the contemporary context.

NARRATIVE *CHRISTUS VICTOR*

What I call narrative *Christus Victor* identifies the victory of Christ in terms of the narratives of the Gospels and Revelation and also distinguishes my formulation from classic *Christus Victor*. The final section of this essay outlines narrative *Christus Victor* as an approach to atonement that expresses the nonviolence of Jesus, does not presume that justice depends on punishment, does not put God in the role of chief avenger, does not make Jesus a model of passive, innocent, voluntary submission to abuse, includes freedom from oppression in its understanding of salvation, and requires oppressors to cease oppression. Narrative *Christus Victor* features an understanding of salvation that includes ethics and that begins in but is certainly not limited to the historical arena in which we live. In other words, narrative *Christus Victor* avoids all the problems of violence identified for classic atonement imagery.

Let us consider again the original survey of atonement images. In particular, let us recall the cosmic battle version of *Christus Victor*, which has received little attention in this chapter. This image featured the forces of God involved in a cosmic battle with the forces of Satan (or evil) for control of the universe. For present purposes, the important issue with classic *Christus Victor* is to recognize and understand of what that cosmic battle consists and where and when it took place.

The book of Revelation is replete with images of this cosmic battle. While many vignettes in Revelation portray this confrontation, chapter 12 contains the specific image of a heavenly battle between the forces of Satan represented by the dragon and the forces of God led by the angel Michael.

But one of the most important points is to see that this confrontation between Michael and the dragon was not an actual battle waged in the cosmos. The imagery and symbols of Revelation, both in chapter 12 and throughout the book, refer to people and events in the historical world of the first century. In other words, Revelation's symbols refer not to the distant future nor to cosmic events outside of history but to events of the first century in the historical world.

In the case of the seven-headed dragon in chapter 12, most scholars recognize that the dragon refers to imperial Rome, whose eponymous city by legend was founded on seven hills, with the horns and crowns referring to a sequence of emperors. The "battle" depicted between forces of God and forces of Satan was really the confrontation *in history* between the church, the earthly institution that represented the rule of God, and the Roman Empire, the earthly structure used to symbolize the rule of Satan. Revelation uses cosmic imagery and symbols to depict the true nature of empire and to encourage the early church to confront it since the resurrection of Jesus has already defeated it.

The same kind of interpretation applies to the seven seals in chapters 6–7. I suggest that the seals correspond to the sequence of Roman emperors from Tiberius (14–37 C.E., seal 1), under whose rule Jesus was crucified, through Caligula (37–40 C.E., seal 2), Claudius (41–54 C.E., seal 3), Nero (54–68 C.E., seal 4), and Vespasian (69–79 C.E., seal 6), to the short reign of Titus (79–81 C.E.) or, more likely, Domitian (81–96 C.E., seal 7). Seal 5 coincides with the gap between Nero and Vespasian when three pretenders (Galbo, Otho, and Vitellius) carried the title but failed to consolidate imperial power.

Each seal contains a symbolic reference to elements from the reign of the corresponding emperor. The unsuccessful effort to conquer by the rider on the white horse—he came out "conquering and to conquer"—makes an oblique reference to the death and resurrection of Jesus that occurred during the reign of Tiberius. Since Jesus did not stay dead, the imagery implies, the rider—Tiberius—had a victory in appearance only. The following symbols are more obvious. The blood-red horse, the sword, and taking peace from the earth in seal 2 refer to the threats posed by Caligula. In addition to Caligula's provocations against the Jews, in 40 C.E. he sent an army to install a statue of himself arrayed as a Roman god on the altar of the Temple of Jerusalem. This army posed a major threat to the city, but Caligula died before the threat was carried out. The symbols of famine in seal 3 refer to the famine during the reign of Claudius that is mentioned in Acts 11:28, while the double-ugly riders and multiple means of destruction in seal 4 portray Nero, whose infamy still lives. Changing the point of view from earth to heaven in seal 5 corresponds to the eighteen-month interlude between Nero and Vespasian, when the three pretenders each obtained the title but did not succeed in consolidating power as emperor. The multiple symbols in the first scene of seal 6 portray the breakdown of order and the overwhelming sense of despair and tragedy felt by the heirs of David when his city—Jerusalem—was sacked and destroyed in 70 C.E. by an army commanded by Emperor Vespasian's son Titus.[13]

The entirety of chapter 7 also belongs to seal 6, which pointedly depicts the celebration of the two throngs as the counterpoint to the devastation of the first scene of seal 6. Twelve is the number of Israel's tribes, and 144,000 is the product of 12 times 12 times 1,000. It is a large number symbolizing that the people of God stands in continuity with God's people Israel. In the first century, this number would have seemed much larger than it does for us in the computer age on the cusp of the third millennium. Its size should be read as a parallel to the "countless multitude," which includes people of every ethnic and national group in the people of God. These two throngs, which show that the people of God includes both Israelites and Gentiles around the world, celebrate the victory of the reign of God over the forces of evil. For those who perceive the resurrection of Jesus, the celebration loudly proclaims, the rule of God has already triumphed over the accumulation of evil experienced under the rule of Rome. In the midst of the worst imaginable tragedy from an earthly perspective—even the destruction of the holy city—the two multitudes are depicted in celebration. For the reader of Revelation, the message of the cheering throngs is that for those who live in the reality of the resurrection of Jesus, the rule of God has already triumphed.

Finally, this celebration leads to the seventh seal, which does not advance the chronology but rather begins a new cycle of seven. Ceasing the count at seven and beginning a new series of seven places the time of the seventh seal in the author's present. According to my sequence, that would be perhaps during the short reign of Titus (79–81 C.E.) or, more likely, during the reign of Domitian (81–96 C.E.).

Putting the declarations of cosmic victory together with the historical antecedents of the symbols shows that Revelation delivers a cosmic and eschatological perspective on events in the history of the first century. The image in Revelation 12 depicts the same history in another way. Rome, the seven-headed dragon, whose ten horns and seven crowns encompass the emperors and pretenders just mentioned, confronts the beautiful woman with a crown of twelve stars. She is Israel, who produced Jesus the Messiah, and is also the church, who is pursued by Rome. In this set of symbols as well, the resurrection of Jesus gives the victory to the earthly representatives of the reign of God over the forces of evil symbolized by Rome.

The Gospels present the same story as that told in Revelation, but from a different standpoint. Revelation tells the story of Jesus from the perspective of the heavenly throne room and the future culmination of the reign of God. The Gospels narrate that same story from the earthly vantage point of the folks who got dust on their sandals as they walked the roads of Palestine with Jesus. Both accounts locate the victory of the reign of God on earth and in history—narrative *Christus Victor*—and make quite clear that the triumph occurred not through the sword and military might but nonviolently, through death and resurrection. The point is that the violence that causes Jesus' death comes from the side of evil, which means that the victory of the reign of God occurs nonviolently. The intrinsically nonviolent character of the victory eliminates what is usually called the triumphalism of the church. As intrinsically nonviolent, its stance to the other or toward those who differ and are different can only be nonviolent.[14] To be otherwise is to cease to be a witness to the reign of God and to join the forces of evil who oppose the reign of God.

At the same time, reading that story in the Gospels shows that Jesus was not a passive victim whose purpose was to get himself killed in order to satisfy a big cosmic legal requirement. Rather, Jesus was an activist whose mission was to make the rule of God visible. And his acts demonstrated what the reign of God looked like—defending poor people, raising the status of women, raising the status of Samaritans, performing healings and exorcisms, preaching the reign of

God, and more. His mission was to make the reign of God present in the world in his person and in his teaching, and to invite people to experience the liberation it presented.

And when Jesus made the reign of God visible and present in that way, it was so threatening that the assembled array of evil forces killed him. These forces include imperial Rome, which carried ultimate legal authority for his death, with some assistance from religious authorities in Jerusalem, as well as Judas, Peter, and other disciples, who could not even watch with him, and the mob that howled for his death. In the resurrection the reign of God is victorious over all these forces of evil that killed Jesus.

As sinners, in one way or another, we are all part of those sinful forces that killed Jesus. Jesus died making the reign of God present for us while we were still sinners. To acknowledge our human sinfulness is to become aware of our participation in the forces of evil that killed Jesus, including their present manifestations in such powers as militarism, nationalism, racism, sexism, heterosexism, and poverty that still bind and oppress.

And because God is a loving God, God invites us to join the rule of God in spite of the fact that we participated with and are captive to the powers that killed Jesus. God invites us to join the struggle of those seeking liberation from the forces that bind and oppress. This invitation envisions both those who are oppressed and their oppressors. When the oppressed accept God's invitation, they cease collaborating with the powers that oppress and join the forces who represent the reign of God in making a visible witness against oppression. And when the oppressors accept God's invitation, they reject their collaboration with the powers of oppression and join the forces who represent the reign of God in witnessing against oppression. Thus, under the reign of God, former oppressed and former oppressors join together in witnessing to the reign of God.

Anselm removed the devil from the salvation equation. Narrative *Christus Victor* restores that deletion, but with a difference. In narrative *Christus Victor* the image of the devil is not that of an individual, personal being. Rather, "the devil" is the Roman Empire, which symbolizes all the institutions and structures and powers of the world that do not recognize the rule of God. Following Walter Wink's understanding of the powers, this devil is the symbol for the accumulation of all that does not recognize the authority of the reign of God.[15] In his contemporary construction of *Christus Victor*, James Cone wrote that the powers of evil confronted by the reign of God include "the American system," symbolized by government officials who "oppress the poor, humiliate the weak, and make heroes out of rich capitalists"; "the Pentagon, which bombed and killed helpless people in Vietnam and Cambodia and attributed such obscene atrocities to the accidents of war"; and the system symbolized in "the police departments and prison officials, which shoots and kills defenseless blacks for being *black* and for demanding their right to exist."[16] The victorious Christ has rescued us from the forces of evil and invites us to be transformed by the rule of God. While that transformation is never complete in the present eschaton, our participation in evil has now become involuntary and our lives take on the character of opposition to, rather than cooperation with, the forces of evil.

Earlier it was shown how Anselmian atonement correlates with feudal society and the ecclesiology that identified with the social order. It is now also possible to see that narrative *Christus Victor* belongs to, and in fact only makes sense when perceived within, the ecclesiological status of the early church that perceived itself to be different from the empire and the prevailing social order. This context is the setting for the confrontation *in history* depicted in narrative *Christus Victor*, which makes sense only if one assumes that the church, as a representative of the reign of God, confronts the social order or poses an alternative to the social order. According to my hypothesis, *Christus Victor* dropped out of the picture when the church came to support the world's social order, to accept the intervention of political authorities in churchly affairs, and to look to political authorities for support and protection. With the historical antecedents of Revelation soon forgotten, all that seemed to remain was cosmic imagery of confrontation that did not match the political reality. Thus, eventually the motif I have called narrative *Christus Victor* could fade away without a sense of loss, to be replaced by Anselm's satisfaction motif, which reflected the medieval social and ecclesiological conditions.

The image of narrative *Christus Victor* avoids all the problematic elements in classic atonement images. It reflects the ecclesiological worldview of the early rather than the medieval church. It is grounded in assumptions of nonviolence—the nonviolence of Jesus—rather than violence. In particular, it does not assume retribution or the assumption that injustice is balanced by the violence of punishment. It does not put God in the role of chief avenger, nor picture God as a child abuser. And it is abundantly obvious that God did not kill Jesus nor need the death of Jesus in any way. Jesus does suffer, but it is not as an act of passive submission to undeserved suffering. Jesus carries out a mission to make the rule of God present and visible, a mission to bring and to give life. When this mission threatens the forces of evil, they retaliate with violence, killing Jesus. This suffering is not something willed by nor needed by God, and it is not directed

Godward. To the contrary, the killing of Jesus is the ultimate contrast between the nonviolent reign of God and the rule of evil.

Earlier, a question used to analyze the atonement motifs was, Who needs the death of Jesus? Bringing that question to narrative *Christus Victor* focuses its profound difference from satisfaction atonement. The question has a nonanswer in narrative *Christus Victor*. God does not need the death because this motif does not make use of the idea of retribution. In narrative *Christus Victor*, the death pays God nothing and is not Godward directed. If anything or anyone "needs" the death, it is the forces of evil who kill Jesus. They "need" the death as part of the futile effort to annihilate the reign of God. The death of Jesus is thus very pointedly not something needed by God or God's honor. It is rather what the forces of evil—the devil—do to Jesus. Rather than being a divine requirement, the death of Jesus is the ultimate indication of the difference between the reign of God and the reign of evil. The reign of the devil attempts to rule by violence and death, whereas the reign of God rules and ultimately conquers through nonviolence.

If Christians are troubled by the violence associated with Christianity during its two-thousand-year history, the first step is to recognize the extent to which formulas of classic theology have contributed to violence both overt and systemic. This essay has provided data for that acknowledgment. The second step away from Christianity as a violent religion would be to construct theology that specifically reflects the nonviolence of its namesake, Jesus Christ. As a suggestion in that direction, I offer narrative *Christus Victor* as both nonviolent atonement and narrative Christology. Finally, step three would be to live out the theology of its nonviolent namesake. That commitment is a call to every Christian. One dimension of enacting that call would be to make nonviolence an intrinsic and integrating principle across the curriculum of Christian colleges and within each discipline by anyone anywhere who seeks to follow the way of peace with mind as well as body.

Christ as Good Shepherd. Early Christian Mosaic, Ravenna, Italy. Photo: Scala/Art Resource, N.Y.

16

The Cross of Resurrection and Communal Redemption

Rita Nakashima Brock

On the red brick walls outside the chapel on the campus of the Central American University in San Salvador are the words of Archbishop Oscar Romero: "If I am killed, I shall arise in the Salvadoran people." Inside, large brightly colored wooden plaques dominate the chancel. To the left and right are paintings of angels; in the middle hangs a tall cross. On the lower section of the cross, a resurrected Archbishop Romero lifts his arms in blessing, dressed in his vestments, a miter, and white robes. A green corn plant sprouts below him. The arms of the cross are vibrant with images of his community, engaged in the ordinary activities of life. The images revive a medieval style of resurrection crosses, which itself was a revival of an earlier Byzantine style.[1]

Just to the right, near the chancel, is a large portrait of the two women and six Jesuit priests assassinated at the university by the military in 1989. Behind their faces, the gaunt, bare torso of Jesus hovers in shadows like a protective ghost. His arms extend in the pose of crucifixion, and his thumbs are tied in the characteristic torture method used by the Salvadoran military.

At the rear, above the doors, the *Via Dolorosa* is mounted on the red-brick inner walls. A series of large, simple charcoal drawings depicts victims tortured by the military, drawn by an artist as he found them tossed on the streets. Young women and men lie in contorted heaps, in small groups or alone, mostly naked. Their thumbs are tied like Jesus; bullet holes riddle their limp bodies.

In this essay I use this set of images, as well as others, to trace a theological and historical trajectory in which iconographies and theologies of the cross shifted from life to death and from resurrection to violence.[2] In examining these shifts, I contend that violence never saves, for it only has the power to destroy or prevent something worse. It cannot create life or restore broken relationships. I propose instead an understanding of salvation as a complex process that is accomplished in communities of resurrection.

THE CHANCEL RESURRECTION CROSS: THE ANASTASIC ERA

It took Jesus a thousand years to die. An image of Jesus dead does not appear in Europe until 960–970.[3] Once he dies, that is all he seems to do. The crucifixion is one of the most recognizable images in all of Western art. His death becomes the screen onto which is projected every imaginable human suffering—an image so characteristic of Western Christianity that it is nearly impossible to imagine a time when his crucifixion did not claim the center of Christian art and piety. But there was such a time.[4]

That earlier time believed in Jesus' resurrection and the promise of paradise delivered by baptism. It lasted from the origins of Christianity until the end of the tenth century, a millennium I call the Anastasic Era, for *anastasis*, resurrection. During that time, the incarnation, transfiguration, miracles, and resurrection of Jesus were the central focus of Christian faith and art, a focus revived in the resurrection crosses in El Salvador.[5]

Anastasic Christians focused predominantly on Jesus' victory over death, following Paul in Romans 6, who makes clear death no longer has power over either the risen Christ or over baptized Christians. By descending into the grave, Jesus had taken away death's power. When he rose on Easter, Jesus unlocked paradise, closed after the banishment of Adam and Eve.[6] His blessings were conferred through the Holy Spirit in the church via baptism, the central ritual of the Anastasic Era, which catechumens undertook en masse at Easter after several years of testing and instruction and weeks of Lenten austerities. As birth began the journey of earthly life, rebirth via baptism began the journey toward eternal life. The newly baptized were called "infants," Jesus at baptism is depicted in

Doubleday, 1973), William R. Jones posited a seminal critique of black theologians' reliance on theodicy, identifying it as a rhetorical prison that does not permit them to question seriously the idea of God's goodness. Both Jones and Pinn advocate some form of *humanism* as a way for black people to exercise an additional faith option.

7. Cf. Rita Nakashima Brock, *Journeys by Heart: A Christology of Erotic Power* (New York: Crossroad, 1988); and Joanne Carlson Brown and Carole R. Bohn, eds., *Christianity, Patriarchy, and Abuse: A Feminist Critique* (New York: Pilgrim, 1989).

8. Delores S. Williams, *Sisters in the Wilderness: The Challenge of Womanist God-Talk* (Maryknoll, N.Y.: Orbis, 1993); and idem, "Black Women's Surrogacy Experience and the Christian Notion of Redemption," in Paula M. Cooey et al., eds., *After Patriarchy: Feminist Transformations of the World Religions* (Maryknoll, N.Y.: Orbis, 1991), 1–14, reprinted in chapter 1 of this volume; see also Jacquelyn Grant, "The Sin of Servanthood and the Deliverance of Discipleship," in Emily Townes, ed., *A Troubling in My Soul: Womanist Perspectives on Evil and Suffering* (Maryknoll, N.Y.: Orbis, 1993), 199–218.

9. Postmodernity is that period of social, political, and economic development in the West after World War II. Culturally, it is marked by the invention of television, which signaled the beginning of the age of information. Advocates of postmodernism resist "metanarratives" of history (usually advanced by dominant cultures) purporting a *telos* that mystifies power arrangements and generally supports the status quo. Postmodernism has given rise to the debate on multiculturalism as a viable alternative to "master narrative" theories of history that seek to control the content of knowledge and the dissemination of information. See Jean-François Lyotard, *The Postmodern Condition: A Report on Knowledge*, Theory and History of Literature, vol. 10 (Minneapolis: University of Minnesota Press, 1984).

10. Carl E. Braaten and Robert W. Jenson, eds., *Christian Dogmatics*, vol. 2 (Philadelphia: Fortress Press, 1984), 14–15.

11. See Gustaf Aulén, *Christus Victor: An Historical Study of the Three Main Types of the Idea of the Atonement* (New York: Macmillan, 1969).

12. Steven E. Ozment, *The Reformation in the Cities: The Appeal of Protestantism to Sixteenth-Century Germany and Switzerland* (New Haven: Yale University Press, 1975), 134.

13. Williams, *Sisters in the Wilderness*, 199–200.

14. Brock, *Journeys by Heart*. See also, idem, "And a Little Child Will Lead Us: Christology and Child Abuse," in Brown and Bohn, eds., *Christianity, Patriarchy, and Abuse*.

15. Kelly Brown Douglas, *The Black Christ* (Maryknoll, N.Y.: Orbis, 1994), 31.

16. Ibid., 22.

17. Jacquelyn Grant, *White Women's Christ and Black Women's Jesus* (Atlanta: Scholars, 1989), 212.

18. Ibid., 209.

19. Ibid., 219. Grant cites her forerunner, Jarena Lee, a nineteenth-century proto-womanist and preacher in the AME Church.

20. Williams, "Black Women's Surrogacy Experience."

21. The "Re-Imagining Conference" (4–7 Nov 1993), held in Minneapolis, was an international gathering of women participating in the World Council of Churches' Ecumenical Decade in Solidarity with Women and consisted of, among other things, an audiotaped lecture/discussion series. The quotations in this section cite Williams's lecture and the question-and-answer session that came after it in the session titled "Re-Imagining Jesus," taped on 5 Nov 1993. Other participants included Korean feminist theologian Kwok Pui-lan and Lutheran feminist theologian and preacher Barbara Lundblad.

await a salvation promised, but lived it in their baptized lives. Hence, Christians were expected to exhibit confidence that they were new beings in Christ, assured of paradise and possessed of the Holy Spirit. Gregory of Nyssa declared, "We are free from any necessity, and not in bondage to any power, but have decision in our own power as we please; for virtue is a voluntary thing, subject to no dominion."[11] Moral behavior demonstrated that baptism had reoriented Christians to ordinary life, and worship enacted this sanctified existence. Anastasic piety was shaped by the joy and confidence granted by the Spirit, the moral obligations of community life, and an affirmation of the spiritually renewing capacities of ordinary life and its ritual activities.

Anastasic art gradually included North African and Asian influences characteristic of Byzantine art. This less naturalistic style uses simplified anatomical forms in formal frontal postures to emphasize the spiritual nature of the subject. The direct gaze of the figures addresses the viewer, inviting devotion instead of conveying narrative action. The faithful encounter a serene presence inviting response. This is religious art, rather than art about religious subjects.[12]

Art historians suggest that the absence of crucifixions is due to Christians feeling that a criminal death was shameful and that dying was incompatible with claims of Jesus' divinity.[13] The Romans used crucifixion to terrorize and control subject populations by conducting them in public. Christians may have eschewed showing the crucifixion to avoid reinforcing the Roman strategy.[14] Irenaeus regards the manner of Jesus' death as less significant than his need to die in order to reopen paradise. Hence, he "naturalizes" or universalizes the death by making it like all deaths. Jesus' saving power was in his miracles, teaching, and victory over death.[15]

THE CRUCIFIED CHRIST AND THE ATONEMENT ERA

Some suggest that, before representations of Jesus' death, Christianity lacked a realistic concern with violence and failed to imagine God's compassion for human suffering.[16] The crucified Christ is read as a sign of divine solidarity with human pain. However, the first images of crucifixion emerge after Christian violence against pagans.

In the early eighth century, the Western church began to force conversion to Christianity. Boniface traveled to Saxony with a papal commission to missionize pagans. To demonstrate the superiority of Christ over Saxon gods, he hacked down the sacred oak of Thor and built a church from its planks. Charlemagne, a generation later, conducted a thirty-three-year terror campaign to convert the Saxons to his version of Christianity. In Charlemagne's Roman Empire of the West, refusal to be baptized carried the death penalty, the first use of violence to missionize. Charlemagne also destroyed their sacred trees.[17] Carolingian theologians forced a new theology of the Eucharist upon the Saxons by asserting that the dead Christ was on their table, judging them of their sins. While Saxon theologians held to the traditional understanding of it as the feast of the risen Christ, imperial coercion and a century of debate eventually pushed the church toward this new Eucharist, focused on death.[18]

One of the first crucifixes appears around 960–970 in Saxony, the Gero Cross, now in the Cologne Cathedral. This three-dimensional, life-sized sculpture is hewn from wood:

> The body sags, the belly protrudes, one hip and the slightly bent knees are pushed to the left....Christ's head has fallen forwards on to his chest....The eyes are closed; the hair spreads over the shoulders....The strong movements...create an overwhelming sense of hanging on the cross. The Death of Christ is here an elemental occurrence. It was never presented thus in Byzantine art.[19]

Pressed by violence into conversion and forced to imagine a dead Christ on their Eucharist table, the Saxons created an early image of Jesus' death on the cross.

The Saxon crucifixion witnesses to their tragic experience of Christianity. For the Saxons and for other Anastasic Christians, Jesus' suffering was a source of grief.[20] Violence was sin. Even soldiers or civilians who killed in self-defense were required to do penance. But this ethical position against violence began to change after the time of the Gero Cross.

In the eleventh century, the Carolingian Empire was in decline. Local castellans plundered the countryside and churches with impunity. In the absence of social order, bishops called Peace Councils, demanding that the castellans take vows not to destroy church properties. Through these councils, the church attempted to prohibit violence.[21] Church officials recruited soldiers into service to enforce the *pax Dei*. Through such measures, the eleventh-century church accrued the authority to regulate violence and used armed force against enemies of the peace.[22]

In November 1095, Pope Urban II called a Peace Council in Clermont, France, and declared a universal, binding Truce of God. At the Peace Council's conclusion, preaching to the armed nobles, bishops, monks, and laity, the Pope announced an armed pilgrimage to Jerusalem, the first crusade. He called on Christians to cease killing each other and to fight to free Jerusalem and the churches of the East from the Saracens (that is, Muslims). Thus, the crusades began in western European Christian society as a strategy for keeping social order, not because of a threat from Muslims or Jews.[23] In follow-up letters, the Pope wrote:

> No one must doubt that if he dies on this expedition for the love of God and his brothers his sins will surely be forgiven and he will gain a share of eternal life.... If any among you travel for the... liberty of the churches, they will be relieved of the penance for all of their sins.[24]

With crosses sewn on their garments, thousands responded to the call. The armed pilgrims, however, did not initially travel east. They went north to the Rhineland, where they killed approximately ten thousand Jews in the spring of 1096—nearly a third of the Jewish population in Europe. In 1099, they slaughtered forty thousand in two days in Jerusalem.[25]

During this first crusade, Anselm of Canterbury, the Pope's close associate and a crusade supporter, published *Cur Deus Homo?* Anselm wrote, "Man absolutely cannot give himself more fully to God than when he commits himself to death for God's honor."[26] He exhorted Christians to imitate Christ's self-offering because God's justice demanded it. Not to do so would be to sin against God. On the death of Jesus, he commented:

> The life of this man [Christ] was so sublime, so precious, that it can suffice to pay what is owed for the sins of the whole world.... Did he not give up His life for the honor of God? He freely gave to God for his honor of such a kind... which can make compensation for all the debts of all human beings.[27]

The death of Christ became a gift, voluntarily offered to pay humanity's debt of sin. Satisfaction was made to God the Father by this execution, which God the Son voluntarily endured because no ordinary human possessed the merit to pay the debt. The boundless merit of Christ's substitutionary payment blesses all humanity. Anselm fails even to mention the resurrection.

Once violence ceased to be a sin, Western Christianity turned toward divinely sanctioned violence. Killing in the name of Christ became a holy act, preached by bishops, supported by taxes, celebrated by poets and artists, institutionalized as penance, enacted by ritual, legalized by canon law, and legitimated by theologians.[28] The fastest route to paradise was to kill or be killed.[29] Christian war was a penitential act, instead of a reason for doing penance. Holy war superceded just war.[30] Death by torture saved life. God took pleasure in the murder of human beings deemed "other," whose vile and filthy race was contrasted with the pure elect.

The substitutionary theory of the atonement engenders a series of substitutions. Crusaders slaughtered Jews and Eastern Christians as substitutes for Muslims, who were substitutes for the original "Christ-killers." Jesus substitutes for sinful humanity to pay the debt owed God. God is a substitute for Satan as the cause of Jesus' death. Personal suffering and self-sacrifice substitute for the moral virtues of self-restraint and serenity. And committing violence substitutes for spiritual rebirth as the route to paradise. This atonement makes everything, reality and myth, "at-one" without distinction.[31]

A century after the Gero Cross, crucifixes began to escalate in grotesqueness and number. As the crusades multiplied and the disastrous fourteenth century arrived, Jesus took on the starved, sore-infested body of a plague victim. He died in agony in proportion to the growing emphasis on violence, sin, and suffering.

The resurrection fades in importance, superceded by redemptive violence. Jesus saves by suffering unto death. In the fourteenth century, for the first time, images of God the Father appear. God, old and in royal attire, impassively or sorrowfully accepts, approves, and presents his dead Son to the viewer.[32] The Trinity is a dyad, the dying Son, grasped in the Father's arms. The Holy Spirit, a small dove, flits ineffectively between them. The life-sustaining power of the Spirit in the church all but disappears in this intimate Father-Son relationship, fused by sacrificial violence. Jesus is a victim, raised by the Father who wills his death. At the same time, paradise disappears as the destination of the dead, superceded by purgatory.[33]

During the medieval period, the central Christian ritual of rebirth had been replaced by a ritual of salvific death—soteriology through violence.[34] The eucharistic mass became the reenactment of crucifixion, gratitude for Jesus' suffering and dying to save humanity. In some images of the crucifixion, Jesus literally dies waist-deep inside a chalice.[35]

The crucifixion of Jesus evolved from a past event to be mourned into a justification for violence and became a central image for devotion. In the Eucharist he died eternally, elevating death to the same eternal status as life. Believers communed with his death through killing and conquest, austerities and self-sacrifice, self-inflicted pain and ritual reenactment. Christians worshiped before images of suffering and violence.

A generation after Anselm, Peter Abelard raised questions about his theory of the atonement. Abelard did not believe Christ gave satisfaction to God to repay the debt of sinfulness required by the justice of God. Abelard proposed a reconciliation theory.[36] Responsibility for Jesus' death lay in human sinfulness, not in

God's need to be repaid the debt of sin. Humanity was estranged from God by sin. Salvation was necessary for us, not for God, who offered grace freely out of love.

God's love was revealed especially in crucifixion, which offered the estranged soul reconciliation. Abelard emphasized that redemption came from knowing divine love in its deepest abyss, revealed in the willing suffering of Jesus Christ, who bore the penalty of human sin. Individuals bore responsibility for choosing to sin; hence, only inner transformation could free the human soul to receive God's love and to love others. Understanding divine love transforms the inner person, who finds his or her sin exposed in the agony of Jesus and, with that knowledge, repents and turns toward God. This inner change reorients the conscience, not through fear of punishment, but through love. In being infused with this love, the soul was set free to follow Christ's example of self-sacrificing love, to love enemies as well as neighbor.

Most liberal Christians are Abelardians. Liberals reject the idea that God was the cause of Jesus' death and prefer Abelard's affirmation of divine love and individual moral responsibility.[37] Abelard seems an improvement over Anselm. However, he and Anselm disassociate the death of Jesus from context and history, universalize its saving significance, and valorize suffering. This process begins with the Gospels, in their softening of Roman responsibility and their anti-Judaism.[38] As Rome became the patron of Christianity, blame shifted increasingly toward the "Jews." Johannine paternal-family metaphors framed the relationship of Jesus to God in intimate terms, which provided language to spiritualize Jesus' death.

Abelard suggests that we come to know love most fully by being moved by torture and execution as an act of self-sacrificing love for us, which then becomes the model for our own lives.[39] Self-sacrifice, however, is generated by the mystical confusions and fusions of violence. Violence forms intense emotional bonds, such as the bonds of comrades in war, but these are not necessarily ties of love.[40] In intimate relationships, these bonds can be mistaken for love because violence fuses selves by destroying boundaries. If self-annihilation, whether willed or coerced, is love, then it is identical with violence. Abelard confuses the trauma of violence with healthy, life-affirming love that resists violence and works for justice.[41]

Abelard affirms the Trinity, so that God always acts with power as Father, wisdom as Son, and love or beneficence as Spirit. The Holy Spirit is the presence of God in human beings, and love, he suggests, is impotent. This follows from his definition of love as self-sacrifice. If love is defined as loss of self, the redeemed soul must surrender all power to resist violence because thought of self is not love. Hence, Abelard embeds helplessness in salvation and romanticizes and sanctifies suffering, an effective way to entrench victims in systems of violence.

Abelard's theory also reinforces the isolation of violence. For Abelard, all sin is against God and personal conscience, not against neighbor. He emphasizes inner transformation and individual moral intent, which parallels later existentialist theories of subjectivity, faith, and personal-guilt piety. The focus on the inner subjective state of the perpetrator and victim is especially problematic in situations of intimate violence because they often love each other.

Intimate violence is the framework of meaning in atonement theology. Jesus is reduced to a relationship to his abuser whom he loves, whom he forgives, and to whom he is so fused in identity as to be nearly at one. This reframing of his death as a story of intimate violence betrays Jesus and his movement for divine justice. The torture and execution of Jesus has been inflicted on many, often in his name. The crucifixion is a reminder of the human legacy of violence, not of salvation.

The *Via Dolorosa*: The Modern Era

The Modern Era did not invent genocide; it perfected technologies for propaganda and killing. In the last century, humanity faced into the abyss of our own extinction. For those who refuse to go gladly into that night, understanding violence and its impacts have taken on great urgency.

Violence succeeds by mystifying accurate perception and historical memory and isolating human beings from community bonds and moral responsibility.[42] In deflecting the causes of Jesus' death onto the wrong people and minimizing or "naturalizing" it, the Anastasic Era buried the historical memory of how he died. Responsibility for Jesus' death was theologized as nonbelievers in collusion with supernatural forces. The execution of Jesus as an enemy of the state was gradually transmogrified into an intimate interaction between Father and Son, opaque and mysterious, behind which the agents of Jesus' death disappear.

This theological process bears a striking resemblance to the psychological effects of rape, child abuse, physical deprivation, captivity, torture, and war.[43] The marks of embedded trauma are evident: the extreme isolation, singularity, and opacity of the experience; the narcissism of individual experience and romance of suffering; the feeling of helplessness; the loss of boundaries and fusion of victim with the perpetrator; the near obsession with the power and drama of violence; the piety of guilt, repentance, and obedience; and the narrowing of meaning to the framework of violence.[44]

Violence in its worst forms is socially organized and transpersonal, in which individual intent rarely matters. Under dire conditions, a person or community may resort to violence, but violence is always unholy because it threatens not just the individual soul, but the entire social nexus of life. Effective resistance to violence comes through community capacities to maintain accurate, integrated memory, to enable recovery from and make restitution for harm, and to negotiate the complex and ambiguous responses to violence that result from its eruptions. A community must expect restitution for harm from those who inflict it, regardless of their intentions, rather than focusing justice on the punishment of perpetrators. In the absence of means for restitution, nonviolent responses to harm must be ritualized and enacted communally.

The restoration of life is never an individual process, even for individuals. When our soteriology focuses on individual subjective states, it falls short of what is necessary to restore right relationships and frame meaning in ways for life to flourish. Salvation comes from communal practices that affirm incarnation, the Spirit in life, and its ongoing promise of resurrection and paradise. From that affirmation flows a commitment to restorative justice and steady, active love, embraced in a common life with all its difficulties and rewards. Religious institutions that sanctify life are essential to this salvation. Such communities of remembrance and hope enable human thriving amidst all the powers in their own times and places arrayed against them.[45]

CONCLUSION: AN ECCLESIAL SOTERIOLOGY

The three sets of images in the chapel in San Salvador affirm the Spirit incarnate in the flesh. The images together present the historical memory of the community in relation to its affirmation of life and the priestly, pastoral, and prophetic work of the church.

The chancel cross image reflects the iconography of the Anastasic Era. The cross affirms resurrection as salvation—the priestly sanctification of life. The Archbishop is *"presente!"*—arisen in the hearts of his people, blessing them. The images on the cross bear witness to paradise, recovered in the ordinary tasks and sustaining relationships of life, sanctified and embodied in ritual. They remind the faithful that worship occurs in the presence of resurrection. The promise of paradise is the restoration of a world devastated by war—a community engaged in common activities where love is tenacious, generous, and fierce. While unfulfilled, the work of justice and peace is never defeated when such ordinary paradise is sanctified in ritual and memory. Incarnation is true, the Spirit lives in the flesh, known in the presence of living beings. Ordinary life holds miracles; there is more to human existence than cold, hard facts that end in death.

The portrait of the women, men, and Jesus echoes Renaissance images. Crucifixions emerged as remembrances of human suffering: terror, plague, war, and genocide. In this portrait, Jesus hovers over the risen martyrs, as if to say, "Whatever the terrorists of the world may do, God has gone before us and is with us always." This accompaniment, too, is a sacred task of the church, its pastoral work of giving comfort, of facing pain with compassion and care. The church heals wounded souls, knits broken relationships, calls the repentant to a new life, and offers company and dignity to the dying.

The *Via Dolorosa*, in stark black and white, is like modern documentary. The images bear witness to the community's memory of a government campaign of terror against its own people, supported by the U.S. government. These stations of the cross are a road to torture and murder. They invoke outrage at carnage, sorrow for loss, resolve to hold fast to the truth of what happened, and commitment to stop such injustice. And this, too, is the sacred work of the church: to shelter truth and accurate, integrative memory, to raise prophetic voices against injustice and violence, and to organize communities to resist the principalities and powers of this world.

The three sets of images do not harmonize well. Their styles clash. They allow no easy integration, no cheap reconciliation. The heart holds contrary motions, shifting from love and joy to outrage and sorrow and back—we must recognize the complexity of life in order to save it. Restoring worlds destroyed by violence is difficult, long, and absolutely necessary. In their grating tensions and complex remembrance, these images hold a world of meaning, wisdom for life, truth about how deeply we need each other, about how deeply what we do matters.

17

Theology of the Cross

Challenge and Opportunity for the Post-Christendom Church

Douglas John Hall

As a non-Lutheran for whom Martin Luther has been, since I first encountered him half a century ago, the most *interesting* historically prominent Christian of them all, I have gradually come to the conclusion that, of all the major voices of the Protestant Reformation, Luther's is the least familiar. That seems obvious enough where Anglo-Saxon Protestants are concerned, but sometimes I have the impression Luther remains something of a stranger even among the churches that call themselves by his name. Perhaps, like many renowned figures of history, Luther's fame has obscured his reality.[1]

We English-speaking Protestants of WASPish origin usually *think* we know Luther. After all, he did "launch" the Reformation with his famous Hallowe'en prank there in Wittenberg nearly five centuries ago. But we tend, most of us, to lump Luther together with all the other heroes of our religious past—Zwingli and Calvin and Knox and the English reformers right down to Wesley. And the truth is, he's significantly different from all of them.

Luther's "difference" can be discussed in many ways. For instance, it can be said that he is still a late-medieval man and a mystic, whereas the other reforming spirits (including Melanchthon!) were "modern," trained in the humanist tradition and tending toward rationalism. Or that Luther, though a scholar, never lost touch with his peasant origins, whilst Calvin and the others were already part of the emerging middle classes. And so forth.

But what really separates Anglo-Christianity from Luther, I think, is his *theology*. There are shadings and nuances in his way of articulating Christian faith that the typical English-speaking Protestant finds puzzling—even uncomfortable. And this discomfort isn't limited to Presbyterians and Methodists and Anglicans. Many avowed Lutherans in North America feel it, too. For Luther's most basic ideas are conspicuously "out of sync" with the culture by which we are all shaped today, no matter what our denominational tag.

Take what's usually regarded as the central claim of the man: "justification by grace through faith"—*sola gratia, sola fide*. Who, in our success-driven society, really believes that—and behaves accordingly? The somewhat-informed church-going Protestant may dutifully deplore "works-righteousness," but will he or she be satisfied with a son or daughter who isn't a high achiever?

Or consider Luther's paradoxical notion that Christians are "*at the same time justified and sinners*" (*simul justus et peccator*). In a country like the United States of America, where "*true* belief" admits of neither intellectual doubt nor moral duplicity, what kind of concession to backsliding is that?

And what of Luther's conception of the authority of the Bible? Certainly the Bible was indispensable for the Saxon Reformer. His *sola Scriptura* (by Scripture alone) was as adamant as Calvin's. But no one who knows him even a little could ever accuse Luther of encouraging fundamentalism. He was fond of quoting the then-popular saying, "The Bible has a wax nose." You can twist it to your own preference in . . . noses! Besides, Scripture is only "the cradle" of Christ, he insisted. Don't confuse it with the Baby. Only the living Christ himself is Truth—and, sorry, you may possess a Bible but you can't possess *him*!

LUTHER'S *THEOLOGIA CRUCIS*: A SPIRIT AND METHOD FOR THEOLOGY

I could go on in that vein, but all this "difference" in Martin Luther is summed up in one great underlying distinction: the distinction that he himself, early in his reforming career, designated by two Latin terms, *theologia crucis* and *theologia gloriae*—usually translated "theology of the cross" and "theology of glory." Luther wanted his theology to be (and it usually was) a theology of the cross. There's a temptation to the theology of glory in all of us, even Luther; but he at least knew that it's a matter of *temptation*, and many Christians, apparently, do not.[2]

By "theology of glory" Luther meant what some of us call *triumphalism*. Religious triumphalism is the kind of belief that imagines itself the only true belief, the only "orthodoxy." In the language of a popular song of my youth, this theology "accentuates the positive, eliminates the negative, and doesn't mess with Mr. In-between."[3] So, for instance, the great "positives" of resurrection, redemption, sanctification, and the triumph of God's righteousness are "accentuated," and crucifixion, divine judgment, continuing sinfulness, and the reality of evil are "eliminated." (Except, of course, as they apply to other people!) Whether in old-fashioned doctrinal language or in the psychologized lingo of the church-going middle classes, the theology of glory offers a full package of Positive Spiritual Reinforcement—for those whose economic and other *material* sorts of reinforcement are firmly in place.

The theology of the cross, on the other hand, is not able to shut its eyes to all the things that are wrong with the world—and with ourselves, our human selves, our *Christian* selves. It doesn't accentuate *the negative*, as its critics sometimes claim; but it does want to acknowledge the presence and reality of that which negates and threatens life. Death and doubt and the demonic are still with us, and Luther never tired of talking about them and struggling with them. Any faith that depends on *denying* all that darkness isn't faith at all in the biblical sense of the term; it's credulity, repression, and self-deception. The "Word of the Cross" doesn't *banish* the darkness; it "lightens" it—which means that the gospel both reveals "the darkness" for what it truly is and provides enough light for us to make our way within it, one step at a time.[4]

If I had to characterize Luther on the basis of the approaches offered in the aforementioned song of my adolescence, I'd say that he intends neither to over-emphasize "the positive" nor to overlook "the negative." His main quest it to understand how, as disciples of the crucified One, we can live with "Mr. In-between"—or, to put it more learnedly, how we can live faithfully in the midst of what Reinhold Niebuhr called "the ambiguities of historical existence." For Luther, neither those who say it's all bad nor those who say it's all good represent rightly the biblical view of the human condition. Life is a voyage on the great murky sea of In-between; and the trick is how to navigate one's frail bark with eyes wide open to the real perils of the depths, yet with courage and expectancy. Only Luther, among the great founders of the Protestant way, as I see it, does justice to the ambivalence and contrarieties of life; only he consistently refuses to offer us religious "answers" that sit lightly to our never-ending human questions.

The theology of the cross isn't just about Jesus' crucifixion and its meaning for us, though the cross of Calvary is of course its central symbol—its window on the world. The *theologia crucis* refers, rather, to a whole spirit and method of "doing" theology; and, as Jürgen Moltmann put it succinctly in his book *The Crucified God*, "*Theologia crucis* is not a single chapter in theology, but the key-signature for all Christian theology."[5] It has as much to do with our understanding of God and the world and humankind and the church as it does with Jesus as the Christ and the doctrine of atonement.

I have found that the best way of capturing the *spirit* of this theological tradition is by considering the three so-called "theological virtues" named by Paul in the famous passage about love (*agape*) in 1 Corinthians 13: faith, hope, and love. But in order to bring out the deeper meaning of these positive Christian "virtues," it's necessary to make explicit what they negate, what they rule out. Without these clarifying negations, faith, hope, and love too easily devolve into pious platitudes.

So let's put it this way: the theology of the cross is a theology of (1) faith—*not sight*; (2) hope—*not finality or consummation*; and (3) love—*not power*.

A THEOLOGY OF FAITH

Faith means trust—trust in God, trust in the absence of conclusive proof, trust in the presence of a good deal that normally makes for distrust! Paul, whose affirmation in 1 Corinthians 1 and 2 ("We preach Christ crucified") is the most explicit biblical source of this theology, continually contrasted "faith" with what he called "sight." Luther was fond of quoting especially Hebrews 11:1: "Now faith is the assurance of things hoped for, the conviction of things *not seen*." If as Christians we think we "see" something ultimate, absolute, it is only "through a glass darkly" (1 Cor. 13:12, KJV).

A theology of *faith* therefore has to be a modest theology. As trust, faith knows periods of real confidence (*con + fide*), but it is consistently denied certitude—the unflinching sureness of those who believe they've "seen." Indeed, the faith that is "not sight" knows moments of serious doubt (Luther experienced many such— *Anfechtungen*, he called them: periods of utter abandonment). Such faith, being conscious of its own incompleteness, is neither threatened by nor scornful of the faiths of others; on the contrary, unlike the religiously sure-of-themselves, it is ready to listen to all seekers after God and Truth.

Just here is one of the many reasons why the theology of the cross represents (as I indicated in my title) both challenge and opportunity for the Christian

Movement as it enters its post-Christendom phase. Faith that is *faith* and doesn't pretend to be "sight" is modest enough to know (*a*) that it is one alternative among many, (*b*) that its public witness must be thoughtful and not just declaratory, and (*c*) that it may and must dialogue with other faiths. A triumphalistic religious community that confronts its world as the one body that really "sees" and "knows" is destined to be a divisive—and perhaps a violent—influence in our diverse and volatile global context today. Only a faith that is conscious of how far short it falls of ultimate truth and goodness ("sight") can contribute to the peace and justice of a planet as diverse and as fragile as ours.

A Theology of Hope

Christian hope has to be distinguished from every worldview, religious or secular, that presents the goal of history as though it were already accomplished—at least in the religious or political theories of the worldview in question. While the gospel proclaims that God's victory over sin, evil, and death has been achieved already *in Christ*, it does not interpret the resurrection triumph of God in Jesus as though the cross—and all the creational and human suffering for which the cross of Jesus stands—were simply a thing of the past. That is precisely the temptation of the theology of glory, and therefore those under the spell of that theology, in whatever form, tend to treat the existing suffering of the world, including individual pain and death, less than seriously.

In fact, a good deal of religion in the world today (some of it allegedly Christian) must be blamed for retarding or subverting changes that are demanded by persons and groups, often working in secular agencies, who care deeply about creation and human civilization. For one thing, too much religion is still fixated on "heaven" as the great and glorious goal of existence, thus relegating earthly troubles to second place at best. More subtly, religion provides its adherents, especially among the more affluent peoples of Earth, with a panoply of well-being that effectively insulates them against the suffering of many creatures, human and extra-human.

To be concrete, many have argued that the main function of religion in the United States seems to be to undergird the "national philosophy of optimism"[6] with a super-optimism born of faith and producing "peace of mind." But this optimism is not to be confused with Christian hope. Hope, as it is conceived of under the sign of the cross, is not based on the capacity of humans (some of them!) to think positively, cheerfully, "hopefully"; it is based on faith in the grace and providence of God. God, who brought Jesus again from the dead, is at work in the world to fulfill the promises of creation, appearances to the contrary. Such hope doesn't have to turn away from all the seemingly hopeless things that occur in order to sustain its hope. It can be honest about the way the developed nations are despoiling nature and oppressing the materially deprived; it can face the reality of our ongoing wars, of devastating pandemics like AIDS, of the worldwide marginalization of women, of racial tension, and so forth. Hope that is fashioned "beneath the cross of Jesus" will even, despite itself, be driven to greater and greater honesty about the data of despair, the realities that make for earthly hopelessness.

And that kind of honesty is ethically extremely important. For unless human beings have the courage to confront what is wrong with their world, they will never be in a position to help to right the wrong. So, far from being an attitude of blessed contentment, lulled by the feeling that "God's in his heaven, all's right with the world," Christian hope is a catalyst of involvement, participation, action! It grabs us by the throat and thrusts us into the life of our tumultuous times, making us *responsible* for our world in a way we never associated with . . . religion.

A THEOLOGY OF LOVE

The theology of the cross is a theology of love, not of power. The contrast between love and power is both dramatic and subtle. Some people like to speak about the "power of love," as though love were just another kind of power, maybe the most powerful. But if it's a power, love is the only power that, to achieve its aim, must become weak. A love that "comes on strong," trying to take the beloved by storm, is a contradiction in terms. Love that's real has to accommodate itself to the condition of the beloved.

That is what God, in the crucified Christ, has done and is doing. As Reinhold Niebuhr put it, "The crux of the cross is its revelation of the fact that the final power of God over humankind is derived from the self-imposed weakness of God's love."[7] Paul Tillich was fond of quoting Luther on the same theme: "If God had come in power, He would not have won our hearts. 'God made himself small for us in Christ.'"[8]

So much religion—including the Christian religion—has been driven by the illusion that it could make a difference only if it were able to compete with the other great powers of the world, including governments and political ideologies and other religions. Christendom throughout its more than 1,500-year history vulnerable to or threatened by torture; and (3) an organized movement against torture that actually exposed the clandestine centers of torture in the country and the identities of official torturers. None of this was easy, and the successes were mixed with occasional failure. The words and actions of eucharistic practice tap into and release the performance of the body of Christ, a performative creativity that enacts the sociality of the body of Christ toward a comprehensive liberating social form (the kingdom). The disciplines of the torture state should meet, in the practice of the Eucharist, a counterpower, one that unleashes worlds of life amid the deathly unmaking of worlds that war and torture spew forth.

CONCLUSION: "WE ARE HUMAN BEINGS!"

As the body of Christ in the American torture state, we are called to perform the body of Christ as a liberating counter-politics in order to end torture and the states that resort to it. We do this, of course, through movements, organizing, consciousness raising, committee work, and with sighs too deep for words. But if this is not merely to be the work of politically inclined folk, but also of the marrow of Christian faith *qua* Christian, I say let us etch that performance against the American torture state ever more obviously and dramatically into the liturgical practice of the Eucharist, in which the body of Christ is re-membered in our midst and for all of us. In closing, allow me to propose an experiment, to offer a suggestion of how this might be done. It is a suggestion on which I know many readers can improve.

Living in memory of the tortured, imperially executed Jesus of Nazareth, who surely screamed when broken under the whip—remembering this Jesus, I wonder, will Christians now separate themselves from the screams, whimpers, groans, and howling of the tortured today? I say let's not; at least on occasion, let us place the screaming—the unmade, unworlded speech—in our eucharistic performance of remembrance, and in our re-membering of a tortured and executed Jesus.

But that would be only the half of it. Because the performance of the Eucharist is one we also do in expectation, in hope of a feast, a time when the tortured and all that is repressive is somehow judged and healed, let us also envision an accompanying performance of renewal. I envision the recorded audio voice of Salvadoran Archbishop Romero being played,[38] where Romero is in a cell forced to listen to his priest and other detainees and friends being tortured, during which

18

The Cross as Military Symbol for Sacrifice

Jürgen Moltmann

AT THE BEGINNING OF CHRISTIANITY there are two crosses: One is a real cross, the other a symbol. One is a murderous gallows of terror and oppression, the other a dream-cross of an emperor. One is for victims of violence, the other for violent conquerors. The one is full of blood and tears, the other empty. The first stands on Golgotha, and Jesus hangs on it, the other is the victorious dream of the Emperor Constantine in the year 312 C.E. What has the second to do with the first? How could the memory of a victim of injustice and violence be changed into a symbol of victorious injustice and violence?

THE CROSS AS SYMBOL OF VIOLENT CHRISTIAN EMPIRE

When Emperor Constantine saw a cross at night and heard the voice, "In hoc signo vinces" (In this sign you shall conquer), he ordered his soldiers to paint a cross on their shields, and lo, they fought and won the battle at the Milvian bridge and conquered Rome for their Lord and master. This—and not Golgotha—was the beginning of the Christian Empire, destined to conquer the world for Christ and his anointed Caesar. One can still see the cross associated with military victory depicted on the ceilings of old Byzantine churches: There is Christus Pantocrator

(Christ the Almighty Ruler) in heaven, and here is the anointed emperor as
Christ's representative on earth. And because there is only one God and one
Christ in heaven, there can be only one ruler and one empire on earth. This
Christian Empire claims that it will be the kingdom of peace that will never end
(in reference to the book of Daniel, chapters 7, 14 and 27). Salvation is inside
this Christian Empire, damnation outside. In the Crusades and Holy Wars, non-
Christian people were confronted with only two alternatives: baptism or death.

The saint of this Christian Empire was St. George, depicted as slaying the
barbarian dragon and rescuing the innocent virgin Church. St. George was changed
from a Christian martyr and victim who died under the Roman Empire (c. 304)
into a military hero of the new Christian Empire of Constantine. The guarding
angel of the Christian Empire became the Archangel Michael, slaying the evil
dragon in heaven. The dragon became the symbol for the enemies of Christ and
the Christian Empire, and following this line of logic, the enemies of the Christian
Empire became enemies of God. Wars became "holy wars," military campaigns
became "crusades," and whoever gave his life in the battles became a martyr
and his death a sacrifice. The future of world history was seen in the apocalyptic
colors of the "last battle" between God and the devil, Christ and Antichrist, the
good guys and the bad guys, the kingdom of heaven and the kingdom of evil,
the empire of freedom and the scoundrel states; in one word: *Armageddon*. The
cross as symbol of military victory and violent world domination was born in an
emperor's dream, lasted for centuries, and is still effective today.

When Hernando Cortez called his soldiers to conquer Tenochtitlán, the city
of the Aztecs, in 1521, he raised the flag with the cross and cried out: *"In hoc signo
vinces."* They killed Moctezuma, destroyed the capital of the Aztecs, and built
what is now known as Mexico City. The triumphal dream-cross of Constantine
continued as the symbol of Christian Empires: Charles the Great subjugated the
Saxons with cross and sword; Otto the Great did the same with the Slovenians.
Knights of the Cross, St. George's Knights, Temple Knights, Knights of Malta,
and other Christian conquerors set up this cross in "barbarian" countries and
brought the "heathen" peoples into a supposedly saving kingdom, or *Heilige Reich*.
Their intended world domination was also later called "the Christian Civilization,"
"the realm of freedom," and multiple other titles. One can find the imperial cross
in the orders and medals of most of the Christian nations: The Iron Cross in
Germany, the Victoria Cross in Britain, the St. George Cross in Russia, the Cross
of the League of Honor in France, and so forth. You can see the victorious cross
on most of the flags of Christian nations. The decorative golden crosses on the
necklaces of beautiful women are banal remnants of the holy triumphant cross.

Decorative and military victory crosses, however, don't depict an actual crucified person—ever since Constantine's time, they are empty.

"They Died That We May Live"

After Constantine, those who sacrificed their lives in the "holy" or existential wars of Christian Empires and Nations were understood in a Christlike manner: The soldiers' deaths were not without religious meaning, and they did not die in vain. Their deaths were sacrifices for their fatherland; they died for us. And such self-sacrifice is a saving act. The first model of self-sacrifice was that of the Christian martyr in the times of Christian origins who gave his or her life for Christ and with Christ for the gospel and the faith. The martyr followed her or his conscience and, in discipleship of Christ, stood at the side of poor and oppressed people. The Constantinian change of affairs turned the Christian martyr into the Christian soldier. The death of the military hero became the cornerstone of the Christian Empire, the Christian nation, and, in modern times, "the Holy Fatherland" of World War II Germany. The crown of the martyr was changed into the medal of honor for bravery and victory. In this way, the death of the soldier received a religious halo, and it was sanctified and glorified by the understanding that they died that we may live. They died for us.

At this point I can't hold back my bitter critique: The soldier's death was glorified in this type of national religion—whether they wanted it or not, whether they volunteered or were drafted against their will. In postwar Germany we asked, "For every one soldier who received the Iron Knight's Cross, the *Ritterkreuz,* how many others were killed or sacrificed?" With the beginning of modern times, the universal Christian Empire was replaced with imperial Christian Nations. Since the French Revolution, "the Nation" has come to mean one's ethnic "Fatherland," land of the Germans, the French, or the Russians, and it has been adored as Holy: "*Heilig Vaterland / in Gefahren / Deine Söhne sich um Dich scharen . . .*" (Holy Fatherland, in danger, your sons gather around you[1]), as a very religious national song in my youth began. The Nation became what the church was previously supposed to be: a redeemer. An example of this is described in Ernest Lee Tuveson's 1968 book, *Redeemer Nation: The Idea of America's Millennial Role.*[2] He who gave his life for this Nation gave his life to God and was saved. The death of the soldier was seen and memorialized as a Christlike death for the salvation of the world.

In World War I, "Golgotha" was repeated in the particularly bloody battles of Verdun and Flanders. Every meaningless death in this war was interpreted as a noble sacrifice. It was as though there were no *victims* at all, only *heroes*. The original Christian religion changed quickly into a national war-religion; the God of Jesus was replaced by the War-God demanding more and more sacrifices, victimizing millions, and swallowing up the young generations of the nations.

Pastoral care in World War II Germany was strangely centered on a *military theology of the cross*. In 1942 Catholic bishops sent a circular letter to Catholic soldiers on the Russian front, saying:

> When the Lord calls you in this war to a soldier's death, the death of a confessor, give up your life in the cross of the Lord as an expiatory sacrifice for our sins and the redemption of our people. When the Lord calls you in the dark Gethsemane hour, in the suffering of wounds or in imprisonment—take it upon yourselves as the cross in the passion of the Lord.[3]

Glorification of the war and sanctifications of the soldier's sacrifice on the front by bishops of the Protestant national churches were even worse because they conveyed the message that Christ is present in the soldier who gives his life for his friends, and anyone who is killed in the noble cause of his Fatherland will be forever engraved in the memory of his people. One can still find monuments of Christlike dying soldiers in the memorials of World War I. The four million dead German soldiers of World War II are buried under iron crosses in German war cemeteries with large crosses at the center of the cemetery that are reminiscent of Golgotha. The Organization for the Care of War Graves (*Kriegsgräberfürsorge*) is still claiming property rights over the corpses themselves in order to make them soldiers forever. Most of these soldiers were drafted against their will and were victimized by meaningless orders in an unjust war. They never wanted to sacrifice themselves; they struggled only to survive.

After World War I, a particular form of German war poetry arose. One of the most read poets was Ernst Jünger. He developed a whole "war religion" with a strange enthusiasm to kill and be killed, an enthusiasm for death. Fascists followed him; one of Franco's generals created the Spanish fascists' battle cry: "*Viva la muerte!*" (long live death). Today we hear similar words from extremist Islamic terrorists who support suicide missions that attack mass civilian populations: "You love life—we love death." Ernst Jünger produced a sacrifice religion for wartimes: "The deepest fortune of men is to be sacrificed, and the highest imperative is to show goals worthy of sacrificing life."[4] The religious role of the officer is the role of the priest and the role of his soldiers is to be the slaughtered sacrifice.

THE CROSS AS MILITARY SYMBOL

I am personally concerned, and shall end this short essay with my life-and-death story. When Germany started the murderous World War II in 1939, I was thirteen years old. Older-age youth of our school were drafted first, and were soon killed in action. Their names were written on a wall below a line from the German poet Hölderlin: "And for you, beloved Fatherland, no one is giving his life in vain."[5] In 1943 there were already too many names under this sentence, and they moved these senseless words to a more remote place. In 1944 my class was drafted. We knew that the war was lost and there was no chance of German victory. We were driven to the front and to our deaths so that Hitler could live a few months longer and, as we found out later, so that the concentration camp murderers could go on killing Jews. We were victimized and the noble appeals of the German war religion made no sense to us. They all knew it—our officers, the generals—but no one dared to doubt the myth of the "German end victory" and the anticipated new "wonder weapons" that could secure a victory; they were obedient to a point of nonsense and absurdity and sent their soldiers to meaningless death.

My father had taught me a certain reverence for my Fatherland, but I didn't want to sacrifice myself, or be sacrificed, for this regime that had betrayed us so much. The "Holy Fatherland" died for me in Bergen-Belsen and Auschwitz. My own father had the conflicting convictions of "I must defend my Fatherland" and "Hitler must not win this war." Ever cognizant of this dilemma, he became an officer and was obedient until the end of the war. Afterward we had a lot of debates. My standpoint was that my true "fatherland" is freedom itself, so there can be no real fatherland in dictatorship; he had trouble understanding this. But, unlike my father, I had been "given" time to formulate my ideas about war, obedience, resistance, and sacrifice for peace in the three years I spent behind barbed wire in prisoner-of-war camps. My resolution after this time was to never again become a victim. During my imprisonment, I found Christ the crucified as my brother in need and my liberator. This was a very different image of the cross than the one presented by the sacrifice religion within wartime Germany. The Son of Man came "to seek out and to save the lost" (Luke 19:10), and he found me in my godforsakenness and took me with himself on the way to the "broad place where there is no oppression anymore" (paraphrased from Job 36:16). Christ crucified liberated me from affirming the terrors produced by those who utilize the cross as military symbol.

19

American Torture and the Body of Christ

Making and Remaking Worlds

Mark Lewis Taylor

WHEN, IN HISTORY, WHAT HAS been called "the star of empire" rises over a nation, marking its powers as global and efficiently sovereign over all other political societies,[1] many in that nation count it a boon to dwell beneath it. Indeed, there is much wealth, also opportunity that goes with a nation's imperial status, but for many peoples within that nation, as well as those on the underside of empires abroad (as Iraqi civilians and many others are today), it is a curse. French sociologist Emmanuel Todd, in his book *After Empire*, has detailed the erosion of citizen life and public vitality that awaits a United States public that continues to live complacently under the star.[2]

The erosions are so many, and are underway at such a fast pace today, it defies my capacity to address them in an essay of this length. I usually let suffice a commentary on the star of empire, imagined as a five-pointed one that, contrary to the glory and brilliance that some see, oozes/drips a bile from each of its five points and so poisons the body politic of the life of the nation that ventures on the imperial quest.[3] These five ominous points of empire are (1) triumphalist unilateralism, (2) war, (3) nationalism, (4) political and economic inequality, and (5) torture. Here, I am focusing only on the fifth poisoning practice, torture. In relation to what is believed by Christians, I will focus on the notion of the body of Christ. Hence, my title, "American Torture and the Body of Christ."

A Tradition of American Torture

The 1984 U.N. Convention against Torture gave the following definition of torture. Torture is

> any act by which severe pain or suffering, whether physical or mental, is intentionally inflicted by or at the instigation of a public official on a person for such purposes as obtaining from him or a third person information or confession, punishing him for an act he has committed, or intimidating him or other persons.[4]

Based on this definition, or versions similar to it, more than ten international and United States laws and conventions thus prohibit torture.[5]

Nevertheless, the United States has used torture in its covert and counter-insurgency campaigns abroad for decades. It has taught torture and admitted to writing manuals of torture.[6] Activists and populations throughout Latin America—for instance, El Salvador, Nicaragua, Mexico, Honduras, Argentina, Chile—and much of the world knows this well.[7] In addition, on the home front, a more than occasional "ethos of torture" has long characterized the treatment of prisoners in U.S. jails, prisons, and police precinct stations. People of color, especially, on the receiving end of prison-guard and police brutality in the United States, know this well.[8] Thus, torture as part of U.S. official policy is nothing new.

One doesn't need only to consult the victims. The United States' running of torture operations, intentionally refining torture procedures in interrogation for maximum impact, and then disseminating the teaching of these practices throughout the world is a matter of published record. One of the most recent and most comprehensive treatments is offered by University of Wisconsin–Madison professor of history Alfred McCoy, in his book *The Question of Torture: CIA Interrogation, from the Cold War to the War on Terror.* In great detail McCoy charts the history of the U.S. Central Intelligence Agency's interrogation practices, particularly the CIA's nervousness during the Cold War over the possibility that the Soviets were using mind-bending drugs for successful extraction of information from recalcitrant detainees. The CIA spread out its contacts through a network of academics and psychiatric practitioners from across U.S. universities such as Yale,

Harvard, Cornell, and the University of Pennsylvania (catching up even a couple of academics at Canada's McGill University[9]) to develop a number of draconian tests used on unsuspecting volunteers. This was all done with the intent of discovering the most devastating modes of interrogation that could strike fear and provoke cooperation in the detainee. The results claimed that while some physical abuse is valuable, psychological abuse is both more destructive and more effective. One of the harsh measures U.S. military personnel often use today is that of forcing detainees to stand for hours on end—a physical hardship, yes, but even more a psychological hardship since its victims often blame themselves for weakening and causing their own physical collapse, and thus for cooperation. These efforts, McCoy argues in his book, provided the fertile soil out of which grew a remarkably similar and predictable pattern of a U.S.-based, CIA-orchestrated-and-disseminated mode of interrogatory torture. After the Cold War period, it reincarnated itself in the Vietnam conflict, where U.S./CIA operation of the notorious Phoenix Program resulted in the detention, torture, and extrajudicial execution of tens of thousands of Vietnamese. When in 1975 the United States was sent packing from Saigon, the operations were taken to Latin America, where the United States was determined to not lose its intensely felt battle with communism. While President Jimmy Carter's human-rights policy initiative closed the major site for torture practices at the School of the Americas in Panama, with Ronald Reagan's presidency U.S. torture manuals and training centers surged strong again, particularly wherever there was an international regime that the United States thought was friendly to Washington, but that was also under threat by leftist forces. "In January 1997, the *Baltimore Sun, Washington Post,* and *New York Times* published extracts from the agency's Honduran handbook, the *Human Resource Exploitation Training Manual— 1983,* describing it as the latest edition of a thousand-page manual distributed to Latin American armies for a twenty-year period." One of these press narratives began as follows: "A newly declassified CIA training manual details torture methods used against suspected subversives in Central America during the 1980s, refuting claims by the Agency that no such methods were taught there."[10]

The details of the U.S. and CIA history McCoy relates from newspapers and government documents are many and sobering. What I want to note here is that in the long-running character of that history from the Cold War to the present, one can discern a consistent thread running throughout the CIA's key torture manuals: a continual propagation of torture. Three manuals in particular show this, and McCoy examines them meticulously. The first is the 1963 *Kubark* manual (or *Kubark Counter-Intelligence Training* manual), which consolidated the results of the psychiatric tests and experiments done on human subjects during the Cold War. The techniques proposed in *Kubark* were continued in the previously mentioned 1983 Honduran manual. Those techniques are refined but basically the same in the more recent "Instructions" orders given by U.S. General Ricardo S. Sanchez for interrogating prisoners at Abu-Ghraib during the Iraqi insurgency there.[11]

Today, citizen fear, nationalism, hyper-patriotism, official willingness to use torture, and our culture of war in the post-9/11 imperial regime have permitted an aggressive new policy of torture, and at many sites: amid abusive U.S. troop incursions into Iraqi homes, at U.S.-guarded prison centers in Iraq and Afghanistan, at U.S. detention centers around the world, and at Guantanamo Bay Detention Center in Cuba, where the United States has housed more than five hundred "illegal enemy combatants," denied them human and civil rights, and subjected them to numerous abuses.[12] Even Michael Ratner, a seasoned international rights lawyer who for many years has prosecuted cases against U.S. officials for mistreatment,[13] has expressed a new level of shock about U.S. policies of abuse after 9/11, policies that include what he documents as "war crimes."[14] The abuses of Abu-Ghraib, Iraq, and elsewhere; the decisions of high officials like Secretary of Defense Donald Rumsfeld to relax rules to allow some forms of torture; and the justifications made by President Bush's legal counselors, such as John Yoo and Attorney General Alberto Gonzales—all this is now stunningly on display in a host of essays and collected works, most notably in Karen Greenberg and Joshua Dratel's *The Torture Papers*.[15] Page after page shows the emergent rationale for using torture in interrogations to get evidence needed to fight terrorism. CIA official Cofer Black put it bluntly at a 2002 Senate Intelligence Committee hearing: "All you need to know is that there was a 'before 9/11' and there was an 'after 9/11'. After 9/11 the gloves come off."[16]

Why Torture? Behind the Intention and Results of Torture

Torture, especially on the level we see it today, requires policy decisions and intentional organization. Former National Security Council adviser Richard Clarke reports that, immediately after his evening speech after the 9/11 attacks, President Bush addressed his White House counterterrorism staff and said, "Any barriers in your way, they are gone." When even Rumsfeld interjected that there were legal restraints on such action, the president shouted back, "I don't care what the international lawyers say, we are going to kick some ass."[17] Further, when CIA head George Tenet was briefing Bush about the later capture of suspected Al-Qaeda operative Abu-Zubayda, he had to inform Bush that it was hard to get information out of the man since he had been wounded in the groin and was groggy from painkillers. At this point, "Bush turned to Tenet and asked: 'Who authorized putting him on pain medication?'" About this statement *New York Times* journalist and author James Risen writes that, wherever this statement sits between joking banter and serious query, "this episode offers the most direct link yet between Bush and the harsh treatment of prisoners by both the CIA and the U.S. military."[18] Similar careful studies and investigations reveal damning evidence that other higher officials—Rumsfeld himself, General Sanchez, Colonel Thomas Pappas—seemed to be fully knowledgeable about mistreatment that violates standing law and conventions against torture. This is evident from the writings of General Antonio Taguba, Colonel Janis Kaprinski, and McCoy.[19] The high officials tend to justify these various modes of "taking off the gloves" as necessary for extracting information from al-Qaeda and those with knowledge of the insurgency in Iraq.

A major problem with the administration's line of reasoning is that—in addition to being a flagrant violation of human dignity according to international law, of the most basic of moral principles, and of the values of almost all religious traditions—torture rarely works. In fact, as experienced FBI interrogator Dan Coleman states about his longtime close work with the CIA on counterterrorism cases, it is actually the extending of due process to detainees and building rapport, some human connection, that "made detainees more compliant, not less." Under torture and abuse, detainees will say anything and they are usually lies, or the lies are nearly impossible to sort out from truth. "Brutalization doesn't work. We know that. Besides, you lose your soul."[20]

Actually, from his survey of the history of U.S. use of torture, McCoy admits that there is one condition under which torture does seem to work for extracting information, such as when a government—as the United States did in its Phoenix Project in Vietnam, and as France did in Algeria at mid-twentieth century—deploys "mass torture." This is a torturing of such large numbers from a population—in the hundreds and thousands—that one is able to sift through the many tales of half-truths to build some composite that provides necessary material. As McCoy points out, mass torture also usually ends up in massive extrajudicial executions since keeping around and maintaining so many broken bodies is just too unwieldy.[21] The problem with this is not only that the torturer loses his or her "soul" in the process, but that the nation allowing mass torture loses its international respect, and also, in spite of gaining information, usually loses the war as a whole, as both the cases of the United States in Vietnam and France in Algeria demonstrate. At present, the United States may not be deploying mass torture, but what it has done is extensive enough that the political fallout and blowback are considerable. McCoy summarizes the state of the present U.S. operations of interrogation and their consequences as of 2006:

> ...the toll from President Bush's orders, as conveyed in these memos and others still secret, would be chilling—some 14,000 Iraqi "security detainees" subjected to harsh interrogation, often with torture; 1,100 "high value" prisoners interrogated, with systematic torture, at Guantánamo and Bagram [Air Base in Afghanistan]; 150 extraordinary, extralegal renditions of terror suspects to nations notorious for brutality; 68 detainees dead under suspicious circumstances; some 36 top Al Qaeda detainees held for years of sustained CIA torture; and 26 detainees murdered under questioning, at least 4 of them by the CIA.[22] Adding to the casualties from this covert war, Bush hinted at torture and extra-judicial execution during his State of the Union address in January 2003, when he spoke about the "3,000 suspected terrorists...arrested in many countries. And many others have met a different fate. They are no longer a problem for the United States." To all these statistics, we should add another casualty—one great nation's international reputation.[23]

This is the ugly consequence, destroying lives, destroying the soul of torturing peoples, as well as the bodies and souls of the tortured. So what positive function of torture might the practice have, such that regimes deploy it? Are they just mistaken?

What torture does do is shore up the power of the state over other entities in the global order and over the citizens a regime wishes to rule. Torture, announced as a necessary practice and then implemented, even sporadically, atomizes a citizenry and increases a state's capacity to rule and to contravene genuine democratic challenges. Torture is known to reduce the language of tortured persons to the babbling sounds of their preverbal childhood. "He howls," notes journalist Jacobo Timmerman recalling his own and others' torture in Argentina.[24] Torture is control over speech, and the fear and haunting power of torture erodes the collective linking by language between citizens that is necessary to citizen collaboration in democracy and for resisting leaders' tendencies to usurp power.

Thus, as theologian William Cavanaugh notes, "Torture breaks down collective links and makes of its victims isolated monads."[25] Philosopher Elaine Scarry, in her book *The Body in Pain,* argues that the tortured person is reduced to inexpressibility, marked especially by her or his inexpressible pain. The sufferer's language is destroyed. Torture "unmakes," as she says, the tortured individual's world.[26] I would add that it makes and extends the world(s) claimed by the state. This isolating and breaking down is a resource for unchecked state power. It excels through fear in controlling and disciplining bodies.

Whether the United States today is on the way to a deployment of "mass torture" on the scale of the Vietnam Phoenix Project of the 1960s and 1970s, or merely working some halfway house toward that extremity, we face a torture state that subverts democracy at home and destabilizes the rest of the world. It is this that makes it so urgent that we find a way to respond, to "Make It Stop," as one North American movement campaign puts it.

MEANINGS OF "AMERICAN TORTURE"

You will have perhaps noted an ambiguity in my use of the phrase "American torture" in this section. When I use the phrase "American torture," there are several overlapping meanings that need to be kept to the fore. First, it refers to the torture policies of the United States of America,[27] post-9/11, and torture by Americans of those who are deemed international enemies of the United States.

Second, it refers to the suffering of torture throughout the American hemisphere, especially in the Caribbean, Central America, and South America, at the hands of the United States or by government elites in those regions wishing to promote U.S. interests. Over 57,000 Latin American officers were trained in the United States Army School of the Americas, located first in Panama, then moved to Fort Benning, Georgia, where it has been renamed in an attempt to avoid its onerous past reputation. Thousands of U.S. peace and justice activists expose that legacy every November with their marches and demonstrations there. They carry thousands of crosses bearing the names of Latin American victims of U.S.-trained squads and officers such as Roberto D'Aubisson, who was implicated in the assassination of Archbishop Oscar Romero of El Salvador.[28] Here "American torture" means torture as experienced by Americans throughout the hemisphere, usually for being on the underside of U.S. interests in controlling Latin America, a concern the United States has announced and exercised since the Monroe Doctrine.

Third, "American torture" refers to those American sufferers of torture *in the United States*. American torture is not just the torturing of other, non-U.S. persons. It is torture *of* U.S. Americans *by* U.S. Americans. Indeed, many modes of harsh interrogation, mistreatment, and torture have long occurred inside the United States prisons. That legacy, combined with the post-9/11 "war on terror," brings the issue home. This is a form of "blowback," not the type Chalmers Johnson writes about in his book by that title, where tortured and repressed foreigners strike back at the United States,[29] but blowback in the form of our U.S. leaders deciding to do to us what we have allowed them to do to others in our name. This is similar to the brilliant arguments of W. E. B. Du Bois and Aimé Cesaire that Europe's self-inflicted world wars were cases of colonial brutality being visited upon Europeans in the form of the barbarisms of Nazism and fascism.[30]

THE SACRALIZATION OF TORTURE

American torture, in *any* of these forms, however, is problematic today also because nationalized forms of Christianity—"Constantinian Christians," as Cornel West has termed them—have, in other contexts and potentially in ours, made a Christian virtue of torture. How so? Situations of fear in which torture is accepted as necessary often lead, as in Argentina's "Dirty War" of the 1970s and 1980s, to a sacralization of victims of torture, such that their enduring of torture is rendered as a way to hallow and sanctify the state. Their deaths are not only an efficient way to rid the state of dissenters and perceived enemies but torture also becomes a ritual that, when repeated, gives the tortured person the role of blessing the state through and by means of his or her drawn-out deaths. Analyst Franz Graziano has documented a torturer in an Argentina torture house: "We are going to make you Christ," says the torturer to his victim on the table of a torture center in what Graziano calls a "theogonic [god-begetting] affair."[31] "El Tijano" ("the Texan"), another notorious torturer in Argentina, told a young female victim, Graciela Geuna: "You're not going to be able to die, little girl, until we want you to. We are God here."[32] The state, in other words, assumes the role of the protective father, protective of order and "freedom from terror," and the victim in this twisted state theology is made a Christ-figure, a scapegoat in the worst sense, whose suffering fuels the protection of the state.

What we must be vigilant over, especially in a Christianized imperial power, is the destructive use of religion for supporting torture *and* thus the dehumanization of religion itself. There is also the fact that torture often drives torturers to develop religious rationalizations of torture, to craft mythologies to charter their acts of torture, and even to form prayers to hallow it, such as the "torturer's prayer" reported by an Argentinean prisoner, in which the torturer asked the Lord to make the torturer's hand "accurate so that the shot will hit its mark and put charity in my heart so that I fire without hatred. . . ."[33] Torturers can reach for the religion at hand that cozies up to state power, and twist it into grotesque pieties and prayers that presume to dispense grace while dissembling the tortured on their tables.

This may become an increasingly grave concern as the current Christian Right, with dreams of christocracy and theocracy, fuses resurgent senses of United States "manifest destiny" with nationalistic dreams of "American greatness."[34] It is a dangerous brew, a precarious and threatening combination of resonances. We must open ourselves to a new mode of performative proactivity amid the torture state. If torture unmakes the world, what is the creativity needed for making and remaking worlds?

HOPE AMID U.S. TORTURE AND EMPIRE: PERFORMING THE BODY OF CHRIST EUCHARISTICALLY

When speaking on these themes, whether in the 1980s and 1990s regarding American torture of peoples to the south, or in the 1990s pertaining to prison abuse and police brutality, I often have received the questions, "What can we do? How can we stop this?" If I am speaking to Christian audiences, I often point to my understanding of grace as a power given to us in the form of what I term, in my book *Remembering Esperanza,* a "reconcilatory liberation"—that is, unity-making liberation always at work, always beckoning us to take stands, do the work, suffer the cost, all to discover, insofar as possible, the grace of a more flourishing life for all peoples.[35] Or, as with my book *The Executed God,* I point to the gospel's way of the cross as (*a*) an "adversarial politics," (*b*) a "performance of creative dramatic action," and (*c*) an "organizing of social and political movements."[36] All these are no mere addenda to grace, but are constitutive of grace and faith as I understand them. Especially important is the second dynamic, though it is not separable from the other two. The performance of faith through creative drama, or what I referred to in *The Executed God* as a "theatric of counter-terror," is a theatric to counter the theatrics of terror of our times. This I take as consonant with Elaine Scarry's call to make and remake the world against the torturer's *un*making. Thus, I am asking here how this making might be done in the way we perform our remembrance of Jesus' body broken on the cross.

My activist colleagues, especially those outside the church, would be perplexed in the extreme that I, indeed anyone, should turn to notions like the body of Christ and the Eucharist as a resource amid the American torture state. "What does the table of the Lord's Supper have to do with the torturer's table?" they might ask. My reply, "Almost everything." But, in order to see its relevance and to experience the liberating power it can have, we are going to have to liberate the eucharistic practice from what it has become in so many North American churches. To address and effectively redress the problematic of American torture, then, I suggest the following three steps.

The Body of Christ as Social

First, Christians need to celebrate our spiritual life in the body of Christ as social. As part of the "body of Christ," we have our life in an ever-richer, more profound social space. Here I am trying to establish the sociality of the notion, "body of Christ." The journey of Jesus' own body as portrayed in the Gospels during the days of passion and resurrection shows the unfolding of this social spirit. The body of Jesus of Nazareth (already in and a part of society and history) crosses boundaries through a radically inclusive love that, in doing justice, puts him at risk with both religious and political/imperial elites. The solitary figure presented in the Gospels, however, is repeatedly uniting with his followers at table, in a whole host of table rituals, and finally in a feast, the Last Supper, that anticipates the great eschatological banquet of the kin(g)dom of God, where all peoples are included and gathered together. Jesus' body is a body-with-others, around the table, in a collective. Even when lifted on his cross, and amid cries of abandonment and isolation, there are many to whom he is joined: the criminals also being executed with him, the women and others at the foot of the cross, as well as the comings and goings of many people on Good Friday, Holy Saturday, and at the narrated empty tomb. Recognition of the resurrected Jesus is presented, as in the Emmaus road incident, amid several walking together, breaking bread with one another, moving on the way—a moving that is a moving alongside, with, and in communion with others.

Precisely this understanding of belongingness to Christ, being a social experience, is often difficult to hold in the U.S. cultural milieu. Here the reigning discourses of the churches fix on "a personal relationship with Jesus," which usually means that the primary experience of grace comes as an individual experience of God that is only secondarily social. As New Testament theologian Herman Ridderbos writes about the Pauline views of new life in Christ, the situation in the New Testament is the reverse and proceeds thus: "Those who by virtue of the corporate bond have been united with Christ...have died and been buried with him, may know themselves to be dead to sin and alive to God...'in the Spirit.' *They are included in this new life-context, no longer in the flesh, but in the Spirit.*"[37]

The Body of Christ as Liberating Sociality

Second, I believe we are forced to ask, "But what kind of collective? What kind of sociality is the body of Christ disclosed in Jesus' way?" A response can be derived by recalling the backdrop of Jesus' passion events, namely the Passover, complete with its remembrances of the emancipation of the Hebrews from their tyranny in Egypt, from slavery, into a structured liberation for flourishing. Jesus, the Galilean Jew, as the Gospels portray him, moved from Galilee to Jerusalem, to the hottest spot in the territory, where remembrance of God's deliverance from the cruel politics of Egypt merged with expectation of a deliverance from the politics of Roman empire and occupation in Palestine. Passion week is understood best, I suggest, as a deliverance of a people, of their bodies, as well as hearts and minds and souls—their fullness of being—from the social, political, and physical cruelties of domination. The drama of Jesus' passion week is painted on the canvas of Passover, its memories of a past deliverance and its hopes for a future one. The meaning of Jesus' ministry in that week, of his teachings, of his death and of his resurrection, needs to be found in his Jewish belonging to that heritage of exodus, in his belonging to a people suffering the death, control, surveillance, occupation, and torture with which Jesus and so many lived, and which he memorably suffered. What kind of sociality marks the body of Christ? It is a sociality of deliverance, of integral liberation for those in need.

Again, in U.S. churches it will not be easy to preach, teach, and be heard if we read Passion week this way. The eucharistic meanings, as usually interpreted and practiced, have been constricted largely to meditations on individual guilt and salvation, mystified on a plane far above earthy domains of relationships, communities, politics, and imperial brutality. In this way we lose not only the politics of liberation so dear to Jesus and Jewish spirituality, but we also lose the earthiness of Christian practice. The bread and wine of the meal, rather than being the food and drink that sustains a community, the body of Christ, ceases to be food and drink and often becomes lost in a fervent prayer for individual forgiveness. In contrast, the passion of Christ, the meaning of the body of Christ, read against the canvas of the liberation of people and their bodies from oppression, provides a very different kind of spirituality of remembrance, one that is earthy, political, social, and alive with meaning for any system that brutalizes and tyrannizes.

Body of Christ as Eucharistic Action: "Acting Up!"

So, third, the Eucharist is a social space of performance. It is a life-context in which the body of Christ "acts up," we might say. This acting up is a corollary of being a community that is marked by a sociality of deliverance. Acting toward liberation is the mark of the body of Christ as the church, as a social presence in history. The bread is broken, the cup lifted, words are spoken. In *Remembering Esperanza*, which sought to think through the Eucharist in relation to the problems of world hunger, the denial/lack of food and drink to so many, I suggested that even the words of institution might be seen as "performative utterances," borrowing a term from philosopher J. L. Austin. The words of institution are not intoned solely as a remembering back, but as that kind of re-membering that is heavily laden with expectation, expectation of deliverance of a groaning people (of hungry people, today), expectation that hearers will perform a distribution of elements not only among themselves but also as food and drink to those in need. Building on this, the eucharistic practice of the body of Christ can be seen as the collective performative force of Christians, moving and on the move, to provide succor and strength to those under repression who are cut off from the social flourishing of soul and body that mark life in the Spirit.

If state torture is an attack on the body that destroys collective life—especially destroying democratic society and virtues, atomizing society, breaking individuals off from one another so that they are subordinate to the state—then torture, from the vantage point of the body of Christ, is seen as the very antithesis of eucharistic practice. It must be affirmed, though, that Christians celebrating the Eucharist in a time of American torture cannot help but be on the move in resistance to it, given what life in the body of Christ is to be.

Again, in his excellent book *Torture and the Eucharist*, Cavanaugh makes the powerful and direct links between the Eucharist and a people suffering torture. His main scene of study is Chile, under the regime of Augusto Pinochet, and the way the church constituted itself during those years of torture and repression. The Eucharist offers, he says, a "counter-politics" that took the form of pursuing three practices in Chile: (1) an announced "excommunication" of Christians who torture or condone torture; (2) an organization of a complex support structure for torture victims, their families, and all poor residents whose activism made them vulnerable to or threatened by torture; and (3) an organized movement against torture that actually exposed the clandestine centers of torture in the country and the identities of official torturers. None of this was easy, and the successes were mixed with occasional failure. The words and actions of eucharistic practice tap into and release the performance of the body of Christ, a performative creativity that enacts the sociality of the body of Christ toward a comprehensive liberating social form (the kingdom). The disciplines of the torture state should meet, in the practice of the Eucharist, a counterpower, one that unleashes worlds of life amid the deathly unmaking of worlds that war and torture spew forth.

CONCLUSION: "WE ARE HUMAN BEINGS!"

As the body of Christ in the American torture state, we are called to perform the body of Christ as a liberating counter-politics in order to end torture and the states that resort to it. We do this, of course, through movements, organizing, consciousness raising, committee work, and with sighs too deep for words. But if this is not merely to be the work of politically inclined folk, but also of the marrow of Christian faith *qua* Christian, I say let us etch that performance against the American torture state ever more obviously and dramatically into the liturgical practice of the Eucharist, in which the body of Christ is re-membered in our midst and for all of us. In closing, allow me to propose an experiment, to offer a suggestion of how this might be done. It is a suggestion on which I know many readers can improve.

Living in memory of the tortured, imperially executed Jesus of Nazareth, who surely screamed when broken under the whip—remembering this Jesus, I wonder, will Christians now separate themselves from the screams, whimpers, groans, and howling of the tortured today? I say let's not; at least on occasion, let us place the screaming—the unmade, unworlded speech—in our eucharistic performance of remembrance, and in our re-membering of a tortured and executed Jesus.

But that would be only the half of it. Because the performance of the Eucharist is one we also do in expectation, in hope of a feast, a time when the tortured and all that is repressive is somehow judged and healed, let us also envision an accompanying performance of renewal. I envision the recorded audio voice of Salvadoran Archbishop Romero being played,[38] where Romero is in a cell forced to listen to his priest and other detainees and friends being tortured, during which time Romero cries out, yelling: "We are human beings!" Then, as I continue to imagine this eucharistic service, while Romero's shouts are being heard by the gathered Eucharist community and amid the continuing groans of the tortured, liturgical dancers in the congregation's midst would move forward from among those gathered, leading all of them forward. They converge around the eucharistic table, the people sing with the dancers, something expressive of a weary people's enduring power. Then, the audiotape is turned off, with no doubt great relief in the sanctuary, stopping the cries of torture. The celebrant's words of institution point to the grace of a people that put a stop to torture.

More songs and hymns could then be sung, pastor and people would share the food and drink performed in this space—and a counter-politics of the Eucharist in the American torture state might be nourished. And perhaps those participants could read, remember, and reconsider the meaning of other words of Romero from the last days of his life, as they might speak to Christians in the U.S. torture state of our time:

> I would like to make a special appeal to the men of the army, and specifically to the ranks of the National Guard, the police and the military. Brothers, you come from our own people. You are killing your own brother peasants when any human order to kill must be subordinate to the law of God which says, "Thou shalt not kill." No soldier is obliged to obey an order contrary to the law of God. No one has to obey an immoral law. It is high time you recovered your consciences and obeyed your consciences rather than a sinful order. The church, the defender of the rights of God, of the law of God, of human dignity, of the person, cannot remain silent before such an abomination. We want the government to face the fact that reforms are valueless if they are to be carried out at the cost of so much blood. In the name of God, in the name of this suffering people whose cries rise to heaven more loudly each day, I implore you, I beg you, I order you in the name of God: stop the repression.[39]

Notes

Introduction: The Cross in Context

1. Paul Tillich, *Dynamics of Faith* (New York: HarperCollins/Perennial Classics, 2001 [1957]), 49.

2. Ibid., 49–50.

3. See Susan L. Nelson's essay in this volume entitled "Imagining the Cross: Through the Eyes of Marian Kolodziej."

4. See J. Denny Weaver's essay in this volume entitled, "Violence in Christian Theology."

5. Christie Cozad Neuger, "Patriarchy Statistics" (presented to "Pastoral Care and Counseling with Women" course taught at United Theological Seminary, St. Paul, Minn., Fall 1993), unpublished. This statistic refers to estimates for abuse within the United States.

6. Brian Nelson, book review of *Proverbs of Ashes* at the "Headline Muse" Web site, 2003. Available from www.headlinemuse.com/Culture/proverbs.htm; accessed 5 May 2006.

7. Rita Nakashima Brock and Rebecca Ann Parker, *Proverbs of Ashes: Violence, Redemptive Suffering and The Search for What Saves Us* (Boston: Beacon, 2001) 25. See also Christine M. Smith, *Risking the Terror: Resurrection in this Life* (Cleveland: Pilgrim, 2001).

8. See Kelly Brown Douglas, *What's Faith Got to Do with It? Black Bodies/Christian Souls* (Maryknoll, N.Y.: Orbis, 2005). See also Orlando Patterson, *Rituals of Blood: Consequences of Slavery in Two American Centuries* (Washington, D.C.: Civitas/Counterpoint, 1998).

9. G. A. Studdert Kennedy, as quoted by Jürgen Moltmann, *The Trinity and the Kingdom*, trans. Margaret Kohl (Minneapolis: Fortress Press, 1993 [1981]), 35.

10. Ibid.

11. Ibid.

12. Information from personal interviews in June 2003 with Zephania Kameeta, Abisai Shejavali, and Paul John Isaak, Lutheran anti-apartheid leaders and theologians reflecting on the Namibian anti-apartheid movement.

13. See Jürgen Moltmann's chapter, "*The Crucified God* Yesterday and Today: 1972–2002."

14. Lewis M. Simons, "Genocide and the Science of Proof," in *National Geographic* (Jan 2006), 28.

15. Stanley Hauerwas, "Why Did Jesus Have to Die? An Attempt to Cross the Barrier of Age," *The Cresset: A Review of Literature, the Arts, and Public Affairs* 69, no. 3 (Feb 2006 [Lent]): 9.

1. Black Women's Surrogacy Experience and the Christian Notion of Redemption

1. Deborah Gray White, *Ar'n't I a Woman? Female Slaves in the Plantation South*, rev. ed. (New York: W. W. Norton, 1999), 33.
2. Ibid., 47.
3. Ibid.
4. Ibid., 48.
5. Ibid.
6. Ibid., 49.
7. Ibid., 55.
8. Ibid.
9. This is not to suggest that such empowerment led to autonomy for slave women. Quite to the contrary. Slave women, like slave men, were always subject to the control of the slave owners. And as White's description of mammy reveals, the empowerment of mammy was also directly related to the attempt of pro-slavery advocates to provide an image of black women that proved that the institution of slavery was vital for molding some black women in accord with the maternal ideals of the Victorian understanding of true womanhood.
10. Some scholars estimate that about 80 percent of slave women worked in the fields; 20 percent worked as house servants. See Robert William Fogel and Stanley L. Engerman, *Time on the Cross: The Economics of American Negro Slavery* (Boston: Little, Brown, 1974), 38–58.
11. bell hooks, *Ain't I a Woman? Black Women and Feminism* (Boston: South End, 1981), 23.
12. Ibid., 22.
13. Bethany Veney, *The Narrative of Bethany Veney: A Slave Woman*, in *Collected Black Women's Narratives*, The Schomburg Library of Nineteenth-Century Black Women Writers, ed. Henry Louis Gates Jr. (New York: Oxford University Press, 1988), 12–13. Pagination from original publication: Boston: George H. Ellis, 1889.
14. H. Mattison, A.M., *Louisa Picquet, The Octoroon: A Tale of Southern Slave Life*, in *Collected Black Women's Narratives*, The Schomburg Library of Nineteenth-Century Black Women Writers, ed. Henry Louis Gates Jr. (New York: Oxford University Press, 1988), 17. Pagination from original publication: New York: H. Mattison, 1861.
15. Mary Prince, *The History of Mary Prince, a West Indian Slave*, ed. Thomas Pringle, in *Six Women's Slave Narratives*, The Schomburg Library of Nineteenth-Century Black Women Writers, ed. Henry Louis Gates Jr. (New York: Oxford University Press, 1988). Pagination from original publication: London: F. Westley and A. H. Davis, 1831.
16. Linda Brent, *Incidents in the Life of a Slave Girl* (Boston: By the Author, Stereotype Foundry, 1861), 6–36.
17. Mattison, *Louisa Picquet, The Octoroon*, 18–21.
18. William Wells Brown, "Narrative of William Wells Brown," in *Puttin' on Ole Massa: The Slave Narratives of Henry Bibb, William Wells Brown, and Solomon Northup*, ed. Gilbert Osofsky (New York: Harper & Row, 1969), 194–95.
19. White, *Ar'n't I A Woman?* 37–38.
20. Ibid., 35.
21. Paula Giddings, *When and Where I Enter: The Impact of Black Women on Race and Sex in America* (New York: Wm. Morrow and Co., 1984), 62.
22. Carter G. Woodson and Lorenzo J. Greene, *The Negro Wage Earner* (Washington, D.C.: The Association for the Study of Negro Life and History, Inc., 1930), 31.
23. Giddings, *When and Where I Enter*, 57–58.
24. hooks, *Ain't I a Woman?* 57.

25. John Langston Gwaltney, *Drylongso* (New York: Random House, 1980), 146–47.

26. Ibid., 151.

27. Ibid., 150.

28. Historian Joel Williamson discusses this in relation to a process of acculturation he says existed among slaves and continued into and beyond the reconstruction. Williamson refers to the slaves as trying to "become more white." See Williamson's article "Black Self-Assertion Before and After Emancipation," in *Key Issues in the Afro-American Experience, Vol. 1 to 1877,* ed. Nathan I. Huggins, Martin Kilson, and Daniel M. Fox (New York: Harcourt Brace Jovanovich, 1971).

29. Woodson and Greene, *The Negro Wage Earner*, 61.

30. Philip S. Foner and Ronald L. Lewis, eds., *The Black Worker: From 1900–1919,* vol. 5 (Philadelphia: Temple University Press, 1980), 55.

31. Ibid.

32. June O. Patten, "Document: Moonlight and Magnolias in Southern Education: The Black Mammy Memorial Institute," *The Journal of Negro History* 65, no. 2 (Spring 1980): 153.

33. White, *Ar'n't I a Woman?* 29.

34. Jürgen Moltmann, "The 'Crucified God': God and the Trinity Today," in *New Questions on God,* ed. Johannes B. Metz (New York: Herder and Herder, 1972), 31–35.

35. Alan Richardson, *Creeds in the Making* (London: Student Christian Movement, 1951), 96–113.

36. Ibid., 21.

37. Ibid.

38. Ibid.

2. Our Mothers' Gardens: Rethinking Sacrifice

This chapter is an adapted and abridged version that combines material from Terrell's book *Power in the Blood?* See introduction and chapters four and five in JoAnne Marie Terrell, *Power in the Blood? The Cross in African American Experience* (Maryknoll, N.Y.: Orbis, 1998), 1–9, 99–144.

1. Editor's note: Emmett Till's 1955 lynching helped galvanize the Civil Rights movement when his brutalized body, in open casket, was pictured in a magazine. He was beaten, shot, and thrown in the Tallahatchie River for allegedly whistling at a white woman. No one has yet been convicted for this crime but the case still circulates in federal and state courts, as of April 2006, and it has become symbolic of all race crimes and lynchings that are never brought to justice.

2. Alice Walker, *The Color Purple* (New York: Simon & Schuster, 1985), 30.

3. I use proto-womanist to describe proactive sentiment, thought, and/or behavior that reflect womanist qualities but that do not derive from womanism or necessarily adhere to the theoretical underpinnings of the various womanist disciplines.

4. Christian theological anthropologies ask this question: What are the qualities of human existence requiring redemption? Typically, they cite universal sin as the purpose of the atonement (conceived as the defining event in human history) and prescribe "brotherly" love in imitation of Christ.

5. Cf. Albert B. Cleage Jr., *The Black Messiah* (New York: Sheed and Ward, 1968); Martin Luther King Jr., *Strength to Love* (Philadelphia: Fortress Press, 1981 [1963]). James H. Cone, *A Black Theology of Liberation* (Philadelphia: J. B. Lippincott, 1970; Maryknoll, N.Y.: Orbis, 1986).

6. Theodicy is an attempt to account for evil in light of belief in the absolute goodness and sovereignty of God. Cf. Anthony Pinn, *Why Lord? Suffering and Evil in Black Theology* (New York: Continuum, 1995). In *Is God a White Racist?* (New York: Anchor Books/

Doubleday, 1973), William R. Jones posited a seminal critique of black theologians' reliance on theodicy, identifying it as a rhetorical prison that does not permit them to question seriously the idea of God's goodness. Both Jones and Pinn advocate some form of *humanism* as a way for black people to exercise an additional faith option.

7. Cf. Rita Nakashima Brock, *Journeys by Heart: A Christology of Erotic Power* (New York: Crossroad, 1988); and Joanne Carlson Brown and Carole R. Bohn, eds., *Christianity, Patriarchy, and Abuse: A Feminist Critique* (New York: Pilgrim, 1989).

8. Delores S. Williams, *Sisters in the Wilderness: The Challenge of Womanist God-Talk* (Maryknoll, N.Y.: Orbis, 1993); and idem, "Black Women's Surrogacy Experience and the Christian Notion of Redemption," in Paula M. Cooey et al., eds., *After Patriarchy: Feminist Transformations of the World Religions* (Maryknoll, N.Y.: Orbis, 1991), 1–14, reprinted in chapter 1 of this volume; see also Jacquelyn Grant, "The Sin of Servanthood and the Deliverance of Discipleship," in Emily Townes, ed., *A Troubling in My Soul: Womanist Perspectives on Evil and Suffering* (Maryknoll, N.Y.: Orbis, 1993), 199–218.

9. Postmodernity is that period of social, political, and economic development in the West after World War II. Culturally, it is marked by the invention of television, which signaled the beginning of the age of information. Advocates of postmodernism resist "metanarratives" of history (usually advanced by dominant cultures) purporting a *telos* that mystifies power arrangements and generally supports the status quo. Postmodernism has given rise to the debate on multiculturalism as a viable alternative to "master narrative" theories of history that seek to control the content of knowledge and the dissemination of information. See Jean-François Lyotard, *The Postmodern Condition: A Report on Knowledge*, Theory and History of Literature, vol. 10 (Minneapolis: University of Minnesota Press, 1984).

10. Carl E. Braaten and Robert W. Jenson, eds., *Christian Dogmatics*, vol. 2 (Philadelphia: Fortress Press, 1984), 14–15.

11. See Gustaf Aulén, *Christus Victor: An Historical Study of the Three Main Types of the Idea of the Atonement* (New York: Macmillan, 1969).

12. Steven E. Ozment, *The Reformation in the Cities: The Appeal of Protestantism to Sixteenth-Century Germany and Switzerland* (New Haven: Yale University Press, 1975), 134.

13. Williams, *Sisters in the Wilderness*, 199–200.

14. Brock, *Journeys by Heart*. See also, idem, "And a Little Child Will Lead Us: Christology and Child Abuse," in Brown and Bohn, eds., *Christianity, Patriarchy, and Abuse.*

15. Jacquelyn Grant, *White Women's Christ and Black Women's Jesus* (Atlanta: Scholars, 1989), 212.

16. Ibid., 209.

17. Ibid., 219. Grant cites her forerunner, Jarena Lee, a nineteenth-century proto-womanist and preacher in the AME Church.

18. Kelly Brown Douglas, *The Black Christ* (Maryknoll, N.Y: Orbis, 1994), 31.

19. Ibid., 22.

20. Williams, "Black Women's Surrogacy Experience."

21. The "Re-Imagining Conference" (4–7 Nov 1993), held in Minneapolis, was an international gathering of women participating in the World Council of Churches' Ecumenical Decade in Solidarity with Women and consisted of, among other things, an audiotaped lecture/discussion series. The quotations in this section cite Williams's lecture and the question-and-answer session that came after it in the session titled "Re-Imagining Jesus," taped on 5 Nov 1993. Other participants included Korean feminist theologian Kwok Pui-lan and Lutheran feminist theologian and preacher Barbara Lundblad.

22. Williams, "Re-Imagining Truth," *The Other Side* (May–June 1994), 53–54.

23. Although black theologians' attempts at reimagining God/Christ are consistent with the Judeo-Christian tradition of anthropomorphizing God, in light of the redirected impetus of the love ethic in nationalist thought it can be argued that the opposite, *theomorphizing blacks* in their own eyes, was a serendipitous effect, which moreover portends specific warrants for the development of womanist Christology.

24. Williams, "Re-Imagining Jesus."

25. Helen Baylor, "Helen's Testimony," *Helen Baylor-Live,* Verity, Recorded 1999, Compact disc.

26. Delores Williams, "A Crucifixion Double-Cross?" in *The Other Side* (Sept–Oct 1993), 25–27, quotation at p. 26.

27. Ibid., 27.

28. Thus, as a black liberation theologian, I would restate the womanist principle in this way: A black liberationist loves black people and *individual* whites. This affirms African Americans' worth apart from whites *and* their right to love whomever they will, or must.

29. Cf. Angela Browne, *When Battered Women Kill* (New York: Free Press, 1989).

30. Yet, in Israelite sacrifice, sin was regarded with such odiousness that the moral onus was placed on the subsequent actions of the one/ones for whom the sacrifice was performed.

3. The Cross and Male Violence

1. World Council of Churches, Project on Overcoming Violence Against Women, www.wcc-coe.org/. See also www.overcomingviolence.org, a Web site of the WCC (Web sites accessed 4 Apr 2006).

2. Ched Myers, *Binding the Strong Man: A Political Reading of Mark's Story of Jesus* (Maryknoll, N.Y.: Orbis, 1988), 257, argues for a nonviolent interpretation of the cross. See also James Poling, *Render unto God: Economic Vulnerability, Family Violence, and Pastoral Theology* (St. Louis: Chalice, 2002), 187–89.

3. For other definitions of Practical Theology, see James Poling, *The Abuse of Power: A Theological Problem* (Nashville: Abingdon, 1991), 186–91; and James Poling and Donald Miller, *Foundations for a Practical Theology of Ministry* (Nashville: Abingdon, 1985), 62–99.

4. Clarice J. Martin, "Black Theodicy and Black Women's Spiritual Autobiography," in *A Troubling in My Soul: Womanist Perspectives on Evil and Suffering,* ed. Emilie M. Townes (Maryknoll, N.Y.: Orbis, 1993), 25.

5. Dr. Martin here quotes from Roger Lunden, Anthony Thistleton, and Clarence Walhout, *The Responsibility of Hermeneutics* (Grand Rapids, Mich.: Wm. B. Eerdmans, 1985), x, xi.

6. I am using a psychoanalytic model of interpretation. See Poling, *The Abuse of Power,* 75–91, for elaboration.

7. Myers, *Binding the Strong Man,* 121.

8. For more detail on narrative theory, see Carrie Doehring, *Taking Care: Monitoring Power Dynamics and Relational Boundaries in Pastoral Care and Counseling* (Nashville: Abingdon, 1995), 141–52.

9. While the majority of victims are women and girls, a significant number of men and boys are also victims of clergy sexual abuse.

10. Paragraph from James Poling and Marie Fortune, *Sexual Abuse by Clergy: A Crisis for the Church* (Decatur, Ga.: Journal of Pastoral Care Publications, 1994), 39.

11. Annie Imbens and Ineke Jonker, *Christianity and Incest,* trans. Patricia McVay (Minneapolis: Fortress Press, 1992), 271.

12. Poling and Fortune, *Sexual Abuse by Clergy,* 39–40.

13. Sharon G. Thornton, *Broken Yet Beloved: A Pastoral Theology of the Cross* (St. Louis: Chalice, 2002), 115. See Douglas John Hall, *Confessing the Faith: Christian Theology in a North American Context* (Minneapolis: Fortress Press, 1996); and Dorothee Soelle, *Theology for Skeptics: Reflections on God*, trans. Joyce L. Irwin (Minneapolis: Fortress Press, 1995).

14. Thornton, *Broken Yet Beloved*, 108.

15. Ibid., 117.

16. Ibid., 116–17.

17. Sharon Rice, M.Div. student at Garrett-Evangelical Theological Seminary, Evanston, Illinois.

18. See Poling, *Abuse of Power*, 169–71; and Poling, *Deliver Us from Evil: Resisting Racial and Gender Oppression* (Minneapolis: Fortress Press, 1996), 157–59. (Martin Luther King Jr., Malcolm X, and Augusto Sandino are examples of activists who lost their lives because they stood with people against injustice.) See also Daniel Day Williams, *Spirit and the Forms of Love* (New York: Harper & Row, 1968), 175; and Rita Nakashima Brock, *Journeys by Heart: A Christology of Erotic Power* (New York: Crossroad, 1988), 55.

19. For an excellent analysis of how boys are socialized and learn about violence and male dominance, see Paul Kivel, *Boys Will Be Men: Raising Our Sons for Courage, Caring, and Community* (Gabriola Island, B.C.: New Society Publishers, 1999). See also Kivel, *Men's Work: How to Stop the Violence That Tears Our Lives Apart* (Center City, Minn.: Hazelden, 1992). There are several activist groups with retraining programs for men, such as www.menstoppingviolence.org, Decatur, Georgia (Web site accessed 4 Apr 2006).

20. For introductory information about conducting groups with abusers, see Mary Nomme Russell, *Confronting Abusive Beliefs: Group Treatment for Abusive Men* (Thousand Oaks, Calif.: Sage Publications, 1995); and George W. Barnard, Kenneth Fuller, Lynn Robbins, and Theodore Shaw, *The Child Molester: An Integrated Approach to Evaluation and Treatment* (New York: Brunner/Mazel, 1989). See Minnesota Center Against Violence and Abuse for organizations that work on prevention of male violence; www.mincava.umn.edu/library/org/ (Web site accessed 4 Apr 2006).

21. Poling, *Render unto God*, 205–08.

22. Ellen K. Wondra, *Humanity Has Been a Holy Thing: Toward a Contemporary Feminist Christology* (Lanham, Md.: University Press of America, 1994), 96.

23. Ibid., 97.

24. Ibid., 326.

25. Ibid., 315.

26. This section is taken from Poling, *Deliver Us from Evil*, 157–59. For more elaboration, see also Poling, *Render unto God*, 198–211.

4. Maternal Sacrifice as a Hermeneutics of the Cross

1. See Mary J. Streufert, "Re-Conceiving Lutheran Christology," Ph.D. diss., Claremont Graduate University, 2004.

2. See, e.g., Delores Williams, *Sisters in the Wilderness: The Challenge of Womanist God-Talk* (Maryknoll, N.Y.: Orbis, 1993).

3. See Streufert, "Re-Conceiving Lutheran Christology."

4. My proposal that maternal sacrifice is one pole in a multipolar understanding of sacrifice comes with caveats. In speaking of the physical and generative sacrifices of mothers specifically, I wish neither to idealize nor to essentialize motherhood, and just as critically, I do not desire to diminish the experiences or capacities of women who do not have children. For examples of motherhood as essential and ideal, see, e.g., Nancy Wilson, *Praise Her in the Gates: The Calling of Christian Motherhood* (Moscow, Idaho: Canon, 2000).

5. See Gen. 1:26–27. See also, for example, 1 Cor. 2:16; Rom. 8:1-17; 12:15; and 13:14.

6. There are also models of Jesus as moral exemplar, teacher of truth, and final scapegoat.

7. President George W. Bush, on "Meet the Press with Tim Russert," NBC–TV, (Web site accessed 8 Feb 2004). Transcript at www.msnbc.msn.com/id/4179618.

8. Richard Lacayo, "One for the Team: Pat Tillman—Football Star, Ranger—did not aspire to heroism. But his life defined it." *Time* 163, no. 18 (3 May 2004): 38–40.

9. As quoted in Alister McGrath, *Historical Theology: An Introduction to the History of Christian Thought* (Oxford: Blackwell, 1998), 284.

10. See ibid.

11. For example, Paul Althaus points out that the theology of the cross is connected to God being God: the paradoxical reality of strength and glory existing in weakness and lowliness. See Althaus, *The Theology of Martin Luther*, trans. Robert C. Schultz (Philadelphia: Fortress Press, 1966), 34.

12. See Heino O. Kadai, "Luther's Theology of the Cross" in *Accents in Luther's Theology: Essays in Commemoration of the 450th Anniversary of the Reformation* (St. Louis: Concordia, 1967), 243.

13. See Günter Gassman and Scott Hendrix, *Fortress Introduction to the Lutheran Confessions* (Minneapolis: Fortress Press, 1999), 83.

14. See Günther Bornkamm, *Jesus of Nazareth*, trans. Irene and Fraser McLusky with James M. Robinson (New York: Harper & Row, 1960), 174.

15. See Ted Peters, *God—The World's Future*, 2nd ed. (Minneapolis: Fortress Press, 2000), 230; and Carl Braaten, *Principles of Lutheran Theology* (Philadelphia: Fortress Press, 1983), 71.

16. See Mary Daly, e.g., *Gyn/Ecology: The Metaethics of Radical Feminism* (Boston: Beacon, 1978), 39.

17. See ibid., 79–80.

18. Rosemary Radford Ruether, *To Change the World: Christology and Cultural Criticism* (New York: Crossroad, 1983), 27.

19. See ibid., 28.

20. See ibid., 15.

21. For more criticism of the violence at the center of the atonement, see also, e.g., Delores S. Williams, *Sisters in the Wilderness*; Elizabeth A. Johnson, "The Word Was Made Flesh and Dwelt among Us: Jesus Research and Christian Faith," in *Jesus: A Colloquium in the Holy Land*, ed. Doris Donnelly (New York: Continuum, 2001), esp. 158–60; and Jacquelyn Grant, "The Sin of Servanthood and the Deliverance of Discipleship," in *A Troubling in My Soul: Womanist Perspectives on Hope, Salvation, and Transformation*, ed. Emilie M. Townes (Maryknoll, N.Y.: Orbis, 1993), 199–218, esp. 208–10.

22. Rita Nakashima Brock and Rebecca Ann Parker, *Proverbs of Ashes: Violence, Redemptive Suffering, and the Search for What Saves Us* (Boston: Beacon, 2001).

23. See Elisabeth Schüssler Fiorenza, *In Memory of Her: A Feminist Theological Reconstruction of Christian Origins* (New York: Crossroad, 1994 [1983]), 118–30, esp. 119–22.

24. Elisabeth Schussler Fiorenza, *Jesus and the Politics of Interpretation* (New York: Continuum, 2000), 95.

25. Gustav Aulen, *Christus Victor: An Historical Study of the Three Main Types of the Idea of Atonement*, trans. A.G. Hebert (New York: SPCK, 1931).

26. See Gregory J. Riley, *One Jesus, Many Christs* (Minneapolis: Fortress Press, 2000), 39. Perseus was the son of Zeus and the virgin Danaë.

27. Ibid., 18.

28. See ibid., 41–56.

29. See ibid., 82–83.

30. This is not to be confused with Christian concepts of hell or the devil.

31. See Riley, *One Jesus, Many Christs*, 27–28.

32. Immortality was reserved for extremely learned philosophers in the ancient Greco-Roman world. See ibid., 93–94.

33. See ibid., 201–02. Jesus as the hero is not the only paradigm for understanding his death in the New Testament. Other scholars have noted Jewish Christians' use of their religious imagery and texts to understand Jesus and his death. See e.g., John Dominic Crossan, *Jesus: A Revolutionary Biography* (San Francisco: HarperSanFrancisco, 1994), 143–52. What is of especial importance here is that death is a requirement, just as it is for the hero. There is no "success" without death. At the heart of the paradigm of the sacrificial lamb is a parallel to the heroic sacrifice.

34. See Sharyn Dowd and Elizabeth Struthers Malbon, "Hearing Mark's Story of Jesus' Death: Overlapping Contexts," paper presented at the meetings of the Society of Biblical Literature, San Antonio, Tex., 2004. They argue that in Mark Jesus is the ransom for others from captive powers, specifically colonial power.

35. As quoted in Susan Maushart, *The Mask of Motherhood: How Becoming a Mother Changes Our Lives and Why We Never Talk about It* (New York: New Press, 1999), 13. Emphasis added.

36. Naomi Wolf, *(misconceptions): Truth, Lies, and the Unexpected on the Journey to Motherhood* (New York: Doubleday, 2001), 7.

37. Catharine MacKinnon, "Can Fatherhood be Optional?" as quoted in ibid., 23.

38. According to Erikson's theory; see Bonnie J. Miller-McLemore, *Also a Mother: Work and Family as Theological Dilemma* (Nashville: Abingdon, 1994), 51.

39. Ibid.

40. See ibid., 145.

41. See ibid., 184.

42. Rebecca Ann Parker, Albertson Lecture, Wenatchee, Wash., 8–10 Feb 2002.

43. Ibid. Also see Brock and Parker, *Proverbs of Ashes*, 210–15. It may very well be, however, that the practice of love at times requires mortal sacrifice. That this is not the only model of redemptive sacrifice is my point here.

44. Cf. Carl Braaten's analysis of liberation theologies' concern with material salvation in *Principles of Lutheran Theology*, 69.

45. Parker, Albertson Lecture.

46. Ibid.

47. See the story of Nicodemus in John 3:1-21.

48. Sandra M. Schneiders, "John 20:11–18: The Encounter of the Easter Jesus with Mary Magdalene—A Transformative Feminist Reading," in *"What Is John?" Readers and Readings of the Fourth Gospel*, ed. Fernando F. Segovia, Society of Biblical Literature Symposium Series 3 (Atlanta: Scholars, 1996): 165.

49. See ibid., 164–65.

50. See ibid., 168. See John 14:18–20.

51. Ibid., 167.

52. See Sharon Welch, *A Feminist Ethic of Risk* (Minneapolis: Fortress Press, 1990).

5. Becoming a Feminist Theologian of the Cross

1. See Kathleen Norris, *Amazing Grace: A Vocabulary of Faith* (New York: Riverhead, 1998), 2.

2. See Douglas John Hall, *Hope against Hope: Toward an Indigenous Theology of the Cross* (Geneva, Switzerland: WSCF, 1971), 1, n. 3.

3. See Walther von Lowenich's groundbreaking study, *Luther's Theology of the Cross* (Minneapolis: Augsburg Books, 1976).

4. Gerhard O. Forde, *On Being a Theologian of the Cross: Reflections on Luther's Heidelberg Disputation, 1518* (Grand Rapids: Eerdmans, 1997).

5. *Luther's Works, Volume 11: Lectures on the Psalms II,* ed. Hilton C. Oswald, trans. Herbert J. Bowman (St. Louis: Concordia, 1976), 103.

6. For a thorough investigation of how Luther's brutish approaches toward the peasants and the Jews relate to his theology of the cross, see chaps. 2–3 in Deanna Thompson, *Crossing the Divide: Luther, Feminism, and the Cross* (Minneapolis: Fortress Press, 2004).

7. Joy Ann McDougall, "Women's Work: Feminist Theology for a New Generation," *Christian Century* (26 July 2005), 20–25.

8. Delores Williams prefers "demonarchy" to "patriarchy" because it highlights the structures that benefit white women and men while simultaneously harming women and men of color. See her illuminating article, "The Color of Feminism: Or Speaking the Black Woman's Tongue," *Feminist Theological Ethics: A Reader,* ed. Lois K. Daly (Louisville: Westminster John Knox, 1994), 42–58.

9. Elisabeth Schüssler Fiorenza also dislikes the limitations of the term *patriarchy* and instead introduced the neologism *kyriarchy* into feminist theological conversation to underscore the pyramidal shape of oppression and to focus on those women at the bottom of a multidimensional structure of oppression. See her description in *Jesus: Miriam's Child, Sophia's Prophet* (New York: Continuum, 1994), 14.

10. Sally B. Purvis, *The Power of the Cross: Foundations for a Feminist Ethic of Community* (Nashville: Abingdon, 1993), 16.

11. Norris, *Amazing Grace,* 167.

12. Rebecca Ann Parker, "The Unblessed Child: Rebecca's Story," in Rita Nakashima Brock and Rebecca Ann Parker, *Proverbs of Ashes: Violence, Redemptive Suffering, and the Search for What Saves Us* (Boston: Beacon, 2001), 199.

13. Serene Jones, *Feminist Theory and Christian Theology: Cartographies of Grace,* Guides to Theological Inquiry (Minneapolis: Fortress Press, 2000), 62.

14. Ibid., 63.

15. Gerhard Ebeling, *Luther: An Introduction to His Thought,* trans. R. A. Wilson (Philadelphia: Fortress Press, 1970), 99.

16. *Luther's Works, Volume 2: Genesis Chapters 6–14,* ed. Jaroslav Jan Pelikan (St. Louis: Concordia, 1960), 145.

17. Jones, *Feminist Theory and Christian Theology,* 63.

18. *Luther's Works, Volume 31: Career of the Reformer I,* ed. Harold J. Grimm, Helmut T. Lehman (Philadelphia: Fortress Press, 1957), 342.

19. See a compilation of fascinating reflections by women to a statue of a crucified woman in Doris Jean Dyke, *The Crucified Woman* (Toronto: United Church Publishing House, 1991).

20. See Flora Keshgegian's enlightening discussion of this point in *Redeeming Memories: A Theology of Healing and Transformation* (Nashville: Abingdon, 2000), 179–89.

21. I propose that there be a variety of female bodies depicted as crucified, not simply one.

22. Gerhard O. Forde, "The Work of Christ," in *Christian Dogmatics, Vol. 2,* ed. Carl E. Braaten and Robert W. Jensen (Philadelphia: Fortress Press, 1984); and Mary Knutson, "Toward a Contemporary Theology of the Cross," Convocation Address (5 Oct 1995), Luther Seminary, St. Paul, Minn.

23. Sallie McFague, *Metaphorical Theology: Models of God in Religious Language* (Philadelphia: Fortress Press, 1982), 159.

24. Forde, "The Work of Christ," 16.

25. Rowan Williams, *Resurrection: Interpreting the Easter Gospel* (Cleveland: Pilgrim, 2003), 154.

26. Gail R. O'Day, Commentary on "John," in *The Women's Bible Commentary*, Carol A. Newsom and Sharon H. Ringe, eds. (Louisville: Westminster John Knox, 1992), 302.

27. *Luther's Works* 31:367.

28. Walter Altmann, *Luther and Liberation: A Latin American Perspective*, trans. Mary M. Solberg (Minneapolis: Fortress Press, 1992), 66.

29. Rowan Williams, *Resurrection*, 40.

30. Ibid., 68.

6. Contextualizing the Cross for the Sake of Subjectivity

1. Lisa Isherwood, *Introducing Feminist Christologies*, Introductions in Feminist Theology (Cleveland: Pilgrim, 2002), 98.

2. Julie Clague, "Divine Transgressions: The Female Christ-Form in Art," *Critical Quarterly* 47, no. 3 (2005): 47–63.

3. Rosemary Radford Ruether, *Introducing Redemption in Christian Feminism*, Introductions in Feminist Theology (Cleveland: Pilgrim, 1998), 98.

4. Suffering involves "a condition of pain, sorrow, and/or anguish, which may be experienced physically, emotionally, or spiritually, personally or corporately. It may be the result of what is termed natural evil, i.e., such things as earthquakes and disease, or the result of historical evil or human action, i.e., such things as war and injustice." See also Flora A. Keshgegian, "Suffering," in *Dictionary of Feminist Theologies*, ed. Letty M. Russell and J. Shannon Clarkson (Louisville: Westminster John Knox, 1996), 278–80. This essay is concerned with theologies of the cross that efface social suffering and that promote social suffering as redemptive.

5. See Joanne Carlson Brown and Carole R. Bohn, eds., *Christianity, Patriarchy, and Abuse: A Feminist Critique* (New York: Pilgrim, 1989), 1–61; and Rita Nakashima Brock and Rebecca Parker, *Proverbs of Ashes: Violence, Redemptive Suffering, and the Search for What Saves Us* (Boston: Beacon, 2001).

6. Delores S. Williams, *Sisters in the Wilderness: The Challenge of Womanist God-Talk* (Maryknoll, N.Y.: Orbis, 1993), 161–70.

7. The shift of women's position from object to subject is elaborated by feminist theologian Elisabeth Schüssler Fiorenza, "For Women in Men's World," in *The Power of Naming: A Concilium Reader in Feminist Liberation Theology*, ed. Elisabeth Schüssler Fiorenza (Maryknoll, N.Y.: Orbis, 1996), 3–13; and, by womanist theologian Stephanie Mitchem, *Introducing Womanist Theology* (Maryknoll, N.Y.: Orbis, 2002), 19–24.

8. Patriarchy is an analytical concept that problematizes the social construction of women's and some men's subordinate status. Patriarchy does not suggest a sex/gender system of universal male dominance, but rather refers to the multiplicative interconnections among gender, race, class, culture, and sexuality that legitimate and justify a complex system of hierarchical relations, as well as ultimately idealize an elite, white, male, Western, heterosexual paradigm of personhood. Patriarchy refers to a multilayered complex system of dominance, which Elisabeth Schüssler Fiorenza renames "kyriarchy" in *But She Said: Feminist Practices of Biblical Interpretation* (Boston: Beacon, 1992), 114–24.

9. This method of critique, recovery, and reconstruction is explained in Anne E. Carr, "The New Vision of Feminist Theology," in *Freeing Theology: The Essentials of Theology in Feminist Perspective*, ed. Catherine Mowry LaCugna (New York: HarperCollins, 1993), 5–29; and Elizabeth Johnson, *She Who Is: The Mystery of God in Feminist Theological Discourse* (New York: Crossroad, 1992), 28–33.

10. Elizabeth A. Johnson, "Redeeming the Name of Christ: Christology," in LaCugna, ed., *Freeing Theology*, 118.

11. The male humanity of Jesus as the incarnation of the alleged male Logos/Word of God has been construed to legitimate androcentric language for God; to justify the christomorphic character of men in bearing a "natural resemblance" to Christ, especially in ordained priestly ministry; and to question the salvation of women by a male savior. See Johnson, "Redeeming," 119–20; idem, "The Maleness of Christ," in Schüssler Fiorenza, ed., *The Power of Naming*, 307–15, esp. 307–08; and idem, *She Who Is*, 151–53.

12. Karen Trimble Alliaume, "The Risks of Repeating Ourselves: Reading Feminist/ Womanist Figures of Jesus," *Cross Currents* 48, no. 2 (1998): 204; Rosemary Radford Ruether, "Christology and Patriarchy," in *Thinking of Christ: Proclamation, Explanation, Meaning*, ed. Tatha Wiley (New York: Continuum, 2003), 125–26.

13. Johnson, *She Who Is*, 86–93.

14. Johnson, "Redeeming," 120–21; idem, *She Who Is*, 94–100; and Elisabeth Schüssler Fiorenza, *Jesus: Miriam's Child, Sophia's Prophet* (New York: Continuum, 1994), 131–62.

15. Other feminist theologians make a similar theological move to challenge a strict physicalist imitation of Jesus by shifting the locus of Christology from the ontological, metaphysical person of Jesus to the ministry of the historical Jesus, especially in light of the biblical prophetic tradition. See Rosemary Radford Ruether, *Sexism and God-Talk: Toward a Feminist Theology* (Boston: Beacon, 1983), 22–23, chap. 5.

16. Johnson, *She Who Is*, 99.

17. Johnson, "Redeeming," 123.

18. Ibid., 125.

19. Ibid., 126. Not only are the roles of women highlighted, but also women signify theologically the in-breaking of the reign of God, in their roles as prophets and witnesses of the resurrection; cf. Ruether, "Christology and Patriarchy," 127–28.

20. Johnson, "Redeeming," 128.

21. Ruether, "Christology and Patriarchy," 132–33.

22. Mary Catherine Hilkert, "*Imago Dei*: Does the Symbol Have a Future?" *The Santa Clara Lectures* 8, no. 3 (Apr 2002): 15, 18, my emphasis.

23. Johnson, "The Maleness of Christ," 313; cf. idem, "Redeeming," 129.

24. Johnson, *She Who Is*, 167; cf. idem, "Redeeming," 131.

25. Johnson, "Redeeming," 124.

26. Ibid., 126, my brackets; cf. 124.

27. Sarah Coakley, "Kenosis and Subversion: On the Repression of 'Vulnerability' in Christian Feminist Thinking," in *Swallowing a Fishbone: Feminist Theologians Debate Christianity*, ed. Daphne Hampson (London: SPCK, 1996), 82–111.

28. Ibid., 107.

29. Ibid., 108. Coakley further develops this argument in "Kenosis: Theological Meanings and Gender Connotations," in *The Work of Love: Creation as Kenosis*, ed. John Polkinghorne (Grand Rapids, Mich.: Wm. B. Eerdmans, 2001), 192–210. This argument begs the question of whether women possess a self, i.e., a modern masculinist subjectivity, to surrender or to expand into God.

30. Johnson, "Redeeming," 127.

31. Ibid., 125.

32. Mitchem, *Introducing Womanist Theology*, 55–57. Mitchem attends to solidarity among womanist, black, and feminist theologies, even as womanist theology claims its distinctive nomenclature and its site of theological reflection; ibid., 87–93, 96–98.

33. Ibid., 60–61.

34. Kelly Brown Douglas, *The Black Christ* (Maryknoll, N.Y.: Orbis, 1994), 110–13.

35. See Jacquelyn Grant, "Subjectification as a Requirement for Christological Construction," in *Lift Every Voice: Constructing Christian Theologies from the Underside*, rev. and exp. ed., ed. Susan Brooks Thistlethwaite and Mary Potter Engel (Maryknoll, N.Y.: Orbis, 1998), 207–20, esp. 209–12; and "'Come to My Help Lord, For I'm in Trouble': Womanist Jesus and the Mutual Struggle for Liberation," in *Reconstructing the Christ Symbol: Essays in Feminist Christology*, ed. Maryanne Stevens (New York: Paulist, 1993), 54–71, esp. 57–66.

36. As Douglas argues, "Symbols and icons are essential tools for pointing to the reality of Christ, and for helping people to see themselves in Christ and Christ in themselves." Douglas, *The Black Christ*, 107–08.

37. Ibid., 108–09.

38. Ibid., 109.

39. Copeland's theology of the cross is consonant with Jon Sobrino's epistemological principle of "the following of Jesus," in which knowing Jesus involves a praxis, especially a praxis of building the reign of God. See Mary Ann Hinsdale, "A Response," in *Christology: Memory, Inquiry, Practice*, ed. Anne M. Clifford and Anthony J. Godzieba (Maryknoll, N.Y.: Orbis, 2003) 197–205.

40. M. Shawn Copeland, "To Live at the Disposal of the Cross: Mystical-Political Discipleship as Christological Locus," in Clifford and Godzieba, eds., *Christology: Memory, Inquiry, Practice*, 180.

41. Ibid., 180.

42. This paragraph closely summarizes ibid., 181–82.

43. Ibid., 185. Mark Lewis Taylor has studied the cross as a major theatrical spectacle of state violence, as well as the parodies of this spectacle in both historical and contemporary religio-political protests. See Taylor, *The Executed God: The Way of the Cross in Lockdown America* (Minneapolis: Fortress Press, 2001).

44. Ibid., 186.

45. This paragraph closely summarizes ibid., 188–89.

46. Ibid., 177–78, 191–92. Copeland notes that writing theology can widen rather than bridge gaps between academic privilege and everyday poverty, between the "black woman above" writing an article and the "black woman below" struggling to secure basic human needs for daily survival.

47. Ibid., 179, 192. To stress that she speaks primarily to privileged peoples, Copeland chooses the Gospel of Luke not only because it underscores active discipleship to bring about the reign of God, but also because it addresses a privileged audience who often prefer charity to social change.

48. Ibid., 193–94, my emphasis.

49. Mitchem defines agency as "the ability of a person or community to work on their own behalf, within or in spite of existing social institutions." Mitchem, *Introducing Womanist Theology*, 20.

50. M. Shawn Copeland, "Wading through Many Sorrows: Toward a Theology of Suffering in Womanist Perspective," in *A Troubling in My Soul: Womanist Perspectives on Evil and Suffering*, ed. Emilie Townes (Maryknoll, N.Y.: Orbis, 1993), 110–11, 118.

51. Ibid., 109, 118.

52. Ibid., 124.

53. M. Shawn Copeland, "Enfleshing Freedom: Theological Anthropology in Womanist Perspective," in *Themes in Feminist Theology for the New Millennium*, vol. 1, ed. Francis A. Eigo (Villanova, Pa.: Villanova University Press, 2002), 87–89.

54. Ibid., 68.

55. Ibid., 71, 78.

56. Ibid., 84.

57. Ibid., 79.

58. Ibid., 87.

59. Ibid.

60. This phrase is borrowed from Rebecca S. Chopp, *Saving Work: Feminist Practices of Theological Education* (Louisville: Westminster John Knox, 1995).

61. Isherwood, *Introducing Feminist Christologies*, 97; cf. 23, 29–31.

62. Linell E. Cady, "Identity, Feminist Theory, and Theology," in *Horizons in Feminist Theology: Identity, Tradition, and Norms*, ed. Rebecca S. Chopp and Sheila Greeve Davaney (Minneapolis: Fortress Press, 1997), 17–32, esp. 23–26.

63. Mary Catherine Hilkert, "Cry Beloved Image," in *In the Embrace of God: Feminist Approaches to Theological Anthropology*, ed. Ann O'Hara Graff (Maryknoll, N.Y.: Orbis, 1995), 190–205, esp. 195–96.

64. "The Pastoral Constitution on the Church in the Modern World," in *Vatican Council II: The Basic Sixteen Documents*, ed. Austin Flannery (Northport, N.Y.: Costello, 1996), 163–282. All parenthetical citations in the chapter list paragraph numbers from the pastoral constitution.

65. Walter Kasper, "The Theological Anthropology of *Gaudium et Spes*," *Communio* 23 (1996): 129–40, at p. 137.

66. Acting as artisans of humanity and hope is central in the recent work of Sharon D. Welch, *After Empire: The Art and Ethos of Enduring Peace* (Minneapolis: Fortress Press, 2004).

7. Lavish Love: A Covenantal Ontology

1. Isak Dinesen, *Anecdotes of Destiny and Ehrengard* (New York: Vintage, 1993), 52. Inclusive language changes are mine.

2. Martin Luther, "The Freedom of a Christian" in *Three Treatises*, trans. W. A. Lambert, rev. Harold J. Grimm (Philadelphia: Fortress Press, 1970), 276.

3. Jesus proclaims that he has come to preach the kingdom of God in three of the four Gospel texts: Matthew, Mark, and Luke. Throughout this chapter, the Gospels are understood to be theological works rather than historical accounts of Jesus' life.

4. Even though Reformed theology has tended to privatize the understanding of election in the last century, its biblical context assumes a social basis for the human relationship to God.

5. See my introduction to this book for further explanation of feminist concerns with cross-centered soteriologies.

6. Over the past century, more and more Lutheran theologians have claimed that the "theology of the cross" is the center for Luther's theology. Mary Solberg notes this in her book *Compelling Knowledge: A Feminist Proposal for an Epistemology of the Cross* (Albany: State University of New York Press, 1997), 188, where she refers to the work of Walther von Loewenich and Alister McGrath who both describe the variety of meanings this term has held and its increasing use over the past century. See Walther von Loewenich, *Luther's Theology of the Cross*, trans. Herbert J. A. Bouman (Belfast: Christian Journals, 1976), 169–73; and Alister E. McGrath, *Luther's Theology of the Cross* (Oxford: Basil Blackwell, 1985), 179.

7. For a full depiction of Luther's theology of the cross, see Solberg, *Compelling Knowledge*.

8. See Jos. E. Vercruysse, "Luther's Theology of the Cross at the Time of the Heidelberg Disputation," *Gregorianum* 57, no. 3 (1976): 523–48. The theology of the cross is never Luther's own explicitly stated focus across his entire career. Bernhard Lohse, who recently published a comprehensive guide to Luther's systematic theology, spends but three pages on the subject of the theology of the cross. See Bernhard Lohse,

Martin Luther's Theology: Its Historical and Systematic Development (Minneapolis: Fortress Press, 1999).

9. C. F. W. Walther, *The Proper Distinction Between Law* and Gospel, trans. W. H. T. Dau (St. Louis: Concordia, 1928), 79.

10. Ibid., 81.

11. Ibid., 83.

12. This quote comes from a course on Lutheran Preaching, "Homiletics," instructors Gracia Grindal and Cathy Malotky, Luther Northwestern Theological Seminary, St. Paul, Minn., Spring 1993. Lecture by Grindal, 19 Apr 1993.

13. See the work of Douglas John Hall and Deanna A. Thompson in this volume and in their respective books *The Cross in Our Context: Jesus and the Suffering World* (Minneapolis: Fortress Press, 2003), and *Crossing the Divide: Luther, Feminism, and the Cross* (Minneapolis: Fortress Press, 2004).

14. Neil Elliott, "The Anti-Imperial Message of the Cross," in *Paul and Empire: Religion and Power Roman Imperial Society*, ed. Richard A. Horsley (Harrisburg: Trinity International, 1997), 167. Here Elliott quotes J. Christiaan Beker, *Paul the Apostle: The Triumph of God in Life and Thought* (Philadelphia: Fortress Press, 1980), 207.

15. Elliott, "The Anti-Imperial Message," 168.

16. Ibid., 182.

17. Stephen J. Patterson, "Consider Yourself Dead: On the Martyrological Understanding of Jesus' Death" in *The Once and Future Faith* (Santa Rosa, Calif.: Polebridge, 2001).

18. Patterson notes that he does not affirm such a martyrdom model without reservation since he acknowledges that "the martyrological tradition has also been used to coax people to die for things far less noble, far less worthy than this very unusual vision of life. From antiquity to modernity one sees this again and again in Christian history," ibid., 186. This is certainly true, as the martyr image has certainly encouraged women to stay in abusive relationships, assuming the role of a passive victim.

19. Patterson furthers this argument in his book *Beyond the Passion: Rethinking the Death and Life of Jesus* (Minneapolis: Fortress Press, 2004).

20. Joanne Marie Terrell, *Power in the Blood? The Cross in the African American Experience* (Maryknoll, N.Y.: Orbis, 1998), 105–06. Here she quotes Abelard in *Exposition to the Romans*, book 2, part 2, in Eugene Fairweather, ed., *A Scholastic Miscellany: Anselm to Ockham* (Philadelphia: Westminster, 1956), 283–84.

21. Terrell, *Power in the Blood?* 106. Terrell here quotes Abelard.

22. Some feminist theologians have questioned whether parental models for God-human relations are appropriate since it may depict God as a parent who never wants her/his children to grow up or have the relationship move in a natural progression to states beyond infant-parent. For this critique, see Rosemary Radford Ruether, *Sexism and God-Talk: Toward a Feminist Theology* (Boston: Beacon, 1993 [reissue]), 69. In the model I propose, however, this is not an issue since the initial connection between the parent and child remains even as the persons and the relationship itself change.

23. Several philosophical and theological movements (among them existentialism and process thought) as well as the sciences of quantum physics and ecology have emphasized these insights on the relational nature of all of existence.

24. Gabriel Marcel, *Being and Having*, trans. Katherine Farrer (Glasgow: University Press, 1949), 167.

25. Cf. Martin Luther, "Sermon on Preparing to Die," in *Martin Luther's Basic Theological Writings,* ed. Timothy F. Lull (Minneapolis: Fortress Press, 1989), 638–54.

26. Karl Barth, *Church Dogmatics* II/2 (Edinburgh: T. & T. Clark, 1957), 161. Inclusive human language changes are mine.

27. Ibid., 167.

28. Ibid. Changes mine.

29. This position brought Barth considerable criticism from other theologians, such as Emil Brunner. See Emil Brunner, *The Christian Doctrine of God: Dogmatics* Vol. 1 (London: Lutterworth, 1949), 346–51.

30. See Dorothee Soelle, *Theology for Skeptics: Reflections on God,* trans. Joyce L. Irwin (Minneapolis: Fortress Press, 1995), 37–50.

31. See Charles Hartshorne, *The Divine Relativity: A Social Conception of God* (New Haven: Yale University Press, 1948), 42.

32. This description of relationship was made famous by Martin Buber's book *I and Thou,* trans. Walter Kaufmann (New York: Simon & Schuster/Touchstone, 1996).

33. Alfred North Whitehead, *Process and Reality,* ed. David Ray Griffin and Donald W. Sherburne (New York: Free Press, 1978), 343.

34. Luther, "The Freedom of a Christian," 290.

35. Walter Rauschenbusch, *A Theology for the Social Gospel* (New York: Macmillan, 1917; Nashville: Abingdon, 1978), 99. All references are to the 1978 edition.

36. Marjorie Hewitt Suchocki, *The Fall to Violence: Original Sin in Relational Theology* (New York: Continuum, 1995), 13.

37. Marjorie Hewitt Suchocki, *God-Christ-Church: A Practical Guide to Process Theology,* rev. ed. (New York: Crossroad, 1989), 14.

38. Martin Luther, "Two Kinds of Righteousness" in *Martin Luther's Basic Theological Writings,* 2nd edition, ed. Timothy F. Lull (Minneapolis: Fortress Press, 2005), 138.

39. For more on this idea, see Christine M. Smith, *Risking the Terror: Resurrection in this Life* (Cleveland: Pilgrim, 2001).

8. The Crucified God: Yesterday and Today: 1972–2002

1. Richard Bauckham, "Preface," in Jürgen Moltmann, *The Crucified God,* SCM Classics Series (London: SCM, 2001), ix.

2. Jürgen Moltmann, *Umkehr zur Zukunft,* (Munich: Chr. Kaiser Verlag, 1970), 14.

3. Bertrand Brasnett, *The Suffering of the Impassible God* (London: SPCK, 1928).

4. Jon Sobrino in Oscar Arnulfo Romero, *Die notwendige Revolution mit einem Beitrag von Jon Sobrino über den Märtyrer der Befreiung* (Mainz: M. Grünewald, 1982), 17.

5. T. Rees in *Hymns and Psalms* (London: Methodist Publishing House, 1983), no. 36, stanza 2.

6. Paul Imhoff and Hubert Biallowons, eds., *Im Gespräch/Karl Rahner* (Munich: Kösel Verlag, 1982), 245.

7. Jürgen Moltmann, *History and the Triune God: Contributions to Trinitarian Theology,* trans. John Bowden (New York: Crossroad, 1992), 122–24.

8. Dorothee Soelle, *Suffering,* trans. Everett R. Kalin (Philadelphia: Fortress Press, 1984).

9. Jürgen Moltmann, *The Coming of God: Christian Eschatology,* trans. Margaret Kohl (Minneapolis: Fortress Press, 1996), 338–39.

9. All That Matters: What an Epistemology of the Cross Is Good For

1. *D. Martin Luthers Werke: Kritische Gesamtausgabe* (Weimar: Hermann Boehlaus Nachfolger, 1883–), 5, 176, 32–33. This authoritative, complete edition of Luther's works—the so-called *Weimar Ausgabe*—is henceforth abbreviated *WA.*

2. According to Joseph E. Vercruysse, Luther himself used the expressions *theologia crucis* and *theologus crucis* (theologian of the cross) in only five texts: "Four of them were written in the spring of 1518 [just before the meeting in Heidelberg], namely the *Asterisci Lutheri adversus Obeliscos Eckii,* the *Lectures on Hebrews,* the *Resolutiones disputationum de indulgentiarum virtute,* and finally the famous Heidelberg Disputation. The fifth one is in the *Operationes in Psalmos,* Luther's second course on the Psalms, held

from 1519 to 1521." See Vercruysse's article, "Luther's Theology of the Cross at the Time of the Heidelberg Disputation," *Gregorianum* 57 (1976): 532–48.

3. Martin Luther, "Heidelberg Disputation," in *Luther's Works, Vol. 31: Career of the Reformer I*, ed. Harold J. Grimm and Helmut T. Lehmann (Philadelphia: Fortress Press, 1957), 41. Hereafter abbreviated as *LW*.

4. Ibid.

5. For a poignant expression of this confidence, see Dietrich Bonhoeffer's poem "Who Am I?" written while he was imprisoned by the Gestapo. That poem's last few words are "thou knowest, O God, I am thine." In *Letters and Papers from Prison*, enlarged edition, ed. Eberhard Bethge (New York: Macmillan, 1972), 345.

6. I am indebted to my former student Tommy P. Valentini for this wonderful turn of phrase.

7. "Experience alone makes a theologian. It is by living—no, rather it is by dying and being damned—that a theologian is made, not by understanding, reading, or speculating." The first sentence is from *LW 54: Table Talk*, ed. Theodore G. Tappert (Philadelphia: Fortress Press, 1967), 7. The second portion of the quotation is found in *WA* 5:163, 28.

8. Gerhard Ebeling, *Luther: An Introduction to His Thought*, trans. R. A. Wilson (Philadelphia: Fortress Press, 1970), 258.

9. Walther von Loewenich, *Luther's Theology of the Cross* (Minneapolis: Augsburg Books, 1976), 64–65.

10. See the collection of essays edited by Yacob Tesfai, *The Scandal of a Crucified World: Perspectives on the Cross and Suffering*, trans. Phillip Berryman (Maryknoll, N.Y.: Orbis, 1994).

11. For a discussion of what Latin American liberation theologians have called an "epistemological break," see, e.g., Jon Sobrino, *The True Church and the Poor*, trans. Matthew J. O'Connell (Maryknoll, N.Y.: Orbis, 1984), 24ff.

12. See Paolo Freire, *Pedagogy of the Oppressed*, 30th Anniversary Edition, trans. Myra Bergman Ramos (New York: Continuum, 2003), for a description of what he calls the "banking method" in teaching and learning.

13. Alfred North Whitehead's observation strikes a resonant chord with me: "Faith in reason is the trust that the ultimate natures of things lie together in a harmony which excludes mere arbitrariness. It is the faith that at the base of things we shall not find mere arbitrary mystery." From *Science in the Modern World* (New York: Macmillan, 1925, 1967), 27.

14. See, for example, Lorraine Code, *What Can She Know? Feminist Theory and the Construction of Knowledge* (Ithaca: Cornell University Press, 1991); Donna Haraway, *Simians, Cyborgs, and Women: The Reinvention of Nature* (New York: Routledge, 1991); Sandra Harding, *Whose Science? Whose Knowledge? Thinking from Women's Lives* (Ithaca: Cornell University Press, 1991); idem, *The Science Question in Feminism* (Ithaca: Cornell University Press, 1986); and Elizabeth Kamarck Minnich, *Transforming Knowledge* (Philadelphia: Temple University Press, 1990).

15. I am only a little dismayed by the failure of secular feminists to warm up to an ethical and epistemological project informed by Christian theological reflection—a failure matched by the thoroughgoing reluctance of Lutheran Christians to speak out or act as if Luther's theology of the cross had any business to do outside narrow academic theological circles. While I think I understand why neither of the interlocutors is eager to come forward, I am unsympathetic and, in the case of the faith community to which I belong, disappointed and chagrined.

16. Mary M. Solberg, *Compelling Knowledge: A Feminist Proposal for an Epistemology of the Cross* (Albany: State University of New York Press, 1997), 74.

17. Ibid., 80.

18. Elizabeth A. Johnson, *Consider Jesus: Waves of Renewal in Christology* (New York: Crossroad, 1990), 50.

19. Solberg, *Compelling Knowledge*, 86.

20. Ibid., 115.

21. Ibid., 118.

22. Jon Sobrino, *Christology at the Crossroads: A Latin American Approach*, trans. John Drury (Maryknoll, N.Y.: Orbis, 1978), 222–23.

23. For a profound treatment of "conversion to the neighbor," see the now classic text by Gustavo Gutiérrez, *A Theology of Liberation: History, Politics, and Salvation*, trans. and ed. Sister Caridad Inda and John Eagleson (Maryknoll, N.Y.: Orbis, 1988, 1973), 118.

24. Luther, "Heidelberg Disputation," *LW* 31:41.

25. Luther, "The Freedom of a Christian," in *LW* 31:344.

10. Reading Ourselves into the Cross Story: Luther and United States Latinos

1. This paper owes a great dose of its genesis to interdisciplinary and intercultural conversations that my husband, the Rev. Dr. Steven Churchill, and I have had, and I owe him much appreciation for them.

2. Martin Luther, "95 Theses," in *Luther's Works, Vol. 31: Career of the Reformer I*, ed. Harold J. Grimm and Helmut T. Lehmann (Philadelphia: Fortress Press, 1957). Hereafter abbreviated as *LW*.

3. Luther, "Preface to the New Testament," *LW, Vol. 35: Word and Sacrament 1*, ed. E. Theodore Bachman (Philadelphia: Fortress Press, 1960), 358.

4. Luther, "A Brief Instruction on What to Look for and Expect in the Gospels," *LW* 35:117–18.

5. Ibid., 119.

6. Ibid., 121.

7. Paul Ricoeur, "Toward a Narrative Theology: Its Necessity, Its Resources, Its Difficulties," in *Figuring the Sacred: Religion, Narrative, and Imagination*, ed. Mark I. Wallace, trans. David Pellauer (Minneapolis: Fortress Press, 1995), 240.

8. Ricoeur, "Philosophy and Religious Language," in *Figuring the Sacred*, 43.

9. Luther, "The Freedom of a Christian," *LW* 31:333.

10. Ricoeur, "Toward a Narrative Theology," in *Figuring the Sacred*, 243.

11. Ricoeur, "Pastoral Praxeology, Hermeneutics, and Identity," in *Figuring the Sacred*, 309.

12. Luther, "A Brief Instruction," *LW* 35:117–18.

13. Gerhard O. Forde, *On Being a Theologian of the Cross: Reflections on Luther's Heidelberg Disputation, 1518* (Grand Rapids, Mich.: Wm. B. Eerdmans, 1997), 8.

14. Ibid., 1, n.1, my emphasis.

15. Timothy F. Lull, ed., *Martin Luther's Basic Theological Writings* (Minneapolis: Fortress Press, 1989), 149.

16. Forde, *On Being a Theologian of the Cross*, 8.

17. Ada María Isasi-Díaz and Fernando F. Segovia, eds., *Hispanic/Latino Theology: Challenge and Promise* (Minneapolis: Fortress Press, 1996), 355.

18. An example of a professional-class Latino who felt marginalized is Professor Justo L. González's recollection of his experience at a "faculty meeting in a white teaching institution . . . when a suggestion [he] had made was completely ignored until, later in the discussion, it was made by a white colleague, at which time it was enthusiastically received." In Justo L. González, *Mañana: Christian Theology from a Hispanic Perspective* (Nashville: Abingdon, 1990), 25.

19. Luther, "A Brief Introduction," *LW* 35:121.

20. See: Ada María Isasi-Díaz, *Mujerista Theology* (Maryknoll, N.Y.: Orbis, 1996); and idem, *En la Lucha = In the Struggle: Elaborating a Mujerista Theology*, 10th Anniversary ed. (Minneapolis: Fortress Press, 2004).

21. Ada María Isasi-Díaz and Yolanda Tarango, *Hispanic Women: Prophetic Voice in the Church* (Minneapolis: Fortress Press, 1992), 31.

22. Ibid., 16.

23. González, *Mañana*, 75.

24. In Carter Lindberg, *Beyond Charity: Reformation Initiatives for the Poor* (Minneapolis: Fortress Press, 1993), 191.

25. Ibid., 192.

26. Ibid.

27. Ibid.

28. Ibid.

11. Imagining the Cross: Through the Eyes of Marian Kolodziej

All images in chapter 11 © 2006 Marian Kolodziej. Used by permission.

1. See Susan Nelson (Dunfee), *Beyond Servanthood: Christianity and the Liberation of Women* (Lanham, Md.: University Press of America, 1988).

2. Sydney B. Carter, "Lord of the Dance," copyright © 1963 Stainer & Bell Ltd. (Carol Stream, Ill.: Hope Publishing Company, 1963).

3. See David Brown, *Tradition and Imagination: Revelation and Change* (New York: Oxford University Press, 1999) for an argument that the Bible itself bears witness to the imagination—and that the incarnation (God—a universal—becomes flesh—to a particular time and place) invites imagining so people can envision how the Word has become flesh and dwells among them.

4. And, of course, Mel Gibson's incorporation of the stations of the cross in his film *The Passion of the Christ* was meant to evoke similar feelings on the part of his viewers.

5. Albert Schweitzer, *The Quest for the Historical Jesus* (New York: Macmillan Co., 1910).

6. See Carolyn Walker Bynum, "Introduction: The Complexity of Symbols," in *Gender and Religions: On the Complexity of Symbols* (Boston: Beacon, 1986).

7. Joanne Carlson Brown and Carole R. Bohn, eds., *Christianity, Patriarchy, and Abuse: A Feminist Critique* (New York: Pilgrim, 1989); Rita Nakashima Brock and Rebecca Ann Parker, *Proverbs of Ashes: Violence, Redemptive Suffering, and the Search for What Saves Us* (Boston: Beacon, 2001).

8. See James Carroll, *Constantine's Sword: The Church and the Jews—A History* (New York: Houghton Mifflin, 2001), for a history of the controversy over the placing of a cross at Auschwitz. For the purpose of this paper, I focus not on the papal cross actually erected—and left for a while—at Auschwitz, but on how one artist, through his imagination, uses the cross to express the trauma he survived. It is not meant to address the question of whether or not it is appropriate to erect a cross on the grounds of KZ Auschwitz.

9. On permanent display in the St. Maximilian Kolbe Retreat Center in Harmeze, Poland, three kilometers from Auschwitz; franciszkanie.pl/harmeze/. Web site accessed 17 Apr 2006.

10. "Plates" here meaning photographic plates—negatives—that would "develop" in the imagination of the viewer.

11. Susan L. Nelson, "The Use of Religious Symbols in the Context of Auschwitz: A Theological Analysis of the Artwork of Marian Kolodziej," presented at the American Academy of Religion Annual Meeting, San Antonio, Texas, November 2004.

12. There is a section of Mr. Kolodziej's exhibit that is devoted to the memory of

Maximilian Kolbe, who died of hunger in the cell after volunteering to take the place of someone else sentenced to die there. Pope John Paul II canonized Kolbe as a martyr in 1981. Mr. Kolodziej uses images of the passion/cross to memorialize Father Kolbe. I have bracketed these images for a later paper and have focused on the images of the passion/cross that Mr. Kolodziej uses to express his own trials at Auschwitz.

13. See Adam Mickiewicz's *Dziady* (Forefather's Eve).

14. Jerzy Popieluszko, *The Way of My Cross* (Chicago: Regnery Books, 1986), 86.

15. Father Popieluszko's sermons proved to be too threatening to the ruling regime. In August of 1984, he was abducted, tortured, and killed. His death was understood both as tragic and as an investment in God's work for justice for the Polish people. Considered a martyr, his death became a symbol of God's victory that was being prepared. And indeed, in 1989, the tight grip of totalitarian rule in Poland was broken.

16. See David Brown, *Tradition and Imagination: Revelation and Change*, 369. Brown speaks of how symbols appropriated apart from their traditional moorings can still have a "traditional" impact on the artist's work despite the artist's intentions.

17. The crucifixion-scene part of this picture was first drawn for Paul Hindesmith's play *Mathis der Maler*, for which Mr. Kolodziej was the set designer. I will interpret it in its present context.

18. Jane Dillenberger, *Style and Content in Christian Art* (New York: Abingdon, 1965), 143–49.

19. Andree Hayum, *The Isenheim Altarpiece: God's Medicine and the Painter's Vision* (Princeton: Princeton University Press, 1989).

20. See Ziva Amishai-Maisels, *Depiction and Interpretation: The Influence of the Holocaust on the Visual Arts* (Oxford: Pergamon, 1993), for a discussion of the use of the cross in Holocaust art.

21. Isaiah 53:3.

22. Human beings know that death is a piece of life. Catastrophic death—death surrounding one daily—is another story.

23. *Christ on the Cold Stone* (Utrecht, Museum Catharijneconvent, INV. ABM bs 692), found in Gabriele Finaldi, *The Image of Christ* (London: National Gallery Co. Ltd./Yale University Press, 2000), 120.

24. Jean Amery, "Torture," in *Art from the Ashes: A Holocaust Anthology*, ed. Lawrence L. Langer (New York: Oxford University Press, 1993), 136.

25. Richard J. Powell, *Homecoming: The Art and Life of William H. Johnson* (New York: W. W. Norton, 1993), 186, plate 167.

26. See Marc Chagall, *White Crucifixion*, 1938; www.canvaz.com/painters/chagall2.htm. Web site accessed 17 Apr 2006.

27. Chaim Potok, *My Name is Asher Lev* (New York: Fawcett Books, 1972), 329–30. There are Jewish artists, however, who have found images in that tradition to express their anguish (and their rage at God). For instance, see Mordecai Ardon's *Sarah* for a retelling of the sacrifice of Isaac where, post-Holocaust, there is no ram and Isaac is indeed dead. See Amishai-Maisels, *Depiction and Interpretation*, chap. 2, "Biblical Imagery," for an analysis of the use of religious imagery in art influenced by the Holocaust.

28. On visiting Kolodziej in his home, I was struck by a crucifix that the artist had hung horizontally from the rafter—the right arm reaching down to all in the room. Perhaps an artist's model; perhaps something more.

29. See Amery, "Torture," 135.

30. Lewis, Alan E., *Between Cross and Resurrection: A Theology of Holy Saturday* (Grand Rapids, Mich.: Wm. B. Eerdmans, 2001), 36–39.

31. Masao Takenaka and Ron O'Grady, *The Bible through Asian Eyes* (Auckland, New Zealand: Pace Publishing; Kyoto, Japan: in association with the Asian Christian Art Association, 1991).

32. Robert Jay Lifton, *The Broken Connection: On Death and the Continuity of Life* (Washington, D.C.: American Psychiatric, 1996), 169.

33. Ibid.

34. Ibid., 170.

35. Ibid., 171.

36. Ibid.

37. Ibid.

38. He says he intentionally drew from the visual vocabulary of Hieronymus Bosch and Peter Brueggel in expressing the grotesque quality of his experience.

39. Robert N. Kraft, *Memory Perceived: Recalling the Holocaust* (Westport, Conn.: Praeger, 2002).

40. Ronnie Janoff-Bulman, "Foreword," in Jeffrey Kauffman, ed., *Loss of the Assumptive World: A Theory of Traumatic Loss* (New York: Brunner-Routledge, 2002), ix–x. See also Ronnie Janoff-Bulman, *Shattered Assumptions: Towards a New Psychology of Trauma* (New York: Free Press, 1992).

41. Janoff-Bulman, "Foreword," x.

42. Ibid.

43. Lawrence L. Langer, *Holocaust Testimonies: The Ruins of Memory* (New Haven: Yale University Press, 1991), 5.

44. Ibid., 6.

45. Ibid.

46. Kolodziej also uses images of hell, apocalypse, and last judgment to convey to the viewer his experience. By looking just at his images of the cross and passion (and these are actually only a few of his images that draw in the passion and the cross; the others also beg interpretation, but must wait for a longer work), we do not get the full range of meanings that religious images offer him to speak of his experience. These other images—because they are hell without heaven, last judgment that is not just, an apocalypse without angels and divine intervention—reinforce what he calls the lack of transcendence in his work and counter the viewer's inclination to invest his use of the cross too hopefully.

47. See Brown, *Tradition and Imagination*, 369. Brown argues that the imagination of which he speaks is rooted in the tradition—or more correctly—in the tradition accommodating itself to different contexts. Thus, it would appear that the tradition, thought transformed imaginatively, retains certain recognizable contours. Brown also speaks of how symbols can be seemingly appropriated apart from their traditional moorings—noting that the images have an impact on the artist's work despite the artist's intentions.

48. One could argue that the multiple meanings of the cross are the efforts of Christian persons to integrate a traumatic event (the cross) into a viable worldview. See Damian Barry Smyth, *The Trauma of the Cross: How the Followers of Jesus Came to Understand the Crucifixion* (New York: Paulist, 1999). It would be appropriate to refer to worldviews in the plural since multiple views of the atonement focus on different ways to integrate the cross and the continued experience of suffering.

12. A Theology of the Cross for the "Uncreators"

1. The Greek word translated into English as "tradition," (paradosis) was, in the New Testament, used first as a verb, meaning "to pass on," as a tradition is passed on (see for example 1 Cor. 15:3). However, that verb also means "to betray" that which is to be passed on. It is, for instance, the verb translated as "betray" when Judas betrayed Jesus into the hands of the Roman soldiers.

2. See Kelly Brown Douglas, *The Black Christ* (Maryknoll, N.Y.: Orbis, 1994).

3. For this insight, I thank Rita Nakashima Brock and Rebecca Anne Parker, keynote address at the Annual Dinner of the Rauschenbusch Center, Seattle, 28 Nov 2005. The material is from their forthcoming book, *Saving Paradise* (Boston: Beacon, 2007).

4. Joseph Sittler, *Gravity and Grace: Reflections and Provocations* (Minneapolis: Augsburg Books, 1986), 106.

5. John B. Cobb Jr. and Herman Daly, *For the Common Good: Redirecting the Economy toward Community, the Environment, and a Sustainable Future* (Boston: Beacon, 1989), 21.

6. Statement by World Meteorological Organization, United Nations Environmental Programme, and Environment Canada at "The Changing Atmosphere: Implications for Global Security" conference, Toronto, June 1988.

7. Ministry of Home Affairs, Housing & Environment, Maldives, 11 March 2003.

8. George Carey, Archbishop of Canterbury, "New Year's Message broadcast on New Year's Eve, 2001," cited in Guy Dauncey with Patrick Mazza, *Stormy Weather: 101 Solutions to Global Climate Change* (Gabriola Island, B.C.: New Society Publishers, 2001).

9. George Monbiot, "World: Who is Paying the Cost of Our Fuel Bills?" *The Guardian Weekly*, 10 Feb 2000.

10. The United Nations Development Programme, *Human Development Report 1998* (New York: Oxford University Press, 1998), 29–30, using data from *Forbes* magazine (1997).

11. Jon Sobrino, Jesuit priest at the University of Central America, San Salvador, in conversation, 1987.

12. Bernardino Mandlate, in a presentation to the United Nations PrepCom for the World Summit on Social Development Plus Ten, New York, February 1999.

13. Martin Luther cited in Douglas John Hall, *Confessing the Faith: Christian Theology in a North American Context* (Minneapolis: Fortress Press, 1996), vi.

14. "Great work" is the term coined by Thomas Berry referring to the ecological dimension of this twofold undertaking. See Thomas Berry, *The Great Work: Our Way into the Future* (New York: Bell Tower, 1999). Some have called the move to sustainable Earth-human relations the fourth great revolution in human history, following the agricultural, industrial, and technological revolutions.

15. Please note that "we," "us," and "our" figure prominently in this essay. They are dangerous pronouns, made much more so when the referent is not specified. Henceforth, in this essay, unless otherwise noted, they refer to citizens of the United States who identify as Christians and who are "relatively privileged in economic terms." With this phrase I am suggesting those of us whose have some degree of choice in how we spend our time, energy, and material goods, because the totality of those resources is not demanded by the need to assure basic minimal requirements of survival with dignity for ourselves and those dependent or interdependent on us, and because we have relative mobility and access to the commonly accepted processes of citizenship.

16. Cynthia Moe-Lobeda, *Healing a Broken World: Globalization and God* (Minneapolis: Fortress Press, 2002), 30–69.

17. Carol Bellamy, executive director of UNICEF, reporting on the U.N. Panel on Humanitarian Issues in Iraq, 12 Aug 1999.

18. Paul Hawken, *The Ecology of Commerce: A Declaration of Sustainability* (New York: HarperBusiness, 1993), 22.

19. David Tracy, public lecture at Seattle University, 2005.

20. Martin Luther, "That These Words of Christ, 'This is My Body,' etc., Still Stand Firm Against the Fanatics," in *Luther's Works, Vol. 37: Word and Sacrament III*, ed. E. Theodore Bachman (Philadelphia: Fortress Press, 1961), 57. Hereafter abbreviated as *LW*.

22. Dietrich Bonhoeffer was a leading German theologian martyred for his leadership in the movement to resist Hitler and fascism. For many and complex reasons, any foray into Bonhoeffer's life and works, for the sake of faithful Christian praxis today, must come with cautionary notes that space precludes elaborating here. They include the following: Rethink his centralizing of suffering in light of feminist and womanist critiques of that centerpiece; contextualize his Christocentrism; heed his later self-criticism of his earlier work, specifically his misgivings regarding *The Cost of Discipleship*. Wayne Floyd, in "Revisioning Bonhoeffer for the Coming Generation: Challenges in Translating the Dietrich Bonhoeffer Works" *Dialog* 34, no. 1 (Winter 1995): 35–36, suggests additional cautions: Avoid quick answers or reductionist questions regarding Bonhoeffer; don't try to make obvious or overt what is cryptic or obscure in his writing; don't try to make his knowledge of the plight of the Jews and of Christian anti-Semitism greater or more insightful than it was.

22. Dietrich Bonhoeffer's theology, partly because it is inherently contextual and experiential, develops over time. Here we do not examine those shifts, but focus on Bonhoeffer as expressed in these two works. They extend the theoethical convictions, claims, and constructions begun in his previous works, but also nuance, critique, and develop them in substantive ways.

23. Dietrich Bonhoeffer, *Letters and Papers from Prison*, ed. Eberhard Bethge, enlarged ed. (New York: Collier Books, 1972), 4.

24. Ibid., 4, 9.

25. Simeon Ilesanmi, address on a panel for the opening plenary of the Society of Christian Ethics, Arlington, Virginia, 7 January 2000.

26. The term *solidarity* is overused and misused. The many problems with it are not easily seen from eyes of privilege. Yet, to lose the norm of solidarity would be a great loss. Problems with this concept and responses to them are sketched in Moe-Lobeda, *Healing a Broken World*, 118–223.

27. Dietrich Bonhoeffer, *No Rusty Swords* (New York: Collins and Harper & Row, 1970), 242.

28. *Se encurvatus en se* (self curved in on self) was Luther's phrase for describing the distortion of human life by sin. We become beings turned in on ourselves, serving self-interest in evident and subtle ways, above all else.

29. Douglas John Hall, *Lighten Our Darkness: Towards an Indigenous Theology of the Cross* (Philadelphia: Westminster, 1976), 149.

30. Winston Persaud, "Luther's 'Theologia Crucis': A Theology of 'Radical Reversal': in response to the Challenge of Marx's *Weltanschauung*," *Dialog* 29, no. 4, Aut 1990, 265–66.

3. Luther, "Heidelberg Disputation," *LW, Vol. 31: Career of the Reformer I*, ed. Harold J. Grimm and Helmut T. Lehmann (Philadelphia: Fortress Press, 1957), 39–58.

32. Dietrich Bonhoeffer, *Sanctorum Communio*, trans. Ronald Gregor Smith, et al. (New York: Harper & Row, 1963), 56.

33. For Bonhoeffer, conformation with the form of Christ implies refusing conformation with ways of life that betray Christ. His use of *"gestaltung"* for "conformation" is a play on the word used by Hitler to mean conforming to fascism. Conformation with the form of Christ crucified, for Bonhoeffer—in response to his context—came to mean both standing on behalf of the persecuted, and assuming the guilt of the Western world. In *Ethics*, he develops the concepts of the church's "deputyship," which has these two implications. This convergence of two meanings assumes very personal meaning for Bonhoeffer. He lives them both: he is imprisoned and executed for an assassination plot that was, in significant part, a defense of (standing on behalf of) those persecuted by the Nazi regime. At the same time, in *Letters and Papers from Prison*, he refers often to his role

as the guilty, assuming the guilt of Germany and of the Western world. In this sense, Bonhoeffer's understanding of the cross bridges the gap between theologies of the cross that see Christ atoning for human sin and theologies of the cross that see Christ executed by imperial power for his allegiance to the compassionate and justice-making reign of God. The cross for Bonhoeffer was both.

34. He writes: "The relation between the divine love and human love is wrongly understood if we say that the divine love [is]...solely for the purpose of setting human love in motion....On the contrary...the love with which [humans] love God and neighbor is the love of God and no other....[T]here is no love which is free or independent from the love of God." Dietrich Bonhoeffer, *Ethics*, ed. Eberhard Bethge, trans. Neville Horton Smith, 1st Touchstone ed. (New York: Simon and Schuster, 1995), 55–56.

35. Note that the New Testament Greek generally translated as "faith in Christ," (*pistis Christou*) in many instances, also may be translated accurately as faith "of" Christ.

36. My feminist and womanist sensibilities and commitments flare, and rightly so, in at least two senses. Is this "conformation with the form of Christ" a reification of servanthood and self-sacrifice, the state to which women, especially women of color, historically have been thrust? At first glance, so it appears. And yet, I think not. On the first count, Bonhoeffer's theology subtly defies the assumption that one sector of society is primarily to serve the other. For him, the state of "being for one another" is given only in the context of also "being with one another." The message for us is not an elevation of servanthood, but a declaration that daring to stand for life in the face of ecological or economic violence—despite the risks entailed—is not work of individuals; it is the work of people woven by the Spirit into a body in which all give and all receive. On the second count, conformation with the form of Christ is not formation toward self-sacrifice per se; it is formation toward a freedom to live as a whole person, to be fully human, to be "the creator's creature," and to help enable that freedom and fullness of life for all. If, in the service of life—rich and full life for all, including self—one is called to action that may endanger life, then that cost is not to be shunned.

37. Luther, *LW*, *Vol. 26: Galatians 1–4*, ed. and trans. Jaroslav Pelikan (St. Louis: Concordia, 1963), as cited by Larry Rasmussen, "Luther and a Gospel of Earth," *Union Seminary Quarterly Review* 51, no. 1–2 (1997): 22.

38. "Mud creatures" is the English translation of the Greek term used by Irenaeus of Lyons, second-century leader of a severely persecuted Christian community, to translate the Hebrew word ('adham) usually rendered "Adam" in the Genesis creation stories.

39. Constitutions, Bylaws, and Continuing Resolutions of the Evangelical Lutheran Church in America (1987), 4.01B02.

40. Bonhoeffer, *Letters and Papers from Prison*, 281–82, 341, 361.

41. Ibid., 361.

42. Luther, "That These Words of Christ," *LW* 37:57.

43. Ibid., 37:58.

44. Luther, the *Weimar Ausgabe* 23.134.34, as cited by Rasmussen, "Luther and a Gospel of Earth," 22, citing Paul Santmire, *The Travail of Nature: The Ambiguous Ecological Promise of Christian Theology* (Philadelphia: Fortress Press, 1985), 129.

45. Ibid., 387.

46. Ibid., 386.

47. Luther, "The Sacrament of the Body and Blood of Christ—Against the Fanatics," in Timothy F. Lull, ed., *Martin Luther's Basic Theological Works* (Minneapolis: Fortress Press, 1989), 321.

48. Luther, "Confession Concerning Christ's Supper," in ibid., 397.

49. Martin Luther, cited in Douglas John Hall, *Confessing the Faith*, vi.

50. Ibid., 2.

13. The Passion of Christ: Grace Both Red and Green

1. For more description of these terms, please see my book entitled *With Roots and Wings: Christianity in an Age of Ecology and Dialogue* (Maryknoll, N.Y.: Orbis, 1995).

2. For readers interested in learning more about process theology, I recommend *A Handbook on Process Theology* (St. Louis: Chalice, 2006), edited by Donna Bowman and myself. It is, to date, the most comprehensive survey of process approaches to Christian theology now available, including sympathetic approaches that arise from Protestant evangelical, feminist, and African American points of view.

3. See Jay McDaniel, *Living from the Center: Spirituality in an Age of Consumerism* (St. Louis: Chalice, 2000).

4. See Anders Nygren, *Agape and Eros*, trans. Philip S. Watson (New York: Harper & Row, 1957 [1930]).

5. See Edward Colline Vacek, *Love, Human and Divine: The Heart of Christian Ethics* (Washington D.C.: Georgetown University Press, 1996).

6. Thomas J. Oord, "The Love Racket: Defining Love and Agape for the Love and Science Research Program," *Zygon* 40, no. 4 (December): 924–28.

14. Saved by What Shouldn't Happen: The Anti-Sacrificial Meaning of the Cross

1. Major portions of this article are drawn from two other publications. See my articles, "Christ Crucified: Why Does Jesus' Death Matter?" *Christian Century* (March 7, 2001), 12–17; and "Christ's Death to End Sacrifice: Visible Victim," *Christian Century* (March 14, 2001), 18–23. The argument outlined here is developed at greater length in my book, *Saved From Sacrifice: A Theology of the Cross* (Grand Rapids, Mich.: Wm. B. Eerdmans, 2006).

2. For the basis of Girard's thought, see René Girard, *Violence and the Sacred*, trans. Patrick Gregory (Baltimore: Johns Hopkins University Press, 1977). For specific background to this discussion, see idem, *I See Satan Fall Like Lightning*, trans. James G. Williams (Maryknoll, N.Y.: Orbis, 2001); idem, *The Girard Reader*, ed. James G. Williams (New York: Crossroad, 1996).

3. *The Passion of the Christ*, a Mel Gibson film, released 11 March 2005 from Newmarket Films and Icon Productions.

4. For Jesus' proclamation of forgiveness, see Matt. 9:2-7 (and parallels) and Luke 7:47-50.

5. C. S. Lewis, *The Lion, the Witch and the Wardrobe: A Story for Children*, illus. Pauline Baynes (New York: Macmillan, 1950).

6. Ibid., 114. The phrase itself is the title of chapter 13.

7. Ibid.,132–33. The phrase is the title of chapter 15.

8. John 14:27: "Peace I leave with you; my peace I give to you. I do not give to you as the world gives."

15. Violence in Christian Theology

1. An earlier version of this article appeared in *Teaching Peace: Nonviolence and the Liberal Arts*, ed. J. Denny Weaver and Gerald Biesecker-Mast (Lanham, Md.: Rowman & Littlefield, 2003), 39–52. Portions of the chapter in *Teaching Peace* draw on my article, "Violence in Christian Theology," *CrossCurrents* 51, no. 2 (Summer 2001): 150–76, and reprinted by permission. Both draw on my book *The Nonviolent Atonement* (Grand Rapids, Mich.: Wm. B. Eerdmans, 2001).

2. John Howard Yoder, *The Politics of Jesus: Vicit Agnus Noster*, 2nd ed. (Grand Rapids, Mich.: Wm. B. Eerdmans, 1993), 5–8, 15–19.

3. These are more fully developed in *Teaching Peace*, chap. 2.

4. Anselm, "Why God Became Man," in *A Scholastic Miscellany: Anselm to Ockham*, ed. and trans. Eugene R. Fairweather, The Library of Christian Classics (Philadelphia: Westminster, 1956), 107–10.

5. Joanne Carlson Brown and Rebecca Parker, "For God So Loved the World?" in *Christianity, Patriarchy, and Abuse: A Feminist Critique*, ed. Joanne Carlson Brown and Carole R. Bohn (New York: Pilgrim, 1989), 1–30; Julie M. Hopkins, *Towards a Feminist Christology: Jesus of Nazareth, European Women, and the Christological Crisis* (Grand Rapids, Mich.: Wm. B. Eerdmans, 1995), 50–52; Rita Nakashima Brock, *Journeys by Heart: A Christology of Erotic Power* (New York: Crossroad, 1988), 55–57; Carter Heyward, *Saving Jesus from Those Who Are Right: Rethinking What It Means to be Christian* (Minneapolis: Fortress Press, 1999), 151; and Delores S. Williams, *Sisters in the Wilderness: The Challenge of Womanist God-Talk* (Maryknoll, N.Y.: Orbis, 1993), 161–67.

6. For an analysis of retributive justice, with restorative justice as the suggested alternative, see Howard Zehr, *Changing Lenses: A New Focus for Crime and Justice* (Scottdale, Pa.: Herald, 1990).

7. R. W. Southern, *Saint Anselm: A Portrait in a Landscape* (Cambridge: Cambridge University Press, 1990), 221–27.

8. The seminal treatment of the changes in the church symbolized by Constantine is John Howard Yoder, "The Constantinian Sources of Western Social Ethics," in *The Priestly Kingdom: Social Ethics as Gospel* (Notre Dame, Ind.: University of Notre Dame Press, 1984), 135–47; as well as Yoder's essays, "The Disavowal of Constantine: An Alternative Perspective on Interfaith Dialogue," in *The Royal Priesthood: Essays Ecclesiological and Ecumenical*, ed. Michael G. Cartwright (Grand Rapids, Mich.: Wm. B. Eerdmans, 1994), 242–61; and "The Otherness of the Church," in *The Royal Priesthood*, 53–64. H. A. Drake has shown that Constantine himself pursued a policy of tolerance, and that the changes he symbolizes and the move toward enforcing one prescribed faith actually occurred in the decades following Constantine (H. A. Drake, *Constantine and the Bishops: The Politics of Intolerance* [Baltimore: Johns Hopkins University Press, 2000]).

9. James H. Cone, *God of the Oppressed*, rev. ed. (Maryknoll, N.Y.: Orbis. 1997), 42–49, 211–12.

10. Brown and Parker, "For God So Loved the World?"; Hopkins, *Towards a Feminist Christology*, 50–52; Brock, *Journeys by Heart*, 55–57; and Heyward, *Saving Jesus*, 151.

11. Cone, *God of the Oppressed*, 211–12.

12. Williams, *Sisters in the Wilderness*, 60–83, 161–67, 178–99.

13. No scholarly consensus exists on the correlation of seals with emperors. While my particular suggestion here is quite plausible, the argument for narrative *Christus Victor* does not depend on accepting this particular interpretation. The vitally important point is to recognize that the antecedents of Revelation's symbols are located in the first century (however identified) and not in the distant future or our present age.

14. Susan Biesecker-Mast, "Nonviolence, Anabaptism, and the Impossible in Communication" in *Teaching Peace*, 115–24, uses rhetorical analysis to expose triumphalism and to display the necessity of a nonviolent stance toward the other.

15. For the full description of the powers, see the first volume of Walter Wink's trilogy on the powers, *Naming the Powers: The Language of Power in the New Testament* (Philadelphia: Fortress Press, 1984).

16. Cone, *God of the Oppressed*, 212–13.

16. The Cross of Resurrection and Communal Redemption

1. Archbishop Oscar Arnulfo Romero y Galdamez was assassinated by the Salvadoran military in March 1980. I was given a tour of the chapel in the spring of 1993. The artist, Fernando Llort, developed the painting style used in the chapel from pre-Renaissance styles of art to capture "unbreakable innocence and a discrete and

cultured magic" in his work. The medieval resurrection crosses were inspired by art that crusaders looted from Eastern Christian churches.

2. This essay is based on research for a forthcoming book, *Saving Paradise*, coauthored with Rebecca Ann Parker (Boston: Beacon, 2007).

3. Art historians note that the Gero Cross, carved in oak between 960–970 and found now in the Cathedral in Cologne, Germany, is the oldest existing image of Jesus' death.

4. Art historians, noting the absence of crucifixion images in early Christian art, suggest it appears symbolically through other images, for example, Gertrude Schiller, *Iconography of Christian Art: The Passion of Jesus Christ*, vol. 2, trans. Janet Seligman (London: Lund Humphries Pub., 1972), 1–9. Diane Apostolos-Cappadona, *Dictionary of Christian Art* (New York: Continuum, 1995), 91–94, instead correlates shifts in the iconography of Jesus to developments in Christology. See also Peter and Linda Murray, *The Oxford Companion to Christian Art and Architecture* (New York: Oxford University Press, 1996), 126–27, for discussions of the evolution of crucifixion images.

5. The earliest Christian images, found in the third-century Dura-Europos house church and the catacombs, lack images of the passion of Jesus. W. H. C. Frend, *The Archaeology of Early Christianity: A History* (Minneapolis: Fortress Press, 1996), 98–199; and J. Stevenson, *The Catacombs: Rediscovered Monuments of Early Christianity* (London: Thames and Hudson, 1978), 85–108.

6. Irenaeus, *Against Heresies*, Book III, 366–68, in *Ante-Nicene Christian Library: Translations of the Writings of the Fathers Down to A.D. 325*, vol. 5, *The Writings of Irenaeus*. vol. 1, trans. Alexander Roberts and Rev. W. H. Rambaut (Edinburgh: T & T Clark, 1868).

7. Stevenson, *The Catacombs*, notes that the catacombs contain frequent images of the Virgin and Magi, but none of the passion. The church of Maria Maggiore in Rome has the oldest existing narrative sequence of the nativity. For information about early baptism, see Peter Cramer, *Baptism and Change in the Early Middle Ages, c. 200–1150* (New York: Cambridge University Press, 1993).

8. In the catacomb of Peter and Marcellinus, "the participants call to the servants, Irene (Peace) and Agape (Love): DA CALDA ('give it warm') or MISCE MI ('mix it for me'!)," Stevenson, *The Catacombs*, 95. Schiller, *Iconography*, v. 2, 24–27, notes in Anastasic Last Suppers that the majority of images show Jesus announcing his betrayal.

9. Jean Delumeau, *History of Paradise: The Garden of Eden in Myth and Tradition* (New York: Continuum, 1995), notes that Origen, following Philo, sees Eden allegorically. Ephraem of Syria, 4th c., identifies the Pishon with the Danube, a historical place (Delumeau, 40). Augustine formulated the dominant view until the Reformation period—Eden was both historically real and spiritually symbolic (Delumeau, 18). Christoph Auffarth, "Paradise Now—But for the Wall Between, Some Remarks on Paradise in the Middle Ages," in Gerard P. Luttikhuizen, ed., *Paradise Interpreted: Representations of Biblical Paradise in Judaism and Christianity* (Leiden: Koninklijke Brill NV, 1999), 178. Colleen McDannell and Bernhard Lang, *Heaven: A History*, 2nd ed. (New Haven: Yale University Press, 2001), ignores the late antique spatial and temporal distinctions between paradise and heaven and collapses them, using a typology of "anthropomorphic" and "theocentric" heaven.

10. Peter Brown, *Power and Persuasion in Late Antiquity: Towards a Christian Empire* (Madison: University of Wisconsin Press, 1992), notes the high value placed on self-control, serenity, and dignity under pressure.

11. Georges Florovsky, *The Byzantine Fathers of the Fifth Century* (Vaduz, Europa; Belmont, Mass.: Büchervertriebsanstalt, 1987), 201.

12. Andre Grabar, *Byzantium: Byzantine Art in the Middle Ages*, trans. Betty Forster (London: Methuan, 1966); and Ernst Kitzinger, *Byzantine Art in the Making: Main Lines of Stylistic Development in Mediterranean Art 3rd–7th Century* (Cambridge: Harvard University Press, 1995).

13. Several prominent art historians in the mid-twentieth century suggested that early Christian iconography used the "emperor mystique" to convey Jesus' power, which crucifixion would contradict. Thomas F. Mathews, *The Clash of the Gods: A Reinterpretation of Early Christian Art* (Princeton: Princeton University Press, 1993), challenges this prevailing "emperor mystique" theory.

14. "Crucifixion was a horrible and degrading punishment inflicted upon slaves or...non-Roman citizens." Murray, *The Oxford Companion*, 126, also suggests the prohibition of graven images is involved, but this would not explain other early images of Jesus.

15. Irenaeus claims Jesus had a twenty-year ministry and died at the elderly age of fifty, in order to sanctify all stages of human life. *Against Heresies*, Book III, 366–68.

16. See, for example, Ellen M. Ross, *The Grief of God: Images of Suffering Jesus in Late Medieval England* (New York: Oxford University Press, 1997). The absence of violence may reflect, however, a desire not to retraumatize victims. Mathews, *The Clash of the Gods*, chap. 3, notes the miracles are an innovation in Christian art and demonstrate divine care for the suffering of ordinary people through images of Jesus healing and resurrecting the dead.

17. "In the thousand-year history of Christianity's missionary efforts in Europe, I doubt if there is any page as brutal as that of Charlemagne's thirty-three year war of conversion and conquest of the Saxons of northern Germany" (G. Ronald Murphy, *The Saxon Savior: The Germanic Transformation of the Gospel in the Ninth-Century Heliand* [New York: Oxford University Press, 1989], 11). "The most marked feature of the rise of the Christian church in western Europe was the imposition of human administrative structures...at the expense of the landscape itself. St. Martin attacked those points at which the natural and divine were held to meet; he cut down the sacred tree....His successors...imposed rhythms of work and leisure that ignored the slow turning of the sun, the moon, and the planets through the heavens, and that reflected, instead a purely human time, linked to the deaths of outstanding individuals. What is at stake in sixth-century Gaul...is nothing less than a conflict of views on the relations between man and nature" (Brown, *The Cult of the Saints*, 124–25, cited in James C. Russell, *The Germanization of Early Medieval Christianity: A Sociohistorical Approach to Religious Transformation* [New York: Oxford University Press, 1994], 177). This hostility to nature resulted in Europe's deforestation with the expansion of empire and anti-pagan wars.

18. A study of this debate about the Eucharist is found in Rachel Fulton's *From Judgment to Passion: Devotion to Christ and the Virgin Mary, 800–1200* (New York: Columbia University Press, 2002).

19. Schiller, *Iconography of Christian Art*, v. 2, 141.

20. Eugenia, a pilgrim to Jerusalem, 5th c., on the Friday before Easter: "All the people are so crowded there....The bishop's chair is placed before the Cross, and from noon to three, nothing is done except that Biblical passages are read...of the Passion....Prayers are always interspersed,...fitting to the day....There is such emotion and weeping by all the people that it is a wonder; for there is no one, old or young, who does not on this day weep for these three hours more than can be imagined because the Lord has suffered for us." From Patricia Wilson-Kastner, G. Ronald Kastner, Ann Millin, Rosemary Rader, eds., *A Lost Tradition: Women Writers of the Early Church* (Washington, D.C.: University Press of America, 1981), 122–23.

21. "Traditionally, the Church had been averse to the shedding of blood. *Ecclesia abhorrent a sanguine* was a principle ever present in patristic writings and conciliar legislation....Even killing a pagan was a homicide. From the fourth century to the eleventh century, the Church as a rule imposed disciplinary measures on those who killed in war, or at least recommended that they do penance." Thomaš Mastnak,

Crusading Peace: Christendom, the Muslim World, and Western Political Order (Berkeley: University of California Press, 2002), 16.

22. Ibid., 45.

23. Since the 1950s, this has been the prevailing view in historical scholarship. See H. E. J. Cowdrey, "Pope Urban II's Preaching," in *The Crusades and Latin Monasticism, 11th–12th Centuries* (Brookfield, N.Y.: Ashgate, 1999), 17–20.

24. Edward Peters, ed. *The First Crusade: The Chronicle of Fulcher of Chartres and Other Source Materials* (Philadelphia: University of Pennsylvania Press, 1998), 44–46. Versions of Urban's sermon emerge four to twenty years later. His letters differ little in tone or theology from his reported comments and begin to appear within a year of the event.

25. James Carroll, *Constantine's Sword: The Church and the Jews, A History* (Boston: Houghton Mifflin, 2001), 247–88.

26. Anselm of Canterbury, *Why God Became Man*, ed. and trans. Joseph M. Colleran (Albany, N.Y.: Magi, 1969), Book 2, chap 11, 136. His treatise is a rational argument for the reasonableness of sacrifice.

27. Ibid., Book 2, chap. 18, 155–56.

28. Anthony W. Bartlett, *Cross Purposes: The Violent Grammar of the Christian Atonement* (Harrisburg: Trinity International, 2001); Thomas Madden, ed., *The Crusades: The Essential Readings* (Oxford: Blackwell, 2002); Mastnak, *Crusading Peace*; and Christoph T. Maier, *Crusade Propaganda and Ideology: Model Sermons for the Preaching of the Cross* (Cambridge: Cambridge University Press, 2000).

29. During the siege of Antioch, an unexpected form of "paradise now" was developed for "soldiers being rewarded by God's taking them immediately after death...into paradise." Auffarth, "Paradise Now," 179.

30. Mastnak, *Crusading Peace*, 62–64, notes an important distinction between justifications for defensive war, i.e., just-war theory, and this new idea of holy war as aggressive conquest and colonization.

31. "The pilgrims...moved within the mental world of those images formed [of the Promised Land]....The pilgrimage was a journey through fantasy....Because the boundary between fantasy and...reality was very thin and fluid,...the nets entangling Jerusalem were not merely symbolic....Those who destroyed [Jerusalem], the army of the new chosen people, had already built an image of the New Jerusalem in their minds' eye." Mastnak, *Crusading Peace*, 46–47.

32. Schiller, *Iconography*, v. 2, 219–25.

33. "The Church's response to the need among the laity...was the invention of Purgatory to fill the void between the individual's demise and the universal end of time. Now...hell and...paradise were under the control of the Church, extending her realm into the afterlife. The doors of paradise were locked once again...." Auffarth, "Paradise Now," 179.

34. "In the mid-eleventh century,...so dramatic an operation [as baptism] begins to become puzzling. In the puzzlement,...there is a loss of innocence: the innocence of the sacramental symbol. In the tentative theology of Abelard we can see some of the anxiety which comes of loss. It is akin to the anxiety of 'not quite getting there' which Abelard finds in the pagan philosophers of Antiquity, whose knowledge was not yet made good by revelation; whose wish to be baptized was, as it were, not yet accomplished by baptism itself." Cramer, *Baptism and Change*, i.

35. "The demonstration of the chalice with the host which in the late Middle Ages replaces the *signum Christi* as the sign of triumph, corresponds in the Trinity image to the transformation of the God-like Son into the Man of Sorrows." Schiller, *Iconography*, v. 2, 223.

36. Abelard's theory is called the moral influence theory, which somewhat distorts his position. Richard E. Weingart, *The Logic of Divine Love: A Critical Analysis of the Soteriology of Peter Abelard* (Oxford: Clarendon, 1970), 126.

37. Carroll and Bartlett are contemporary thinkers who explicitly draw on Abelardian themes. Liberation theologians, too, agree that human sinfulness caused Jesus' death.

38. On Johannine anti-Judaism, related to the absence of atonement in the Gospel, see Rita Nakashima Brock and Rebecca Ann Parker, "Enemy and Ally: Contending with the Gospel of John's Anti-Judaism," in *Walk in the Ways of Wisdom: Essays in Honor of Elisabeth Schüssler Fiorenza*, ed. Shelly Matthews, Cynthia Kittridge, and Melanie Johnson (Harrisburg: Trinity International, 2003).

39. "So that we might persist strongly in the agony of suffering for Christ's sake, he is always to be before our eyes and his passion ought always to be an example for us lest we fail." Abelard, *Sermon* ix.447d, cited in Weingart, *The Logic*.

40. Christopher Hedges, *War Is a Force That Gives Us Meaning* (New York: Anchor Books, 2003).

41. Riley-Smith, "Crusading as an Act of Love," in Madden, *The Crusades*, analyses this confusion of violence, self-sacrifice, and love. For a contemporary analysis of the confusions, see Judith Herman, *Trauma and Recovery: The Aftermath of Violence from Domestic Abuse to Political Terror* (New York: Basic Books, 1992).

42. Hedges, *War Is a Force*; and Herman, *Trauma and Recovery*.

43. Studies of trauma have emerged in a variety of disciplines, from the humanities to the social and biological sciences. Herman, *Trauma and Recovery*, draws parallels between war-induced post-traumatic stress and intimate violence.

44. Hedges, *War Is a Force*; Herman, *Trauma and Recovery*; and Elaine Scarry, *The Body in Pain: The Making and Unmaking of the World* (New York: Oxford University Press, 1987).

45. The second, and central, of three sections of Rita Nakashima Brock and Rebecca Ann Parker, *Proverbs of Ashes: Violence, Redemptive Suffering and the Search for What Saves Us* (Boston: Beacon, 2001), entitled "Pentecost," focuses on redemptive communities that create the conditions for the saving and renewing of life described in the third section, "Epiphany."

17. Theology of the Cross: Challenge and Opportunity for the Post-Christendom Church

1. If you would like to renew your acquaintance with the course of Luther's life, look at James A. Nestingen's very readable book, *Martin Luther: A Life* (Minneapolis: Augsburg Books, 2003).

2. For an extensive treatment of the theology of the cross, see my book *The Cross in Our Context: Jesus and the Suffering World* (Minneapolis: Fortress Press, 2003).

3. "Ac-cent-tchu-ate the Positive (Mister In-between)," written by Johnny Mercer and Harold Arlen (New York: Edwin H. Morris & Co., 1944), and sung in a popular version by Bing Crosby and the Andrews Sisters in the movie *Here Come the Waves*.

4. That's why I called my first larger book *Lighten Our Darkness: Towards an Indigenous Theology of the Cross* (Philadelphia: Westminster, 1976); rev. ed., with foreword by David J. Monge (Lima, Ohio: Academic Renewal, 2001).

5. Jürgen Moltmann, *The Crucified God*, trans. R. A. Wilson and John Bowden (London: SCM, 1974), 72.

6. Sydney Hook, on the cover of Robert L. Heilbronner, *The Future as History* (New York: Harper Torchbooks, 1959).

7. Robert McAfee Brown, ed., *The Essential Reinhold Niebuhr: Selected Essays and Addresses* (New Haven: Yale University Press, 1986), 22.

8. Paul Tillich, from a sermon entitled "The Yoke of Religion," in *The Shaking of the Foundations {Sermons}* (New York: C. Scribner's Sons, 1948), 93–103.

18. The Cross as Military Symbol for Sacrifice

1. Translated by Ingeborg G. Larsen.

2. See Ernest Lee Tuveson, *Redeemer Nation: The Idea of America's Millennial Role* (Chicago: University of Chicago Press, 1968; Midway reprint, 1980).

3. Quoted in *Zur Debatte. Themen der Katholischen Akademie*, München 3/2005, 13 (translation mine). Heinrich Missala, *Wie der Krieg zur Schule Gottes wurde*. Verquickung der katholischen Kirche mit der Wehrmacht, Publik Forum Bücher Oberursel 2000; Hans Prolingheuer / Thomas Breuer (Hg), *Dem Führer gehorsam: Christen an der Front*, Die Verstrickung beider Kirchen in den Zweiten Weltkrieg, Publik Forum Bücher 2002.

4. Ernst Jünger, *Der Arbeiter* (Hamburg, 1932), 71 (translation mine).

5. Friedrich Hölderlin, *Hyperion* (Zürich: Atlantis Verlag, 1944), 164 (translation mine).

19. American Torture and the Body of Christ: Making and Remaking Worlds

1. Political philosopher Michael Doyle has defined empires as "political relationships of political control by some political societies over the effective sovereignty of other political societies." Michael W. Doyle, *Empires*, Cornell Studies in Comparative History (London and Ithaca: Cornell University Press, 1986), 19.

2. Emmanuel Todd, *After the Empire: The Breakdown of the American Order*, trans. C. Jon Delogu (New York: Columbia University Press, 2003), 79-99.

3. Mark Lewis Taylor, *Religion, Politics, and the Christian Right: Post-9/11 Powers and American Empire* (Minneapolis: Fortress Press, 2005), 2–9.

4. General Assembly of the United Nations, "Declaration Against Torture," 9 Dec 1975, cited from Edward Peters, *Torture* (New York: Basil Blackwell, 1985), 2.

5. Karen J. Greenberg and Joshua L. Dratel, "Appendix C," in *The Torture Papers: The Road to Abu-Ghraib* (Cambridge, UK: Cambridge University Press, 2005), 1241.

6. "Pentagon Admits Use of Torture Manuals," *National Catholic Reporter*, 4 Oct 1976.

7. Sue Branford, "The Salvador Option," *Newsweek*, 31 Jan 2005, vol. 134, Issue 4724/4725, 18.

8. Bonnie Kerness, "America's Abuse of Prisoners Didn't Begin in Iraq," *Newark Star Ledger*, 18 Jan 2004, A16. Kerness is coordinator of the American Friends Service Committee's Prison Watch Project.

9. Alfred W. McCoy, *A Question of Torture: CIA Interrogation, from the Cold War to the War on Terror* (New York: Metropolitan Books, 2006), 32–38.

10. Cited in ibid., 106, n.127.

11. Ibid., 12, 153–55.

12. Michael Ratner and Ellen Ray, *Guantánamo: What the World Should Know* (White River Junction, Vt.: Chelsea Green, 2004).

13. Such as for Haitians held in Guantanamo detention center and those who have suffered U.S. bombings and sanctions in Iraq since 1991.

14. Ratner and Ray, *Guantánamo*, xvii.

15. In addition to Greenberg and Dratel (n. 5, above) see also Mark Danner, *Torture and Truth: America, Abu Ghraib and the War on Terror* (New York: NYRB, 2004).

16. Cited in Jane Mayer, "Outsourcing Torture," *The New Yorker*, 14 Feb 2005, Vol. 81, Issue 1, 106-123.

17. Richard A. Clarke, *Against All Enemies: Inside America's War on Terror* (New York: Free Press, 2004), 24. Also commented on in McCoy, *A Question of Torture*, 113.

18. James Risen, *State of War: The Secret History of the CIA and the Bush Administration* (New York: Free Press, 2006), 22.

19. McCoy, *A Question of Torture*, 138–40, 142–44. General Janis Kaprinski was the supervising commander of the Abu-Ghraib facility before General Sanchez ordered its key interrogation operations to be handled by military Special Access Programs.

20. Mayer, 112.

21. Ibid., 198–203.

22. See McCoy, 125 n. 42, for sources.

23. Ibid., 125.

24. Jacobo Timmerman, *Prisoner without a Name, Cell without a Number*, trans. Tony Talbot (New York: Vintage Books, 1988), 32–33.

25. William T. Cavanaugh, *Torture and Eucharist: Theology, Politics and the Body of Christ* (London: Blackwell Publishing Ltd., 1998), 34.

26. Elaine Scarry, *The Body in Pain: The Making and Unmaking of the World* (New York: Oxford University Press, 1986), 27–59.

27. The United States consistently arrogates to itself, from the whole hemisphere of North, Caribbean and Latin American nations, the name "America."

28. Assassinated 24 Mar 1980.

29. Chalmers Johnson, *Blowback: The Costs and Consequences of American Empire* (New York: Henry Holt, 2000).

30. W. E. B. Du Bois, "The Souls of White Folk," in *Darkwater: Voices from Within the Veil,* (New York: Humanity Books, 2003 [1920]); Aimé Cesaire, *Discourse on Colonialism,* trans. Joan Pinkham (New York: Monthly Review, 2000).

31. Franz Graziano, *Divine Violence: Spectacle, Psychosexuality, and Radical Christianity in the Argentine "Dirty War"* (Boulder: Westview, 1996), 205. Graziano is citing Elvira Orphée, *La última conquista de El Angel* (Buenos Aires: Javier Vergara Editor, 1984), 60.

32. Marguerite Feitlowitz, *A Lexicon of Terror: Argentina and the Legacies of Torture* (New York: Oxford University Press, 1998), 9-10.

33. Cited in William T. Cavanaugh, *Torture and Eucharist: Theology, Politics and the Body of Christ (Challenges in Contemporary Theology)* (Oxford: Blackwell, 1998) 24, n. 6.

34. For this contemporary trend, see Taylor, *Religion, Politics, and the Christian Right,* 1–14, 53–62.

35. Mark Lewis Taylor, *Remembering Esperanza: A Cultural-Political Theology of North American Praxis* (Minneapolis: Fortress Press, 2005/Maryknoll, NY: Orbis, 1990).

36. Mark Lewis Taylor, *The Executed God: The Way of the Cross in Lockdown America* (Minneapolis: Fortress Press, 2001).

37. Herman Ridderbos, *Paul: An Outline of His Theology*, trans. John Richard de Witt (Grand Rapids, Mich.: Wm. B. Eerdmans, 1975). Emphasis mine.

38. More specifically, the actor Raul Julia as Romero in the movie *Romero,* DVD, directed by John Duigan (1989; New York: Lion's Gate Studio, 2000).

39. For the full sermon, see www.thirdworldtraveler.com/Human%20Rights%20D ocuments/Archbishop_Romero.html. Accessed 28 Mar 2006.

For Further Reading

Classics and Historical Studies on the Cross and Atonement Theory

Abelard, Peter. "Exposition of the Epistle to the Romans (An Excerpt from the Second Book)." Trans. Gerald E. Moffatt. In *A Scholastic Miscellany: Anselm to Ockham*. Ed. Eugene R. Fairweather, 276–287. Philadelphia: Westminster, 1956.

Anselm. *Cur Deus Homo*. In *Anselm of Canterbury*, vol. 3. Ed. and trans. Jasper Hopkins and Herbert Richardson, 39–137. Toronto: Edwin Mellen, 1976.

Aquinas, Thomas. *Summa Theologica*, vol. IV. 2277–78. Trans. Fathers of the English Dominican Province. Westminster, Md.: Christian Classics, 1981 (reprint). This can be found in other editions of the *Summa*: IIIa, question 48, article 2.

Athanasius. *De incarnatione Verbi*, VIII, 4-IX, 1; and *contra Arianos*, III, 33. In *The Christian Theology Reader*, ed. Alister McGrath, 331–33. 2nd ed. Oxford: Blackwell, 2001.

Aulén, Gustav. *Christus Victor: An Historical Study of the Three Main Types of the Idea of Atonement*. Trans. A. G. Hebert. New York: SPCK, 1931.

Calvin, John. *Institutes of the Christian Religion*, book 2, chaps. 1–17. This can be found in any edition of *The Institutes*. An abbreviated form may be found in *Calvin's Institutes: A New Compend*. Ed. Hugh T. Kerr. Louisville: Westminster, 1989, 55–80.

————. *Consilium de peccato et redemptione*. In *The Christian Theology Reader*, ed. Alister McGrath, 348–49. 2nd ed. Oxford: Blackwell, 2001.

Franks, R. S. *The Work of Christ: A Historical Study*. London/New York: Nelson, 1965.

Girard, René. *Violence and the Sacred*. Trans. Patrick Gregory. Baltimore: Johns Hopkins University Press, 1977.

Irenaeus of Lyons. *Against the Heresies*. Trans. and annotated by Dominic J. Unger, with further revisions by John J. Dillon. New York: Paulist, 1992. See esp. V.i.1.

Luther, Martin. "Heidelberg Disputation." In *Luther's Works, Vol. 31: Career of the Reformer I*, ed. Harold J. Grimm and Helmut T. Lehmann, 39–58. Philadelphia: Fortress Press, 1957. This contains Luther's classic discussion of what is means to be a "theologian of the cross."

Moltmann, Jürgen. *The Crucified God*. Trans. R. A. Wilson and John Bowden. London: SCM, 1974.

Schleiermacher, Friedrich. *The Christian Faith*. Ed. H. R. Mackintosh and J. S. Stewart. Edinburgh: T. & T. Clark, 1928. See esp. 374–463.

Sykes, S. W., ed. *Sacrifice and Redemption*. Cambridge: Cambridge University Press, 1991.

Womanist, Asian-Feminist, Mujerista, and Feminist Readings

Brown, Joanne Carlson, and Rebecca Parker. "For God So Loved the World?" In *Christianity, Patriarchy, and Abuse: A Feminist Critique*, ed. Joanne Carlson Brown and Carole R. Bohn, 1–30. New York: Pilgrim, 1989.

Copeland, M. Shawn. "To Live at the Disposal of the Cross: Mystical-Political Discipleship as Christological Locus." In *Christology: Memory, Inquiry, Practice*, ed. Anne M. Clifford and Anthony J. Godzieba, 177–205. Maryknoll, N.Y.: Orbis Books, 2003.

————. "Wading Through Many Sorrows: Toward a Theology of Suffering in Womanist Perspective." In *A Troubling in My Soul: Womanist Perspectives on Evil and Suffering*, ed. Emilie Townes, 109–29. Maryknoll, N.Y.: Orbis Books, 1993.

Douglas, Kelly Brown. *The Black Christ*. Maryknoll, N.Y.: Orbis Books, 1994.

————. *What's Faith Got to Do With It? Black Bodies/Christian Souls*. Maryknoll, N.Y.: Orbis Books, 2005. See esp. 53–70, where Douglas discusses atonement and soteriological history in relation to power issues and lynching.

Brock, Rita Nakashima. "And a Little Child Will Lead Us: Christology and Child Abuse." In *Christianity, Patriarchy, and Abuse: A Feminist Critique*, ed. Joanne Carlson Brown and Carole R. Bohn, 42–61. New York: Pilgrim, 1989.

————. *Journeys by Heart: A Christology of Erotic Power*. New York: Crossroad, 1988.

————, and Rebecca Ann Parker. *Proverbs of Ashes: Violence, Redemptive Suffering and the Search for What Saves Us*. Boston: Beacon, 2001.

Grant, Jacquelyn. "The Sin of Servanthood and the Deliverance of Discipleship." In *A Troubling in My Soul: Womanist Perspectives on Evil and Suffering*, ed. Emily Townes, 199–218. Maryknoll, N.Y.: Orbis Books, 1993.

————. "Subjectification as a Requirement for Christological Construction." In *Lift Every Voice: Constructing Christian Theologies from the Underside*, ed. Susan Brooks Thistlethwaite and Mary Potter Engel, 207–20. Rev. and exp. ed. Maryknoll, N.Y.: Orbis Books, 1998.

————. *White Women's Christ and Black Women's Jesus: Feminist Christology and Womanist Response*. American Academy of Religion Academy Series no. 64. Atlanta: Scholars Press, 1989.

Isasi-Díaz, Ada María. *En la Lucha / In the Struggle: Elaborating a Mujerista Theology*. Tenth anniversary ed. Minneapolis: Fortress Press, 2004.

Ray, Darby Kathleen. *Deceiving the Devil: Atonement, Abuse, and Ransom*. Cleveland: Pilgrim, 1998.

Smith, Christine M. *Risking the Terror: Resurrection in this Life*. Cleveland: Pilgrim, 2001.

Solberg, Mary M. *Compelling Knowledge: A Feminist Proposal for an Epistemology of the Cross*. Albany: State University of New York Press, 1997.

Stevens, Maryanne, ed. *Reconstructing the Christ Symbol: Essays in Feminist Christology.* New York: Paulist, 1993. This volume contains essays by Rosemary Radford Ruether, Rita Nakashima Brock, Jacquelyn Grant, Marina Herrera, Elizabeth A. Johnson, and Eleanor McLaughlin.

Terrell, Joanne Marie. *Power in the Blood? The Cross in the African American Experience.* Maryknoll, N.Y.: Orbis Books, 1998.

Thompson, Deanna. *Crossing the Divide: Luther, Feminism, and the Cross.* Minneapolis: Fortress Press, 2004.

Other Contemporary Theological Readings on the Cross, Race, Violence, and Atonement

Boersma, Hans. *Violence, Hospitality, and the Cross: Reappropriating the Atonement Tradition.* Grand Rapids, Mich.: Baker Academic, 2004.

Cavanaugh, William T. *Torture and Eucharist: Theology, Politics, and the Body of Christ.* Challenges in Contemporary Theology series. Oxford: Blackwell, 1998.

Cleage. Albert B., Jr. *The Black Messiah.* New York: Sheed and Ward, 1968.

Cone, James H. *A Black Theology of Liberation.* Philadelphia: J. B. Lippincott, 1970.

Finlan, Stephen. *Problems with Atonement: The Origins of, and Controversy about, the Atonement Doctrine.* Collegeville, Minn.: Liturgical Press, 2005.

Forde, Gerhard. *On Being a Theologian of the Cross: Reflections on Luther's Heidelberg Disputation, 1518.* Grand Rapids, Mich.: Wm. B. Eerdmans, 1997.

Girard, René. *I See Satan Fall Like Lightning.* Trans. James G. Williams. Maryknoll, N.Y.: Orbis Books, 2001.

Hall, Douglas John. *The Cross in Our Context: Jesus and the Suffering World.* Minneapolis: Fortress Press, 2003.

———. *God and Human Suffering: An Exercise in the Theology of the Cross.* Minneapolis: Augsburg, 1986.

———. *Lighten Our Darkness: Toward an Indigenous Theology of the Cross.* Revised and with a foreword by David J. Monge. Lima, Ohio: Academic Renewal Press, 2001.

Heim, S. Mark. *Saved from Sacrifice: A Theology of the Cross.* Grand Rapids, Mich.: Wm. B. Eerdmans, 2006.

Hill, Charles E., and Frank A. James III, eds. *The Glory of the Atonement: Biblical, Historical, & Practical Perspectives: Essays in Honor of Roger R. Nicole.* Downers Grove, Ill.: InterVarsity, 2004.

Patterson, Orlando. *Rituals of Blood: Consequences of Slavery in Two American Centuries.* Washington, D.C.: Civitas/Counterpoint, 1998.

Patterson, Stephen J. *Beyond the Passion: Rethinking the Death and Life of Jesus.* Minneapolis: Fortress Press, 2004.

Pinn, Anthony. *Why Lord? Suffering and Evil in Black Theology.* New York: Continuum, 1995.

Taylor, Mark Lewis. *The Executed God: The Way of the Cross in Lockdown America.* Minneapolis: Fortress Press, 2001.

Weaver, J. Denny. *The Nonviolent Atonement.* Grand Rapids, Mich.: Wm. B. Eerdmans, 2001.

———. "Violence in Christian Theology." In *Teaching Peace: Nonviolence and the Liberal Arts,* ed. J. Denny Weaver and Gerald Biesecker-Mast, 39–52. Lanham, Md.: Rowman & Littlefield, 2003.

Index of Names

Index of Subjects

.

Made in the USA
Lexington, KY
15 January 2012